Semantic Web for the Working Ontologist

Second Edition

Semantic Web for the Working Ontologist

Effective Modeling in RDFS and OWL

Second Edition

Dean Allemang

Jim Hendler

ELSEVIER

AMSTERDAM • BOSTON • HEIDELBERG • LONDON • NEW YORK • OXFORD
PARIS • SAN DIEGO • SAN FRANCISCO • SINGAPORE • SYDNEY • TOKYO

Morgan Kaufmann Publishers is an imprint of Elsevier

Acquiring Editor: Todd Green
Development Editor: Robyn Day
Project Manager: Sarah Binns
Designer: Kristen Davis

Morgan Kaufmann Publishers is an imprint of Elsevier.
225 Wyman Street, Waltham, MA 02451, USA

This book is printed on acid-free paper.

Notices

Knowledge and best practice in this field are constantly changing. As new research and experience broaden our understanding, changes in research methods, professional practices, or medical treatment may become necessary.

Practitioners and researchers must always rely on their own experience and knowledge in evaluating and using any information, methods, compounds, or experiments described herein. In using such information or methods they should be mindful of their own safety and the safety of others, including parties for whom they have a professional responsibility.

To the fullest extent of the law, neither the Publisher nor the authors, contributors, or editors, assume any liability for any injury and/or damage to persons or property as a matter of products liability, negligence or otherwise, or from any use or operation of any methods, products, instructions, or ideas contained in the material herein.

Library of Congress Cataloging-in-Publication Data
Allemang, Dean.
  Semantic Web for the working ontologist : effective modeling in RDFS and OWL / Dean Allemang, Jim Hendler. – 2nd ed.
     p. cm.
  Includes index.
  ISBN 978-0-12-385965-5
  1. Web site development. 2. Semantic Web. 3. Metadata. I. Hendler, James A. II. Title.
  TK5105.888.A45 2012
  025.042′7–dc22

                         2011010645

British Library Cataloguing-in-Publication Data
A catalogue record for this book is available from the British Library.

For information on all Morgan Kaufmann publications, visit
our Web site at www.mkp.com or www.elsevierdirect.com

Printed in the United States of America

11 12 13 14 15   5 4 3 2 1

Contents

Preface to the second edition

Since the first edition of *Semantic Web for the Working Ontologist* came out in June 2008, we have been encouraged by the reception the book has received. Practitioners from a wide variety of industries—health care, energy, environmental science, life sciences, national intelligence, and publishing, to name a few—have told us that the first edition clarified for them the possibilities and capabilities of Semantic Web technology. This was the audience we had hoped to reach, and we are happy to see that we have.

Since that time, the technology standards of the Semantic Web have continued to develop. SPARQL, the query language for RDF, became a Recommendation from the World Wide Web Consortium and was so successful that version 2 is already nearly ready (it will probably be ratified by the time this book sees print). SKOS, which we described as an example of modeling "in the wild" in the first edition, has raced to the forefront of the Semantic Web with high-profile uses in a wide variety of industries, so we gave it a chapter of its own. Version 2 of the Web Ontology Language, OWL, also appeared during this time.

Probably the biggest development in the Semantic Web standards since the first edition is the rise of the query language SPARQL. Beyond being a query language, SPARQL is a powerful graph-matching language which pushes its utility beyond simple queries. In particular, SPARQL can be used to specify general inferencing in a concise and precise way. We have adopted it as the main expository language for describing inferencing in this book. It turns out to be a lot easier to describe RDF, RDFS, and OWL in terms of SPARQL.

The "in the wild" sections became problematic in the second edition, but for a good reason—we had too many good examples to choose from. We're very happy with the final choices, and are pleased with the resulting "in the wild" chapters (9 and 13). The Open Graph Protocol and Good Relations are probably responsible for more serious RDF data on the Web than any other efforts. While one may argue (and many have) that FOAF is getting a bit long in the tooth, recent developments in social networking have brought concerns about privacy and ownership of social data to the fore; it was exactly these concerns that motivated FOAF over a decade ago. We also include two scientific examples of models "in the wild"—QUDT (Quantities, Units, Dimensions, and Types) and The Open Biological and Biomedical Ontologies (OBO). QUDT is a great example of how SPARQL can be used to specify detailed computation over a large set of rules (rules for converting units and for performing dimensional analysis). The wealth of information in the OBO has made them perennial favorites in health care and the life sciences. In our presentation, we hope to make them accessible to an audience who doesn't have specialized experience with OBO publication conventions. While these chapters logically build on the material that precedes them, we have done our best to make them stand alone, so that impatient readers who haven't yet mastered all the fine points of the earlier chapters can still appreciate the "wild" examples.

We have added some organizational aids to the book since the first edition. The "Challenges" that appear throughout the book, as in the first edition, provide examples for how to use the Semantic Web technologies to solve common modeling problems. The "FAQ" section organizes the challenges by topic, or, more properly, by the task that they illustrate. We have added a numeric index of all the challenges to help the reader cross-reference them.

We hope that the second edition will strike a chord with our readers as the first edition has done.

On a sad note, many of the examples in Chapter 5 use "Elizabeth Taylor" as an example of a "living actress." During postproduction of this book, Dame Elizabeth Taylor succumbed to congestive heart failure and died. We were too far along in the production to make the change, so we have kept the examples as they are. May her soul rest in peace.

PREFACE TO THE FIRST EDITION

In 2003, when the World Wide Web Consortium was working toward the ratification of the Recommendations for the Semantic Web languages, RDF, RDFS, and OWL, we realized that there was a need for an industrial-level introductory course in these technologies. The standards were technically sound, but, as is typically the case with standards documents, they were written with technical completeness in mind rather than education. We realized that for this technology to take off, people other than mathematicians and logicians would have to learn the basics of semantic modeling.

Toward that end, we started a collaboration to create a series of trainings aimed not at university students or technologists but at Web developers who were practitioners in some other field. In short, we needed to get the Semantic Web out of the hands of the logicians and Web technologists, whose job had been to build a consistent and robust infrastructure, and into the hands of the practitioners who were to build the Semantic Web. The Web didn't grow to the size it is today through the efforts of only HTML designers, nor would the Semantic Web grow as a result of only logicians' efforts.

After a year or so of offering training to a variety of audiences, we delivered a training course at the National Agriculture Library of the U.S. Department of Agriculture. Present for this training were a wide variety of practitioners in many fields, including health care, finance, engineering, national intelligence, and enterprise architecture. The unique synergy of these varied practitioners resulted in a dynamic four-day investigation into the power and subtlety of semantic modeling. Although the practitioners in the room were innovative and intelligent, we found that even for these early adopters, some of the new ways of thinking required for modeling in a World Wide Web context were too subtle to master after just a one-week course. One participant had registered for the course multiple times, insisting that something else "clicked" each time she went through the exercises.

This is when we realized that although the course was doing a good job of disseminating the information and skills for the Semantic Web, another, more archival resource was needed. We had to create something that students could work with on their own and could consult when they had questions. This was the point at which the idea of a book on modeling in the Semantic Web was conceived. We realized that the readership needed to include a wide variety of people from a number of fields, not just programmers or Web application developers but all the people from different fields who were struggling to understand how to use the new Web languages.

It was tempting at first to design this book to be the definitive statement on the Semantic Web vision, or "everything you ever wanted to know about OWL," including comparisons to program modeling languages such as UML, knowledge modeling languages, theories of inferencing and logic, details of the Web infrastructure (URIs and URLs), and the exact current status of all the developing standards (including SPARQL, GRDDL, RDFa, and the new OWL 1.1 effort). We realized, however, that not only would such a book be a superhuman undertaking, but it would also fail to serve our primary purpose of putting the tools of the Semantic Web into the hands of a generation of intelligent practitioners who could build real applications. For this reason, we concentrated on a particular essential skill for constructing the Semantic Web: building useful and reusable models in the World Wide Web setting.

Many of these patterns entail several variants, each embodying a different philosophy or approach to modeling. For advanced cases such as these, we realized that we couldn't hope to provide a single, definitive answer to how these things should be modeled. So instead, our goal is to educate domain practitioners so that they can read and understand design patterns of this sort and have the intellectual tools to make considered decisions about which ones to use and how to adapt them. We wanted to focus on those trying to use RDF, RDFS, and OWL to accomplish specific tasks and model their own data and domains, rather than write a generic book on ontology development. Thus, we have focused on the "working ontologist" who was trying to create a domain model on the Semantic Web.

The design patterns we use in this book tend to be much simpler. Often a pattern consists of only a single statement but one that is especially helpful when used in a particular context. The value of the pattern isn't so much in the complexity of its realization but in the awareness of the sort of situation in which it can be used.

This "make it useful" philosophy also motivated the choice of the examples we use to illustrate these patterns in this book. There are a number of competing criteria for good example domains in a book of this sort. The examples must be understandable to a wide variety of audiences, fairly compelling, yet complex enough to reflect real modeling situations. The actual examples we have encountered in our customer modeling situations satisfy the last condition but either are too specialized—for example, modeling complex molecular biological data; or, in some cases, they are too business-sensitive—for example, modeling particular investment policies—to publish for a general audience.

We also had to struggle with a tension between the coherence of the examples. We had to decide between using the same example throughout the book versus having stylistic variation and different examples, both so the prose didn't get too heavy with one topic, but also so the book didn't become one about how to model—for example, the life and works of William Shakespeare for the Semantic Web.

We addressed these competing constraints by introducing a fairly small number of example domains: William Shakespeare is used to illustrate some of the most basic capabilities of the Semantic Web. The tabular information about products and the manufacturing locations was inspired by the sample data provided with a popular database management package. Other examples come from domains we've worked with in the past or where there had been particular interest among our students. We hope the examples based on the roles of people in a workplace will be familiar to just about anyone who has worked in an office with more than one person, and that they highlight the capabilities of Semantic Web modeling when it comes to the different ways entities can be related to one another.

Some of the more involved examples are based on actual modeling challenges from fairly involved customer applications. For example, the ice cream example in Chapter 7 is based, believe it or not, on a workflow analysis example from a NASA application. The questionnaire is based on a number of customer examples for controlled data gathering, including sensitive intelligence gathering for a military application. In these cases, the domain has been changed to make the examples more entertaining and accessible to a general audience.

We have included a number of extended examples of Semantic Web modeling "in the wild," where we have found publicly available and accessible modeling projects for which there is no need to sanitize the models. These examples can include any number of anomalies or idiosyncrasies, which would be confusing as an introduction to modeling but as illustrations give a better picture about how these systems are being used on the World Wide Web. In accordance with the tenet that this book does not include everything we know about the Semantic Web, these examples are limited to the modeling issues that arise around the problem of distributing structured knowledge over the Web. Thus, the treatment focuses on how information is modeled for reuse and robustness in a distributed environment.

By combining these different example sources, we hope we have struck a happy balance among all the competing constraints and managed to include a fairly entertaining but comprehensive set of examples that can guide the reader through the various capabilities of the Semantic Web modeling languages.

This book provides many technical terms that we introduce in a somewhat informal way. Although there have been many volumes written that debate the formal meaning of words like *inference, representation,* and even *meaning,* we have chosen to stick to a relatively informal and operational use of the terms. We feel this is more appropriate to the needs of the ontology designer or application developer for whom this book was written. We apologize to those philosophers and formalists who may be offended by our casual use of such important concepts.

We often find that when people hear we are writing a new Semantic Web modeling book, their first question is, "Will it have examples?" For this book, the answer is an emphatic "Yes!" Even with a wide variety of examples, however, it is easy to keep thinking "inside the box" and to focus too heavily on the details of the examples themselves. We hope you will use the examples as they were intended: for illustration and education. But you should also consider how the examples could be changed, adapted, or retargeted to model something in your personal domain. In the Semantic Web, Anyone can say Anything about Any topic. Explore the freedom.

Second Printing: Since the first printing there have been advances in several of the technologies we discuss such as SPARQL, OWL 2, and SKOS that go beyond the state of affairs at the time of first printing. We have created a web site that covers developing technology standards and changing thinking about the best practices for the Semantic Web. You can find it at http://www .workingontologist.org/.

Acknowledgments

The second edition builds on the work of Semantic Web practitioners and researchers who have moved the field forward in the past two years—they are too numerous to thank individually. But we would like to extend special recognition to James "Chip" Masters, Martin Hepp, Ralph Hodgson, Austin Haugen, and Paul Tarjan, whose work on various ontologies allowed them to be mature enough to serve as examples "in the wild."

We also want to thank TopQuadrant, Inc. for making their software TopBraid Composer™ available for the preparation of the book. All examples were managed using this software, and the figures that show RDF data were laid out using its graphic capabilities. The book would have been much harder to manage without it.

Once again, Mike Uschold contributed heroic effort as a reviewer of several of the chapters. We also wish to thank John Madden, Scott Henninger, and Jeff Stein for their reviews of various parts of the second edition.

The faculty staff and students at the Tetherless World Constellation at RPI have also been a great help. The inside knowledge from members of the various W3C working groups they staff, the years of experience in Semantic Web among the staff, and the great work done by Peter Fox and Deborah McGuinness served as inspiration as well as encouragement in getting the second edition done.

We especially want to thank Todd Green and the staff at Elsevier for pushing us to do a second edition, and for their patience when we missed deadlines that meant more work for them in less time.

Most of all, we want to thank the readers who provided feedback on the first edition that helped us to shape the book as it is now. We write books for the readers, and their feedback is essential. Thank you for the work you put in on the web site—you have been heard, and your feedback is incorporated into the second edition.

About the authors

Dean Allemang is the chief scientist at TopQuadrant, Inc.—the first company in the United States devoted to consulting, training, and products for the Semantic Web. He codeveloped (with Professor Hendler) TopQuadrant's successful Semantic Web training series, which he has been delivering on a regular basis since 2003.

He was the recipient of a National Science Foundation Graduate Fellowship and the President's 300th Commencement Award at Ohio State University. He has studied and worked extensively throughout Europe as a Marshall Scholar at Trinity College, Cambridge, from 1982 through 1984 and was the winner of the Swiss Technology Prize twice (1992 and 1996).

He has served as an invited expert on numerous international review boards, including a review of the Digital Enterprise Research Institute—the world's largest Semantic Web research institute, and the Innovative Medicines Initiative, a collaboration between 10 pharmaceutical companies and the European Commission to set the roadmap for the pharmaceutical industry for the near future.

Jim Hendler is the Tetherless World Senior Constellation Chair at Rensselaer Polytechnic Institute where he has appointments in the Departments of Computer Science and Cognitive Science and the Assistant Dean for Information Technology and Web Science. He also serves as a trustee of the Web Science Trust in the United Kingdom. Dr. Hendler has authored over 200 technical papers in the areas of artificial intelligence, Semantic Web, agent-based computing, and Web science.

One of the early developers of the Semantic Web, he was the recipient of a 1995 Fulbright Foundation Fellowship, is a former member of the US Air Force Science Advisory Board, and is a Fellow of the IEEE, the American Association for Artificial Intelligence and the British Computer Society. Dr. Hendler is also the former chief scientist at the Information Systems Office of the US Defense Advanced Research Projects Agency (DARPA) and was awarded a US Air Force Exceptional Civilian Service Medal in 2002. He is the Editor-in-Chief emeritus of *IEEE Intelligent Systems* and is the first computer scientist to serve on the Board of Reviewing Editors for *Science* and in 2010, he was chosen as one of the 20 most innovative professors in America by *Playboy* magazine, Hendler currently serves as an "Internet Web Expert" for the US government, providing guidance to the Data.gov project.

What is the Semantic Web?

This book is about something we call the Semantic Web. From the name, you can probably guess that it is related somehow to the World Wide Web (WWW) and that it has something to do with semantics. Semantics, in turn, has to do with understanding the nature of meaning, but even the word *semantics* has a number of meanings. In what sense are we using the word *semantics?* And how can it be applied to the Web?

This book is for a working ontologist. That is, the aim of this book is not to motivate or pitch the Semantic Web but to provide the tools necessary for working with it. Or, perhaps more accurately, the World Wide Web Consortium (W3C) has provided these tools in the forms of standard Semantic Web languages, complete with abstract syntax, model-based semantics, reference implementations, test cases, and so forth. But these are like any tools—there are some basic tools that are all you need to build many useful things, and there are specialized craftsman's tools that can produce far more specializes outputs. Whichever tools are needed for a particular task, however, one still needs to understand how to use them. In the hands of someone with no knowledge, they can produce clumsy, ugly, barely functional output, but in the hands of a skilled craftsman, they can produce works of utility, beauty, and durability. It is our aim in this book to describe the craft of building Semantic Web systems. We go beyond only providing a coverage of the fundamental tools to also show how they can be used together to create semantic models, sometimes called *ontologies,* that are understandable, useful, durable, and perhaps even beautiful.

WHAT IS A WEB?

The idea of a web of information was once a technical idea accessible only to highly trained, elite information professionals: IT administrators, librarians, information architects, and the like. Since the widespread adoption of the World Wide Web, it is now common to expect just about anyone to be familiar with the idea of a web of information that is shared around the world. Contributions to this web come from every source, and every topic you can think of is covered.

Essential to the notion of the Web is the idea of an open community: Anyone can contribute their ideas to the whole, for anyone to see. It is this openness that has resulted in the astonishing comprehensiveness of topics covered by the Web. An information "web" is an organic entity that grows from the interests and energy of the communities that support it. As such, it is a hodgepodge of different analyses, presentations, and summaries of any topic that suits the fancy of anyone with the energy to publish a web page. Even as a hodgepodge, the Web is pretty useful. Anyone with the patience and savvy to dig through it can find support for just about any inquiry that interests them. But the Web often feels like it is "a mile wide but an inch deep." How can we build a more integrated, consistent, deep Web experience?

SMART WEB, DUMB WEB

Suppose you consult a web page, looking for a major national park, and you find a list of hotels that have branches in the vicinity of the park. In that list you see that Mongotel, one of the well-known hotel chains, has a branch there. Since you have a Mongotel rewards card, you decide to book your room there. So you click on the Mongotel web site and search for the hotel's location. To your surprise, you can't find a Mongotel branch at the national park. What is going on here? "That's so dumb," you tell your browsing friends. "If they list Mongotel on the national park web site, shouldn't they list the national park on Mongotel's web site?"

Suppose you are planning to attend a conference in a far-off city. The conference web site lists the venue where the sessions will take place. You go to the web site of your preferred hotel chain and find a few hotels in the same vicinity. "Which hotel in my chain is nearest to the conference?" you wonder. "And just how far off is it?" There is no shortage of web sites that can compute these distances once you give them the addresses of the venue and your own hotel. So you spend some time copying and pasting the addresses from one page to the next and noting the distances. You think to yourself, "Why should I be the one to copy this information from one page to another? Why do I have to be the one to copy and paste all this information into a single map?

Suppose you are investigating our solar system, and you find a comprehensive web site about objects in the solar system: Stars (well, there's just one of those), planets, moons, asteroids, and comets are all described there. Each object has its own web page, with photos and essential information (mass, albedo, distance from the sun, shape, size, what object it revolves around, period of rotation, period of revolution, etc.). At the head of the page is the object category: planet, moon, asteroid, comet. Another page includes interesting lists of objects: the moons of Jupiter, the named objects in the asteroid belt, the planets that revolve around the sun. This last page has the nine familiar planets, each linked to its own data page.

One day, you read in the newspaper that the International Astronomical Union (IAU) has decided that Pluto, which up until 2006 was considered a planet, should be considered a member of a new category called a "dwarf planet"! You rush to the Pluto page and see that indeed, the update has been made: Pluto is listed as a dwarf planet! But when you go back to the "Solar Planets" page, you still see nine planets listed under the heading "Planet." Pluto is still there! "That's dumb." Then you say to yourself, "Why didn't someone update the web pages consistently?"

What do these examples have in common? Each of them has an apparent representation of data, whose presentation to the end user (the person operating the Web browser) seems "dumb." What do we mean by "dumb"? In this case, "dumb" means inconsistent, out of synchronized, and disconnected. What would it take to make the Web experience seem smarter? Do we need smarter applications or a smarter Web infrastructure?

Smart web applications

The Web is full of intelligent applications, with new innovations coming every day. Ideas that once seemed futuristic are now commonplace; search engines make matches that seem deep and intuitive; commerce sites make smart recommendations personalized in uncanny ways to your own purchasing patterns; mapping sites include detailed information about world geography, and they can plan routes and measure distances. The sky is the limit for the technologies a web site can draw on. Every information technology under the sun can be used in a web site, and many of them are. New sites with new capabilities come on the scene on a regular basis.

But what is the role of the Web infrastructure in making these applications "smart"? It is tempting to make the infrastructure of the Web smart enough to encompass all of these technologies and more. The smarter the infrastructure, the smarter the Web's performance, right? But it isn't practical, or even possible, for the Web infrastructure to provide specific support for all, or even any, of the technologies that we might want to use on the Web. Smart behavior in the Web comes from smart applications on the Web, not from the infrastructure.

So what role does the infrastructure play in making the Web smart? Is there a role at all? We have smart applications on the Web, so why are we even talking about enhancing the Web infrastructure to make a smarter Web if the smarts aren't in the infrastructure?

The reason we are improving the Web infrastructure is to allow smart applications to perform to their potential. Even the most insightful and intelligent application is only as smart as the data that is available to it. Inconsistent or contradictory input will still result in confusing, disconnected, "dumb" results, even from very smart applications. The challenge for the design of the Semantic Web is not to make a web infrastructure that is as smart as possible; it is to make an infrastructure that is most appropriate to the job of integrating information on the Web.

The Semantic Web doesn't make data smart because smart data isn't what the Semantic Web needs. The Semantic Web just needs to get the right data to the right place so the smart applications can do their work. So the question to ask is not "How can we make the Web infrastructure smarter?" but "What can the Web infrastructure provide to improve the consistency and availability of Web data?"

Connected data is smarter data

Even in the face of intelligent applications, disconnected data result in dumb behavior. But the Web data don't have to be smart; that's the job of the applications. So what can we realistically and productively expect from the data in our Web applications? In a nutshell, we want data that don't surprise us with inconsistencies that make us want to say, "This doesn't make sense!" We don't need a smart Web infrastructure, but we need a Web infrastructure that lets us connect data to smart Web applications so that the whole Web experience is enhanced. The Web *seems* smarter because smart applications can get the data they need.

In the example of the hotels in the national park, we'd like there to be coordination between the two web pages so that an update to the location of hotels would be reflected in the list of hotels at any particular location. We'd like the two sources to stay synchronized; then we won't be surprised at confusing and inconsistent conclusions drawn from information taken from different pages of the same site.

In the mapping example, we'd like the data from the conference web site and the data from the hotels web site to be automatically understandable to the mapping web site. It shouldn't take interpretation by a human user to move information from one site to the other. The mapping web site already has the smarts it needs to find shortest routes (taking into account details like toll roads and one-way streets) and to estimate the time required to make the trip, but it can only do that if it knows the correct starting and endpoints.

We'd like the astronomy web site to update consistently. If we state that Pluto is no longer a planet, the list of planets should reflect that fact as well. This is the sort of behavior that gives a reader confidence that what they are reading reflects the state of knowledge reported in the web site, regardless of how they read it.

None of these things is beyond the reach of current information technology. In fact, it is not uncommon for programmers and system architects, when they first learn of the Semantic Web, to exclaim proudly, "I implemented something very like that for a project I did a few years back. We used…." Then they go on to explain how they used some conventional, established technology such as relational databases, XML stores, or object stores to make their data more connected and consistent. But what is it that these developers are building?

What is it about managing data this way that made it worth their while to create a whole subsystem on top of their base technology to deal with it? And where are these projects two or more years later? When those same developers are asked whether they would rather have built a flexible, distributed, connected data model support system themselves than have used a standard one that someone else optimized and supported, they unanimously chose the latter. Infrastructure is something that one would rather buy than build.

SEMANTIC DATA

In the Mongotel example, there is a list of hotels at the national park and another list of locations for hotels. The fact that these lists are intended to represent the presence of a hotel at a certain location is not explicit anywhere; this makes it difficult to maintain consistency between the two representations. In the example of the conference venue, the address appears only as text typeset on a page so that human beings can interpret it as an address. There is no explicit representation of the notion of an address or the parts that make up an address. In the case of the astronomy web page, there is no explicit representation of the status of an object as a planet. In all of these cases, the data describe the presentation of information rather than describe the entities in the world.

Could it be some other way? Can an application organize its data so that they provide an integrated description of objects in the world and their relationships rather than their presentation? The answer is "yes," and indeed it is common good practice in web site design to work this way. There are a number of well-known approaches.

One common way to make Web applications more integrated is to back them up with a relational database and generate the web pages from queries run against that database. Updates to the site are made by updating the contents of the database. All web pages that require information about a particular data record will change when that record changes, without any further action required by the Web maintainer. The database holds information about the entities themselves, while the relationship between one page and another (presentation) is encoded in the different queries.

Consider the case of the national parks and hotel. If these pages were backed by the same database, the national park page could be built on the query "Find all hotels with location = national park," and the hotel page could be built on the query "Find all hotels from chain = Mongotel." If Mongotel has a location at the national park, it will appear on both pages; otherwise, it won't appear at all. Both pages will be consistent. The difficulty in the example given is that it is organizationally very unlikely that there could be a single database driving both of these pages, since one of them is published and maintained by the National Park Service and the other is managed by the Mongotel chain.

The astronomy case is very similar to the hotel case, in that the same information (about the classification of various astronomical bodies) is accessed from two different places, ensuring consistency of information even in the face of diverse presentation. It differs in that it is more likely that an astronomy club or university department might maintain a database with all the currently known information about the solar system.

In these cases, the Web applications can behave more robustly by adding an organizing query into the Web application to mediate between a single view of the data and the presentation. The data aren't any less dumb than before, but at least what's there is centralized, and the application or the web pages can be made to organize the data in a way that is more consistent for the user to view. It is the web page or application that behaves smarter, not the data. While this approach is useful for supporting data consistency, it doesn't help much with the conference mapping example.

Another approach to making Web applications a bit smarter is to write program code in a general-purpose language (e.g., C, Perl, Java, Lisp, Python, or XSLT) that keeps data from different places up to date. In the hotel example, such a program would update the National Park web page whenever a change is made to a corresponding hotel page. A similar solution would allow the planet example to be more consistent. Code for this purpose is often organized in a relational database application in the form of *stored procedures;* in XML applications, it can be affected using a transformational language like XSLT.

These solutions are more cumbersome to implement since they require special-purpose code to be written for each linkage of data, but they have the advantage over a centralized database that they do not require all the publishers of the data to agree on and share a single data source. Furthermore, such approaches could provide a solution to the conference mapping problem by transforming data from one source to another. Just as in the query/presentation solution, this solution does not make the data any smarter; it just puts an informed infrastructure around the data, whose job it is to keep the various data sources consistent.

The common trend in these solutions is to move away from having the presentation of the data (for human eyes) be the primary representation of the data; that is, they move from having a web site be a collection of pages to having a web site be a collection of data, from which the web page presentations are generated. The application focuses not on the presentation but on the subjects of the presentation. It is in this sense that these applications are semantic applications; they explicitly represent the relationships that underlie the application and generate presentations as needed.

A distributed web of data

The Semantic Web takes this idea one step further, applying it to the Web as a whole. The current Web infrastructure supports a distributed network of web pages that can refer to one another with global links called Uniform Resource Locators (URLs). As we have seen, sophisticated web sites replace this structure locally with a database or XML backend that ensures consistency within that page.

The main idea of the Semantic Web is to support a distributed Web at the level of the data rather than at the level of the presentation. Instead of having one web page point to another, one data item can point to another, using global references called Uniform Resource Identifiers (URIs). The Web infrastructure provides a data model whereby information about a single entity can be distributed over the Web. This distribution allows the Mongotel example and the conference hotel example to work like the astronomy example, even though the information is distributed over web sites controlled by more than one organization. The single, coherent data model for the application is not held inside one application but rather is part of the Web infrastructure. When Mongotel publishes information about its hotels and their locations, it doesn't just publish a human-readable presentation of this information but instead a distributable, machine-readable description of the data. The data model that the Semantic Web infrastructure uses to represent this distributed web of data is called the Resource Description Framework (RDF) and is the topic of Chapter 3.

This single, distributed model of information is the contribution that the Semantic Web infrastructure brings to a smarter Web. Just as is the case with data-backed Web applications, the Semantic Web infrastructure allows the data to drive the presentation so that various web pages (presentations) can provide views into a consistent body of information. In this way, the Semantic Web helps data not be so dumb.

Features of a Semantic Web

The World Wide Web was the result of a radical new way of thinking about sharing information. These ideas seem familiar now, as the Web itself has become pervasive. But this radical new way of thinking has even more profound ramifications when it is applied to a web of data like the Semantic Web. These ramifications have driven many of the design decisions for the Semantic Web Standards and have a strong influence on the craft of producing quality Semantic Web applications.

Give me a voice …

On the World Wide Web, publication is by and large in the hands of the content producer. People can build their own web page and say whatever they want on it. A wide range of opinions on any topic can be found; it is up to the reader to come to a conclusion about what to believe. The Web is the ultimate example of the warning *caveat emptor* ("Let the buyer beware"). This feature of the Web is so instrumental in its character that we give it a name: the *AAA Slogan*: "**A**nyone can say **A**nything about **A**ny topic."

In a web of documents, the AAA slogan means that anyone can write a page saying whatever they please, and publish it to the Web infrastructure. In the case of the Semantic Web, it means that our data infrastructure has to allow any individual to express a piece of data about some entity in a way that can be combined with information from other sources. This requirement sets some of the foundation for the design of RDF.

It also means that the Web is like a data wilderness—full of valuable treasure, but overgrown and tangled. Even the valuable data that you can find can take any of a number of forms, adapted to its own part of the wilderness. In contrast to the situation in a large, corporate data center, where one database administrator rules with an iron hand over any addition or modification to the database, the Web has no gatekeeper. Anything and everything can grow there. A distributed web of data is an organic system, with contributions coming from all sources. While this can be maddening for someone trying to make sense of information on the Web, this freedom of expression on the Web is what allowed it to take off as a bottom-up, grassroots phenomenon.

... *So I may speak!*

In the early days of the document Web, it was common for skeptics, hearing for the first time about the possibilities of a worldwide distributed web full of hyperlinked pages on every topic, to ask, "But who is going to create all that content? Someone has to write those web pages!"

To the surprise of those skeptics, and even of many proponents of the Web, the answer to this question was that *everyone* would provide the content. Once the Web infrastructure was in place (so that Anyone could say Anything about Any topic), people came out of the woodwork to do just that. Soon every topic under the sun had a web page, either official or unofficial. It turns out that a lot of people had something to say, and they were willing to put some work into saying it. As this trend continued, it resulted in collaborative "crowdsourced" resources like Wikipedia and the Internet Movie DataBase (IMDB)—collaboratively edited information sources with broad utility.

The document Web grew because of a virtuous cycle that is called the *network effect*. In a network of contributors like the Web, the infrastructure made it *possible* for anyone to publish, but what made it *desirable* for them to do so? At one point in the Web, when Web browsers were a novelty, there was not much incentive to put a page on this new thing called "the Web"; after all, who was going to read it? Why do I want to communicate to them? Just as it isn't very useful to be the first kid on the block to have a fax machine (whom do you exchange faxes with?), it wasn't very interesting to be the first kid with a Web server.

But because a few people did have Web servers, and a few more got Web browsers, it became more attractive to have both web pages and Web browsers. Content providers found a larger audience for their work; content consumers found more content to browse. As this trend continued, it became more and more attractive, and more people joined in, on both sides. This is the basis of the network effect: The more people who are playing now, the more attractive it is for new people to start playing.

A good deal of the information that populates the Semantic Web started out on the document Web, sometimes in the form of tables, spreadsheets, or databases, and sometimes as organized group efforts like Wikipedia. Who is doing the work of converting this data to RDF for distributed access? In the earliest days of the Semantic Web there was little incentive to do so, and it was done primarily by vanguards who had an interest in Semantic Web technology itself. As more and more data is available in RDF form, it becomes more useful to write applications that utilize this distributed data. Already there are several large, public data sources available in RDF, including an RDF image of Wikipedia called dbpedia, and a surprisingly large number of government datasets. Small retailers publish information about their offerings using a Semantic Web format called RDFa. Facebook allows content managers to provide structured data using RDFa and a format called the Open Graph Protocol. The presense of these sorts of data sources makes it more useful to produce data in linked form for the Semantic Web. The Semantic Web design allows it to benefit from the same network effect that drove the document Web.

What about the round-worlders?

The network effect has already proven to be an effective and empowering way to muster the effort needed to create a massive information network like the World Wide Web; in fact, it is the only method that has actually succeeded in creating such a structure. The AAA slogan enables the network effect that made the rapid growth of the Web possible. But what are some of the ramifications of such an open system? What does the AAA slogan imply for the content of an organically grown web?

For the network effect to take hold, we have to be prepared to cope with a wide range of variance in the information on the Web. Sometimes the differences will be minor details in an otherwise agreed-on area; at other times, differences may be essential disagreements that drive political and cultural discourse in our society. This phenomenon is apparent in the document web today; for just about any topic, it is possible to find web pages that express widely differing opinions about that topic. The ability to disagree, and at various levels, is an essential part of human discourse and a key aspect of the Web that makes it successful. Some people might want to put forth a very odd opinion on any topic; someone might even want to postulate that the world is round, while others insist that it is flat. The infrastructure of the Web must allow both of these (contradictory) opinions to have equal availability and access.

There are a number of ways in which two speakers on the Web may disagree. We will illustrate each of them with the example of the status of Pluto as a planet:

They may fundamentally disagree on some topic. While the IAU has changed its definition of *planet* in such a way that Pluto is no longer included, it is not necessarily the case that every astronomy club or even national body agrees with this categorization. Many astrologers, in particular, who have a vested interest in considering Pluto to be a planet, have decided to continue to consider Pluto as a planet. In such cases, different sources will simply disagree.

Someone might want to intentionally deceive. Someone who markets posters, models, or other works that depict nine planets has a good reason to delay reporting the result from the IAU and even to spreading uncertainty about the state of affairs.

Someone might simply be mistaken. Web sites are built and maintained by human beings, and thus they are subject to human error. Some web site might erroneously list Pluto as a planet or, indeed, might even erroneously fail to list one of the eight "nondwarf" planets as a planet.

Some information may be out of date. There are a number of displays around the world of scale models of the solar system, in which the status of the planets is literally carved in stone; these will continue to list Pluto as a planet until such time as there is funding to carve a new description for the ninth object. Web sites are not carved in stone, but it does take effort to update them; not everyone will rush to accomplish this.

While some of the reasons for disagreement might be, well, disagreeable (wouldn't it be nice if we could stop people from lying?), in practice there isn't any way to tell them apart. The infrastructure of the Web has to be able to cope with the fact that information on the Web will disagree from time to time and that this is not a temporary condition. It is in the very nature of the Web that there be variations and disagreement.

The Semantic Web is often mistaken for an effort to make everyone agree on a single ontology—but that just isn't the way the Web works. The Semantic Web isn't about getting everyone to agree, but rather about coping in a world where not everyone will agree, and achieving some degree of inter-operability nevertheless. There will always be multiple ontologies, just as there will always be multiple web pages on any given topic. The Web is innovative because it allows all these multiple viewpoints to coexist.

To each their own

How can the Web infrastructure support this sort of variation of opinion? That is, how can two people say different things, about the same topic? There are two approaches to this issue. First, we have to talk a bit about how one can make any statement at all in a web context.

The IAU can make a statement in plain English about Pluto, such as "Pluto is a dwarf planet," but such a statement is fraught with all the ambiguities and contextual dependencies inherent in natural language. We think we know what "Pluto" refers to, but how about "dwarf planet"? Is there any possibility that someone might disagree on what a "dwarf planet" is? How can we even discuss such things?

The first requirement for making statements on a global web is to have a global way of identifying the entities we are talking about. We need to be able to refer to "the notion of Pluto as used by the IAU" and "the notion of Pluto as used by the American Federation of Astrologers" if we even want to be able to discuss whether the two organizations are referring to the same thing by these names.

In addition to Pluto, another object was also classified as a "dwarf planet." This object is sometimes known as UB313 and sometimes known by the name Xena. How can we say that the object known to the IAU as UB313 is the same object that its discoverer Michael Brown calls "Xena"?

One way to do this would be to have a global arbiter of names decide how to refer to the object. Then Brown and the IAU can both refer to that "official" name and say that they use a private "nickname" for it. Of course, the IAU itself is a good candidate for such a body, but the process to name the object has taken over two years. Coming up with good, agreed-on global names is not always easy business.

In the absence of such an agreement, different Web authors will select different URIs for the same real-world resource. Brown's Xena is IAU's UB313. When information from these different sources is brought together in the distributed network of data, the Web infrastructure has no way of knowing that these need to be treated as the same entity. The flip side of this is that we cannot assume that just because two URIs are distinct, they refer to distinct resources. This feature of the Semantic Web is called the *Nonunique Naming Assumption;* that is, we have to assume (until told otherwise) that some Web resource might be referred to using different names by different people. It's also crucial to note that there are times when unique names might be nice, but it may be impossible. Some other organization than the IAU, for example, might decide they are unwilling to accept the new nomenclature.

There's always one more

In a distributed network of information, as a rule we cannot assume at any time that we have seen all the information in the network, or even that we know everything that has been asserted about one single topic. This is evident in the history of Pluto and UB313. For many years, it was sufficient to say that a *planet* was defined as "any object of a particular size orbiting the sun." Given the information available during that time, it was easy to say that there were nine planets around the sun. But the new information about UB313 changed that; if a planet is defined to be any body that orbits the sun of a particular size, then UB313 had to be considered a planet, too. Careful speakers in the late twentieth century, of course, spoke of the "known" planets, since they were aware that another planet was not only possible but even suspected (the so-called "Planet X," which stood in for the unknown but suspected planet for many years).

The same situation holds for the Semantic Web. Not only might new information be discovered at any time (as is the case in solar system astronomy), but, because of the networked nature of the Web, at any one time a particular server that holds some unique information might be unavailable. For this reason, on the Semantic Web we can rarely conclude things like "there are nine planets," since we don't know what new information might come to light.

In general, this aspect of a Web has a subtle but profound impact on how we draw conclusions from the information we have. It forces us to consider the Web as an *Open World* and to treat it using the *Open World Assumption.* An Open World in this sense is one in which we must assume at any time that new information could come to light, and we may draw no conclusions that rely on assuming that the information available at any one point is all the information available.

For many applications, the Open World Assumption makes no difference; if we draw a map of all the Mongotel hotels in Boston, we get a map of all the ones we know of at the time. The fact that Mongotel might have more hotels in Boston (or might open a new one) does not invalidate the fact that it has the ones it already lists. In fact, for a great deal of Semantic Web applications, we can ignore the Open World Assumption and simply understand that a semantic application, like any other web page, is simply reporting on the information it was able to access at one time.

The openness of the Web only becomes an issue when we want to draw conclusions based on distributed data. If we want to place Boston in the list of cities that are not served by Mongotel (e.g., as part of a market study of new places to target Mongotels), then we cannot assume that just because we haven't found a Mongotel listing in Boston, no such hotel exists.

As we shall see in the following chapters, the Semantic Web includes features that correspond to all the ways of working with Open Worlds that we have seen in the real world. We can draw conclusions about missing Mongotels if we say that some list is a comprehensive list of all Mongotels. We can have an anonymous "Planet X" stand in for an unknown but anticipated entity. These techniques allow us to cope with the Open World Assumption in the Semantic Web, just as they do in the Open World of human knowledge.

When will the Semantic Web arrive? It already has. In selecting candidate examples for this second edition, we had to pick and choose from a wide range of Semantic Web deployments. We devote two chapters to in-depth studies of these deployments "in the wild." In Chapter 9, we see how the US government shares data about its operations in a flexible way and how Facebook uses the Semantic Web to link pages from all over the web into its network. Chapter 13 shows how the Semantic Web is used by thousands of e-commerce web pages to make information available to mass markets through major search engines and how scientific communities share key information about engineering, chemistry, and biology. The Semantic Web is here today.

SUMMARY

The aspects of the Web we have outlined here—the AAA slogan, the network effect, nonunique naming, and the Open World Assumption—already hold for the document Web. As a result, the Web today is something of an unruly place, with a wide variety of different sources, organizations, and styles of information. Effective and creative use of search engines is something of a craft; efforts to make order from this include community efforts like social bookmarking and community encyclopedias to automated methods like statistical correlations and fuzzy similarity matches.

For the Semantic Web, which operates at the finer level of individual statements about data, the situation is even wilder. With a human in the loop, contradictions and inconsistencies in the document Web can be dealt with by the process of human observation and application of common sense. With a machine combining information, how do we bring any order to the chaos? How can one have any confidence in the information we merge from multiple sources? If the document Web is unruly, then surely the Semantic Web is a jungle—a rich mass of interconnected information, without any road map, index, or guidance.

How can such a mess become something useful? That is the challenge that faces the working ontologist. Their medium is the distributed web of data; their tools are the Semantic Web languages RDF, RDFS, SPARQL, SKOS, and OWL. Their craft is to make sensible, usable, and durable information resources from this medium. We call that craft *modeling,* and it is the centerpiece of this book.

The cover of this book shows a system of channels with water coursing through them. If we think of the water as the data on the Web, the channels are the model. If not for the model, the water would not flow in any systematic way; there would simply be a vast, undistinguished expanse of water. Without the water, the channels would have no dynamism; they have no moving parts in and of themselves. Put the two together, and we have a dynamic system. The water flows in an orderly fashion, defined by the structure of the channels. This is the role that a model plays in the Semantic Web.

Without the model, there is an undifferentiated mass of data; there is no way to tell which data can or should interact with other data. The model itself has no significance without data to describe it. Put the two together, however, and you have a dynamic web of information, where data flow from one point to another in a principled, systematic fashion. This is the vision of the Semantic Web—an organized worldwide system where information flows from one place to another in a smooth but orderly way.

Fundamental concepts

The following fundamental concepts were introduced in this chapter.

The AAA slogan—Anyone can say Anything about Any topic. One of the basic tenets of the Web in general and the Semantic Web in particular.

Open world/Closed world—A consequence of the AAA slogan is that there could always be something new that someone will say; this means that we must assume that there is always more information that could be known.

Nonunique naming—Since the speakers on the Web won't necessarily coordinate their naming efforts, the same entity could be known by more than one name.

The network effect—The property of a web that makes it grow organically. The value of joining in increases with the number of people who have joined, resulting in a virtuous cycle of participation.

The data wilderness—The condition of most data on the web. It contains valuable information, but there is no guarantee that it will be orderly or readily understandable.

Semantic modeling

What would you call a world in which any number of people can speak, when you never know who has something useful to say, and when someone new might come along at any time and make a valuable but unexpected contribution? What if just about everyone had the same goal of advancing the collaborative state of knowledge of the group, but there was little agreement (at first, anyway) about how to achieve it?

If your answer is "That sounds like the Semantic Web!" you are right (and you must have read Chapter 1). If your answer is "It sounds like any large group trying to understand a complex phenomenon," you are even more right. The jungle that is the Semantic Web is not a new thing; this sort of chaos has existed since people first tried to make sense of the world around them.

What intellectual tools have been successful in helping people sort through this sort of tangle? Any number of analytical tools has been developed over the years, but they all have one thing in common: They help people understand their world by forming an abstract description that hides certain details while illuminating others. These abstractions are called *models,* and they can take many forms.

How do models help people assemble their knowledge? Models assist in three essential ways:

1. *Models help people communicate.* A model describes the situation in a particular way that other people can understand.
2. *Models explain and make predictions.* A model relates primitive phenomena to one another and to more complex phenomena, providing explanations and predictions about the world.
3. *Models mediate among multiple viewpoints.* No two people agree completely on what they want to know about a phenomenon; models represent their commonalities while allowing them to explore their differences.

The Semantic Web standards have been created not only as a medium in which people can collaborate by sharing information but also as a medium in which people can collaborate on models. Models that they can use to organize the information that they share. Models that they can use to advance the common collection of knowledge.

How can a model help us find our way through the mess that is the Web? How do these three features help? The first feature, human communication, allows people to collaborate on their understanding. If someone else has faced the same challenge that you face today, perhaps you can learn from their experience and apply it to yours. There are a number of examples of this in the Web today, of newsgroups, mailing lists, and wikis where people can ask questions and get answers. In the case in which the information needs are fairly uniform, it is not uncommon for a community or a company to assemble a set of "Frequently Asked Questions," or FAQs, that gather the appropriate knowledge as answers to these questions. As the number of questions becomes unmanageable, it is not uncommon to group them by topic, by task, by affected subsystem, and so forth. This sort of activity, by which information is organized for the purpose of sharing, is the simplest and most common kind of modeling, with the sole aim of helping a group of people collaborate in their effort to sort through a complex set of knowledge.

The second feature, explanation and prediction, helps individuals make their own judgments based on information they receive. FAQs are useful when there is a single authority that can give clear answers to a question, as is the case for technical assistance for using some appliance or service. But in more interpretive situations, someone might want or need to draw a conclusion for themselves. In such a situation, a simple answer as given in a FAQ is not sufficient. Politics is a common example from everyday life. Politicians in debate do not tell people how to vote, but they try to convince them to vote in one way or another. Part of that convincing is done by explaining their position and allowing the individual to evaluate whether that explanation holds true to their own beliefs about the world. They also typically make predictions: If we follow this course of action, then a particular outcome will follow. Of course, a lot more goes into political persuasion than the argument, but explanation and prediction are key elements of a persuasive argument.

Finally, the third feature, mediation of multiple viewpoints, is essential to fostering understanding in a web environment. As the web of opinions and facts grows, many people will say things that disagree slightly or even outright contradict what others are saying. Anyone who wants to make their way through this will have to be able to sort out different opinions, representing what they have in common as well as the ways in which they differ. This is one of the most essential organizing principles of a large, heterogeneous knowledge set, and it is one of the major contributions that modeling makes to helping people organize what they know.

Astrologers and the IAU agree on the planethood of Mercury, Venus, Earth, Mars, Jupiter, Saturn, Uranus, and Neptune. The IAU also agrees with astrologers that Pluto is a planet, but it disagrees by calling it a dwarf planet. Astrologers (or classical astronomers) do not accept the concept of dwarf planets, so they are not in agreement with the IAU, which categorizes UB313 and Ceres as such. A model for the Semantic Web must be able to organize this sort of variation, and much more, in a meaningful and manageable way.

MODELING FOR HUMAN COMMUNICATION

Models used for human communication have a great advantage over models that are intended for use by computers; they can take advantage of the human capacity to interpret signs to give them meaning. This means that communication models can be written in a wide variety of forms, including plain language or ad hoc images. A model can be explained by one person, amended by another, interpreted by a third person, and so on. Models written in natural language have been used in all manner of intellectual life, including science, religion, government, and mathematics.

But this advantage is a double-edged sword; when we leave it to humans to interpret the meaning of a model, we open the door for all manner of abuse, both intentional and unintentional. Legislation provides a good example of this. A governing body like a parliament or a legislature enacts laws that are intended to mediate rights and responsibilities between various parties. Legislation typically sets up some sort of model of a situation, perhaps involving money (e.g., interest caps, taxes); access rights (who can view what information, how can information be legally protected); personal freedom (how freely can one travel across borders, when does the government have the right to restrict a person's movements); or even the structure of government itself (who can vote and how are those votes counted, how can government officials be removed from office). These models are painstakingly written in natural language and agreed on through an elaborate process (which is also typically modeled in natural language).

It is well known to anyone with even a passing interest in politics that good legislation is not an easy task and that crafting the words carefully for a law or statute is very important. The same flexibility of interpretation that makes natural language models so flexible also makes it difficult to control how the laws will be interpreted in the future. When someone else reads the text, they will have their own background and their own interests that will influence how they interpret any particular model. This phenomenon is so widespread that most government systems include a process (usually involving a court magistrate and possibly a committee of citizens) whereby disputes over the interpretation of a law or its applicability can be resolved.

When a model relies on particulars of the context of its reader for interpretation of its meaning, as is the case in legislation, we say that a model is *informal.* That is, the model lacks a formalism whereby the meaning of terms in the model can be uniquely defined.

In the document web today, there are informal models that help people communicate about the organization of the information. It is common for commerce web sites to organize their wares in catalogs with category names like "web-cams," "Oxford shirts," and "Granola." In such cases, the communication is primarily one way; the catalogue designer wants to communicate to the buyers the information that will help them find what they want to buy. The interpretation of these words is up to the buyers. The effectiveness of such a model is measured by the degree to which this is successful. If enough people interpret the categories in a way similar enough to the intent of the cataloguer, then they will find what they want to buy. There will be the occasional discrepancy like "Why wasn't that item listed as a *webcam?*" or "That's not granola, that's just plain cereal!" But as long as the interpretation is close enough, the model is successful.

A more collaborative style of document modeling comes in the form of community tagging. A number of web sites have been successful by allowing users to provide meaningful symbolic descriptions of their content in the form of *tags.* A tag in this sense is simply a single word or short phrase that describes some aspect of the content. Examples of tagging systems include Flickr for photos and del.icio.us for Web bookmarks. The idea of community tagging is that each individual who provides content will describe it using tags of their own choosing. If any two people use the same tag, this becomes a common organizing entity; anyone who is browsing for content can access information from both contributors under that tag. The tagging infrastructure shows which tags have been used by many people. Not only does this help browsers determine what tags to use in a search, but it also helps content providers to find commonly used tags that they might want to use to describe new content. Thus, a tagging system will have a certain self-organizing character, whereby popular tags become more popular and unpopular tags remain unpopular—something like evolution by artificial selection of tags.

Tagging systems of this sort provide an informal organization to a large body of heterogeneous information. The organization is informal in the sense that the interpretation of the tags requires human processing in the context of the consumer. Just because a tag is popular doesn't mean that everyone is using it in the same way. In fact, the community selection process actually selects tags that are used in several different ways, whether they are compatible or not. As more and more people provide content, the popular tags saturate with a wide variety of content, making them less and less useful as discriminators for people browsing for content. This sort of problem is inherent in information modeling systems; since there isn't an objective description of the meaning of a symbol outside the context of the provider and consumer of the symbol, the communication power of that symbol degrades as it is used in more and more contexts.

Formality of a model isn't a black-and-white judgment; there can be degrees of formality. This is clear in legal systems, where it is common to have several layers of legislation, each one giving objective context for the next. A contract between two parties is usually governed by some regional law that provides standard definitions for terms in the contract. Regional laws are governed by national laws, which provide constraints and definitions for their terms. National laws have their own structure, in which a constitution or a body of case law provides a framework for new decisions and legislation. Even though all these models are expressed in natural language and fall back on human interpretation in the long run, they can be more formal than private agreements that rely almost entirely on the interpretation of the agreeing parties.

This layering of informal models sometimes results in a modeling style that is reminiscent of Talmudic scholarship. The content of the Talmud includes not only the original scripture but also interpretative comments on the scripture by authoritative sources (classical rabbis). Their comments have gained such respect that they are traditionally published along with the original scripture for comment by later rabbis, whose comments in turn have become part of the intellectual tradition. The original scripture, along with all the authoritative comments, is collectively called the Talmud, and it is the basis of a classical Jewish education to this day.

A similar effect happens with informal models. The original model is appropriate in some context, but as its use expands beyond that context, further models are required to provide common context to explicate the shared meaning. But if this further exposition is also informal, then there is the risk that its meaning will not be clear, so further modeling must be done to clarify that. This results in heavily layered models, in which the meaning of the terms is always subject to further interpretation. It is the inherent ambiguity of natural language at each level that makes the next layer of commentary necessary until the degree of ambiguity is "good enough" that no more levels are needed. When it is possible to choose words that are evocative and have considerable agreement, this process converges much more quickly.

Human communication, as a goal for modeling, allows it to play a role in the ongoing collection of human knowledge. The levels of communication can be quite sophisticated, including the collection of information used to interpret other information. In this sense, human communication is the funda-mental requirement for building a Semantic Web. It allows people to contribute to a growing body of knowledge and then draw from it. But communication is not enough; to empower a web of human knowledge, the information in a model needs to be organized in such a way that it can be useful to a wide range of consumers.

EXPLANATION AND PREDICTION

Models are used to organize human thought in the form of explanations. When we understand how a phenomenon results from other basic principles, we gain a number of advantages. Not least is the feeling of confidence that we have actually understood it; people often claim to "have a grasp on" or "have their head around" an idea when they finally understand it. Explanation plays a major role in this sort of understanding. Explanation also assists in memory; it is easier to remember that putting a lid on a flaming pot can quench the flame if one knows the explanation that fire requires air to burn. Most important for the context of the Semantic Web, explanation makes it easier to reuse a model in whole or in part; an explanation relates a conclusion to more basic principles. Understanding how a pot lid quenches a fire can help one understand how a candle snuffer works. Explanation is the key to understanding when a model is applicable and when it is not.

Closely related to this aspect of a model is the idea of prediction. When a model provides an adequate explanation of a phenomenon, it can also be used to make predictions. This aspect of models is what makes their use central to the scientific method, where falsification of predictions made by models forms the basis of the methodology of inquiry.

Explanation and prediction typically require models with a good deal more formality than is usually required for human communication. An explanation relates a phenomenon to "first principles"; these principles, and the rules by which they are related, do not depend on interpretation by the consumer but instead are in some objective form that stands outside the communication. Such an objective form, and the rules that govern how it works, is called a *formalism*.

Formal models are the bread and butter of mathematical modeling, in which very specific rules for calculation and symbol manipulation govern the structure of a mathematical model and the valid ways in which one item can refer to another. Explanations come in the form of proofs, in which steps from premises (stated in some formalism) to conclusions are made according to strict rules of transformation for the formalism. Formal models are used in many human intellectual endeavors, wherever precision and objectivity are required.

Formalisms can also be used for predictions. Given a description of a situation in some formalism, the same rules that govern transformations in proofs can be used to make predictions. We can explain the trajectory of an object thrown out of a window with a formal model of force, gravity, speed, and mass, but given the initial conditions of the object thrown, we can also compute, and thus predict, its trajectory.

Formal prediction and explanation allow us to evaluate when a model is applicable. Furthermore, the formalism allows that evaluation to be independent of the listener. One can dispute the result that $2 + 2 = 4$ by questioning just what the terms "2," "4," "+," and "=" mean, but once people agree on what they mean, they cannot (reasonably) dispute that this formula is correct.

Formal modeling therefore has a very different social dynamic than informal modeling; because there is an objective reference to the model (the formalism), there is no need for the layers of interpretation that result in Talmudic modeling. Instead of layers and layers of interpretation, the buck stops at the formalism.

As we shall see, the Semantic Web standards include a small variety of modeling formalisms. Because they are formalisms, modeling in the Semantic Web need not become a process of layering interpretation on interpretation. Also, because they are formalisms, it is possible to couch explanations in the Semantic

Web in the form of proofs and to use that proof mechanism to make predictions. This aspect of Semantic Web models goes by the name *inference* and it will be discussed in detail in Chapter 5.

MEDIATING VARIABILITY

In any Web setting, variability is to be expected and even embraced. The dynamics of the network effect require the ability to represent a variety of opinions. A good model organizes those opinions so that the things that are common can be represented together, while the things that are distinct can be represented as well.

Let's take the case of Pluto as an example. From 1930 until 2006, it was considered to be a planet by astronomers and astrologers alike. After the redefinition of *planet* by the IAU in 2006, Pluto was no longer considered to be a planet but more specifically a *dwarf planet* by the IAU and by astronomers who accept the IAU as an authority. Astrologers, however, chose not to adopt the IAU convention, and they continued to consider Pluto a planet. Some amateur astronomers, mostly for nostalgic reasons, also continued to consider Pluto a planet. How can we accommodate all of these variations of opinion on the Web?

One way to accommodate them would be to make a decision as to which one is "preferred" and to control the Web so that only that position is supported. This is the solution that is most commonly used in corporate data centers, where a small group or even a single person acts as the database administrator and decides what data are allowed to live in the corporate database. This solution is not appropriate for the Web because it does not allow for the AAA slogan (see Chapter 1) that leads to the network effect.

Another way to accommodate these different viewpoints would be to simply allow each one to be represented separately, with no reference to one another at all. It would be the responsibility of the information consumer to understand how these things relate to one another and to make any connections as appropriate. This is the basis of an informal approach, and it indeed describes the state of the document web as it is today. A Web search for Pluto will turn up a wide array of articles, in which some call it a planet (e.g., astrological ones or astronomical ones that have not been updated), some call it a dwarf planet (IAU official web sites), and some that are still debating the issue. The only way a reader can come to understand what is common among these things—the notion of a planet, of the solar system, or even of Pluto itself—is through reader interpretation.

How can a model help sort this out? How can a model describe what is common about the astrological notion of a planet, the twentieth-century astronomical notion of a planet, and the post-2006 notion of a planet? The model must also allow for each of these differing viewpoints to be expressed.

Variation and classes

This problem is not a new one; it is a well-known problem in software engineering. When a software component is designed, it has to provide certain functionality, determined by information given to it at runtime. There is a trade-off in such a design; the component can be made to operate in a wide variety of circumstances, but it will require a complex input to describe just how it should behave at any one time. Or the system could be designed to work with very simple input but be useful in only a small number of very specific situations. The design of a software component inherently involves a model of the commonality and variability in the environment in which it is expected to be deployed. In response to this challenge, software methodology has developed the art of object modeling (in the context of Object-Oriented Programming, or OOP) as a means of organizing commonality and variability in software components.

One of the primary organizing tools in OOP is the notion of a hierarchy of classes and subclasses. Classes high up in the hierarchy represent functionality that is common to a large number of components; classes farther down in a hierarchy represent more specific functionality. Commonality and variability in the functionality of a set of software components is represented in a class hierarchy.

The Semantic Web standards also use this idea of class hierarchy for representing commonality and variability. Since the Semantic Web, unlike OOP, is not focused on software representation, classes are not defined in terms of behaviors of functions. But the notion of classes and subclasses remains, and it plays much the same role. High-level classes represent commonality among a large variety of entities, whereas lower-level classes represent commonality among a small, specific set of things.

Let's take Pluto as an example. The 2006 IAU definition of *planet* is quite specific in requiring these three criteria for a celestial body to be considered a planet:

1. It is in orbit around the sun.
2. It has sufficient mass to be nearly round.
3. It has cleared the neighborhood around its orbit.

The IAU goes further to state that a dwarf planet is a body that satisfies conditions 1 and 2 (and not 3); a body that satisfies only condition 1 is a *small solar system body (SSSB)*. These definitions make a number of things clear: The classes SSSB, dwarf planet, and planet are all mutually exclusive; no body is a member of any two classes. However, there is something that all of them have in common: They all are in orbit around the sun.

Twentieth-century astronomy and astrology are not quite as organized as this; they don't have such rigorous definitions of the word *planet*. So how can we relate these notions to the twenty-first-century notion of *planet?*

The first thing we need is a way to talk about the various uses of the word *planet:* the IAU use, the astrological use, and the twentieth-century astronomical use. This seems like a simple requirement, but until it is met, we can't even talk about the relationship among these terms. We will see details of the Semantic Web solution to this issue in Chapter 3, but for now, we will simply prefix each term with a short abbreviation of its source—for example, use `IAU:Planet` for the IAU use of the word, `horo:Planet` for the astrological use, and `astro:Planet` for the twentieth-century astronomical use.

The solution begins by noticing what it is that all three notions of *planet* have in common; in this case, it is that the body orbits the sun. Thus, we can define a class of the things that orbit the sun, which we may as well call *solar system body*, or *SSB* for short. All three notions are subclasses of this notion. This can be depicted graphically as in Figure 2.1.

We can go further in this modeling when we observe that there are only eight `IAU:Planet`s, and each one is also a `horo:Planet` and an `astro:Planet`. Thus, we can say that `IAU:Planet` is a subclass of both `horo:Planet` and `astro:Planet`, as shown in Figure 2.2. We can continue in this way, describing the relationships among all the concepts we have mentioned so far: `IAU:DwarfPlanet` and `IAU:SSSB`. As we go down the tree, each class refers to a more restrictive set of entities. In this way, we can model the commonality among entities (at the high level) while respecting their variation (at a low level).

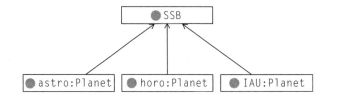

FIGURE 2.1

Subclass diagram for different notions of *planet*.

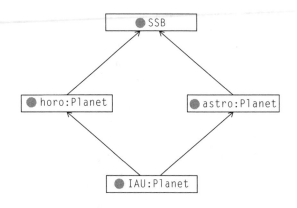

FIGURE 2.2

More detailed relationships between various notions of *planet*.

Variation and layers

Classes and subclasses are a fine way to organize variation when there is a simple, known relationship between the modeled entities and it is possible to determine a clear ordering of classes that describes these relationships. In a Web setting, however, this usually is not the case. Each contributor can have something new to say that may fit in with previous statements in a wide variety of ways. How can we accommodate variation of sources if we can't structure the entities they are describing into a class model?

The Semantic Web provides an elegant solution to this problem. The basic idea is that any model can be built up from contributions from multiple sources. One way of thinking about this is to consider a model to be described in layers. Each layer comes from a different source. The entire model is the combination of all the layers, viewed as a single, unified whole.

Let's have a look at how this could work in the case of Pluto. Figure 2.3 illustrates how different communities could assert varying information about Pluto. In part (a) of the figure, we see some information about Pluto that is common among astrologers—namely, that Pluto signifies rebirth and regeneration and that the preferred symbol for referring to Pluto is the glyph indicated. Part (b) shows some information that is of concern to astronomers, including the composition of the body Pluto and their preferred symbol. How can this variation be accommodated in a web of information? The simplest way is to simply merge the two models into a single one that includes all the information from each model, as shown in part (c).

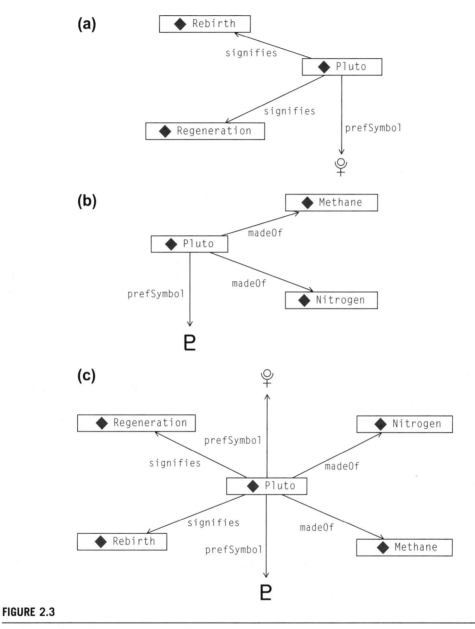

FIGURE 2.3

Layers of modeled information about Pluto.

Merging models in this way is a conceptually simple thing to do, but how does it cope with variability? In the first place, it copes in the simplest way possible: It allows the astrologers and the astronomers to both have their say about Pluto (remember the AAA slogan!). For any party that is interested in both of these things (perhaps someone looking for a spiritual significance for elements?), the information can be viewed as a single, unified whole.

But merging models in this way has a drawback as well. In Figure 2.3(c), there are two distinct glyphs, each claiming to be the "preferred" symbol for Pluto. This brings up issues of consistency of viewpoints. On the face of it, this appears to be an inconsistency because, from its name, we might expect that there can be exactly one preferred symbol (prefSymbol) for any body. But how can a machine know that? For a machine, the name prefSymbol can't be treated any differently from any other label—for instance, madeOf or signifies. In such a context, how can we even tell that this is an inconsistency? After all, we don't think it is an inconsistency that Pluto can be composed of more than one chemical compound or that it can signify more than one spiritual theme. Do we have to describe this in a natural language commentary on the model?

Detailed answers to questions like these are exactly the reason why we need to publish models on the Semantic Web. When two (or more!) viewpoints come together in a web of knowledge, there will typically be overlap, disagreement, and confusion before there is synergy, cooperation, and collaboration. If the infrastructure of the Web is to help us to find our way through the wild stage of information sharing, an informal notion of how things fit together, or should fit together, will not suffice. It is easy enough to say that we have an intuition that states there is something special about prefSymbol that makes it different from madeOf or signifies. If we can inform our infrastructure about this distinction in a sufficiently formal way, then it can, for instance, detect discrepancies of this sort and, in some cases, even resolve them.

This is the essence of modeling in the Semantic Web: providing an infrastructure where not only can anyone say anything about any topic but the infrastructure can help a community work through the resulting chaos. A model can provide a framework (like classes and subclasses) for representing and organizing commonality and variability of viewpoints when they are known. But in advance of such an organization, a model can provide a framework for describing what sorts of things we can say about something. We might not agree on the symbol for Pluto, but we can agree that it should have just one preferred symbol.

EXPRESSIVITY IN MODELING

There is a trade-off when we model, and although anyone can say anything about any topic, not everyone will want to say certain things. There are those who are interested in saying details about individual entities, like the preferred symbol for Pluto or the themes in life that it signifies. Others (like that IAU) are interested in talking about categories, what belongs in a category, and how you can tell the difference. Still others (like lexicographers, information architects, and librarians) want to talk about the rules for specifying information, such as whether there can be more than one preferred label for any entity. All of these people have contributions to make to the web of knowledge, but the kinds of contributions they make are very different, and they need different tools. This difference is one of *level of expressivity*.

The idea of different levels of expressivity is as well known in the history of collaborative human knowledge as modeling itself. Take as an example the development of models of a water molecule, as

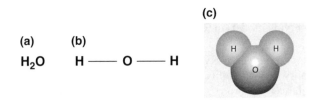

(a)   **(b)**

H_2O H ——— O ——— H

(c)

FIGURE 2.4

Different expressivity of models of a water molecule.

shown in Figure 2.4. In part (a), we see a model of the water molecule in terms of the elements that make up the molecule and how many of each is present—namely, two hydrogen atoms and one oxygen atom. This model expresses important information about the molecule, and it can be used to answer a number of basic questions about water, such as calculating the mass of the molecule (given the masses of its component atoms) and what components would have to be present to be able to construct water from constituent parts.

In Figure 2.4(b), we see a model with more expressivity. Not only does this model identify the components of water and their proportions, but it also shows how they are connected in the chemical structure of the molecule. The oxygen molecule is connected to each of the hydrogen molecules, which are not (directly) connected to one another at all. This model is somewhat more expressive than the model in part (a); it can answer further questions about the molecule. From (b), it is clear that when the water molecule breaks down into smaller molecules, it can break into single hydrogen atoms (H) or into oxygen-hydrogen ions (OH) but not into double-hydrogen atoms (H_2) without some recombination of components after the initial decomposition.

Finally, the model shown in Figure 2.4(c) is more expressive still in that it shows not only the chemical structure of the molecule but also the physical structure. The fact that the oxygen atom is somewhat larger than the hydrogen atoms is shown in this model. Even the angle between the two hydrogen atoms as bound to the oxygen atom is shown. This information is useful for working out the geometry of combinations of water molecules, as is the case, for instance, in the crystalline structure of ice.

Just because one model is more expressive than another does not make it superior; different expressive modeling frameworks are different tools for different purposes. The chemical formula for water is simpler to determine than the more expressive, but more complex, models, and it is useful for resolving a wide variety of questions about chemistry. In fact, most chemistry textbooks go for quite a while working only from the chemical formulas without having to resort to more structural models until the course covers advanced topics.

The Semantic Web provides a number of modeling languages that differ in their level of expressivity; that is, they constitute different tools that allow different people to express different sorts of information. In the rest of this book, we will cover these modeling languages in detail. The Semantic Web standards are organized so that each language level builds on the one before so the languages themselves are layered. The following are the languages of the Semantic Web from least expressive to most expressive.

RDF—The Resource Description Framework. This is the basic framework that the rest of the Semantic Web is based on. RDF provides a mechanism for allowing anyone to make a basic statement about anything and layering these statements into a single model. Figure 2.3 shows the basic capability of merging models in RDF. RDF has been a recommendation from the W3C since 1999.

RDFS—The RDF Schema language. RDFS is a language with the expressivity to describe the basic notions of commonality and variability familiar from object languages and other class systems—namely classes, subclasses, and properties. Figures 2.1 and 2.2 illustrated the capabilities of RDFS. RDFS has been a W3C recommendation since 2004.

RDFS-Plus. RDFS-Plus is a subset of OWL that is more expressive than RDFS but without the complexity of OWL. There is no standard in progress for RDFS-Plus, but there is a growing awareness that something between RDFS and OWL could be industrially relevant. We have selected a particular subset of OWL functionality to present the capabilities of OWL incrementally. RDFS-Plus includes enough expressivity to describe how certain properties can be used and how they relate to one another. RDFS-Plus is expressive enough to show the utility of certain constructs beyond RDFS, but it lacks the complexity that makes OWL daunting to many beginning modelers. The issue of uniqueness of the preferred symbol is an example of the expressivity of RDFS-Plus.

OWL. OWL brings the expressivity of logic to the Semantic Web. It allows modelers to express detailed constraints between classes, entities, and properties. OWL was adopted as a recommendation by the W3C in 2004, with a second version adopted in 2009.

SUMMARY

The Semantic Web, just like the document web that preceded it, is based on some radical notions of information sharing. These ideas—the AAA slogan, the open world assumption, and nonunique naming—provide for an environment in which information sharing can thrive and a network effect of knowledge synergy is possible. But this style of information gathering creates a chaotic landscape rife with confusion, disagreement, and conflict. How can the infrastructure of the Web support the development from this chaotic state to one characterized by information sharing, cooperation, and collaboration?

The answer to this question lies in modeling. Modeling is the process of organizing information for community use. Modeling supports this in three ways: It provides a framework for human communication, it provides a means for explaining conclusions, and it provides a structure for managing varying viewpoints. In the context of the Semantic Web, modeling is an ongoing process. At any point in time, some knowledge will be well structured and understood, and these structures can be represented in the Semantic Web modeling language. At the same time, other knowledge will still be in the chaotic, discordant stage, where everyone is expressing himself differently. And typically, as different people provide their own opinions about any topic under the sun, the Web will simultaneously contain organized and unorganized knowledge about the very same topic. The modeling activity is the activity of distilling communal knowledge out of a chaotic mess of information. This was nicely illustrated in the Pluto example.

The next several chapters of the book introduce each of the modeling languages of the Semantic Web and illustrate how they approach the challenges of modeling in a Semantic Web context. For each modeling language—RDF, RDFS, and OWL—we will describe the technical details of how the language works, with specific examples "in the wild" of the standard in use.

Fundamental concepts

The following fundamental concepts were introduced in this chapter.

Modeling—Making sense of unorganized information.

Formality/Informality—The degree to which the meaning of a modeling language is given independent of the particular speaker or audience.

Commonality **and** *Variability*—When describing a set of things, some of them will have somem things in common (commonality), and some will have important differences (variability). Managing commonality and variability is a fundamental aspect of modeling in general, and of Semantic Web models in particular.

Expressivity—The ability of a modeling language to describe certain aspects of the world. More expressive modeling language can express a wider variety of statements about the model. Modeling languages of the Semantic *Web—RDF, RDFS,* and OWL—differ in their levels of expressivity.

RDF—The basis of the Semantic Web

RDF, RDFS, and OWL are the basic representation languages of the Semantic Web, with RDF serving as the foundation. RDF addresses one fundamental issue in the Semantic Web: managing distributed data. All other Semantic Web standards build on this foundation of distributed data. RDF relies heavily on the infrastructure of the Web, using many of its familiar and proven features, while extending them to provide a foundation for a distributed network of data.

The Web that we are accustomed to is made up of documents that are linked to one another. Any connection between a document and the thing(s) in the world it describes is made only by the person who reads the document. There could be a link from a document about Shakespeare to a document about Stratford-upon-Avon, but there is no notion of an entity that is Shakespeare or linking it to the thing that is Stratford.

In the Semantic Web we refer to the things in the world as *resources;* a *resource* can be anything that someone might want to talk about. Shakespeare, Stratford, "the value of X," and "all the cows in Texas" are all examples of things someone might talk about and that can be resources in the Semantic Web. This is admittedly a pretty odd use of the word *resource,* but alternatives like *entity* or *thing,* which might be more accurate, have their own issues. In any case, *resource* is the word used in the

Semantic Web standards. In fact, the name of the base technology in the Semantic Web (RDF) uses this word in an essential way. *RDF* stands for *Resource Description Framework.*

In a web of information, anyone can contribute to our knowledge about a resource. It was this aspect of the current Web that allowed it to grow at such an unprecedented rate. To implement the Semantic Web, we need a model of data that allows information to be distributed over the Web.

DISTRIBUTING DATA ACROSS THE WEB

Data are most often represented in tabular form, in which each row represents some item we are describing, and each column represents some property of those items. The cells in the table are the particular values for those properties. Table 3.1 shows a sample of some data about works completed around the time of Shakespeare.

Let's consider a few different strategies for how these data could be distributed over the Web. In all of these strategies, some part of the data will be represented on one computer, while other parts will be represented on another. Figure 3.1 shows one strategy for distributing information over many machines. Each networked machine is responsible for maintaining the information about one or more complete rows from the table. Any query about an entity can be answered by the machine that stores its corresponding row. One machine is responsible for information about "Sonnet 78" and *Edward II,* whereas another is responsible for information about *As You Like It.*

This distribution solution provides considerable flexibility, since the machines can share the load of representing information about several individuals. But because it is a distributed representation of data, it requires some coordination between the servers. In particular, each server must share information about the columns. Does the second column on one server correspond to the same information as the second column on another server? This is not an insurmountable problem, and, in fact, it is a fundamental problem of data distribution. There must be some agreed-on coordination between the servers. In this example, the servers must be able to, in a global way, indicate which property each column corresponds to.

Table 3.1 Tabular Data about Elizabethan Literature and Music

ID	Title	Author	Medium	Year
1	*As You Like It*	Shakespeare	Play	1599
2	*Hamlet*	Shakespeare	Play	1604
3	*Othello*	Shakespeare	Play	1603
4	"Sonnet 78"	Shakespeare	Poem	1609
5	*Astrophil and Stella*	Sir Phillip Sidney	Poem	1590
6	*Edward II*	Christopher Marlowe	Play	1592
7	*Hero and Leander*	Christopher Marlowe	Poem	1593
8	*Greensleeves*	Henry VIII Rex	Song	1525

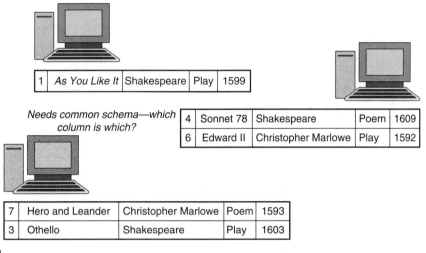

FIGURE 3.1

Distributing data across the Web, row by row.

Figure 3.2 shows another strategy, in which each server is responsible for one or more complete columns from the original table. In this example, one server is responsible for the publication dates and medium, and another server is responsible for titles. This solution is flexible in a different way from the solution of Figure 3.1. The solution in Figure 3.2 allows each machine to be responsible for one kind of information. If we are not interested in the dates of publication, we needn't consider information from that server. If we want to specify something new about the entities (say, how many pages the manuscript is), we can add a new server with that information without disrupting the others.

This solution is similar to the solution in Figure 3.1 in that it requires some coordination between the servers. In this case, the coordination has to do with the identities of the entities to be described. How do I know that row 3 on one server refers to the same entity as row 3 on another server? This solution requires a global identifier for the entities being described.

The strategy outlined in Figure 3.3 is a combination of the previous two strategies, in which information is neither distributed row by row nor column by column but instead is distributed cell by cell. Each machine is responsible for some number of cells in the table. This system combines the flexibility of both of the previous strategies. Two servers can share the description of a single entity (in the figure, the year and title of *Hamlet* are stored separately), and they can share the use of a particular property (in Figure 3.3, the Mediums of rows 6 and 7 are represented on different servers).

This flexibility is required if we want our data distribution system to really support the AAA slogan that "Anyone can say Anything about Any topic." If we take the AAA slogan seriously, any server needs to be able to make a statement about any entity (as is the case in Figure 3.2), but also any server needs to be able to specify any property of an entity (as is the case in Figure 3.1). The solution in Figure 3.3 has both of these benefits.

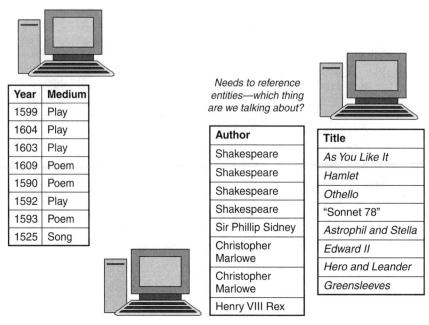

FIGURE 3.2

Distributing data across the Web, column by column.

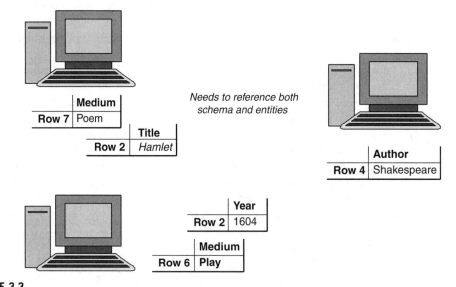

FIGURE 3.3

Distributing data across the Web, cell by cell.

Table 3.2 Sample Triples

Subject	Predicate	Object
Row 7	Medium	Poem
Row 2	Title	Hamlet
Row 2	Year	1604
Row 4	Author	Shakespeare
Row 6	Medium	Play

But this solution also combines the costs of the other two strategies. Not only do we now need a global reference for the column headings, but we also need a global reference for the rows. In fact, each cell has to be represented with three values: a global reference for the row, a global reference for the column, and the value in the cell itself. This third strategy is the strategy taken by RDF. We will see how RDF resolves the issue of global reference later in this chapter, but for now, we will focus on how a table cell is represented and managed in RDF.

Since a cell is represented with three values, the basic building block for RDF is called the *triple*. The identifier for the row is called the *subject* of the triple (following the notion from elementary grammar, since the subject is the thing that a statement is about). The identifier for the column is called the *predicate* of the triple (since columns specify properties of the entities in the rows). The value in the cell is called the *object* of the triple. Table 3.2 shows the triples in Figure 3.3 as subject, predicate, and object.

Triples become more interesting when more than one triple refers to the same entity, such as in Table 3.3. When more than one triple refers to the same thing, sometimes it is convenient to view the triples as a *directed graph* in which each triple is an edge from its subject to its object, with the predicate as the label on the edge, as shown in Figure 3.4. The graph visualization in Figure 3.4 expresses the same information presented in Table 3.3, but everything we know about Shakespeare (either as subject or object) is displayed at a single node.

Table 3.3 Sample Triples

Subject	Predicate	Object
Shakespeare	wrote	King Lear
Shakespeare	wrote	Macbeth
Anne Hathaway	married	Shakespeare
Shakespeare	livedIn	Stratford
Stratford	isIn	England
Macbeth	setIn	Scotland
England	partOf	UK
Scotland	partOf	UK

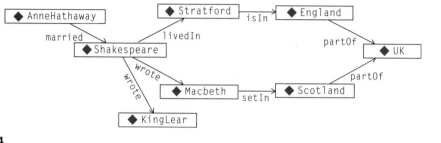

FIGURE 3.4

Graph display of triples from Table 3.3. Eight triples appear as eight labeled edges.

MERGING DATA FROM MULTIPLE SOURCES

We started off describing RDF as a way to distribute data over several sources. But when we want to use that data, we will need to merge those sources back together again. One value of the triples representation is the ease with which this kind of merger can be accomplished. Since information is represented simply as triples, merged information from two graphs is as simple as forming the graph of all of the triples from each individual graph, taken together. Let's see how this is accomplished in RDF.

Suppose that we had another source of information that was relevant to our example from Table 3.3—that is, a list of plays that Shakespeare wrote or a list of parts of the United Kingdom. These would be represented as triples as in Tables 3.4 and 3.5. Each of these can also be shown as a graph, just as in the original table, as shown in Figure 3.5.

What happens when we merge together the information from these three sources? We simply get the graph of all the triples that show up in Figures 3.4 and 3.5. Merging graphs like those in Figures 3.4 and 3.5 to create a combined graph like the one shown in Figure 3.6 is a straightforward process—but only when it is known which nodes in each of the source graphs match.

Table 3.4 Triples about Shakespeare's Plays		
Subject	**Predicate**	**Object**
Shakespeare	Wrote	*As You Like It*
Shakespeare	Wrote	*Henry V*
Shakespeare	Wrote	*Love's Labour's Lost*
Shakespeare	Wrote	*Measure for Measure*
Shakespeare	Wrote	*Twelfth Night*
Shakespeare	Wrote	*The Winter's Tale*
Shakespeare	Wrote	*Hamlet*
Shakespeare	Wrote	*Othello*
		etc.

Table 3.5 Triples about the Parts of the United Kingdom

Subject	Predicate	Object
Scotland	part Of	The UK
England	part Of	The UK
Wales	part Of	The UK
Northern Ireland	part Of	The UK
Channel Islands	part Of	The UK
Isle of Man	part Of	The UK

NAMESPACES, URIS, AND IDENTITY

The essence of the merge comes down to answering the question "When is a node in one graph *the same node* as a node in another graph?" In RDF, this issue is resolved through the use of Uniform Resource Identifiers (*URIs*).

In the figures so far, we have labeled the nodes and edges in the graphs with simple names like *Shakespeare* or *Wales*. On the Semantic Web, this is not sufficient information to determine whether two nodes are really the same. Why not? Isn't there just one thing in the universe that everyone agrees refers to as *Shakespeare?* When referring to agreement on the Web, never say, "everyone." Somewhere, someone will refer not to the historical Shakespeare but to the title character of the feature film *Shakespeare in Love,* which bears very little resemblance to the historical figure. And "Shakespeare" is one of the more stable concepts to appear on the Web; consider the range of referents for a name like "Washington" or "Bordeaux." To merge graphs in a Semantic Web setting, we have to be more specific: In what sense do we mean the word *Shakespeare?*

RDF borrows its solution to this problem from foundational Web technology—in particular, the URI. The syntax and format of a URI are familiar even to casual users of the Web today because of the special, but typical, case of the URL—for example, *http://www.WorkingOntologist.org/Examples/ Chapter3/Shakespeare#Shakespeare*. But the significance of the URI as a global identifier for a Web resource is often not appreciated. A URI provides a global identification for a resource that is common across the Web. If two agents on the Web want to refer to the same resource, recommended practice on the Web is for them to agree to a common URI for that resource. This is not a stipulation that is particular to the Semantic Web but to the Web in general; global naming leads to global network effects.

URIs and URLs look exactly the same, and, in fact, a URL is just a special case of the URI. Why does the Web have both of these ideas? Simplifying somewhat, the URI is an identifier with global (i.e., "World Wide" in the "World Wide Web" sense) scope. Any two Web applications in the world can refer to the same thing by referencing the same URI. But the syntax of the URI makes it possible to "dereference" it—that is, to use all the information in the URI (which specifies things like server name, protocol, port number, file name, etc.) to locate a file (or a location in a file) on the Web.[1] This

---

[1]We are primarily discussing files here, but a URI can refer to other resources. The Wikipedia article on URIs includes more than 50 different resource types that can be referenced by URIs—see *http://en.wikipedia.org/wiki/URI_ scheme*.

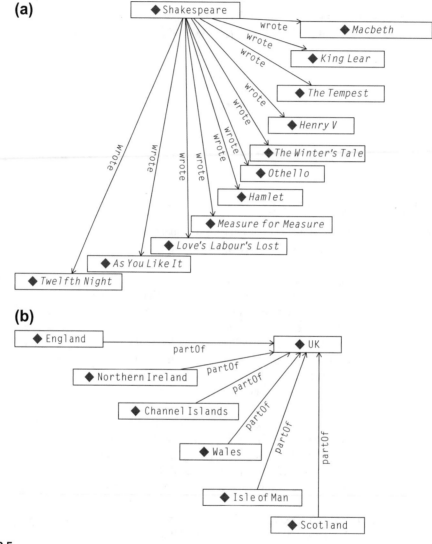

FIGURE 3.5

Graphic representation of triples describing (a) Shakespeare's plays and (b) parts of the United Kingdom.

dereferencing succeeds if all these parts work; the protocol locates the specified server running on the specified port and so on. When this is the case, we can say that the URI is not just a URI, but it also is a URL. From the point of view of modeling, the distinction is not important. But from the point of view of having a model on the Semantic Web, the fact that a URI can potentially be dereferenced allows the models to participate in a global Web infrastructure.

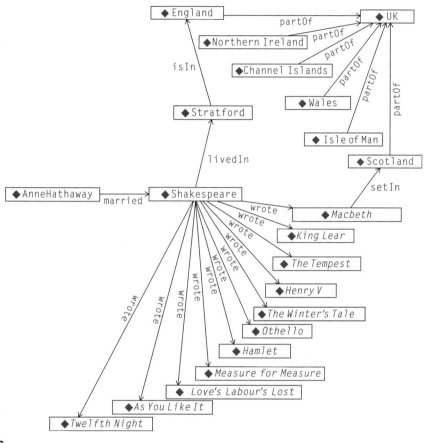

FIGURE 3.6

Combined graph of all triples about Shakespeare and the United Kingdom.

RDF applies the notion of the URI to resolve the identity problem in graph merging. The application is quite simple: A node from one graph is merged with a node from another graph—exactly, if they have the same URI. On the one hand, this may seem disingenuous, "solving" the problem of node identity by relying on another standard to solve it. On the other hand, since issues of identity appear in the Web in general and not just in the Semantic Web, it would be foolish not to use the same strategy to resolve the issue in both cases.

Expressing URIs in print

URIs work very well for expressing identity on the World Wide Web, but they are typically a bit of a pain to write out in detail when expressing models, especially in print. So for the examples in this book, we use a simplified version of a URI abbreviation scheme called *qnames*. In its simplest form, a URI expressed as a qname has two parts: a namespace and an identifier, written with a colon between. So the qname representation for the identifier *England* in the namespace *geo* is simply `geo:England`. The RDF/XML standard includes elaborate rules that allow programmers to map namespaces to other URI representations (such as the familiar *http://* notation). For the examples in this book, we will use the simple qname form for all URIs. It is important, however, to note that qnames are *not* global identifiers on the Web; only fully qualified URIs (e.g., *http://www.WorkingOntologist.org/Examples/Chapter3/Shakespeare#Shakespeare*) are global Web names. Thus, any representation of a qname must, in principle, be accompanied by a declaration of the namespace correspondence.

It is customary on the Web in general and part of the XML specification to insist that URIs contain no embedded spaces. For example, an identifier "part of" is typically not used in the web. Instead, we follow the InterCap convention (sometimes called CamelCase), whereby names that are made up of multiple words are transformed into identifiers without spaces by capitalizing each word. Thus, "part of" becomes `partOf`, "Great Britain" becomes `GreatBritain`, "Measure for Measure" becomes `MeasureForMeasure`, and so on.

There is no limitation on the use of multiple namespaces in a single source of data, or even in a single triple. Selection of namespaces is entirely unrestricted as far as the data model and standards are concerned. It is common practice, however, to refer to related identifiers in a single namespace. For instance, all of the literary or geographical information from Table 3.4 or Table 3.5 would be placed into one namespace per table, with a suggestive name—say, *lit* or *geo*—respectively. Strictly speaking, these names correspond to fully qualified URIs—for example, *lit* stands for *http://www.WorkingOntologist.com/Examples/Chapter3/Shakespeare#*, and *geo* stands for *http://www.WorkingOntologist.com/Examples/Chapter3/geography#*.

For the purposes of explaining modeling on the Semantic Web, the detailed URIs behind the qnames are not important, so for the most part, we will omit these bindings from now on. In many examples, we will take this notion of abbreviation one step further; in the cases when we use a single namespace throughout one example, we will assume there is a *default* namespace declaration that allows us to refer to URIs simply with a symbolic name preceded by a colon (`:`), such as `:Shakespeare`, `:JamesDean`, `:Researcher`.

Table 3.6 Plays of Shakespeare with Qnames		
Subject	**Predicate**	**Object**
lit:Shakespeare	lit:wrote	lit:AsYouLikeIt
lit:Shakespeare	lit:wrote	lit:HenryV
lit:Shakespeare	lit:wrote	lit:LovesLaboursLost
lit:Shakespeare	lit:wrote	lit:MeasureForMeasure
lit:Shakespeare	lit:wrote	lit:TwelfthNight
lit:Shakespeare	lit:wrote	lit:WintersTale
lit:Shakespeare	lit:wrote	lit:Hamlet
lit:Shakespeare	lit:wrote	lit:Othello
		etc.

Table 3.7 Geographical Information as Qnames

Subject	Predicate	Object
geo:Scotland	geo:partOf	geo:UK
geo:England	geo:partOf	geo:UK
geo:Wales	geo:partOf	geo:UK
geo:NorthernIreland	geo:partOf	geo:UK
geo:ChannelIslands	geo:partOf	geo:UK
geo:IsleOfMan	geo:partOf	geo:UK

Using qnames, our triple sets now look as shown in Tables 3.6 and 3.7. Compare Table 3.6 with Table 3.4, and compare Table 3.7 with Table 3.5. But it isn't always that simple; some triples will have to use identifiers with different namespaces, as in the example in Table 3.8, which was taken from Table 3.3.

In Table 3.8, we introduced a new namespace, *bio:,* without specifying the actual URI to which it corresponds. For this model to participate on the Web, this information must be filled in. But from the point of view of modeling, this detail is unimportant. For the rest of this book, we will assume that the prefixes of all qnames are defined, even if that definition has not been specified explicitly in print.

Standard namespaces

Using the URI as a standard for global identifiers allows for a worldwide reference for any symbol. This means that we can tell when any two people anywhere in the world are referring to the same thing.

This property of the URI provides a simple way for a standard organization (like the W3C) to specify the meaning of certain terms in the standard. As we will see in coming chapters, the W3C standards provide definitions for terms such as `type`, `subClassOf`, `Class`, `inverseOf`, and so forth. But these standards are intended to apply globally across the Semantic Web, so the standards

Table 3.8 Triples Referring to URIs with a Variety of Namespaces

Subject	Predicate	Object
lit:Shakespeare	lit:wrote	lit:KingLear
lit:Shakespeare	lit:wrote	lit:MacBeth
bio:AnneHathaway	bio:married	lit:Shakespeare
bio:AnneHathaway	bio:livedWith	lit:Shakespeare
lit:Shakespeare	bio:livedIn	geo:Stratford
geo:Stratford	geo:isIn	geo:England
geo:England	geo:partOf	geo:UK
geo:Scotland	geo:partOf	geo:UK

refer to these reserved words in the same way as they refer to any other resource on the Semantic Web, as URIs.

The W3C has defined a number of standard namespaces for use with Web technologies, including `xsd:` for XML schema definition; `xmlns:` for XML namespaces; and so on. The Semantic Web is handled in exactly the same way, with namespace definitions for the major layers of the Semantic Web. Following standard practice with the W3C, we will use qnames to refer to these terms, using the following definitions for the standard namespaces.

> *rdf*: Indicates identifiers used in RDF. The set of identifiers defined in the standard is quite small and is used to define types and properties in RDF. The global URI for the *rdf* namespace is *http://www.w3.org/1999/02/22-rdf-syntax-ns#*.
>
> *rdfs*: Indicates identifiers used for the RDF Schema language, RDFS. The scope and semantics of the symbols in this namespace are the topics of future chapters. The global URI for the *rdfs* namespace is *http://www.w3.org/2000/01/rdf-schema#*.
>
> *owl*: Indicates identifiers used for the Web Ontology Language, OWL. The scope and semantics of the symbols in this namespace are the topics of future chapters. The global URI for the *owl* namespace is *http://www.w3.org/2002/07/owl#*.

These URIs provide a good example of the interaction between a URI and a URL. For modeling purposes, any URI in one of these namespaces (e.g., *http://www.w3.org/2000/01/rdf-schema# subClassOf,* or `rdfs:subClassOf` for short) refers to a particular term that the W3C makes some statements about in the RDFS standard. But the term can also be dereferenced—that is, if we look at the server *www.w3.org,* there is a page at the location `2000/01/rdf-schema` with an entry about `subClassOf`, giving supplemental information about this resource. From the point of view of modeling, it is not necessary that it be possible to dereference this URI, but from the point of view of Web integration, it is critical that it is.

IDENTIFIERS IN THE RDF NAMESPACE

The RDF data model specifies the notion of triples and the idea of merging sets of triples as just shown. With the introduction of namespaces, RDF uses the infrastructure of the Web to represent agreements

Table 3.9 Using `rdf:type` to Describe Playwrights

Subject	Predicate	Object
lit:Shakespeare	rdf:type	lit:Playwright
lit:Ibsen	rdf:type	lit:Playwright
lit:Simon	rdf:type	lit:Playwright
lit:Miller	rdf:type	lit:Playwright
lit:Marlowe	rdf:type	lit:Playwright
lit:Wilder	rdf:type	lit:Playwright

Table 3.10 Defining Types of Names

Subject	Predicate	Object
lit:Playwright	rdf:type	bus:Profession
bus:Profession	rdf:type	hr:Compensation

on how to refer to a particular entity. The RDF standard itself takes advantage of the namespace infrastructure to define a small number of standard identifiers in a namespace defined in the standard, a namespace called *rdf.*

rdf:type is a property that provides an elementary typing system in RDF. For example, we can express the relationship between several playwrights using type information, as shown in Table 3.9. The subject of rdf:type in these triples can be any identifier, and the object is understood to be a type. There is no restriction on the usage of rdf:type with types; types can have types ad infinitum, as shown in Table 3.10.

When we read a triple out loud (or just to ourselves), it is understandably tempting to read it (in English, anyway) in subject/predicate/object order so that the first triple in Table 3.9 would read, "Shakespeare type Playwright." Unfortunately, this is pretty fractured syntax no matter how you inflect it. It would be better to have something like "Shakespeare has type Playwright" or maybe "The type of Shakespeare is Playwright."

This issue really has to do with the choice of name for the rdf:type resource; if it had been called rdf:isInstanceOf instead, it would have been much easier to read out loud in English. But since we never have control over how other entities (in this case, the W3C) chose their names, we don't have the luxury of changing these names. When we read out loud, we just have to take some liberties in adding in connecting words. So this triple can be pronounced, "Shakespeare [has] type Playwright," adding in the "has" (or sometimes, the word "is" works better) to make the sentence into somewhat correct English.

rdf:Property is an identifier that is used as a type in RDF to indicate when another identifier is to be used as a predicate rather than as a subject or an object. We can declare all the identifiers we have used as predicates so far in this chapter as shown in Table 3.11.

Table 3.11 rdf:Property Assertions for Tables 3.5 to 3.8

Subject	Predicate	Object
lit:wrote	rdf:type	rdf:Property
geo:partOf	rdf:type	rdf:Property
bio:married	rdf:type	rdf:Property
bio:livedIn	rdf:type	rdf:Property
bio:livedWith	rdf:type	rdf:Property
geo:isIn	rdf:type	rdf:Property

CHALLENGE: RDF AND TABULAR DATA

We began this chapter by motivating RDF as a way to distribute data over the Web—in particular, tabular data. Now that we have all of the detailed mechanisms of RDF (including namespaces and triples) in place, we can revisit tabular data and show how to represent it consistently in RDF.

CHALLENGE 1

Given a table from a relational database, describing products, suppliers, and stocking information about the products (see Table 3.12), produce an RDF graph that reflects the content of Table 3.12 in such a way that the information intent is preserved but the data are now amenable for RDF operations like merging and RDF query.

Solution

Each row in the table describes a single entity, all of the same type. That type is given by the name of the table itself, *Product*. We know certain information about each of these items, based on the columns in the table itself, such as the model number, the division, and so on. We want to represent these data in RDF.

Since each row represents a distinct entity, each row will have a distinct URI. Fortunately, the need for unique identifiers is just as present in the database as it is in the Semantic Web, so there is a (locally) unique identifier available—namely, the primary table key, in this case the column called *ID*. For the Semantic Web, we need a globally unique identifier. The simplest way to form such an identifier is by having a single URI for the database itself (perhaps even a URL if the database is on the Web). Use that URI as the namespace for all the identifiers in the database. Since this is a database for a manufacturing company, let's call that namespace mfg:.

Table 3.12 Sample Tabular Data for Triples

				Product		
ID	Model Number	Division	Product Line	Manufacture Location	SKU	Available
1	ZX-3	Manufacturing support	Paper machine	Sacramento	FB3524	23
2	ZX-3P	Manufacturing support	Paper machine	Sacramento	KD5243	4
3	ZX-3S	Manufacturing support	Paper machine	Sacramento	IL4028	34
4	B-1430	Control engineering	Feedback line	Elizabeth	KS4520	23
5	B-1430X	Control engineering	Feedback line	Elizabeth	CL5934	14
6	B-1431	Control engineering	Active sensor	Seoul	KK3945	0
7	DBB-12	Accessories	Monitor	Hong Kong	ND5520	100
8	SP-1234	Safety	Safety valve	Cleveland	HI4554	4
9	SPX-1234	Safety	Safety valve	Cleveland	OP5333	14

Then we can create an identifier for each line by concatenating the table name "Product" with the unique key and expressing this identifier in the `mfg:` namespace, resulting in identifiers `mfg:Product1`, `mfg:Product2`, and so on.

Each row in the table says several things about that item—namely, its model number, its division, and so on. To represent this in RDF, each of these will be a property that will describe the Products. But just as is the case for the unique identifiers for the rows, we need to have global unique identifiers for these properties. We can use the same namespace as we did for the individuals, but since two tables could have the same column name (but they aren't the same properties!), we need to combine the table name and the column name. This results in properties like `mfg:Product_ModelNo`, `mfg:Product_Division`, and so on.

With these conventions in place, we can now express all the information in the table as triples. There will be one triple per cell in the table—that is, for *n* rows and *c* columns, there will be $n \times c$ triples. The data shown in Table 3.12 have 7 columns and 9 rows, so there are 63 triples, as shown in Table 3.13.

The triples in the table are a bit different from the triples we have seen so far. Although the subject and predicate of these triples are RDF resources (complete with qname namespaces!), the objects are not resources but literal data—that is, strings, integers, and so forth. This should come as no surprise, since, after all, RDF is a data representation system. RDF borrows from XML all the literal data types as possible values for the object of a triple; in this case, the types of all data are strings or integers.

The usual interpretation of a table is that each row in the table corresponds to one individual and that the type of these individuals corresponds to the name of the table. In Table 3.12, each row corresponds to a Product. We can represent this in RDF by adding one triple per row that specifies the type of the individual described by each row, as shown in Table 3.14.

The full complement of triples from the translation of the information in Table 3.12 is shown in Figure 3.7. The types (i.e., where the predicate is `rdf:type`, and the object is the class `mfg:Product`) are shown as links in the graph; triples in which the object is a literal datum are shown (for sake of compactness in the figure) within a box labeled by their common subject.

Table 3.13 Triples Representing Some of the Data in Table 3.12

Subject	Predicate	Object
mfg:Product1	mfg:Product_ID	1
mfg:Product1	mfg:Product_ModelNo	ZX-3
mfg:Product1	mfg:Product_Division	Manufacturing support
mfg:Product1	mfg:Product_Product_Line	Paper machine
mfg:Product1	mfg:Product_Manufacture_Location	Sacramento
mfg:Product1	mfg:Product_SKU	FB3524
mfg:Product1	mfg:Product_Available	23
mfg:Product2	mfg:Product_ID	2
mfg:Product2	mfg:Product_ModelNo	ZX-3P
mfg:Product2	mfg:Product_Division	Manufacturing support
mfg:Product2	mfg:Product_Product_Line	Paper machine
mfg:Product2	mfg:Product_Manufacture_Location	Sacramento
mfg:Product2	mfg:Product_SKU	KD5243
mfg:Product2	mfg:Product_Available	4...

Table 3.14 Triples Representing Type of Information from Table 3.12

Subject	Predicate	Object
mfg:Product1	rdf:type	mfg:Product
mfg:Product2	rdf:type	mfg:Product
mfg:Product3	rdf:type	mfg:Product
mfg:Product4	rdf:type	mfg:Product
mfg:Product5	rdf:type	mfg:Product
mfg:Product6	rdf:type	mfg:Product
mfg:Product7	rdf:type	mfg:Product
mfg:Product8	rdf:type	mfg:Product
mfg:Product9	rdf:type	mfg:Product

HIGHER-ORDER RELATIONSHIPS

It is not unusual for someone who is building a model in RDF for the first time to feel a bit limited by the simple subject/predicate/object form of the RDF triple. They don't want to just say that *Shakespeare wrote Hamlet,* but they want to qualify this statement and say that *Shakespeare wrote Hamlet in 1604* or that *Wikipedia states that Shakespeare wrote Hamlet in 1604.* In general, these are cases in which it is, or at least seems, desirable to make a statement about another statement. This process is called *reification.* Reification is not a problem specific to Semantic Web modeling; the same issue arises in other data modeling contexts like relational databases and object systems. In fact, one approach to reification in the Semantic Web is to simply borrow the standard solution that is commonly used in relational database schemas, using the conventional mapping from relational tables to RDF given in the preceding challenge. In a relational database table, it is possible to simply create a table with more columns to add additional information about a triple. So the statement *Shakespeare wrote Hamlet* is expressed (as in Table 3.1) in a single row of a table, where there is a column for the author of a work and another column for its title. Any further information about this event is done with another column (again, just as in Table 3.1). When this is converted to RDF according to the example in the Challenge, the row is represented by a number of triples, one triple per column in the database. The subject of all of these triples is the same: a single resource that corresponds to the row in the table.

An example of this can be seen in Table 3.13, where several triples have the same subject and one triple apiece for each column in the table. This approach to reification has a strong pedigree in relational modeling, and it has worked well for a wide range of modeling applications. It can be applied in RDF even when the data have not been imported from tabular form. That is, the statement *Shakespeare wrote Hamlet in 1601* (disagreeing with the statement in Table 3.2) can be expressed with these three triples:

```
bio:n1 bio:author lit:Shakespeare.
bio:n1 bio:title "Hamlet".
bio:n1 bio:publicationDate 1601.
```

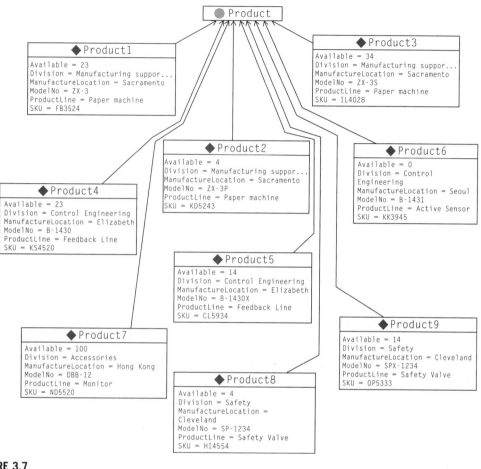

FIGURE 3.7

Graphical version of the tabular data from Table 3.12.

This approach works well for examples like *Shakespeare wrote Hamlet in 1601*, in which we want to express more information about some event or statement. It doesn't work so well in cases like *Wikipedia says Shakespeare wrote Hamlet*, in which we are expressing information about the statement itself, *Shakespeare wrote Hamlet*. This kind of metadata about statements often takes the form of provenance (information about the source of a statement, as in this example), likelihood (expressed in some quantitative form like probability, such as *It is 90 percent probable that Shakespeare wrote* Hamlet), context (specific information about a project setting in which a statement holds, such as *Kenneth Branagh played Hamlet in the movie*), or time frame (Hamlet *plays on Broadway January 11 through March 12*). In such cases, it is useful to explicitly make a statement about a statement. This process, called *explicit reification*, is supported by the W3C RDF standard with three resources called `rdf:subject`, `rdf:predicate`, and `rdf:object`.

Let's take the example of *Wikipedia says Shakespeare wrote Hamlet.* Using the RDF standard, we can refer to a triple as follows:

```
q:n1 rdf:subject lit:Shakespeare;
     rdf:predicate lit:wrote;
     rdf:object lit:Hamlet.
```

Then we can express the relation of Wikipedia to this statement as follows:

```
web:Wikipedia m:says q:n1.
```

Notice that just because we have asserted the reification triples about q:n1, it is not necessarily the case that we have also asserted the triple itself:

```
lit:Shakespeare lit:wrote lit:Hamlet.
```

This is as it should be; after all, if an application does not trust information from Wikipedia, then it should not behave as though that triple has been asserted. An application that does trust Wikipedia will want to behave as though it had.

ALTERNATIVES FOR SERIALIZATION

So far, we have expressed RDF triples in subject/predicate/object tabular form or as graphs of boxes and arrows. Although these are simple and apparent forms to display triples, they aren't always the most compact forms, or even the most human-friendly form, to see the relations between entities.

The issue of representing RDF in text doesn't only arise in books and documents about RDF; it also arises when we want to publish data in RDF on the Web. In response to this need, there are multiple ways of expressing RDF in textual form.

N-Triples

The simplest form is called *N-Triples* and corresponds most directly to the raw RDF triples. It refers to resources using their fully unabbreviated URIs. Each URI is written between angle brackets ($<$ and $>$). Three resources are expressed in subject/predicate/object order, followed by a period (.). For example, if the namespace mfg corresponds to *http://www.WorkingOntologist.org/Examples/Chapter3 Manufacture#*, then the first triple from Table 3.14 is written in N-Triples as follows:

```
<http://www.WorkingOntologist.org/Examples/Chapter3Manufacture#

http://www.WorkingOntologist.org/Examples/Chapter3/Manufacture#Product1

http://www.WorkingOntologist.org/Examples/Chapter3/Manufacture#Product
```

It is difficult to print N-Triples on a page in a book—the serialization does not allow for new lines within a triple (as we had to do here, to fit it in the page). An actual ntriple file has the whole triple on a single line.

Turtle

In this book, we use a more compact serialization of RDF called *Turtle*. Turtle combines the apparent display of triples from N-Triples with the terseness of qnames. We will introduce Turtle in this section and describe just the subset required for the current examples. We will describe more of the language as needed for later examples. For a full description of Turtle, see the W3C Turtle team submission.[1]

Since Turtle uses qnames, there must be a binding between the (local) qnames and the (global) URIs. Hence, Turtle begins with a preamble in which these bindings are defined; for example, we can define the qnames needed in the Challenge example with the following preamble:

```
@prefix mfg:
<http://www.WorkingOntologist.com/Examples/Chapter3/Manufac
    turing#>
@prefix rdf: http://www.w3.org/1999/02/22-rdf-syntax-ns#
```

Once the local qnames have been defined, Turtle provides a very simple way to express a triple by listing three resources, using qname abbreviations, in subject/predicate/object order, followed by a period, such as the following:

```
mfg:Product1 rdf:type mfg:Product .
```

The final period can come directly after the resource for the object, but we often put a space in front of it, to make it stand out visually. This space is optional.

It is quite common (especially after importing tabular data) to have several triples that share a common subject. Turtle provides for a compact representation of such data. It begins with the first triple in subject/predicate/object order, as before; but instead of terminating with a period, it uses a semicolon (;) to indicate that another triple with the same subject follows. For that triple, only the predicate and object need to be specified (since it is the same subject from before). The information in Tables 3.13 and 3.14 about `Product1` and `Product2` appears in Turtle as follows:

```
mfg:Product1 rdf:type mfg:Product;
    mfg:Product_Division "Manufacturing support";
    mfg:Product_ID "1";
    mfg:Product_Manufacture_Location "Sacramento";
    mfg:Product_ModelNo "ZX-3";
    mfg:Product_Product_Line "Paper Machine";
    mfg:Product_SKU "FB3524";
    mfg:Product_Available "23" .
mfg:Product2 rdf:type mfg:Product;
    mfg:Product_Division "Manufacturing support";
    mfg:Product_ID "2";
    mfg:Product_Manufacture_Location "Sacramento";
    mfg:Product_ModelNo "ZX-3P";
    mfg:Product_Product_Line "Paper Machine";
    mfg:Product_SKU "KD5243";
    mfg:Product_Available "4" .
```

[1]http://www.w3.org/TeamSubmission/turtle/

When there are several triples that share both subject and predicate, Turtle provides a compact way to express this as well so that neither the subject nor the predicate needs to be repeated. Turtle uses a comma (,) to separate the objects. So the fact that Shakespeare had three children named Susanna, Judith, and Hamnet can be expressed as follows:

```
lit:Shakespeare b:hasChild b:Susanna, b:Judith, b:Hamnet.
```

There are actually three triples represented here—namely:

```
lit:Shakespeare b:hasChild b:Susanna.
lit:Shakespeare b:hasChild b:Judith.
lit:Shakespeare b:hasChild b:Hamnet.
```

Turtle provides some abbreviations to improve terseness and readability; in this book, we use just a few of these. One of the most widely used abbreviations is to use the word *a* to mean `rdf:type`. The motivation for this is that in common speech, we are likely to say, "`Product1` is *a* Product" or "Shakespeare is *a* playwright" for the triples,

```
mfg:Product1 rdf:type mfg:Product.
lit:Shakespeare rdf:type lit:Playwright.
```

respectively. Thus we will usually write instead:

```
mfg:Product1 a mfg:Product.
lit:Shakespeare a lit:Playwright.
```

RDF/XML

While Turtle is convenient for human consumption and is more compact for the printed page, many Web infrastructures are accustomed to representing information in HTML or, more generally, XML. For this reason, the W3C has recommended the use of an XML serialization of RDF called RDF/XML. The information about `Product1` and `Product2` just shown looks as follows in RDF/XML. In this example, the subjects (`Product1` and `Product2`) are referenced using the XML attribute `rdf:about`; the triples with each of these as subjects appear as subelements within these definitions. The complete details of the RDF/XML syntax are beyond the scope of this discussion and can be found in *http://www.w3.org/TR/rdf-syntax-grammar/*.

```
<rdf:RDF
xmlns:mfg="http://www.WorkingOntologist.com/Examples/Chapter3/
Manufacturing#"
    xmlns:rdf="http://www.w3.org/1999/02/22-rdf-syntax-
    ns#">
    <mfg:Product
```

```
rdf:about="http://www.WorkingOntologist.com/Examples/Chapter3/
Manufacturing#Product1">
    <mfg:Available>23</mfg:Available>
    <mfg:Division>Manufacturing support</mfg:Division>
    <mfg:ProductLine>Paper machine</mfg:ProductLine>
    <mfg:SKU>FB3524</mfg:SKU>
    <mfg:ModelNo>ZX-3</mfg:ModelNo>
    <mfg:ManufactureLocation>Sacramento</mfg:Manufacture
    Location>
    </mfg:Product>
    <mfg:Product
rdf:about="http://www.WorkingOntologist.com/Examples/Chapter3/
Manufacturing#Product2">
    <mfg:SKU>KD5243</mfg:SKU>
    <mfg:Division>Manufacturing support</mfg:Division>
    <mfg:ManufactureLocation>Sacramento</mfg:Manufacture
    Location>
    <mfg:Available>4</mfg:Available>
    <mfg:ModelNo>ZX-3P</mfg:ModelNo>
    <mfg:ProductLine>Paper machine</mfg:ProductLine>
    </mfg:Product>
</rdf:RDF>
```

The same information is contained in the RDF/XML form as in the Turtle, including the declarations of the qnames for `mfg:` and `rdf:`. RDF/XML includes a number of rules for determining the fully qualified URI of a resource mentioned in an RDF/XML document. These details are quite involved and will not be used for the examples in this book.

BLANK NODES

So far, we have described how RDF can represent sets of triples, in which each subject, predicate, and object is either a source or (in the case of the object of a triple) a literal data value. Each resource is given an identity according to the Web standard for identity, the URI. RDF also allows for resources that do not have any Web identity at all. But why would we want to represent a resource that has no identity on the Web?

Sometimes we know that something exists, and we even know some things about it, but we don't know its identity. For instance, suppose we want to represent the fact that Shakespeare had a mistress, whose identity remains unknown. But we know a few things about her; she was a woman, she lived in England, and she was the inspiration for "Sonnet 78."

It is simple enough to express these statements in RDF, but we need an identifier for the mistress. In Turtle, we could express them as follows:

```
lit:Mistress1 rdf:type bio:Woman;
    bio:LivedIn geo:England.
lit:Sonnet78 lit:hasInspiration lit:Mistress1.
```

But if we don't want to have an identifier for the mistress, how can we proceed? RDF allows for a "blank node," or *bnode* for short, for such a situation. If we were to indicate a bnode with a ?, the triples would look as follows:

```
? rdf:type bio:Woman;
    bio:livedIn geo:England.
lit:Sonnet78 lit:hasInspiration ?.
```

The use of the bnode in RDF can essentially be interpreted as a logical statement, "there exists." That is, in these statements we assert "there exists a woman, who lived in England, who was the inspiration for 'Sonnet78.'"

But this notation (which does *not* constitute a valid Turtle expression) has a problem: If there is more than one blank node, how do we know which "?" references which node? For this reason, Turtle instead includes a compact and unambiguous notation for describing blank nodes. A blank node is indicated by putting all the triples of which it is a subject between square brackets ([and]), so:

```
[ rdf:type bio:Woman;
  bio:livedIn geo:England ]
```

It is customary, though not required, to leave blank space after the opening bracket to indicate that we are acting *as if* there were a subject for these triples, even though none is specified.

We can refer to this blank node in other triples by including the entire bracketed sequence in place of the blank node. Furthermore, the abbreviation of "a" for rdf:type is particularly useful in this context. Thus, our entire statement about the mistress who inspired "Sonnet 78" looks as follows in Turtle:

```
lit:Sonnet78 lit:hasInspiration [a :Woman;
                                 bio:livedIn geo:England].
```

This expression of RDF can be read almost directly as plain English: that is, "Sonnet78 has [as] inspiration a Woman [who] lived in England." The identity of the woman is indeterminate. The use of the bracket notation for blank nodes will become particularly important when we come to describe OWL, the Web Ontology Language, since it makes very particular use of bnodes.

Ordered information in RDF

The children of Shakespeare appear in a certain order on the printed page, but from the point of view of RDF, they are in no order at all; there are just three triples, one describing the relationship between Shakespeare and each of his children. What if we do want to specify an ordering. How would we do it in RDF?

RDF provides a facility for ordering elements in a list format. An ordered list can be expressed quite easily in Turtle as follows:

```
lit:Shakespeare b:hasChild (b:Susanna b:Judith b:Hamnet).
```

This translates into the following triples, where _:a, _:b, and _:c are bnodes:

```
lit:Shakespeare b:hasChild _:a.
_:a rdf:first b:Susanna.
_:a rdf:rest _:b.
_:b rdf:first b:Judith.
_:b rdf:rest _:c.
_:c rdf:rest rdf:nil.
_:c rdf:first b:Hamnet.
```

This rendition preserves the ordering of the objects but at a cost of considerable complexity of representation. Fortunately, the Turtle representation is quite compact, so it is not usually necessary to remember the details of the RDF triples behind it.

SUMMARY

RDF is, first and foremost, a system for modeling data. It gives up in compactness what it gains in flexibility. Every relationship between any two data elements is explicitly represented, allowing for a very simple model of merging data. There is no need to arrange the columns of tables so that they "match up" or to worry about data "missing" from a particular column. A relationship (expressed in a familiar form of subject/predicate/object) is either present or it is not. Merging data is thus reduced to a simple matter of considering all such statements from all sources, together in a single place.

The only challenge that remains in such a system is the challenge of *identity*. How do we have a global notation for the identity of any entity? Fortunately, this problem is not unique to the RDF data model. The infrastructure of the Web itself has the same issue and has a standard solution: the URI. RDF borrows this solution.

Since RDF is a Web language, a fundamental consideration is the distribution of information from multiple sources, across the Web. On the Web, the AAA slogan holds: Anyone can say Anything about Any topic. RDF supports this slogan by allowing any data source to refer to resources in any namespace. Even a single triple can refer to resources in multiple namespaces.

As a data model, RDF provides a clear specification of what has to happen to merge information from multiple sources. It does not provide algorithms or technology to implement those processes. These technologies are the topic of the next chapter.

Fundamental concepts

The following fundamental concepts were introduced in this chapter.

RDF (Resource Description Framework)—This distributes data on the Web.

Triple—The fundamental data structure of RDF. A triple is made up of a subject, predicate, and object.

Graph—A nodes-and-links structural view of RDF data.

Merging—The process of treating two graphs as if they were one.

URI (Uniform Resource Indicator)—A generalization of the URL (Uniform Resource Locator), which is the global name on the Web.

namespace—A set of names that belongs to a single authority. Namespaces allow different agents to use the same word in different ways.

qname—An abbreviated version of a URI, it is made up of a namespace identifier and a name, separated by a colon.

rdf:type—The relationship between an instance and its type.

rdf:Property—The type of any property in RDF.

Reification—The practice of making a statement about another statement. It is done in RDF using `rdf:subject`, `rdf:predicate`, and `rdf:object`.

N-Triples, Turtle, RDF/XML—The serialization syntaxes for RDF.

Blank nodes—RDF nodes that have no URI and thus cannot be referenced globally. They are used to stand in for anonymous entities.

Semantic Web application architecture

So far, we have seen how RDF can represent data in a distributed way across the Web. As such, it forms the basis for the Semantic Web, a web of data in which Anyone can say Anything about Any topic. The focus of this book is modeling on the Semantic Web: describing and defining distributed data in such a way that the data can be brought back together in a useful and meaningful way. In a book about only modeling, one could say that there is no room for a discussion of system architecture—the components of a computer system that can actually use these models in useful applications. But this book is for the working ontologist who builds models so that they can be used. But used for what? These models are used to build some application that takes advantage of information distributed over the Web. In short, to put the Semantic Web to work, we need to describe, at least at a high level, the structure of a Semantic Web application—in particular, the components that comprise it, the kinds of inputs it gets (and from where), how it takes advantage of RDF, and why this is different from other application architectures.

Many of the components of a Semantic Web application are provided both as supported products by companies specializing in Semantic Web technology and as free software under a variety of licenses. New software is being developed both by research groups as well as product companies on an ongoing basis. We do not describe any particular tools in this chapter, but rather we discuss the types of components that make up a Semantic Web deployment and how they fit together.

RDF Parser/Serializer We have already seen a number of serializations of RDF, including the W3C standard serialization in XML. An RDF parser reads text in one (or more) of these formats and interprets it as triples in the RDF data model. An RDF serializer does the

51

reverse; it takes a set of triples and creates a file that expresses that content in one of the serialization forms.

RDF Store We have seen how RDF distributes data in the form of triples. An RDF store (sometimes called a triple store) is a database that is tuned for storing and retrieving data in the form of triples. In addition to the familiar functions of any database, an RDF store has the additional ability to merge information from multiple data sources, as defined by the RDF standard.

RDF Query Engine Closely related to the RDF store is the RDF query engine. The query engine provides the capability to retrieve information from an RDF store according to structured queries.

Application An application has some work that it performs with the data it processes: analysis, user interaction, archiving, and so forth. These capabilities are accomplished using some programming language that accesses the RDF store via queries (processed with the RDF query engine).

Most of these components have corresponding components in a familiar relational data-backed application. The relational database itself corresponds to the RDF store in that it stores the data. The database includes a query language with a corresponding query engine for accessing this data. In both cases, the application itself is written using a general-purpose programming language that makes queries and processes their results. The parser/serializer has no direct counterpart in a relational data-backed system, at least as far as standards go. There is no standard serialization of a relational database that will allow it to be imported into a competing relational database system without a change of semantics. (This is a key advantage of RDF stores over traditional data stores.)

In the following sections, we examine each of these capabilities in detail. Since new products in each of these categories are being developed on an ongoing basis, we describe them generically and do not refer to specific products.

RDF PARSER/SERIALIZER

How does an RDF-based system get started? Where do the triples come from? There are a number of possible answers for this, but the simplest one is to find them directly on the Web.

Google can find millions of files with the extension .rdf. Any of these could be a source of data for an RDF application. But these files are useless unless we have a program that can read them. That program is an RDF parser. RDF parsers take as their input a file in some RDF format. Most parsers support the standard RDF/XML format, which is compatible with the more widespread XML standard. An RDF parser takes such a file as input and converts it into an internal representation of the triples that are expressed in that file. At this point, the triples are stored in the triple store and are available for all the operations of that store.

The triples at this point could also be serialized back out, either in the same text form or in another text form. This is done using the reverse operation of the parser: the serializer. It is possible to take a "round-trip" with triples using a parser and serializer; if you serialize a set of triples, then you parse the resulting string with a corresponding parser (e.g., a Turtle parser for a Turtle serialization), and the result is the same set of triples that the process began with. Notice that this is not necessarily true if you start with a text file that represents some triples. Even in a single format, there can be many distinct files that represent the same set of triples. Thus, it is not, in general, possible to read in an RDF file, export it again, and be certain that the resulting file will be identical (character by character) to the input file.

Other data sources

Parsers and serializers based on the standard representations of RDF are useful for the systematic processing and archiving of data in RDF. While there are considerable data available in these formats, even more data are not already available in RDF. Fortunately, for many common data formats (e.g., tabular data), it is quite easy to convert these formats into RDF triples.

We already saw how tabular data can be mapped into triples in a natural way. This approach can be applied to relational databases or spreadsheets. Tools to perform a conversion based on this mapping, though not strictly speaking parsers, play the same role as a parser in a semantic solution: They connect the triple store with sources of information in the form of triples. Most RDF systems include a table input converter of some sort. Some tools specifically target relational databases, including appropriate treatment of foreign key references, whereas others work more directly with spreadsheet tables. Tools of this sort are called *converters,* since they typically convert information from some form into RDF and often into a standard form of RDF like Turtle. This allows them to be used with any other RDF. Another rich source of data for the Semantic Web can be found in existing web pages—that is, in HTML pages. Such pages often include structured information, like contact information, descriptions of events, product descriptions, publications, and so on. This information can be combined in novel ways on the Semantic Web once it is available in RDF.

A related approach to encoding information in web pages is a trend that goes by the name of *microformats.* The idea of a microformat is that some web page authors might be willing to embed structured information in their web pages. To enable them to do this, a standard vocabulary (usually embedded in HTML as special tag attributes that have no impact on how a browser displays a page) is developed for commonly used items on a web page. Some of the first microformats were for business cards (including, in the controlled vocabulary, names, positions, companies, and phone numbers) and events (including location, start time, and end time). One limitation of microformats is the need to specify a controlled vocabulary and provide a parser that can process that vocabulary. Wouldn't it be better if, instead, someone (like the W3C) would simply specify a single syntax for marking up HTML pages with RDF data? Then there would be a single processing script for all microformats.

The W3C has proposed just such a format called RDFa. The idea behind RDFa is quite simple: Use the attribute tags in HTML to embed information that can be parsed into RDF. Just like microformats, RDFa has no effect on how a browser displays a page. A number of search engines (Google and Yahoo!) and retailers (BestBuy, Overstock.com) have begun to adopt RDFa to provide machine processable Semantic Web data. Facebook has adopted a variant of RDFa as part of the Open Graph Protocol—a network of information available in Facebook.

RDFa provides two advantages for sharing data on the Web. First, from the point of view of data consumers, it is easier to harvest the RDF data from pages that were marked up with structured data extraction in mind, than from sources that were developed without this intention. But, more important, from the point of view of the content author, it allows them to express the intended meaning of a web page inside the web page itself. This ensures that the RDF data in the document matches the intended meaning of the document itself. This really is the spirit of the word *semantic* in the Semantic

Web—that page authors be given the capability of expressing what they mean in a web page for a machine to read and use.

RDF STORE

A database is a program that stores data, making them available for future use. An RDF data storage solution is no different; the RDF data are kept in a system called an *RDF store*. It is typical for an RDF data store to be accompanied by a parser and a serializer to populate the store and publish information from the store, respectively. Just as is the case for conventional (e.g., relational) data stores, an RDF store may also include a query engine, as described in the next section. Conventional data stores are differentiated based on a variety of performance features, including the volume of data that can be stored, the speed with which data can be accessed or updated, and the variety of query languages supported by the query engine. These features are equally relevant when applied to an RDF store.

In contrast to a relational data store, an RDF store includes as a fundamental capability, the ability to merge two data sets together. Because of the flexible nature of the RDF data model, the specification of such a merge operation is clearly defined. Each data store represents a set of RDF triples; a merger of two (or more) data sets is the single data set that includes all and only the triples from the source data sets. Any resources with the same URI (regardless of the originating data source) are considered to be equivalent in the merged data set. Thus, in addition to the usual means of evaluating a data store, an RDF store can be evaluated on the efficiency of the merge process.

RDF store implementations range from custom programmed database solutions to fully supported off-the-shelf products from specialty vendors. Conceptually, the simplest relational implementation of a triple store is as a single table with three columns, one each for the subject, predicate, and object of the triple. Table 4.1 shows some data about Los Angeles Metro stations, organized in this way.

This representation should look familiar, as it is exactly the representation we used to introduce RDF triples in Chapter 3. Since this fits in a relational database representation, it can be accessed using conventional relational database tools such as SQL. An experienced SQL programmer would have no problem writing a query to answer a question like "List the dc:title of every instance of metro:Metro in the table." As an implementation representation, it has a number of apparent

Table 4.1 Names and Addresses of Los Angeles Metro Stations

Subject	Predicate	Object
metro:item0	rdf:type	metro:Metro
metro:item0	dc:title	"Allen Station"
metro:item0	simile:address	"395 N. Allen Av., Pasadena 91106"
metro:item1	rdf:type	metro:Metro
metro:item1	dc:title	"Chinatown Station"
metro:item1	simile:address	"901 N. Spring St., Los Angeles 90012–1862"
metro:item2	rdf:type	metro:Metro
metro:item2	dc:title	Del Mar Station
metro:item2	simile:address	"230 S. Raymond Av., Pasadena 91105–2014"

problems, including the replication of information in the first column and the difficulty of building indices around string values like URIs.

It is not the purpose of this discussion to go into details of the possible optimizations of the RDF store. These details are the topic of the particular (sometimes proprietary) solutions provided by a vendor of an off-the-shelf RDF store. In particular, the issue of building indices that work on URIs can be solved with a number of well-understood data organization algorithms. Serious providers of RDF stores differentiate their offerings based on the scalability and efficiency of these indexing solutions.

RDF data standards and interoperability of RDF stores

RDF stores bear considerable similarity to relational stores, especially in terms of how the quality of a store is evaluated. A notable distinction of RDF stores results from the standardization of the RDF data model and RDF/XML serialization syntax. Several competing vendors of relational data stores dominate the market today, and they have for several decades. While each of these products is based on the same basic idea of the relational algebra for data representation, it is a difficult process to transfer a whole database from one system to another. That is, there is no standard serialization language with which one can completely describe a relational database in such a way that it can be automatically imported into a competitor's system. Such a task is possible, but it typically requires a database programmer to track down the particulars of the source database to ensure that they are represented faithfully in the target system.

The standardization effort for RDF makes the situation very different when it comes to RDF stores. Just as for relational stores, there are several competing vendors and projects. In stark contrast to the situation for relational databases, the underlying RDF data model is shared by all of these products, and, even more specifically, all of them can import and export their data sets in any of the standard formats (RDF/XML or Turtle). This makes it a routine task to transfer an RDF data set—or several RDF data sets—from one RDF store to another. This feature, which is a result of an early and aggressive standardization process, makes it much easier to begin with one RDF store, secure in the knowledge that the system can be migrated to another as the need arises. It also simplifies the issue of federating data that are housed in multiple RDF stores, possibly coming from different vendor sources.

RDF query engines

An RDF store is typically accessed using a query language. In this sense, an RDF store is similar to a relational database or an XML store. Not surprisingly, in the early days of RDF, a number of different query languages were available, each supported by some RDF-based product or open-source project. From the common features of these query languages, the W3C has undertaken the process of standardizing an RDF query language called SPARQL. We cover the details of the SPARQL query language in the next chapter.

An RDF query engine is intimately tied to the RDF store. To solve a query, the engine relies on the indices and internal representations of the RDF store: the more finely tuned the store is to the query engine, the better its performance. For large-scale applications, it is preferable to have an RDF store and query engine that retain their performance even in the face of very large data sets. For smaller applications, other features (e.g., cost, ease of installation, platform, open-source status, and built-in integration with other enterprise systems) may dominate.

The SPARQL query language includes a protocol for communicating queries and results so that a query engine can act as a web service. This provides another source of data for the semantic web—the so-called *SPARQL endpoints* provide access to large amounts of structured RDF data. It is even possible to provide SPARQL access to databases that are not triple stores, effectively translating SPARQL queries into the query language of the underlying store. The W3C has recently begun the process to standardize a translation from SPARQL to SQL for relational stores.

Comparison to relational queries

In many ways, an RDF query engine is very similar to the query engine in a relational data store: It provides a standard interface to the data and defines a formalism by which data are viewed. A relational query language is based on the relational algebra of joins and foreign key references. RDF query languages look more like statements in predicate calculus. Unification variables are used to express constraints between the patterns.

A relational query describes a new data table that is formed by combining two or more source tables. An RDF query (whether in SPARQL or another RDF query language) can describe a new graph that is formed by describing a subset of a source RDF graph. That graph, in turn, may be the result of having merged together several other graphs. The inherently recursive nature of graphs simplifies a number of detailed issues that arise in table-based queries. For instance, an RDF query language like SPARQL has little need for a subquery construct; in many cases, the same effect can be achieved with a single query. Similarly, there is nothing corresponding to the special case of an SQL "self-join" in SPARQL.

In the special case in which an RDF store is implemented as a single table in a relational database, any graph pattern match in such a scenario will constitute a self-join on that table. Some end-developers choose to work this way in a familiar SQL environment. Oracle takes another approach to making RDF queries accessible to SQL programmers by providing its own SPARQL extension to its version of SQL, optimized for graph queries. Their SPARQL engine is smoothly integrated with the table/join structure of their SQL scripting language.

APPLICATION CODE

Database applications include more than just a database and query engine; they also include some application code, in an application environment, that performs some analysis on or displays some information from the database. The only access the application has to the database is through the query interface, as shown in Figure 4.1.

An RDF application has a similar architecture, but it includes the RDF parser and serializer, converters, the RDF merge functionality, and the RDF query engine. These capabilities interact with the application itself and the RDF store as shown in Figure 4.2.

The application itself can take any of several forms. Most commonly, it is written in a conventional programming language (Java, C, Python, and Perl are popular options). In this case, the RDF capabilities are provided as API bindings for that language. It is also common for an RDF store to provide a scripting language as part of the query system, which gives programmatic access to these capabilities in a way that is not unlike how advanced dialects of SQL provide scripting capabilities for relational database applications.

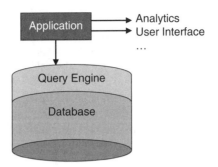

FIGURE 4.1

Application architecture for a database application.

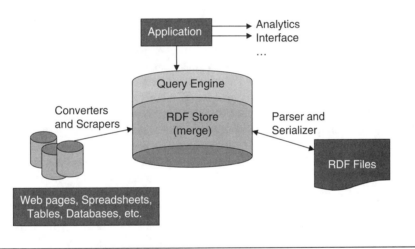

FIGURE 4.2

Application architecture for an RDF application.

Regardless of the method by which the RDF store makes these functionalities available to the application, it is still the responsibility of the application to use them. Here are some examples of typical RDF applications:

- *Calendar integration*—shows appointments from different people and teams on a single calendar view
- *Map integration*—shows locations of points of interest gathered from different web sites, spreadsheets, and databases all on a single map
- *Annotation*—allows a community of users to apply keywords (with URIs) to information *(tagging)* for others to consult
- *Content management*—makes a single index of information resources (documents, web pages, databases, etc.) that are available in several content stores.

The application will decide what information sources need to be scraped or converted (e.g., diary entries in XML, lists of addresses from a web page, directory listings of content servers).

Depending on the volatility of the data, some of this process may even happen offline (e.g., locations of subway stations in New York, entries in the Sears catalog, analyses of common chemical structures, etc., don't change very rapidly; these sorts of data could be imported into RDF entirely outside of an application context), whereas other data (like calendar data of team members, transactional sales data, experimental results) will have to be updated on a regular basis. Some data can remain in the RDF store itself (private information about this team, order information, patented chemical formulas); other data could be published in RDF form for other applications to use (train timetables, catalog specials, FDA findings about certain chemicals).

Once all the required data sources have been converted, fetched, or parsed, the application uses the merge functionality of the RDF store to produce a single, federated graph of all the merged data. It is this federated graph that the application will use for all further queries. There is no need for the queries themselves to be aware of the federation strategy or schedule; the federation has already taken place when the RDF merge was performed.

From this point onward, the application behaves very like any other database application. A web page to display the appointments of any member of a team will include a query for that information. Even if the appointments came from different sources and the information about team membership from still another source, the query is made against the federated information graph.

RDF-backed web portals

When the front end of an application is a web server, the architecture (shown in Figure 4.1) is well known for a database-backed web portal. The pages are generated using any of a number of technologies (e.g., CGI, ASP, JSP, ZOPE) that allow web pages to be constructed from the results of queries against a database. In the earliest days of the web, web pages were typically stored statically as files in a file system. The move to database-backed portals was made to allow web sites to reflect the complex interrelated structure of data as it appears in a relational database.

The system architecture outlined in Figure 4.2 can be used the same way to implement a Semantic Web portal. The RDF store plays the same role that the database plays in database-backed portals. It is important to note that because of the separation between the presentation layer in both Figures 4.1 and 4.2, it is possible to use all the same technologies for the actual web page construction for a Semantic Web portal as those used in a database-backed portal. But, in contrast to conventional data-backed web portals, and because of the distributed nature of the RDF store that backs a Semantic Web portal, information on a single RDF-backed web page typically comes from multiple sources. The merge capability of an RDF store supports this sort of information distribution as part of the infrastructure of the web portal. When the portal is backed by RDF, there is no difference between building a distributed web portal and one in which all the information is local. Using RDF, federated web portals are as easy as siloed portals.

DATA FEDERATION

The RDF data model was designed from the beginning with data federation in mind. Information from any source is converted into a set of triples so that data federation of any kind—spreadsheets and XML, database tables and web pages—is accomplished with a single mechanism. As shown in Figure 4.2, this strategy of federation converts information from multiple sources into a single format and then combines all the information into a single store. This is in contrast to a federation strategy in which the application queries each source using a method corresponding to that format. RDF does not refer to a file format or a particular language for encoding data but rather to the data model of representing information in triples. It is this feature of RDF that allows data to be federated in this way. The mechanism for merging this information, and the details of the RDF data model, can be encapsulated into a piece of software—the RDF store—to be used as a building block for applications.

The strategy of federating information first and then querying the federated information store separates the concerns of data federation from the operational concerns of the application. Queries written in the application need not know where a particular triple came from. This allows a single query to seamlessly operate over multiple data sources without elaborate planning on the part of the query author. This also means that changes to the application to federate further data sources will not impact the queries in the application itself.

This feature of RDF applications forms the key to much of the discussion that follows. In our discussion of RDFS and OWL, we will assume that any federation necessary for the application has already taken place; that is, all queries and inferences will take place on the *federated graph*. The federated graph is simply the graph that includes information from all the federated data sources over which application queries will be run.

SUMMARY

The components described in this chapter—RDF parsers, serializers, stores, and query engines—are not semantic models in themselves but the components of a system that will include semantic models. Even the information represented in RDF is not necessarily a semantic model. These are the building blocks that go into making and using a semantic model. The model will be represented in RDF, to be sure. As we shall see, the semantic modeling languages of the W3C, RDFS, and OWL are built entirely in RDF, and they can be federated just like any other RDF data.

Where do semantic models fit into the application architecture of Figure 4.2? As data expressed in RDF, they will be housed in the RDF store, along with all other data. But semantic models go beyond just including data that will be used to answer a query, like the list of plays that Shakespeare wrote or the places where paper machines are kept. Semantic models also include meta-data; data that help to organize other data. When we federate information from multiple sources, the RDF data model allows us to represent all the data in a single, uniform way. But it does nothing to resolve any conflicts of meaning between the sources. Do two states have the same definitions of "marriage"? Is the notion of "writing" a play the same as the notion of "writing" a song? It is the semantic models that give answers to questions like these. A semantic model acts as a sort of glue between disparate, federated data sources so we can describe how they fit together.

Just as Anyone can say Anything about Any topic, so also can anyone say anything about a model; that is, anyone can contribute to the definition and mapping between information sources. In this way, not only can a federated, RDF-based, semantic application get its information from multiple sources, but it can even get the instructions on how to combine information from multiple sources. In this way, the Semantic Web really is a web of meaning, with multiple sources describing what the information on the Web means.

Fundamental concepts

The following fundamental concepts were introduced in this chapter:

RDF parser/serializer—A system component for reading and writing RDF in one of several file formats.

RDF store—A database that works in RDF. One of its main operations is to merge RDF graphs.

RDF query engine—This provides access to an RDF store, much as an SQL engine provides access to a relational store.

SPARQL—The W3C standard query language for RDF.

SPARQL endpoint—An application that can answer a SPARQL query, including one where the native encoding of information is not in RDF.

Application interface—The part of the application that uses the content of an RDF store in an interaction with some user.

Converter—A tool that converts data from some form (e.g., tables) into RDF.

RDFa—Standard for encoding and retrieving RDF metadata from HTML pages.

Querying the Semantic Web—SPARQL

5

CHAPTER OUTLINE

RDF provides a simple way to represent distributed data. The triple is the simplest way to represent a named connection between two things. But a representation of data is useless without some means of accessing that data. The standard way to access RDF data uses a query language called SPARQL. SPARQL stands for **SPARQL P**rotocol **A**nd **R**DF **Q**uery **L**anguage (yes, the "S" in "SPARQL" stands for "SPARQL," sigh). The SPARQL query language works closely with the structure of RDF itself. SPARQL query patterns are represented in a variant of Turtle (the same language that we use to express

RDF throughout this book). The queried RDF graph can be created from one kind of data or merged from many; in either case, SPARQL is the way to query it.

This chapter gives examples of the SPARQL query language. Most of the examples are based on version 1.0 of the standard, released in 2008. At the time of this writing, a new version of SPARQL is under development. The advanced examples will use features from the new standard (version 1.1) and will be indicated in the heading of each section as **(SPARQL 1.1)**. Features described in sections without this indication are available in both SPARQL 1.0 as well as SPARQL 1.1. Since this recommendation is still in progress, the final version might deviate in small ways from the examples given here.

SPARQL is a query language and shares many features with other query languages like XQUERY and SQL. But it differs from each of these query languages in important ways (as they differ from one another). Since we don't want to assume that a reader has a background in any specific query language (or even query languages at all), we begin with a gentle introduction to querying data. We start with the most basic information retrieval system, which we call a *Tell-and-Ask* system.

TELL-AND-ASK SYSTEMS

A Tell-and-Ask system is a simple system—you *tell* it some facts, and then it can answer questions you *ask* based on what you told it. Consider the following simple example:

> **Tell:** James Dean played in the movie *Giant*.

Then you could ask questions like:

> **Ask:** Who played in *Giant*?
> **Answer:** James Dean
> **Ask:** James Dean played in what?
> **Answer:** *Giant*

You might tell it some more things, too, like:

> **Tell:** James Dean played in *East of Eden*.
> James Dean played in *Rebel Without a Cause*.

Then if you ask:

> **Ask:** James Dean played in what?
> **Answer:** *Giant, East of Eden, Rebel Without a Cause.*

One could imagine a sophisticated Tell-and-Ask system that understands natural language and can cope with questions like

> **Ask:** What movies did James Dean star in?
> **Answer:** *Giant, East of Eden, Rebel Without a Cause.*

Instead of using the simplified language in these examples. As we shall see, most real Tell-and-Ask systems don't do anything with natural language processing at all. In more complex Tell-and-Ask systems, it can be quite difficult to be very specific about just what you really want to ask, so they usually use languages that are quite precise and technical.

On the face of it, it might seem that Tell-and-Ask systems aren't very interesting. They don't figure out anything you didn't tell them yourself. They don't do any calculations, they don't do any analysis. But this judgment is premature; even very simple Tell-and-Ask systems are quite useful. Let's have a look at one—a simple address book.

You have probably used an address book at some point in your life. Even a paper-and-pencil address book is a Tell-and-Ask system, though the process of telling it something (i.e., writing down an address) and the process of asking it something (looking up an address) take a lot of human effort. Let's think instead of a computer program that does the job of an address book. How does it work?

Like a paper address book, you tell it names and addresses (and probably phone numbers and email addresses and other information). Unlike the sample Tell-and-Ask system that we used to talk about James Dean and movies, you probably don't talk to your address book in anything that remotely resembles English; you probably fill out a form, with a field for a name, and another for the parts of the address, and so on. You "tell" it an address by filling in a form.

How do you ask a question? If you want to know the address of someone, you type in their name, perhaps into another form, very similar to the one you filled in to tell it the information in the first place. Once you have entered the name, you get the address.

The address book only gives you back what you told it. It does no calculations, and draws no conclusions. How could this be an interesting system? Even without any ability to do computations, address books are useful systems. They help us organize certain kinds of information that is useful to us and to find it when we need it. It is a simple Tell-and-Ask system—you tell it things, then you ask questions.

Even the address book is a bit more advanced than the simplest Tell-and-Ask system. When you look up an address in an address book, you usually get a lot more information than just the address. It is as if you asked a whole set of questions:

> **Ask:** What is the address of Maggie Smith?
> **Ask:** What is the phone number of Maggie Smith?
> **Ask:** What is the email address of Maggie Smith?
> And so on.

How can we make our address book system a bit more useful? There are a number of ways to enhance its behavior (and many of these are available in real address book applications). One way to make the address book "smarter" is to require less of the user who is asking questions. For instance, instead of typing in "Maggie Smith" when looking for an address, the system could let you just type in "Maggie," and look for any address where the name of the addressee *contains* the word "Maggie." Now it is as if you have asked

> **Ask:** What is the address of everyone whose name includes "Maggie"?
> You might get more answers if you do this—if, for instance, you also have an address for Maggie King, you'll get both addresses in response to your question.
> You can go even further—you can ask your question based on some other information. You could ask about the address instead of the name, by filling in information in the address field:
> **Ask:** Who lives at an address that contains "Downing"?

Common tell-and-ask infrastructure—spreadsheets

The address book was an example of a special-purpose tell-and-ask system; it is aimed at a single task, and has a fixed structure to the information you can tell it and ask it about. A spreadsheet is an example of a tell-and-ask system that is highly configurable and can be applied to a large number of situations. Spreadsheets are often cited as the most successful "killer application" ever; putting data management into the hands of intelligent people without the need to learn any heavy-duty technical skills. Spreadsheets apply the notion of WYSIWYG (What You See Is What You Get) to data management; a visual representation of data.

The "language" for telling information to a spreadsheet and asking information of a spreadsheet is visual; information is entered into a particular row and column and is retrieved by visually inspecting the table.

Since spreadsheets are primarily a visual presentation of data, you don't communicate with them in any particular language—much less natural language. You don't write "where does Maggie live?" to a spreadsheet; instead you search for Maggie in the "Name" column, and look into the "address" column to answer your question.

Spreadsheets become more cumbersome when the data aren't conveniently represented in a single table. Probably the simplest example of data that don't fit into a table is multiple values. Suppose we have more than one email address for Maggie Smith. How do we deal with this? We could have multiple email columns, like this:

Name	Email1	Email2
Maggie Smith	MSmith@acme.com	maggie@gmail.com

This solution works as long as nobody has three email addresses, etc. Another solution is to have a new row for Maggie, for each email address

Name	Email
Maggie Smith	MSmith@acme.com
Maggie Smith	maggie@gmail.com

This is a bit confusing, in that it is unclear whether we have one contact named "Maggie Smith" with two emails, or two contacts who happen to have the same name, one with each email address.

Spreadsheets also start to break down when an application requires highly interconnected data. Consider a contacts list that maintains names of people and the companies they work for. Then they maintain separate information for the companies—billing information, contract officer, etc. If this information is put into a single table, the relationship between the company and its information will be duplicated for each contact that works at that company, as illustrated in the table below:

Name	Email	Company	Contract Officer	Headquarters
Maggie Smith	MSmith@acme.com	ACME Product Inc.	Cynthia Wiley	Pittsburgh
Maggie King	MKing@acme.com	ACME Product Inc.	Cynthia Wiley	Pittsburgh

Both Maggies work for ACME, where the Contract Officer is Cynthia and the headquarters is in Pittsburgh. Duplicating information in this manner is error-prone as well as wasteful; for instance, if ACME gets a new contract officer, all the contact records for people who work for ACME need to be changed.

A common solution to this problem is to separate out the company information from the contact information into two tables, e.g.:

Name	Email	Company
Maggie Smith	MSmith@acme.com	ACME Product Inc.
Maggie King	MKing@acme.com	ACME Product Inc.

Company	Contract Officer	Headquarters
ACME Product Inc.	Cynthia Wiley	Pittsburgh

This sort of solution is workable in modern spreadsheet software, but begins to degrade the main advantages of spreadsheets; we can no longer use visualization to answer questions. Its structure relies on cross-references that are not readily visible by examining the spreadsheet. In fact, this sort of solution moves the tell-and-ask system from spreadsheets into a more structured form of tell-and-ask system, a relational database.

Advanced tell-and-ask infrastructure—relational database

Relational databases form the basis for most large-scale tell-and-ask systems. They share with spreadsheets a tabular presentation of data, but include a strong formal system (based on a mathematical formalism called the "relational algebra") that provides a systematic way to link tables together. This facility, along with some well-defined methodological support, allows relational databases to represent highly structured data, and respond to very detailed, structured questions.

> **Tell:** Maggie King works for Acme Product Inc.
> **Tell:** The contract officer for Acme Product Inc. is Cynthia Wiley
> **Tell:** Cynthia Wiley's email address is CJWiley@acme.com
> **Ask:** What is the email address for the contract officer at the company where Maggie King works?
> **Answer:** CJWiley@acme.com

This sort of detailed structure comes at a price—asking a question becomes a very detailed process, requiring a specialized language. Such a language is called a *query language*.

In the query language for relational databases, links from one table to another are done by cross-referencing a closer rendering of the question above, in a query language for a relational database, would be:

> **Ask:** What is the email address for the person matched by the "contract officer" reference for the company matched by the "works for" reference for the person whose name is "Maggie King"?
> **Answer:** CJWiley@acme.com

This might seem like a needlessly wordy way to ask the question, but this is how you pose questions precisely enough to recover information from a complex database structure.

RDF AS A TELL-AND-ASK SYSTEM

RDF is also a tell-and-ask system. Like a relational database, RDF can represent complex structured data. Also like a relational database, RDF requires a precise query language to specify questions. Unlike a relational database, the cross-references are not visible to the end user, and there is no need to explicitly represent them in the query language.

As discussed in previous chapters, in RDF, relationships are represented as triples. Asserting a triple amounts to TELLing the triple store a fact.

Tell: James Dean played in the movie *Giant*.

How do we **ASK** questions of this? Even with a single triple, there are already some questions we could ask:

Ask: What did James Dean play in?
Ask: Who played in *Giant*?
Ask: What did James Dean do in *Giant*?

All of these questions can be asked in SPARQL in a simple way, by replacing part of the triple with a question word, like Who, What, Where, etc. SPARQL doesn't actually distinguish between question words, so we can choose words that make sense in English. In SPARQL, question words are written with a question mark at the start, e.g., *?who, ?where, ?when*, etc.

Ask: James Dean played in ?what
Answer: *Giant*
Ask: ?who played in *Giant*
Answer: James Dean
Ask: James Dean ?what *Giant*
Answer: played in

This is the basic idea behind SPARQL—that you can write a question that looks a lot like the data, with a question word standing in for the thing you want to know. Like query languages for relational databases and spreadsheets, SPARQL makes no attempt to mimic the syntax of natural language, but it does use the idea that a question can look just like a statement, but with a question word to indicate what we want to know.

SPARQL—QUERY LANGUAGE FOR RDF

The syntax of SPARQL actually looks like Turtle. So these examples really look more like this:

```
Tell:   :JamesDean :playedIn :Giant .
Ask:    :JamesDean :playedIn ?what .
Answer: :Giant
Ask:    ?who :playedIn :Giant .
Answer: :JamesDean
Ask:    :JamesDean ?what :Giant .
Answer: :playedIn
```

Before we go further, let's talk a bit about the syntax of a SPARQL query. We'll start with a simple form, the SELECT query. Readers familiar with SQL will notice a lot of overlap with SPARQL syntax (e.g., keywords like SELECT and WHERE). This is not coincidental; SPARQL was designed to be easily learned by SQL users.

A SPARQL SELECT query has two parts; a set of question words, and a question pattern. The keyword WHERE indicates the selection pattern, written in braces. We have already seen some question patterns, e.g.,

```
WHERE {:JamesDean :playedIn ?what .}
WHERE {?who :playedIn :Giant .}
WHERE {:JamesDean ?what :Giant .}
```

The query begins with the word SELECT followed by a list of the question words. So the queries for the questions above are

```
SELECT ?what WHERE {:JamesDean ?playedIn ?what .}
SELECT ?who WHERE {?who :playedIn :Giant .}
SELECT ?what WHERE {:JamesDean ?what :Giant .}
```

It might seem that listing the question words in the SELECT part is redundant—after all, they appear in the patterns already. To some extent, this is true, but we'll see later how modifying this list can be useful.

RDF (and SPARQL) deals well with multiple values. If we TELL the system that James Dean played in multiple movies, we can do this without having to make any considerations in the representation:

Tell: `:JamesDean :playedIn :Giant .`
Tell: `:JamesDean :playedIn :EastOfEden .`
Tell: `:JamesDean :playedIn :RebelWithoutaCause .`

Now if we ASK a question with SPARQL

Ask: SELECT `?what` **WHERE** `{:JamesDean :playedIn ?what}`
Answer: `:Giant, :EastOfEden, :RebelWithoutaCause.`

The WHERE clause of a SPARQL query can be seen as a *graph pattern*, that is, a pattern that is matched against the data graph. In this case, the pattern has just one triple, `:JamesDean` as the subject, `:playedIn` as the predicate, and a question word as the object. The action of the query engine is to find all matches for the pattern in the data, and to return all the values that the question word matched.

We can see this as a graph—Figure 5.1 shows the James Dean data in the form of a graph, and the WHERE clause as a graph pattern. There are three matches for this pattern in the graph, where a match has to match resources in the pattern exactly, but anything can match the question word.

Suppose we follow the data along further. Each of these movies is directed by someone. Some of them might be directed by more than one person, as shown in Figure 5.2. Who were the directors that

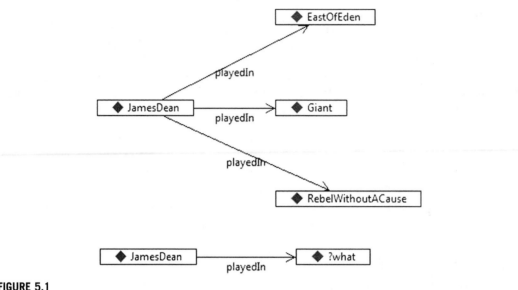

FIGURE 5.1

James Dean data in a graph, and a query to fetch it.

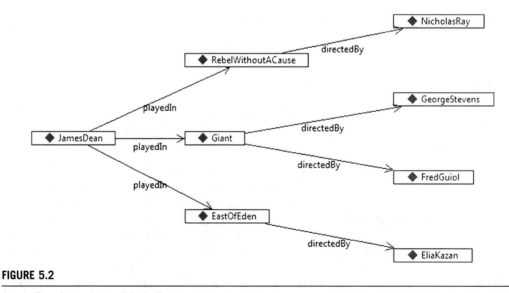

FIGURE 5.2

James Dean's movies and their directors.

FIGURE 5.3

Graphic version of a query to find James Dean's directors.

James Dean worked with? We can query this by asking who directed the movies that James Dean played in. The graph pattern for this query has two triples:

```
:JamesDean :playedIn ?what .
?what :directedBy ?who .
```

Since the variable *?what* appears in both triples, the graph pattern is joined at that point. We can draw a graph pattern the same way we draw a graph. Figure 5.3 shows this graph pattern. There are two triples in the pattern and two triples in the diagram.

This graph pattern has two question words, so the query engine will find all matches for the pattern, with both question words being free to match any resource. This results in several matches:

```
?what=:Giant                 ?who=:GeorgeStevens
?what=:Giant                 ?who=:FredGuiol
?what=:EastOfEden            ?who=:EliaKazan
?what=:RebelWithoutaCause    ?who=:NicholasRay
```

When we have more than one question word, we might actually only be interested in one of them. In this case, we asked what directors James Dean had worked with; the movies he played in were just a means to that end. This is where the details of the SELECT clause come in—we can specify which question words we are interested in. So the complete query to find James Dean's directors looks like this:

Ask:
```
SELECT ?who
WHERE {:JamesDean :playedIn ?what .
       ?what :directedBy ?who .}
```
Answer:
```
:GeorgeStevens,    :EliaKazan,    :NicholasRay,    :FredGuiol
```

Since a query in SPARQL can have several question words and several answers, it is convenient to display the answers in a table with one column for each question word and one row for each answer.

?who
:GeorgeStevens
:EliaKazan
:NicholasRay
:FredGuiol

If we decide to keep both question words in the SELECT, we will have more columns in the table

Ask:

```
SELECT ?what ?who
WHERE {:JamesDean :playedIn ?what .
       ?what :directedBy ?who .}
```

?what	?who
:Giant	:GeorgeStevens
:Giant	:FredGuiol
:EastOfEden	:EliaKazan
:RebelWithoutaCause	:NicholasRay

Naming question words in SPARQL

In English, we have a handful of question words—who, what, where, etc. A question doesn't make sense if we use some other word. But in SPARQL, a question word is just signaled by the *?* at the start—any word would do just as well. If we look at the output table above, the question words *?who* and *?what* are not very helpful in describing what is going on in the table. If we remember the question, we know what they mean (*?what* is a movie, and *?who* is its director). But we can make the table more understandable, even out of the context of the question, by selecting descriptive question words. It is customary in SPARQL to do this, to communicate the intention of a question word to someone who might want to read the query. For example, we might write this query as

Ask:

```
SELECT ?movie ?director
WHERE {:JamesDean :playedIn ?movie .
       ?movie :directedBy ?director .}
```

Answer:

?movie	?director
:Giant	:GeorgeStevens
:Giant	:FredGuiol
:EastOfEden	:EliaKazan
:RebelWithoutaCause	:NicholasRay

The graph pattern we just saw was a simple chain—James Dean played in some movie that was directed by someone. Graph patterns in SPARQL can be as elaborate as the graphs they match against. For instance, given a more complete set of information about James Dean movies we could find the actresses who worked with him with a graph pattern:

Ask:

```
SELECT ?actress ?movie
WHERE {:JamesDean :playedIn ?movie .
       ?actress :playedIn ?movie .
       ?actress rdf:type :Woman }
```

Answer:

?actress
:AnnDoran
:ElizabethTaylor
:CarrollBaker
:JoVanFleet
:JulieHarris
:MercedesMcCambridge
:NatalieWood

Figure 5.4 shows a fragment of the data graph, and the graph pattern, with the result for the question word *?actress* indicated in the third 'column' of the figure. Notice that Rock Hudson is not a match; while he indeed played in *Giant,* there is no match for the third triple,

```
:RockHudson rdf:type :Woman.
```

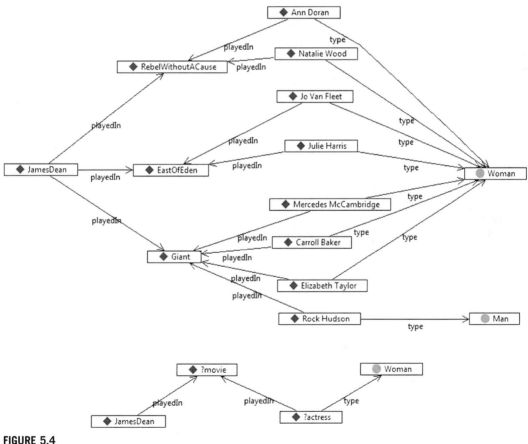

FIGURE 5.4

Information about James Dean's co-stars, and a query to fetch some of it.

Remember that *?actress* is just a question word like *?who*, renamed to be more readable; the only reason *?actress* doesn't match `:RockHudson` is because the data do not support the match. That is, the meaning of *?actress* is not given by its name, but instead by the structure of the graph pattern.

With this observation, one might wonder how we know that *?movie* is sure to come up with movies? And indeed this is a consideration; in this example, the only things that James Dean played in were movies, so it really isn't an issue. But on the Semantic Web, we could have more information about things that James Dean played in. So we really should restrict the value of the question word *? movie* to be a member of the class movie. We can do this by adding one more triple to the pattern:

Ask:
```
SELECT ?actress
WHERE {:JamesDean :playedIn ?movie .
       ?movie rdf:type :Movie .
       ?actress :playedIn ?movie .
       ?actress rdf:type :Woman }
```

This query pattern is shown graphically in Figure 5.5.
Triples like

```
?movie rdf:type :Movie .
```

can seem a bit confusing at first—with two uses of the word *movie*, what does this mean? But now that we know that *?movie* is just a generic question word with a name that prints well in a table, we can see that this triple is how we tell SPARQL what we really mean by *?movie*. The meaning isn't in the name, so we have to put it in a triple.

You might come upon a model that gives properties the same name as the class of entity they are intended to point to—so that instead of a property called `:directedBy` in this example, a model might call it simply `:director`. In such a case, the query to find the people who directed James Dean movies would look like this:

```
SELECT ?director
WHERE {:JamesDean :playedIn ?movie .
       ?movie :director ?director .}
```

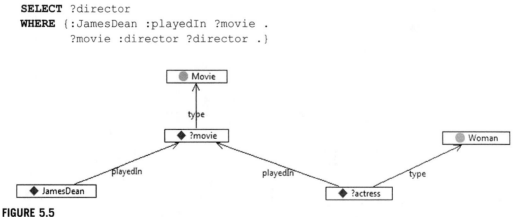

FIGURE 5.5

Extended query pattern that includes the fact that ?movie has type Movie.

This can look a bit daunting—what is the difference between *?director* and :director? As we've already seen, :director refers to a particular resource (using the default namespace—that's what the ":" means) On the other hand, *?director* is a question word—it could have been *?foo* or *?bar* just as easily, but we chose *?director* to remind us of its connection with a movie director, when we see it out of the context of the query. If you have to write (or read!) a query written for a model that names its properties in this way, don't panic! Just remember that the *?* marks a question word—the name *?director* is just there to let you (and whoever else reads the query) know what *?director* is expected to mean. If you are creating your own model, we recommend that you use property names like :directedBy instead of :director so that you don't invite this confusion in the people who want to query data using your model.

Query structure vs. data structure

In Figure 5.4, we saw how the graph pattern in a query looks a lot like the data graph it matches against. This is true of graph patterns in general. The complexity of a question that can be specified with SPARQL is limited only by the complexity of the data. We could, for instance, ask about actresses who played in a movie with James Dean who themselves were in a movie directed by John Ford:

Ask:
```
SELECT ?actress ?movie
WHERE {:JamesDean :playedIn ?movie .
       ?actress :playedIn ?movie .
       ?actress a :Woman .
       ?actress :playedIn ?anotherMovie .
       ?anotherMovie :directedBy :JohnFord .}
```
Answer:

?actress
NatalieWood
CarrollBaker

Figure 5.6 shows this query as a graph. In the text version of the query, we often see the same question word appear in multiple triples, and some of them even refer to the same kind of thing (?movie, *?anotherMovie*). In the graph version, we see that these are the points where two triples must refer to the same thing. For instance, we know that James Dean and *?actress* played in the same movie, because both triples use the same question word (*?movie*) for that movie. Similarly, that *?actress* is the same one who played in *?anotherMovie*, because there the same question word *?actress* appears in those two triples. All these relationships are visibly apparent in Figure 5.6, where we see that *?movie* is the connection between James Dean and *?actress*, *?actress* is the connection between *?movie* and *?anotherMovie*, and *?anotherMovie* is the connection between *?actress* and John Ford.

If we look at the information supporting the answer "Natalie Wood," we see that the data graph looks just like the graph pattern—this should come as no surprise, since that is how the pattern works. But we can use this feature to our advantage when writing queries. One way to write a complex query like the one in Figure 5.6 is to walk through the question we want to answer, writing down triples as we

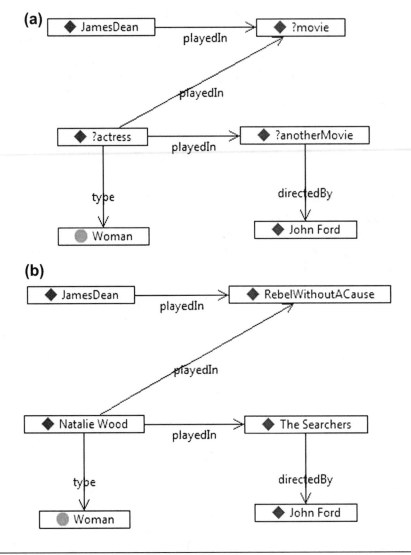

FIGURE 5.6

Data about James Dean and Natalie Wood, and a query to fetch that data.

go until we have the full query. But another way is to start with the data. Suppose we have an example of what we want to search for, for example, we know that Natalie Wood played in *The Searchers*, which was directed by John Ford. Next, we show how we can use the close match between graphs and patterns to construct the pattern from the example.

Since the example from the data graph matches the graph pattern triple for triple, we already know a lot about the graph pattern we want to create. The only thing we need to specify is which values from the example we want to keep as literal values in the pattern, and which ones we want to replace with question words. In Figure 5.7(a) the boxed x on certain resources (James Dean, John Ford, and Woman) indicates those that will stay as they are; all other resources (Natalie Wood, *The Searchers, Rebel Without a Cause*) will be replaced with question words. We have to decide what question words to use; there could be a lot of them. Remember that as far as the SPARQL query engine is concerned, the names of the question words aren't important, so we can call them whatever we like as long as we make sure to use the same question word when we need the same value to be used in the answer. For this example, we'll call them *?q1, ?q2,* etc. Figure 5.7(b) shows the query pattern graphically.

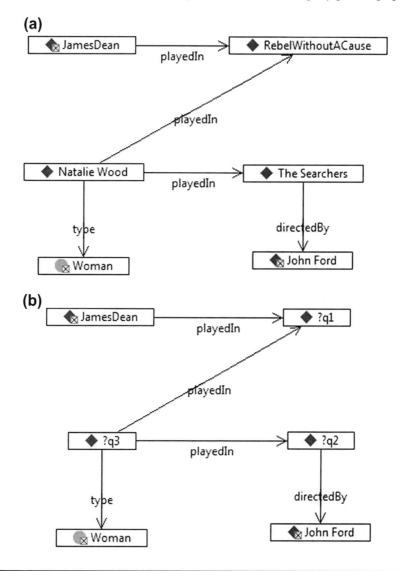

FIGURE 5.7

Creating a graph pattern from a data graph. Resources marked with X appear as themselves in the query.

Now we can create our SPARQL query by simply copying down the graph pattern in Turtle. Each arrow in the graph becomes a triple. If a particular entity (either a literal resource or a question word) participates in more than one triple in the graph, then it will appear more than one time in the Turtle rendering of the pattern. The graph diagram in Figure 5.7(b) has five connecting arrows; the corresponding query will have the same number of triples:

```
{        :JamesDean :playedIn ?q1 .
         ?q3 :playedIn ?q1 .
         ?q3 rdf:type :Woman .
         ?q3 :playedIn ?q2 .
         ?q2 :directedBy :JohnFord .}
```

To complete the query, simply SELECT the question word(s) you want to report on, and perhaps give it a meaningful name. This brings us back to a query very like the original query (differing only in the names of the unselected question words)—but this time, it was generated from a pattern in the data.

```
SELECT ?actress
WHERE  {:JamesDean :playedIn ?q1 .
         ?actress :playedIn ?q1 .
         ?actress rdf:type :Woman .
         ?actress :playedIn ?q2 .
         ?q2 :directedBy :JohnFord .}
```

As we saw above, there are two matches for this query in the sample data, Natalie Wood (no surprise there—after all, it was her performance that we used as a model for this query) and Carroll Baker. Carroll Baker is similar to Natalie Wood, in that she is also a woman, she also played alongside James Dean in a movie, and she was also directed by John Ford. She is similar to Natalie Wood in exactly the features specified in the query.

This method for creating queries can be seen as a sort of "more like this" capability; once you have one example of something you are interested in, you can ask for "more like this," where the notion of "like this" is made specific by including particular triples in the example, and hence in the graph pattern.

For example, we just wrote a query that found actresses who played in James Dean movies and also played in movies directed by John Ford. How do we know that the results are limited to actresses? In the example, Natalie Wood is an actress. But she is one of the resources that we replaced by a question word—how do we know that all the things that the pattern matches will also be actresses? We know this because we included the triple

```
?q3 rdf:type :Woman .
```

in the example, and hence in the pattern.

What would happen if we left that triple out? Natalie Wood is, of course, still a Woman in the data graph, but we haven't included that fact in our example. So that fact does not get copied into the query. Our new query looks like this:

```
SELECT ?q3
WHERE {:JamesDean :playedIn ?q1 .
        ?q3 :playedIn ?q1 .
        ?q3 :playedIn ?q2 .
        ?q2 :directedBy :JohnFord .}
```

It has one fewer triple than the previous query. What is the difference if we run this query against the data? Now we get another answer—Raymond Massey (who also played in *East of Eden*). It would be misleading (but perfectly fine from the point of view of the SPARQL query language) to name this question word *?actress* in this situation—we might want to call it *?actor* instead (with the convention that women can also be actors; if we don't like that convention, we might just keep the meaningless name *?q3*).

So when we say we want to match "more like this" from the example of Natalie Wood, in the first case, we meant "Women who played with James Dean in some movie, and who played in a movie directed by John Ford." In the second case, we just asked for "Anyone who played with James Dean in some movie, and who played in a movie directed by John Ford." How did we specify the difference? By including (or excluding) the triple that asserts that Natalie Wood is a woman. When we include it, "more like this" includes the fact that the result must be a Woman. When we exclude it, "more like this" does not include this stipulation.

Ordering of triples in SPARQL queries

In the previous section, we copied down a graph pattern that was expressed in graphical form into Turtle. The process was straightforward—for each triple in the graph (i.e., each arrowhead), write down one triple in Turtle. But this process left out one variation—in what order do you write down the triples?

One of the beauties of the RDF data model is that its semantics are specified by the graph—the order in which triples are written down makes no difference to an RDF data graph. And to a large extent, this is also true for a graph pattern. To be specific, a graph pattern written in one order will produce the same results (when matched against the same data graph) as another graph pattern, with all the same triples, written in a different order. This means that, as far as the pattern matches are concerned, it makes no difference what order the triples are written in; the graph pattern is the same either way.

But there can be other ramifications of the ordering of the triples in the Turtle rendering of the graph. Most query engines process the queries in top-to-bottom order, constraining the set of possible matches for all variables as the query is processed. This suggests a heuristic for writing graph patterns that are easier for the query engine to process than others. If we take our most recent query as an example:

```
SELECT ?q3
WHERE {:JamesDean :playedIn ?q1 .
        ?q3 :playedIn ?q1 .
        ?q3 :playedIn ?q2 .
        ?q2 :directedBy :JohnFord .}
```

The first triple in this query matches three values for *?q1* (since James Dean played in just three movies). If each movie has *N* actors in it, then the second triple will match *Nx3* actors.

If we write the query differently, say

```
SELECT  ?q3
WHERE  {?q3 :playedIn ?q1 .
        :JamesDean :playedIn ?q1 .
        ?q3 :playedIn ?q2 .
        ?q2 :directedBy :John Ford. }
```

The meaning of this query in terms of results is the same—it matches exactly the same triples as the previous query. But in this case, the first triple in this query will match all pairs of values for *?q3* and *?q1* in which someone played in something. If we have *N* people and *M* movies, this could be on the order of *NxM* matches. The second triple invalidates a large number of these, since for many of them, *?q1* does not match (i.e., James Dean didn't play in that movie). But the query engine has to remember the *NxM* intermediate results—a difference that can make quite a difference in the execution time for a query. Even if James Dean had played in a larger number of movies, the number is likely to be far less than *M*. This suggests a simple heuristic for ordering triples in a query:

Order triples in a query so that the fewest number of new variables are introduced in each new triple. In this case, the heuristic suggests starting the query either with

```
:JamesDean :playedIn ?q1 .
?q3 :playedIn ?q1 .
```

or with

```
?q2 :directedBy :JohnFord.
?q3 :playedIn ?q2 .
```

since in each case, a single new variable is introduced at each triple.

While this heuristic can sometimes dramatically improve the processing speed of a query, it is important to remember that it won't change the results that are matched. The meaning of the query is given by the matches for the graph pattern, and the presentation order of the triples does not have an impact on that match. Another way in which ordering can have an impact is when multiple graph patterns interact. As we shall see in "Subqueries (SPARQL 1.1)," later in this chapter, SPARQL allows for circumstances in which a query pattern includes another one as an optional subpattern. Even in this situation, the ordering of the triples has no impact on the results of the query, but the ordering of the subgraphs can have an impact.

Querying for properties and schema

In all of our examples so far, we have used question words only for the subjects and objects of triples. But the SPARQL pattern matching paradigm allows predicates to be matched as well.

A simple exploitation of this is to answer the question, "What do you know about James Dean?" This can be done with a graph pattern of a single triple:

Ask:
```
SELECT ?property ?value
WHERE {:JamesDean ?property ?value}
```
Answer:

?property	?value
bornOn	1931-02-08
diedOn	1955-09-30
playedIn	RebelWithoutaCause
playedIn	EastOfEden
playedIn	Giant
rdf:type	Man
rdfs:label	James Dean

This is a powerful feature for exploring data sets that you aren't very familiar with. And since we are on the Semantic Web, that is likely to happen frequently. You might not know what properties are defined for James Dean, but this query will find them for you, and show you the values.

You don't have to ask for the values—you can just ask for the properties. This will tell you what sort of information is available, without reporting all of the details:

Ask:
```
SELECT ?property
WHERE {:JamesDean ?property ?value}
```
Answer:

?property
bornOn
diedOn
playedIn
playedIn
playedIn
rdf:type
rdfs:label

This query effectively asks for metadata about James Dean—it is asking, "what are the sorts of things this dataset knows about James Dean?"

Notice that the result :playedIn appears three times in the answers. This is because there are actually three different matches for the graph pattern in the data graph. SPARQL includes the keyword *DISTINCT* to filter out the duplicate results.

Ask:
```
SELECT DISTINCT ?property
WHERE {:JamesDean ?property ?value}
```
Answer:

?property
bornOn
diedOn
playedIn
rdf:type
rdfs:label

This ability to query for properties used in the data distinguishes SPARQL from many other query languages. Among other things, this makes it possible to reverse-engineer schema information from the data itself. For example, we can change the query about properties used to describe James Dean to find all properties used to describe any actor.

Ask:

```
SELECT DISTINCT ?property
WHERE {?q0 a :Actor .
       ?q0 ?property ?object .}
```

Answer:

?property
bornOn
diedOn
playedIn
rdf:type
rdfs:label
produced
sang
wrote

What if we don't know about the class :Actor? We can ask about that as well:

Ask:

```
SELECT DISTINCT ?class
WHERE {?class rdfs:subClassOf :Person}
```

Answer:

?class
:Actor
:Actress
:Man
:Woman
:Politician
:Producer

If we don't know anything about the data at all, we can find the classes used in the data

```
SELECT DISTINCT ?class
WHERE {?q0 a ?class}
```

Or find all the properties used anywhere in the data

```
SELECT DISTINCT ?property
WHERE {?q0 ?property ?q1}
```

Queries of this sort take advantage of a number of distinctive features of RDF; first, that it is possible to match any part of the data (subjects, predicates, objects) with a question word, and that RDFS, the schema language of RDF (Chapter 7), is also expressed in RDF. These two features of RDF/SPARQL make RDF "self-describing" in a way that goes beyond most representation languages.

Variables, bindings, and filters

In the last example, we showed how we can use *DISTINCT* to remove some rows from the result set. We can use this idea to pose more detailed questions using SPARQL.

James Dean and many of his co-stars died very young, while others enjoyed long lives and careers. We might want to find out which of the actors who played in *Giant* lived for more than five years after the movie was made. We'll start by finding the date of death of every actor in *Giant* with the query:

Ask:
```
SELECT ?actor ?deathdate
WHERE {?actor :playedIn :Giant .
       ?actor :diedOn ?deathdate .}
```
Answer:

Actor	deathdate
RockHudson	1985-10-02
JamesDean	1955-10-30
...	

This is useful information, and the answer lies in the table, but the query hasn't really answered our question—who lived on past November 24, 1961 (five years after the production date of *Giant*)?

You can define your own conditions under which rows will be excluded from the results, using the keyword *FILTER*. The idea of FILTER is that you can define a Boolean test that determines whether that row will be included in the results or not. We can filter out the names of the actors who lived on by adding a FILTER to the query, as follows:

Ask:
```
SELECT ?actor
WHERE {?actor :playedIn :Giant .
       ?actor :diedOn ?deathdate .
       FILTER (?deathdate > "1961-11-24"^^xsd:date)}
```
Answer:

Actor
RockHudson
...

So far, we have referred to things like *?property*, *?q0*, *?deathdate*, etc. as "question words," paralleling the use of words like *who*, *what*, *where*, etc. in English. But in SPARQL these things are normally referred to as *variables*—that's what we'll call them from now on. A FILTER defines a Boolean condition on one or more of the variables in the query that determines which rows in the result will be kept and which will be discarded. In this example, the test compares the variable *?deathdate* to the particular date November 24, 1961. Rows for which this condition is true (like Rock Hudson) are kept; others (like James Dean) are discarded.

A note about syntax; the FILTER is a Boolean test, not a graph pattern, so it isn't written like a graph pattern in braces; instead, it is written in parentheses. The tests that are available in the FILTER clause are taken from similar tests available in XQuery, and are outlined in detail in the SPARQL standard.[1] In general, arithmetic and comparisons on all XML data types (integers, floats, strings, dates, etc.) are allowed, as well as some useful functions like REGEX (regular expression matching for strings), and Boolean functions for AND, OR, and NOT (which is indicated by an exclamation point "!").

Earlier, we pointed out that a variable does not get its meaning from its name, but from triples in the graph pattern. Just because we call a variable *?actress* doesn't mean that it will only match women—we need to include a triple relating it to :Woman. A common error among beginning SPARQL users is to use a variable with a meaningful name in a FILTER, assuming that it has been bound to something. For example, to find actors who played in *East of Eden*, who were born in 1930 or later, one might write:

Ask:
```
    SELECT ?actor
    WHERE {?actor :playedIn :EastOfEden .
            FILTER (?birthday > "1930-01-01"^^xsd:date)}
```
Answer:
(none)

Why are there no answers? Because the variable *?birthday* is not mentioned anywhere in the graph pattern, and has no value at all. Remembering that variables are just meaningless question words, this query is equivalent to

```
    SELECT ?actor
    WHERE {?actor :playedIn :EastOfEden .
            FILTER (?q0 > "1930-01-01"^^xsd:date)}
```

where the meaningful variable *?birthdate* has been replaced by the meaningless (but equivalent) variable *?q0*. There is nothing in this graph pattern to indicate what *?q0* is supposed to mean; there is nothing in the original query to indicate what *?birthdate* is supposed to mean. The correct way to write this query is:

---

[1]http://www.w3.org/TR/sparql11-query/

```
SELECT ?actor
WHERE  {?actor :playedIn :EastOfEden .
        ?actor :bornOn ?birthday .
        FILTER (?birthday > "1930-01-01"^^xsd:date)}
```

There is now a triple in the pattern that provides meaning for the variable *?birthday,* and the variable has a value that can be compared to the date Jan 1, 1930. This query will find the actors in *East of Eden* who were born after 1930. The syntax of FILTER does not prohibit this sort of incorrect use of variables. A rule of thumb is that you cannot reference a variable in a FILTER that hasn't already been referenced in the graph pattern. A query can have more than one FILTER clause—to find the people born during the 1960s, we can say

```
SELECT ?person
WHERE  {?person a :Person .
        ?person :bornOn ?birthday .
        FILTER (?birthday > "Jan 1, 1960"^^xsd:date)
        FILTER (?birthday < "Dec 31, 1969"^^xsd:date)}
```

The meaning of multiple filters is that *all* tests must hold true, for the binding to make it into the result set. Notice again that the fact that *?person* is a :Person is not enforced by the variable name *?person,* but by the first triple,

```
?person a :Person.
```

Optional matches

So far, we have talked about single graph patterns. Every triple in the graph pattern must match in the data set in order for the match to succeed; if any triple fails to match, then no row appears in the result set at all.

For example, consider a query we looked at earlier about dates of death:

Ask:
```
SELECT ?actor ?deathdate
WHERE  {?actor :playedIn :Giant .
        ?actor :diedOn ?deathdate .}
```
Answer:

actor	deathdate
RockHudson	1985-10-02
JamesDean	1955-10-30
. . .	

Elizabeth Taylor does not appear in this list, because she has not died, and thus has no entry for :diedOn. It isn't that there is some reserved *null* value for unassigned values; there simply is no triple in the data set of the form

```
:ElizabethTaylor :diedOn ?x .
```

Since the whole graph pattern does not match, no match is found for *any* variable in the pattern; the row for Elizabeth Taylor simply doesn't show up in the result set.

A row in a result set (like this one) includes a value for each selected variable (here, actor and deathdate); this value is called the *binding* of the variable in that row, and we say that in a particular row, the variable is *bound* to that value. So in the first row of this result set, *?actor* is bound to RockHudson and *?deathdate* is bound to 1985-10-02. In the case of Elizabeth Taylor, we say that there is no binding of the variable *?actor* to `ElizabethTaylor` (since one of the triples in the pattern fails to match in her case).

But it is a reasonable question to ask—"who played in *East of Eden*, and when did they die (if applicable)?" SPARQL provides a capability for this with the keyword *OPTIONAL*, which specifies another graph pattern, which is not required to match in order for the overall match to succeed. The OPTIONAL (sub) pattern can bind variables when it does match, but will not invalidate the match if it does not.

Ask:
```
SELECT ?actor ?deathdate
WHERE {?actor :playedIn :Giant .
       OPTIONAL {?actor :diedOn ?deathdate .}}
```
Answer:

Actor	deathdate
RockHudson	1985-10-02
JamesDean	1955-10-30
Elizabeth Taylor	*(no binding)*
...	

It is difficult to write the results of such a query in tabular form, since in a table, we have to put something in the table next to Elizabeth Taylor's name (even if that something is just a blank!). The actual SPARQL result set does not have any particular value for the variable *?deathdate* for this match—it simply has no binding at all. We have chosen to display that in the answer with "(no binding)."

Negation (SPARQL 1.1)

We have already seen how graph patterns provide a flexible way to describe desired results from a data graph. But sometimes it is convenient to specify that there are certain triples that *aren't* in the data set.

In our previous example, we found the death dates of actors who played in *Giant*. Examination of that table can tell us which actors are living, by looking for the "(no binding)" in the *deathdate* column. But it is reasonable to want to ask the question—which actors from *Giant* are still living?

We can use the SPARQL *UNSAID* keyword for this. UNSAID introduces a subgraph; the meaning of UNSAID is that the overall graph pattern will match just if the UNSAID pattern does *not* match.

```
SELECT ?actor
WHERE {?actor :playedIn :Giant .
         UNSAID {?actor :diedOn ?deathdate .} }
```

This finds all of the living actors who played in *East of Eden*.

UNSAID can be used to query about set differences. For instance, some actors are also producers; we might be interested in just those actors who are not members of the class :Producer. This can be done easily with UNSAID:

```
SELECT ?actor
WHERE {?actor a :Actor .
         UNSAID {?actor a :Producer} }
```

Notice that interpreting UNSAID as negation makes a closed-world assumption; we haven't actually found the actors who are not also producers; we have found the actors for which there are no data in this data set to say that they are producers. Since this is the Semantic Web, and anyone can say anything about any topic, we might come to learn that someone is a producer, but we didn't know it before. Using the keyword "UNSAID" (vs. a proposed alternative syntax, "NOT EXISTS") reminds us of this subtlety. The "UNSAID" and "NOT EXISTS" keywords are available only in SPARQL 1.1.

Yes/No queries

SELECT queries in SPARQL select bindings for variables (hence the word "select"). It is also possible to ask Yes/No questions of a graph—for instance, one could ask if Elizabeth Taylor is still alive? (Yes). Or if any actor who played in *Giant* was born after 1950? (No). Questions of this sort can be used by reporting software to decide whether to include a particular section in a report, or by decision support software to make recommendations.

SPARQL includes a keyword ASK for questions of this sort. They keyword appears at the very beginning of the query—instead of the word SELECT. For example:

```
ASK WHERE {:ElizabethTaylor :diedOn ?any}
```

This query will produce a **true** answer if any match is found for the graph pattern (that is, if we have any date on which Elizabeth Taylor died); in this data set, the result is **false**, since no such date exists. We can combine UNSAID with ASK, and create the query for "Is Elizabeth Taylor alive?" as

```
ASK WHERE {UNSAID {:ElizabethTaylor :diedOn ?any}}
```

The answer to this, happily, is **true**.

We can ASK about more complex graph patterns just as easily—was any actor in *Giant* born after 1950?

```
ASK WHERE {?any :playedIn :Giant.
            ?any :bornOn ?birthday .
            FILTER (?birthday > "1950-01-01"^^xsd:date) }
```

Given *Giant*'s 1956 production date, we shouldn't be surprised at the **false** response to this query.

CONSTRUCT QUERIES IN SPARQL

So far, we have seen that the answers to questions in SPARQL can take the form of a table, or of a single bit (true/false for Yes/No questions). But in the RDF world, answers to queries can take a more flexible form—an answer could take the form of an RDF graph. This is the idea behind CONSTRUCT—we use the expressive power of RDF in the answer to a query, as well as in the question.

Suppose we wanted to find out all the movie directors in our dataset about movies. One way to find this out would be to write a query that finds out all the people that movies were directed by:

Ask:

```
SELECT ?director
WHERE {?m :directedBy ?director}
```

Answer:

?director
:EliaKazan
:FredGuiol
:GeorgeCukor
:GeorgeStevens
:NicholasRay
etc.

This returns the answer as a table. We know that the answer refers to a "director" because we chose that name for a variable. This information is amenable for pasting into a spreadsheet, or even a relational database. But suppose we wanted to convey the answer to this question in a more complete way—we want to convey the fact that these five people are directors, and that by "Director" we have a very specific meaning in mind—a particular URI for "Director." And we might want to convey some further information about them—perhaps a string representation of their names (instead of the qnames we have been using so far—that is, "Elia Kazan" instead of :EliaKazan). How can we convey all of this information in a concise, standard way?

RDF provides a way to do this—we can say that each of these resources is a Director by using triples of the form

```
:EliaKazan rdf:type :Director .
```

We can provide a print name for this resource with a triple of the form

```
:EliaKazan rdfs:label "Elia Kazan" .
```

We can specify these triples in a SPARQL query by using the *CONSTRUCT* keyword. The WHERE clause behaves exactly as before, matching triple patterns against the data. But instead of SELECTing some variables, the CONSTRUCT keyword introduces a graph pattern to be used as a template in constructing a new graph, based on results from the old data graph. For our Directors example, we have

```
CONSTRUCT {?d rdf:type :Director .
          ?d rdfs:label ?name . }
WHERE {?any :directedBy ?d .
       ?d rdfs:label ?name . }
```

Figure 5.8 (a) shows some data triples, while Figure 5.8 (b) the triples that will be constructed by this query. The data include several people and movies directed by them. The query matches for each of these, as well as an `rdfs:label` (not shown). For each director, the CONSTRUCT specifies two triples; one is a `rdf:type` triple, the other a `rdfs:label` triple. For five directors, ten triples were produced. These ten triples are shown in Figure 5.8 (b).

USING RESULTS OF CONSTRUCT QUERIES

A query language provides a way to ask a question. The question is posed to a system that processes the query and replies with an answer. That answer can come in many forms—a Yes or No (ASK), a table (SELECT), or, as we just saw, a set of triples (CONSTRUCT). It is reasonable to wonder, where does this information go? For a Yes/No answer or a table, one can easily imagine a user interface like a web page that displays that information in some form. But one could also imagine integrating the information into another application—putting a table into Excel or injecting it into a database.

In some sense, it isn't the job of the query language to specify this. The query language just provides a formalism to describe the meaning of a query, i.e., it specifies what answers a particular query will return, given the data. Most query languages are accompanied with (often proprietary) scripting languages that provide ways to specify what happens to the results of the queries. Sophisticated RDF query systems provide workbenches where users are afforded a variety of options for what to do with constructed triples:

- Insert the constructed triples back into the original data source that the query was run against,
- Store the constructed triples as a separate graph, for processing further triples,
- Store the constructed triples into a new dataset (in another database) for publication,
- Serialize the results in some standard form, and save them to a file.

Any of these options could be appropriate, depending on a user's future plans for the data. These options are similar to information storage options available in other query systems.

In a web service context, there is another option for what to do with the constructed triples. The "P" in SPARQL stands for "protocol." Since SPARQL was designed as a query language for the Web, it includes a protocol for publishing the results of a query to the web. The protocol can deal with binary results (from Yes/No ASK queries), tabular results (from SELECT queries), and, of course, triples (from CONSTRUCT queries). This means that the output of a SPARQL query could be used on the Web as input for another query (since a SPARQL query retrieves information from a set of triples, and CONSTRUCT provides a set of triples). A server for the SPARQL protocol is called a *SPARQL Endpoint*—it is a service that accepts SPARQL queries, and returns results, according to the details of the protocol. Many SPARQL Endpoints are available today, providing information about a variety of subjects. The movie examples in this chapter were derived from an open SPARQL endpoint called LinkedMDB (The **Linked M**ovie **D**ata**B**ase, http://linkedmdb.org/).

A SPARQL endpoint is the most web-friendly way to provide access to RDF data. The endpoint is identified with a URL and provides flexible access to its data set. It is common to speak of "wrapping"

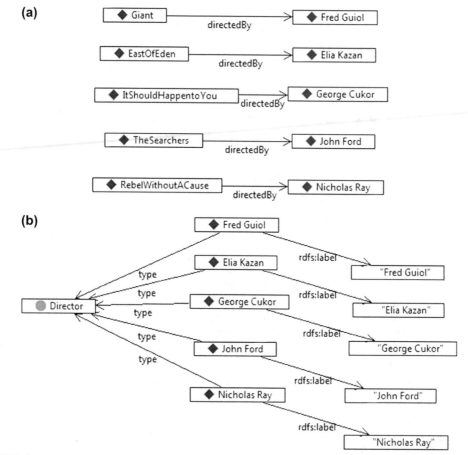

FIGURE 5.8

Constructing a model about directors from a query about movies.

some data set with a SPARQL endpoint—that is, providing a service that responds to the SPARQL protocol, providing access to that data set.

SPARQL RULES—USING SPARQL AS A RULE LANGUAGE

SPARQL CONSTRUCT allows us to specify templates of new information based on patterns found in old information. A specification of this sort is sometimes called a *Rule*, since it provides a way to specify things like "Whenever you see this, conclude that." Examples of rules include data completeness rules ("If John's father is Joe, then Joe's son is John"), logical rules ("If Socrates is a man, and all men are mortal, then Socrates is mortal"), definitions ("If Ted's sister is Maria's mother, then Ted is Maria's uncle"), as well as business rules ("Customers who have done more than $5000 worth of business with us are preferred customers"). Useful rules can often be expressed simply in SPARQL—though there are some subtleties.

Consider the following data:

```
:John a :Man.
:Joe a :Man.
:Eunice a :Woman .
:Maria a :Woman .
:Caroline a :Woman .
:Ted a :Man .
:Socrates a :Man .
:Caroline :hasFather :John .
:Ted :hasBrother :John .
:John :hasFather :Joe .
:Maria :hasMother :Eunice .
:Maria :hasFather :Sargent .
:Ted :hasSister :Eunice .
```

We could write a rule relating father to son as

```
CONSTRUCT {?q1 :hasSon :q2 .}
WHERE {?q2 :hasFather ?q1}
```

But this wouldn't quite work the way we want; while we do construct

```
:Joe :hasSon :John .
```

as desired, we also conclude

```
:Sargent :hasSon :Maria .
```

which is not the usual interpretation of "son".

So, we need to restrict the rule a bit, so that it only applies to men:

```
CONSTRUCT {?q1 :hasSon :q2 .}
WHERE {?q2 a :Man .
       ?q2 :hasFather ?q1}
```

SPARQL allows us to be as specific as we want when writing a rule.

The rule about Socrates is already restricted just to men:

```
CONSTRUCT {?q1 a :Mortal}
WHERE {?q1 a :Man}
```

So we will conclude that Socrates (as well as Ted, John, Joe, and Sargent) are mortal. But Maria and Eunice are off the hook—we'll draw no conclusion about them.

The definition of "uncle" is easy to do in SPARQL

```
CONSTRUCT {?q1 :hasUncle ?q2}
WHERE {?q2 :hasSister ?s .
       ?q1 :hasMother ?s .}
```

But this is both too permissive and too restrictive; for example, we won't conclude that

```
:Caroline :hasUncle :Ted .
```

One way to deal with this would be to write a system of rules—some dealing with completeness of concepts like mother, father, sister, and brother, and another for uncle:

```
CONSTRUCT {?q1 :hasSibling ?q2} WHERE {?q1 :hasBrother ?q2}
CONSTRUCT {?q1 :hasSibling ?q2} WHERE {?q1 :hasSister ?q2}
CONSTRUCT {?q1 :hasParent ?q2} WHERE {?q1 :hasFather ?q2}
CONSTRUCT {?q1 :hasParent ?q2} WHERE {?q1 :hasMother ?q2}
```

Now we can define uncle in terms of siblings and parents:

```
CONSTRUCT {?q1 :hasUncle ?q2}
WHERE {?q2 :hasSibling ?parent .
       ?q2 a :Man .
       ?q1 :hasParent ?parent }
```

and can conclude both relationships:

```
:Caroline :hasUncle :Ted .
:Maria :hasUncle :Ted .
```

(A complete model of family relationships will include quite a few data completeness rules about siblings and parents. In Chapter 7, we'll see a more systematic way to organize a set of rules about these things.)

If we know how much business a customer has done with us, we can write a business rule in SPARQL to sort out our preferred customers.

```
:ACME :totalBusiness 5253.00 .
:PRIME :totalBusiness 12453.00 .
:ABC :totalbusiness 1545.00 .
```

The query

```
CONSTRUCT {?c a :PreferredCustomer}
WHERE {?c :totalBusiness ?tb .
       FILTER (?tb > 5000) }
```

will assert all the preferred customers:

```
:ACME a :PreferredCustomer .
:PRIME a :PreferredCustomer .
```

Later in this section, we'll see how to use aggregators and subqueries to compute things like total business from information about various business transactions.

For many of these queries, it was important to restrict the application of the query to particular sets of individuals—e.g., Uncles and Sons can only be Men. This is a typical sort of restriction—a rule only applies to a particular class of things. In Chapter 7, we'll revisit SPARQL rules, and see how an RDFS class structure can be used to organize a set of interacting SPARQL rules.

CHALLENGE 2: USING SPARL TO TRANSFORM HIERARCHICAL DATA

In the data wilderness, information comes in many forms. Some of the variety stems from all the systems and syntaxes that we use to represent data—spreadsheets, XML, relational databases, and even text documents. RDF, as a general way to represent data, resolves many of the more superficial issues with different data formats. But even within a single system, there are a variety of ways to represent the same information. If we want to deal with data from the wilderness, we often have to transform data to make it easier to use.

We'll start with a simple example. Taking some of the family tree data from the previous example (plus a few more):

```
:Caroline :hasFather :John .
:John :hasFather :Joe .
:Eunice :hasFather :Joe .
:Maria :hasMother :Eunice .
:Maria :hasFather :Sargent .
:Joe :hasSon :Robert .
:Joe :hasSon :Ted .
:Ted :hasSon :Patrick .
```

We could speculate about how a dataset could get to be in such an inconsistent state—with some family relationships relating children to their parents, while others relate parents to their children. The data might originally come from multiple sources, or have been entered using multiple systems or by people following different methodologies. But regardless of how it happened, this is a typical state of affairs in the data wilderness; the data you find are organized in an inconsistent way.

Now suppose we are interested in building a family tree that looks something like Figure 5.9, in which we see children and grandchildren, regardless of gender, all in a single display. The tree is defined in a uniform way— Eunice has parent Joe, Maria has parent Eunice (and Sargent), Caroline has parent John, etc.

FIGURE 5.9

Family tree shown in a uniform manner.

All this information is available in the data set, if you abstract away from gender words (like Son, Daughter, Mother, and Father) and re-order some triples (turning *hasSon* around to be *hasParent*). How can we do this using SPARQL? We can do this by specifying a few rules as SPARQL constructs to map these things into the form we want.

```
CONSTRUCT {?s :hasParent ?o} WHERE {?s :hasMother ?o}
CONSTRUCT {?s :hasParent ?o} WHERE {?s :hasFather ?o}
CONSTRUCT {?s :hasParent ?o} WHERE {?o :hasSon ?s}
CONSTRUCT {?s :hasParent ?o} WHERE {?o :hasDaughter ?s}
```

These queries match all the various forms of *hasSon*, *hasDaughter*, *hasMother*, and *hasFather* and map them all into appropriate triples using *hasParent*. The resulting triples are

```
:Caroline :hasParent :John .
:Eunice :hasParent :Joe .
:John :hasParent :Joe .
:Maria :hasParent :Sargent .
:Maria :hasParent :Eunice .
:Patrick :hasParent :Ted .
:Robert :hasParent :Joe .
:Ted :hasParent :Joe .
```

These provide a uniform representation of the family tree and are amenable for producing a display like that in Figure 5.9.

We can extend this example to compute the gender of the family members, by adding another triple to each query:

```
CONSTRUCT {?s :hasParent ?o .
           ?o a :Woman .}
WHERE {?s :hasMother ?o}
CONSTRUCT {?s :hasParent ?o .
           ?o a :Man .}
WHERE {?s :hasFather ?o}
CONSTRUCT {?s :hasParent ?o .
           ?s a :Man .}
WHERE {?o :hasSon ?s}
CONSTRUCT {?s :hasParent ?o .
           ?s a :Woman .}
WHERE {?o :hasDaughter ?s}
```

Transitive queries (SPARQL 1.1)

Hierarchical data can pose very particular problems when it comes to querying. We can see this using the example of the family tree in Figure 5.9. Suppose we want to query for all members of Joe's family. We can query for his children with a simple graph pattern:

Ask:
```
SELECT ?member
WHERE {?member :hasParent :Joe}
```
Answer:

?member
Eunice
John
Robert
Ted

If we want his grandchildren, we can build a slightly more complicated query:

Ask:
```
SELECT ?member
WHERE {?int :hasParent :Joe .
       ?member :hasParent ?int .}
```
Answer:

?member
Maria
Caroline
Patrick

If we wanted Joe's great-grandchildren, we could make another query, and so on. But what if we want all of his family, regardless of how many generations intervene? SPARQL 1.1 includes a transitivity operator for just this purpose. If we include a * after a property name, then the triple matches any number of chained occurrences of the same property.

Ask:
```
SELECT ?member
WHERE {?member :hasParent* :Joe .}
```
Answer:

?member
Joe
Eunice
Maria
John
Caroline
Robert
Ted
Patrick

Notice that Joe himself is matched—even chains of zero triples will match. If we want to insist that there is at least one triple in the chain (Joe's progeny, not including himself), we can use a + instead:

Ask:

```
SELECT ?member
WHERE {?member :hasParent+ :Joe .}
```

Answer:

?member
Eunice
Maria
John
Caroline
Robert
Ted
Patrick

(SPARQL 1.1 includes a number of variations on this theme, beyond what we cover here. Details can be found in the SPARQL 1.1 standard.)

CHALLENGE 3: USING SPARQL TO RECORD SAMENESS IN THE LINKED MDB

When merging information from multiple sources, it is typical for the same entity to appear in each data source with a different identifier. Even in the case of a single data source, it is not unusual for the same item to appear multiple times, with a different identifier each time. This is especially common when the data source is implemented as a relational database, where common practice involves separating out information based on the role an entity plays in an application.

The **Linked Movie DataBase**[2] (LinkedMDB) is an open data source containing data about movies. The LinkedMDB is based on a relational database containing information about movies, actors, directors, etc. The underlying database includes information about what movies directors *made* as well as what movies actors *played in*. This information is represented in two separate tables—a *director* table and an *actor* table. When converted to triples, this database structure results in two classes in the published SPARQL endpoint with corresponding names—*director* and *actor*.

Members of the classes in the linkedMDB are given numeric URIs—here is a very small excerpt of data from that endpoint:

```
actor:29753
      rdf:type linkedmdb:actor ;
      linkedmdb:actor_name "Clint Eastwood" .

film:38599
      rdf:type linkedmdb:film ;
      dc:title "Unforgiven" ;
      linkedmdb:actor  actor:29753 ;
      linkedmdb:director director:8533 .

director:8533
      rdf:type linkedmdb:director ;
      linkedmdb:director_name "Clint Eastwood" .
```

In this fragment, there is a movie whose `dc:title` is "Unforgiven" (the namespace dc stands for "Dublin Core," a metadata standard used by many libraries worldwide that includes standard terms for titles, authors, publication dates, etc.), stars an actor (number 29753) whose name is "Clint Eastwood," and was directed by a director (number 8533) whose name is "Clint Eastwood." Is the fact that both of these people are named "Clint Eastwood" enough for us to conclude that they are the same person?

Fortunately, there is another triple for each of these resources in the LinkedMBD dataset:

```
actor:29753 foaf:page freebase:9202a8c04000641f8000000000056de6 .
director:8533 foaf:page freebase:9202a8c04000641f8000000000056de6 .
```

Freebase is a linked data resource that (among other things) provides an identity service for resources on the Web. Any data source on the Web can refer to a freebase resource, to unambiguously identify its own resources. Freebase is not the only such service—in the life sciences, there are several such identification services for proteins, genes, and other biological entities, and others exist for a number of areas.

In this case, we can use this information to determine that these two people named "Clint Eastwood" are in fact the same person; since linkedMDB links both of them to the same Freebase resource, they must be the same. But what can we do with that information?

We can use SPARQL to detect identities of this sort, and record it as a new triple.

```
CONSTRUCT {?a skos:exactMatch ?b}
WHERE {?a foaf:page ?page .
       ?b foaf:page ?page .}
```

You can understand this query, even without knowing anything else about the resources in it—`foaf:page` and `skos:exactMatch` (though these will be discussed in Chapters 9 and 10). This query simply says that any two resources with the same `foaf:page` are `skos:exactMatch` to one another. On this data set, we get the following triples:

```
actor:29753 skos:exactMatch director:8533 .
director:8533 skos:exactMatch actor:29753 .
director:8533 skos:exactMatch director:8533 .
actor:29753 skos:exactMatch actor:29753 .
```

These triples indeed encode the identity match that we observed—that the director of *Unforgiven* also played in it. But it brings along some extra baggage—the `exactMatch` appears twice, once relating the actor to the director, and another time relating the director to the actor. Furthermore, we have two rather trivial results, that every actor is an exact match to itself (and the same for directors). These extra results appear because SPARQL finds *every* match for the graph pattern in the data; and all four assignments of *?a* and *?b* to `director:8533` and `actor:29753` satisfy the pattern (they have the same values for `:page`). These extra triples don't really cause any harm—after all, it seems correct to say that something is an exact match to itself—but at the same time, they are somewhat superfluous. In an earlier example, we were able to drop duplicates by using the DISTINCT keyword in SPARQL. In this case, we need something else; since all four of these triples are already distinct (i.e., no two have the same value for all three positions; subject, predicate and object).

We can use a FILTER clause to eliminate many of these spurious values—since we aren't interested in statements that say that an actor is an exact match for himself, we can eliminate these with a filter for matching the same values:

```
CONSTRUCT {?a skos:exactMatch ?b}
WHERE {?a foaf:page ?page .
       ?b foaf:page ?page .
FILTER (?a != ?b)}
```

The comparison != in a filter stands for "not equal"—it evaluates to 'true' just if *?a* and *?b* are not the same. This results in the following triples:

```
actor:29753 skos:exactMatch director:8533 .
director:8533 skos:exactMatch actor:29753 .
```

This is an improvement. And if we didn't know that skos:exactMatch is a symmetric property (see Chapter 10), we would be satisfied at this point that we had filtered out all the spurious triples.

If we want to go one step further, we can sort these triples so that only the first one of the pair is kept. The FILTER clause in SPARQL includes capabilities for managing data types borrowed from XML, so there are many ways to compare values. We can convert a URI to an XML, then compare the strings. We can use this trick to reduce our results to a single triple:

```
CONSTRUCT {?a skos:exactMatch ?b}
WHERE {?a foaf:page ?page .
       ?b foaf:page ?page .
       FILTER (xsd:string (?a) > xsd:string (?b))
}
```

This query will keep a triple only when the subject comes after the object in alphabetical order; this means that of the two triples in the previous result, only the second one is kept:

```
director:8533 skos:exactMatch actor:29753 .
```

In general, there could be many ways to determine that two resources are actually referring to the same thing; having a reference system like Freebase is the easiest way. The need for such reference systems of this kind did not begin with the Semantic Web—it has been around for centuries. The Semantic Web simply provides a means for publishing these systems, and referring to them, on the Web. When there isn't a reference system like Freebase around, more complex means of identifying individuals can be used. The same strategy using SPARQL CONSTRUCT can be used to determine these matches and to record them using skos:exactMatch. For example, suppose that the data set included information about date and place of birth. If it is reasonable to assume in the dataset that two people who share the same name, place, and date of birth are indeed the same persons, then the query

```
CONSTRUCT {?a skos:exactMatch ?b}
WHERE {?a :name ?name .
       ?b :name ?name .
       ?a :birthplace ?bplace .
       ?b :birthplace ?bplace .
       ?a :birthdate ?date .
       ?b :birthdate ?date .
       FILTER (xsd:string (?a) > xsd:string (?b))
}
```

will construct triples asserting the matches between these resources.

The Semantic Web doesn't provide any particular mechanism for determining that one resource refers to the same individual as another; it provides a means for writing down such a conclusion, and publishing it on the Web.

Now that we know that both people named Clint Eastwood are really the same person, we are in a position to answer the question, "Which directors played in movies they directed?" We can answer it with the following query:

[2]http://linkedmdb.org/

Ask:

```
SELECT ?director
WHERE {?dir foaf:made ?m .
       ?dir linkedmdb:director_name ?director .
       ?m linkedmdb:actor ?star .
       ?dir skos:exactMatch ?star . }
```

Answer:

?director
"Clint Eastwood"

CHALLENGE 4: USING SPARQL TO COPY AN EXCERPT OF A DATABASE

An RDF data set is often made up of a very large number of triples. There are a number of reasons why one might want to create a smaller excerpt of such a data set:

- The data set might be available only as a network resource, with inconsistent connectivity. You might want to keep a more robust copy of the information that is used the most.
- The data set might be very large, resulting in slow query time for complex queries. You might want to keep a cache of a small, relevant part of the database for fast queries.
- The data set might contain sensitive information that should not be disclosed to certain audiences. You might want to make a copy of the less sensitive information for public access.

In any case, it can be useful to be able to select a part of a data set for separate storage. This can be done with SPARQL CONSTRUCT queries.

Following on the previous example, suppose we wanted to create a data set that contains information about the film "Unforgiven." We want to include the actors who played in it, its director, producer, and any other information about it.

In the LinkedMDB, *Unforgiven* is given the resource name `film:38599`. How can we select all the information in the LinkedMDB about *Unforgiven*?

Depending on just what we mean by "all" the information, we can start with a simple query:

```
CONSTRUCT {film:38599 ?p ?o . } WHERE {film:38599 ?p ?o . }
```

This apparently trivial query selects all the triples from the data set with `film:38599` as the subject. From the full LinkedMDB, it returns a few dozen results, including the triples:

```
film:38599 rdf:type linkedmdb:film .
film:38599 dc:title "Unforgiven" .
film:38599 linkedmdb:actor actor:29753 .
film:38599 linkedmdb:actor actor:30285 .
film:38599 linkedmdb:director director:8533 .
film:38599 linkedmdb:editor editor:2920 .
```

This is a good start for getting "all" the information about *Unforgiven*. It includes the information about actors and directors we need to figure out that it is one of the movies that Clint Eastwood both directed and starred in. But there could be more information in the data set that is relevant to this movie—for instance, there is the triple

```
director:8522 foaf:made film:38599 .
```

This triple doesn't appear in the results of the query, since in this case, `film:38599` is the object of the triple, not the subject. We can use a very similar query to fetch these triples:

CONSTRUCT `{?s ?p film:38599. }` **WHERE** `{?s ?p film:38599 . }`

This will fetch all the triples in which *Unforgiven* appears as the object, including the `foaf:made` triple above. This is a more comprehensive notion of what it could mean to fetch "all" the information about a particular resource.

But even these triples might not seem like quite enough to tell us all about *Unforgiven*; for example, who is `actor:30285`? In addition to the information about the movie itself, we might want to also identify information about related entities. A more elaborate graph pattern can do this as well:

```
CONSTRUCT {?s ?p ?o}
WHERE {film:38599 ?p1 ?s .
       ?s ?p ?o . }
```

The pattern

```
?s ?p ?o
```

matches every triple in the data set, subject to the bindings so far. In this case, *?s* is already bound from the first triple pattern to anything that is related (in any way) to *Unforgiven*. So in this case, this pattern copies all triples whose subjects are related to *Unforgiven*.

For example, since

```
film:38599 linkedmdb:actor actor:30285 .
```

is in the data set, this query will find all the triples starting with `actor:30285`, including

```
actor:30285 linkedmdb:actor_name "Richard Harris" .
```

If we merge together the results of all of these queries, we can create a comprehensive cache of all information regarding *Unforgiven*. This method was used to create most of the sample files for the examples in this chapter.

ADVANCED FEATURES OF SPARQL

Limits and ordering

Suppose we want to know the movies that James Dean played in, and the dates they were released:

Ask:

```
SELECT ?movie ?date
WHERE {:JamesDean :playedIn ?m.
       ?m rdfs:label ?movie .
       ?m dc:date   ?date . }
```

Answer:

?movie	?date
Giant	1956
EastOfEden	1955
RebelWithoutaCause	1955

These answers come back in no particular order; different SPARQL implementations (and even the same implementation, at different times) are free to produce the results in any order they like.

We can specify an ordering in the query for the results using the directive *ORDER BY.* The ORDER BY directive comes after the graph pattern, and specifies one or more variables to use to determine the order in which the results are returned. The following two examples show how this works, ordering by *?date* and *?movie* (title), respectively:

Ask:

```
SELECT ?title ?date
WHERE {:JamesDean :playedIn ?movie.
       ?movie rdfs:label ?title .
       ?movie dc:date  ?date . }
ORDER BY ?date
```

Answer:

?title	?date
EastOfEden	1955
RebelWithoutaCause	1955
Giant	1956

Ask:

```
SELECT ?title ?date
WHERE {:JamesDean :playedIn ?movie.
       ?movie rdfs:label ?title .
       ?movie dc:date  ?date . }
ORDER BY ?title
```

Answer:

?title	?date
EastOfEden	1955
Giant	1956
RebelWithoutaCause	1955

(Note that SPARQL uses simple notions of ordering for each type of value: numbers in numerical order, strings in alphabetic order, etc.)

Sometimes we don't want all the possible matches to a query—for a user interface, we might want to limit the number of items we display at a time. Or we might want to provide a report of just the highest values—the "top ten" results. To accommodate these sorts of requests, SPARQL includes a LIMIT directive, with which the query can specify the maximum number of results to be fetched. LIMIT works together with ORDER BY to determine which items to return; when LIMIT is used without ORDER BY, the SPARQL implementation is free to fetch any matching results, up to the specified limit.

So to find the earliest James Dean movie, we can ORDER BY *?date* and specify a LIMIT of 1:

Ask:

```
SELECT ?title
WHERE {:JamesDean :playedIn ?m.
        ?m rdfs:label ?title .
        ?m dc:date   ?date . }
ORDER BY ?date
LIMIT 1
```

Answer:

?title
East Of Eden

All three stars (James Dean, Natalie Wood, and Sal Mineo) of *Rebel Without a Cause* died young under tragic circumstances. Which one died first?

Ask:

```
SELECT ?first
WHERE {?who :playedIn :RebelWithoutaCause .
        ?who rdfs:label ?first .
        ?who :diedOn ?date}
ORDER BY ?date
LIMIT 1
```

Answer:

?first
James Dean

By default, SPARQL orders results in ascending order. We can reverse the ordering, and find the star who lived the longest with the keyword DESC (for "descending")

Ask:

```
SELECT ?last
WHERE {?who :playedIn :RebelWithoutaCause .
        ?who rdfs:label ?last .
        ?who :diedOn ?date}
ORDER BY DESC (?date)
LIMIT 1
```

Answer:

?last
Sal Mineo

AGGREGATES AND GROUPING (SPARQL 1.1)

SPARQL 1.1 includes a facility for specifying aggregate functions of data. Specifically, it provides aggregate functions COUNT, MIN, MAX, AVG, and SUM. These aggregates can be used alongside any graph pattern, computing a result for all matches for the pattern.

For example, we could find out how many movies James Dean has played in:

```
SELECT (COUNT (?movie) AS ?howmany)
WHERE {:JamesDean ?playedIn ?movie .}
```

The syntax of SPARQL[3] aggregates appears in the SELECT clause—the aggregate expression appears in parentheses, starting with the aggregate word, followed by the variable to be aggregated (also in parentheses), then the keyword AS followed by a new variable, which will be bound to the aggregated value. In this case, the query result is a single binding for *?howmany*

?howmany
3

Sums work in much the same way—suppose we want to add up the amount of business we have done each year with various customers, and we have data about our sales—which company made the purchase, the amount of the purchase, and the year in which the purchase was made. The data are shown in tabular form here:

Company	Amount	Year
ACME	$1250	2010
PRIME	$3000	2009
ABC	$2500	2009
ABC	$2800	2010
PRIME	$1950	2010
ACME	$2500	2009
ACME	$3100	2010
ABC	$1500	2009
ACME	$1250	2009
PRIME	$2350	2009
PRIME	$1850	2010

---

[3]As the specification for SPARQL 1.1 is still in flux at the time of this writing, some SPARQL implementations use notational variants. In this section, we use the proposed syntax in the emerging recommendation.

As triples, each row is represented as four triples, with an arbitrary URI for the row. Each row is a member of a single class, :Sale. So the first row looks like the triples:

```
:row1 a :Sale .
:row1 :company :ACME .
:row1 :amount 1250 .
:row1 :year 2010 .
```

Using this representation in triples, we can find our total sales using a SUM aggregator:

Ask:

```
SELECT (SUM (?val) AS ?total)
WHERE {?s a :Sale .
         ?s :amount ?val }
```

Answer:

?total
24050.00

With this sort of data, we are interested in breaking this answer down in various ways; how much business did we do with each customer? How much business did we do in a given year? SPARQL allows us to organize the query in these ways, using the notion of GROUP BY. For instance, we can find the amount of business for each year by grouping by years:

Ask:

```
SELECT ?year   (SUM (?val) AS ?total)
WHERE {?s a :Sale .
         ?s :amount ?val .
         ?s :year ?year   }
GROUP BY ?year
```

Answer:

?year	?total
2009	13100.00
2010	10950.00

The GROUP BY keyword comes after the graph pattern and informs the aggregate how to group the sums; instead of summing all the results, it sums results grouped by the specified variable. In this case, the sum is grouped by *?year*. The GROUP BY variable must already have been bound in the graph pattern; these values are used to sort the results for aggregation. Since a variable mentioned in the GROUP BY clause will have the same value for every summand for a particular sum, it is sensible to include it in the SELECT clause (if desired). Other variables (like *?s* and *?val*) will have different values for each summand, and hence won't have a single defined value for a sum; these variables are not available for inclusion in the SELECT clause.

We can sort by more than one variable at a time:

Ask:

```
SELECT ?year ?company  (SUM  (?val) AS ?total)
WHERE {?s a :Sale .
        ?s :amount ?val .
        ?s :year ?year  .
        ?s :company ?company .
}
GROUP BY ?year ?company
```

Answer:

?year	?company	?total
2009	ACME	3750.00
2009	ABC	4000.00
2009	PRIME	5350.00
2010	ACME	4350.00
2010	PRIME	3800.00
2010	ABC	2800.00

This tells us how much business we did with each customer in a particular year. If we'd like to find out customers that did more than $5000 of business in some year, we can show only some of these results, using the keyword HAVING to choose particular results:

Ask:

```
SELECT ?year ?company (SUM (?val) AS ?total)
WHERE {?s a :Sale .
        ?s :amount ?val .
        ?s :year ?year  .
        ?s :company ?company .
}
GROUP BY ?year ?company
HAVING (?total > 5000)
```

Answer:

?year	?company	?total
2009	PRIME	5350.00

PRIME was the only customer who satisfied this criterion, which they did in 2009. The keywords HAVING and FILTER are very similar; both of them introduce a condition that is to be met by the results. FILTER refers to variables bound within a particular graph pattern, hence the FILTER keyword always appears in the pattern (between "{" and "}"), while HAVING refers to variables defined by aggregations in the SELECT clause, and hence always appears outside a graph pattern.

SUBQUERIES (SPARQL 1.1)

A subquery is a query within a query. Since a SPARQL graph pattern can include arbitrary connections between variables and resource identifiers, there isn't as much need to have subquery as there is in other query languages. In fact, for basic SPARQL (i.e., without limit or aggregate functions), there is no need for subquery at all.

But subqueries can be useful when combining limits and aggregates with other graph patterns. A question has to be pretty complex to require a subquery in SPARQL. A subquery limits the scope of things like aggregators, orderings, and limits to just part of the query. Following along the example using customer sales above, we notice that some companies increased their sales from 2009 to 2010, while others decreased. We can use subqueries to find out which ones increased their sales during that time:

Ask:

```
SELECT ?company
WHERE {
    {SELECT ?company ((SUM(?val)) AS ?total09)
        WHERE {
            ?s a :Sale .
            ?s :amount ?val .
            ?s :company ?company .
            ?s :year 2009 . }
        GROUP BY ?company } .
    {SELECT ?company ((SUM(?val)) AS ?total10)
        WHERE {
            ?s a :Sale .
            ?s :amount ?val .
            ?s :company ?company .
            ?s :year 2010 .}
        GROUP BY ?company } .
    FILTER (?total10 > ?total09) . }
```

Answer:

?company
ACME

The two subqueries in this example compute the total sales for years 2009 and 2010, respectively. The FILTER retains only the matches in which the 2010 total exceeds the 2009 totals—customers who did more business in 2010 than in 2009. Each subquery (including GROUP BY etc. at the end) is enclosed in braces. Within the subqueries, variables have their own scope; that is, the variable *?val* in each of these subqueries matches completely different values (in one subquery, it matches the 2009 values; in the other, it matches the 2010 values). This sort of computation requires subqueries, since it involves independent subsets of the data to be compared.

Another application of subqueries is to bring the power of aggregates (available only in SELECT queries) to other SPARQL query constructs (like ASK and CONSTRUCT). Earlier, we saw a query that selected the companies who had done more than $5000 worth of business in a single year.

Suppose we wanted to use this result as part of a CONSTRUCT query—where would we put the aggregation specification? This can be handled uniformly with a subquery, as in the following example:

```
CONSTRUCT {?company a :PreferredCustomer.
           ?company :totalSales ?total .}
WHERE {SELECT ?year ?company  (SUM  (?val) as ?total)
       WHERE {?s a :Sale .
              ?s :amount ?val .
              ?s :year ?year  .
              ?s :company ?company .
       }
       GROUP BY ?year ?company
       HAVING (?total > 5000)}
```

This results in two triples:

```
:PRIME a :PreferredCustomer .
:PRIME :totalSales 5350.00 .
```

The subquery is the same query we saw before, determining which companies did more than $5000 of business in a single year. The CONSTRUCT query creates a graph with just the information about preferred customers—their preferred status as membership in the class :PreferredCustomer, and the total sales as a numeric value.

UNION

A graph pattern is made up of several triples—all of which have to match in order for the pattern to match. In logical terms, this means that there is an implicit "and" operation between the triples. One could correctly read a graph pattern as saying "the first triple matches AND the second triple matches AND the third triple matches ..." But there are times when we might want to say that this triple matches OR that triple matches. For those times, SPARQL provides UNION.

UNION combines two graph patterns, resulting in the set union of all bindings made by each pattern. Variables in each pattern take values independently (just as they do in subqueries), but the results are combined together.

A simple example would be to find out all the actors who played either in *Rebel Without a Cause* or *Giant*. Each of these is a simple query; we can get all the answers by making a UNION of the two queries:

Ask:
```
SELECT ?actor
WHERE {
        {?actor :playedIn :Giant .}
        UNION
        {?actor :playedIn :RebelWithoutaCause .}
        }
```

Answer:

actor
Ann Doran
Carroll Baker
Elizabeth Taylor
James Dean
James Dean
Jim Backus
Mercedes McCambridge
Natalie Wood
Rock Hudson
Sal Mineo
Sal Mineo

Some names appear twice, if the actor appeared in both movies. This repetition can be removed by using the DISTINCT keyword.

UNION can be used in the context of CONSTRUCT as well. In a challenge earlier in this chapter, we used SPARQL to transform hierarchical information, by mapping several related relationships (mother, father, son, daughter) onto a single hierarchy (parent); the resulting triples were shown in Figure 5.9. This involved four CONSTRUCT queries, with an implicit understanding that all the triples resulting from each query would be merged. This is a perfectly fine assumption, if the queries are run in the context of a program that indeed combines all the results (e.g., by adding all the triples to the same triple store). But with UNION, we can specify explicitly that the triples are to be combined. We can take the graph pattern for each of the triples, and combine them all with the UNION operator, thus:

```
CONSTRUCT {?s :hasParent ?o}
WHERE{ {?s :hasMother ?o}
       UNION
       {?s :hasFather ?o}
       UNION
       {?o :hasSon ?s}
       UNION
       {?o :hasDaughter ?s}}
```

The result of this query is the same as the combined results of the queries in the Challenge, i.e., the set of hasParent relationships shown in Figure 5.9.

ASSIGNMENTS (SPARQL 1.1)

Suppose we want to query the full names of the authors of the book "Semantic Web for the Working Ontologist." We can easily find first names and last names, but how do we get the full names? It is a simple enough computation—concatenate the first and last names together, with an embedded space. But the string "James Hendler" is nowhere to be found in the data set. How do we create it?

Tell-and-ask systems typically answer questions based on information that was told to them—this is true for spreadsheets, notebooks, databases, and RDF stores. But many tell-and-ask systems go beyond this, and provide ways for you to specify information that you didn't (directly) tell the system. We have already seen how this can be done with aggregators in SPARQL—the sums, averages, counts, etc., are information that was not directly told to the system, but was computed from information that was already there.

But sometimes we would like to specify a special purpose computation as part of the ask process. Spreadsheets excel at this functionality, with the ability for the user to specify arbitrary formulas that will be calculated and updated whenever data are changed or entered. Databases have stored procedures that execute arbitrary code based on information in the database. SPARQL provides a similar capability through query-time assignments. An *assignment* lets the query write specifically the value of a variable through some computation—"assigning" a value to that variable, rather than matching some value in the data.

Assignments are not supported in the SPARQL 1.0 standard, but will be supported in some form in the 1.1 standard. Assignments are expressed as part of the SELECT clause, with a renaming syntax:

SELECT (*expression* (?other) **AS** ?var)

The *expression* can include arithmetic formulas (using the usual operators $+$, $-$, $*$, $/$, etc.) or a series of function calls. Like stored procedures in relational databases, the function calls can include arbitrary programs in a variety of programming languages. For the examples in this book, we will restrict ourselves to some standard functions, those from the XPATH spec for XML.

Suppose we have some data about books and their authors, including the following data:

```
:DeanAllemang
    rdf:type :Person ;
    :firstName "Dean" ;
    :lastName "Allemang" .

:JimHendler
    rdf:type :Person ;
    :firstName "James" ;
    :lastName "Hendler" .

:WorkingOntologist
    rdf:type :Book ;
    rdfs:label  "Semantic  Web  for  the  Working  Ontologist" ;
    dc:creator :DeanAllemang , :JimHendler .
```

This is where assignments come in. We can match for the first and last names, but we need to do a computation to get the full name. There is a function for concatenate in the XPATH spec—it is called fn:concat. We can use this to compute the full names:

Ask:

```
SELECT (fn:concat (?first, " ", ?last) AS ?fullname)
WHERE {:WorkingOntologist dc:creator ?author .
        ?author :firstName ?first .
        ?author :lastName ?last .
}
```
Answer:

?fullname
James Hendler
Dean Allemang

Assignments are a convenient way to compute information based on other things you are already asking for. But they really show their power when they are used for intermediate computations, so that the results of an assignment can be used to specify parameters for the ongoing search.

As an example, let's consider merging the information about this book with our movie database. One might wonder if there are any actors with names that are like the authors of this book—perhaps one whose name is made up of the first names of the book's authors. We can fetch those first names easily enough:

Ask:

```
SELECT ?n1 ?n2
WHERE { authors:WorkingOntologist dc:creator ?a1 .
        authors:WorkingOntologist dc:creator?a2 .
        ?a1 authors:firstName ?n1 .
        ?a2 authors:firstName ?n2 .}
```

Answer:

?n1	?n2
Dean	Dean
Dean	James
James	Dean
James	James

Now, let's make a full name out of the two first names, by concatenating them together, using the same function from XPATH as in the previous example. At the same time, we'll get rid of the situations where both variables match the same name by filtering them out. This leaves us with:

Ask:

```
SELECT (fn:concat (?n1, " ", ?n2) AS ?probe)
WHERE { authors:WorkingOntologist dc:creator ?a1 .
        authors:WorkingOntologist dc:creator?a2 .
        ?a1 authors:firstName ?n1 .
        ?a2 authors:firstName ?n2 .
        FILTER (?a1 != ?a2) }
```

Answer:

?probe
"Dean James"
"James Dean"

Now, let's use this computed result as a way to query the movie database. We want to find an actor who has one of these as his name. If we consider an actor to be someone who acts in a movie, we can find such an actor by matching a triple for the predicate :playsIn. But this poses a problem—we'd like to use the result *?probe* later on in the graph pattern, but the assignment is only specified as part of the SELECT clause. We can get around this issue by using subqueries:

Ask:

```
SELECT DISTINCT ?who
WHERE {
    SELECT (fn:concat (?n1, " ", ?n2)) AS  ?probe)
    WHERE {
            authors:WorkingOntologist dc:creator ?a1 .
            authors:WorkingOntologist dc:creator ?a2 .
            ?a1 authors:firstName ?n1 .
            ?a2 authors:firstName ?n2 .
            FILTER (?a1 != ?a2)
            } }
    {SELECT ?probe ?who
    WHERE {
            ?who movies:playedIn ?any .
            ?who rdfs:label ?probe .}}}
```

Answer:

?who
movies:JamesDean

Indeed, there is an actor in the database whose full name is made up of the concatenation of the first names of the authors of this book.

Having the assignment happen only in the SELECT clause is inconvenient from the point of view of writing queries of this sort (where we want to use the result of the assignment to restrict another query), but does have the virtue that the meaning of a graph pattern does not depend on the ordering of its conditions. Creating a subquery structure of this sort makes the ordering of the assignments crystal clear; within any particular query, the ordering of the triple patterns has no effect on the meaning of the query.

FEDERATING SPARQL QUERIES

In the previous example, we assumed that all the triples about books and authors, and the triples about movies were available in a single graph. This isn't such a far-fetched assumption, since it is a conceptually simple matter to merge multiple graphs into a single one for the purpose of running queries. But it is certainly not guaranteed that this will be the case; when data sets are very large, it can be impractical to merge them together before querying them. The data sets may be available only on the Web, and access to them could be limited.

For this reason, it is desirable to be able to federate a query across more than one data source. "-Federate" in this sense means to virtually combine the data sources in the query, while leaving each component with its own identity. Multiple data sources can be made available in a variety of ways. Data sources on the Web can be published for remote access as SPARQL endpoints. But even within a single data source, sets of triples can be given names as named graphs. Both endpoints and named graphs can participate in federated SPARQL queries.

When each data set is published via a SPARQL endpoint, SPARQL allows subqueries to be dispatched to different endpoints. The endpoint for the subquery is specified by putting the keyword SERVICE followed by a URL for the SPARQL endpoint before a graph pattern. A similar syntax is used for named graphs, but using the keyword GRAPH, followed by the URL that denotes the named graph. For instance, we could find out what the SPARQL endpoint dbpedia (http://dbpedia.org/sparql) knows about the movies that James Dean played in. As a simple query, we could find out whether there are any entries in dbpedia that have labels matching the names of actors who played in the movie *Giant*:

Ask:

```
SELECT ?entry
WHERE {?actor :playedIn :Giant .
     ?actor rdfs:label ?name .
         SERVICE <http://dbpedia.org/sparql>
             {?entry rdfs:label ?name .}
     }
```

Answer:

?entry
<http://dbpedia.org/resource/Carroll_Baker>
<http://dbpedia.org/resource/Elizabeth_Taylor>
<http://dbpedia.org/resource/James_Dean>
<http://dbpedia.org/resource/Mercedes_McCambridge>
<http://dbpedia.org/resource/Rock_Hudson>
<http://dbpedia.org/resource/Sal_Mineo>

The variable *?name*, which was defined in the second triple, is used again in the subquery; in effect, a value from the local data set has been given to the remote data set (dbpedia) as a predefined binding of a variable. From the point of view of the dbpedia endpoint, *?name* isn't a variable anymore; it is already bound to some value(s) from outside the query ("Giant," "Rebel Without a Cause," and "East of Eden"). The value(s) found for *?entry* in the subquery is available as a result for the full query.

The query we made to the dbpedia service in this example wasn't very interesting—it just found the dbpedia reference for something (someone) we already know about. It would be more interesting if we would ask dbpedia to tell us something we don't already know—for instance, the birth name of these actors:

Ask:

```
SELECT DISTINCT ?name ?realname
WHERE {?actor :playedIn :Giant .
    ?actor rdfs:label ?name .
        SERVICE <http://dbpedia.org/sparql>
            {?entry rdfs:label ?name .
                ?entry dbpedia:birthname ?realname }
    }
```

Answer:

?name	?realname
Elizabeth Taylor	Elizabeth Rosemond Taylor
Rock Hudson	Roy Harold Scherer, Jr.
Sal Mineo	Salvatore Mineo, Jr.

A drawback of this query is that it assumes that `rdfs:label` is an appropriate property for identifying a resource in dbpedia. But dbpedia has information about millions of things—people, movies, places, countries, etc. It includes pretty much anything that has a Wikipedia entry; it is likely that two things could have the same `rdfs:label`. A better way to identify a resource in dbpedia would be to refer to the dbpedia URL directly. This isn't something we can just do in the query—the data source would have to include a link between its resources and dbpedia. For example, if the data source were to include the following triples:

```
:ElizabethTaylor skos:exactMatch dbpedia:Elizabeth_Taylor .
:RockHudson skos:exactMatch dbpedia:Rock_Hudson .
:SalMineo skos:exactMatch dbpedia:Sal_Mineo .
```

Then we could change the query to be

```
SELECT DISTINCT ?name ?realname
WHERE {?actor :playedIn :Giant .
    ?actor skos:exactMatch ?db .
        SERVICE <http://dbpedia.org/sparql>
            { ?db dbpedia:birthname ?realname }
    }
```

Not only is this a shorter query, but it also has less chance of going awry; even if there are other people with names like "Sal Mineo" or "Elizabeth Taylor," the inclusion of the exact match in the data set ensures that the correct resource will be used in the dbpedia query. It is quite common for published data sets to include this sort of linkage to data source like dbpedia to resolve ambiguity—dbpedia has become a de facto registry of names for celebrities, places, works of art, etc., that is, for anything that is mentioned in Wikipedia.

Any number of federated SERVICE specifications are allowed in a SPARQL query, making it possible to write queries that are federated over several data sources.

SUMMARY

The SPARQL query language provides a means for querying information from an RDF data graph. The workhorse of the query is the graph pattern—a smaller graph including both resources and variables, that is matched against a data graph. The graph pattern specifies what information is to be fetched from the graph, and how the entities that match the variables are related to one another.

SPARQL queries can be used to fetch information (like SQL queries) or to transform a graph into a new form (like rules). Both forms use the same notion of graph pattern to specify the desired information.

Fundamental concepts

The following fundamental concepts were introduced in this chapter.

Graph pattern—a graph with wildcards, used to match against a data graph to specify desired results.

Variables (question words)—wildcards in a graph pattern. They can match any resource.

SELECT query—a query form that fetches binding for variables from a graph.

CONSTRUCT query—a query form that builds a new graph based on matches in a data graph, along with a graph template.

Queries as rules—using a CONSTRUCT query to specify rules.

Federated query—querying multiple data sources in a single query.

RDF and inferencing

6

CHAPTER OUTLINE

Suppose you hit the web page of an online clothing retailer, and you search for "chamois" in the category of "Shirts." Your search comes up empty. You are surprised, because you were quite certain that you saw a chamois Henley in the paper catalog that landed in your mailbox. So you look up the unit number in the catalog and do another search, using that. Sure enough, there is the chamois Henley. Furthermore, you find that "Henleys" is shown in the catalog as a kind of "Shirts." You mutter to yourself. "If it comes up under 'Henleys,' it should come up under 'Shirts.' What's the matter with this thing?"

What do we expect from a search like this? We want any search, query, or other access to the data that reference "Shirts" to also look at "Henleys." What is so special about the relationship between "Shirts" and "Henleys" to make us expect this? That is what we *mean* when we say, "'Henleys' is a kind of 'Shirts.'" How can we express this meaning in a way that is consistent and maintainable?

One solution to this problem is to leverage the power of the query; after all, in conventional database applications, it is in the query where relationships among data elements are elaborated. In this case, we could use the transitive query facility in SPARQL (Chapter 5) to write a query to search all the of shirts. If we represent relationships between categories with :subClassOf, we could write:

```
SELECT ?item
WHERE {?class :subClassOf* :Shirts .
       ?item a ?class . }
```

In addition to this approach, the Semantic Web also provides a model of data expression that allows for explicit representation of the relationship between various data items. In this sense, it genuinely allows a data modeler to create data that are more connected, better integrated, and in which the consistency constraints on the data can be expressed *in the data itself*. The data can describe something about the way they should be used.

113

As an alternative to this approach, the Semantic Web stack includes a series of layers on top of the RDF layer to describe consistency constraints in the data. The key to these levels is the notion of *inferencing*. In the context of the Semantic Web, inferencing simply means that given some stated information, we can determine other, related information that we can also consider as if it had been stated. In the Henleys/Shirts example, we would *infer* that any members of the class "Henleys" is also a member of the class "Shirts." Inferencing is a powerful mechanism for dealing with information, and it can cover a wide range of elaborate processing. For the purposes of making our data more integrated and consistent, very simple inferences are often more useful than elaborate ones. As a simple example, in Chapter 5, we saw how to write a set of queries to maintain relationship information in a family tree, whether the information was originally expressed about chidren, brothers, sisters, mothers, sons, etc. It is this sort of mundane consistency completion of data that can be done with inferencing in the Semantic Web. Although inferencing of this sort seems trivial from the point of view of the natural world (after all, doesn't everyone *just know* that this is the way families work?), it is the lack of just this sort of correlation that keeps data inconsistent.

INFERENCE IN THE SEMANTIC WEB

To make our data seem more connected and consistently integrated, we must be able to add relationships into the data that will constrain how the data are viewed. We want to be able to express the relationship between "Henleys" and "Shirts" that will tell us that any item in the "Henleys" category should also be in the "Shirts" category. We want to express the fact about locations that says that if a hotel chain has a hotel at a particular location, then that location is served by a hotel in that chain. We want to express the list of planets in terms of the classifications of the various bodies in the solar system.

Many of these relationships are familiar to information modelers in many paradigms. Let's take the relationship between "Henleys" and "Shirts" as an example. Thesaurus writers are familiar with the notion of *broader term*. "Shirts" is a broader term than "Henleys." Object-oriented programmers are accustomed to the notion of *subclasses* or *class extensions*. "Henleys" is a subclass of, or extends, the class "Shirts." In the RDF Schema language, to be described in the next chapter, we say, "Henleys" subClassOf "Shirts." It is all well and good to say these things, but what do they mean?

Thesauri take an informal stance on what these things mean in a number of contexts. If you use a broader term in a search, you will also find all the entries that were tagged with the narrower term. If you classify something according to a broad term, you may be offered a list of the narrower terms to choose from to focus your classification.

> Many readers may be familiar with terms like *class* and *subclass* from Object-Oriented Programming (OOP). There is a close historical and technical relationship between the use of these and other terms in OOP and their use in the Semantic Web, but there are also important and subtle differences. OOP systems take a more formal, if programmatic, view of class relationships than that taken by thesauri and taxonomies. An object whose type is "Henleys" will respond to all messages defined for object of type "Shirts." Furthermore, the action associated with this call will be the same for all "Shirts," unless a more specific behavior has been defined for "Henley," and so on. The Semantic Web also takes a formal view of these relationships, but in contrast to the programmatic definition found in OOP, the Semantic Web defines the meaning of these things in terms of *inference*.

The Semantic Web infrastructure provides a formal and elegant specification of the meaning of the various terms like subClassOf. For example, the meaning of "*B* is a SubClassOf *C*" is "Every member of class *B* is also a member of class *C*." This specification is expressed in the form of an inference. From the information "*x* is a member of *B*," one can derive the new information, "*x* is a member of *C*."

For the next several chapters, we will introduce terms that can be used in an RDF model, along with a statement of what each term means. This statement of meaning will be given in the form of an inference pattern: "Given some initial information, the following new information can be derived." This is how the RDF Schema language (RDFS, Chapter 6) and the Web Ontology Language (OWL, Chapter 10) work.

Our first example is one that we can use with the Henleys and Shirts example. The meaning for rdfs:subClassOf is given by the following inference:

```
IF
?A rdfs:subClassOf ?B.
AND
?x rdf:type ?A.
THEN
?x rdf:type ?B.
```

In plain English, this says that if one class A is a subclass of another class B, anything of type A is also of type B. This simple statement is the entire definition of the meaning of subClassOf in the RDF Schema language. We will refer to this rule as the *type propagation* rule. This very simple interpretation of the subclass relationship makes it a workhorse for RDFS modeling (and also for OWL modeling, as described in subsequent chapters). It closely corresponds to the IF/THEN construct of programming languages: IF something is a member of the subclass, THEN it is a member of the superclass.

The Semantic Web definition of subClassOf is similar to the definition of subclass or extension in OOP. In OOP, an instance of some class responds to the same methods in the same way that instances of its superclass do. In Semantic Web terms, this is because that instance is also a member of the superclass, and thus must behave like any such member. For example, the reason why an instance of class "Henleys" responds to methods defined in "Shirts" is because the instance actually *is* also a member of class "Shirts."

This similarity only goes so far. For example, it breaks down when, in the OOP system, the subclass defines an override for a method defined in the superclass. In Semantic Web terms, the instances of "Henleys" are still instance of "Shirts" and should respond accordingly. But in most OOP semantics, this is not the case; the definitions at "Henleys" take precedence over those at "Shirts," and thus "Henleys" need not actually behave like "Shirts" at all. In the logic of the Semantic Web, this is not allowed.

SPARQL and inference

Often, we can express the inference rules of RDFS (and OWL) by using SPARQL CONSTRUCT. For example, since a CONSTRUCT query specifies new triples based on a graph pattern of triples found in the data, in the case of the type propagation rule, we can specify the type propagation rule with the following SPARQL CONSTRUCT query:

```
CONSTRUCT {?r rdf:type ?B}
WHERE    {?A rdfs:subClassOf ?B .
          ?r rdf:type ?A}
```

SPARQL provides a precise and compact way to express inference rules of this sort. We will use this SPARQL notation throughout the rest of the book to describe much of the inferencing in RDFS and OWL. It is a clean, concise way to specify inferences, provide ample examples of SPARQL queries, and show the relationship between SPARQL and these other Semantic Web languages.

Using SPARQL to define inference isn't just a convenience for writing a book—SPARQL can be used as the basis for an inference language itself. One proposal for such an inference language is called **SPARQL** **I**nferencing **N**otation (SPIN).[1] SPIN includes a number of constructs for managing inferencing with SPARQL, but for the purposes of this book, SPIN is simply a way to specify that a particular CONSTRUCT query is to be used as a definition for inferences for a particular model. For example, if we want to say that the type propagation rule holds for all members of the class Shirt, we can specify this in SPIN as

```
:Shirt spin:rule "CONSTRUCT {?this rdf:type ?B}
                  WHERE    {?A rdfs:subClassOf ?B .
                            ?this rdf:type ?A}" .
```

The variable *?this* has special meaning in SPIN; it refers to a member of the class that the query is attached to by spin:rule. In this example, *?this* refers to any member of the class :Shirt. We will use SPIN from time to time to elaborate how inferences in RDFS and OWL are related to constructions that can be specified in SPARQL.

Virtues of inference-based semantics

Inference patterns constitute an elegant way to define the meaning of a data construct. But is this approach really useful? Why is it a particularly effective way to define the meaning of constructs in the Semantic Web?

Since our data are living in the Web, a major concern for making our data more useful is to have them behave in a consistent way when combined with data from multiple sources. The strategy of basing the meaning of our terms on inferencing provides a robust solution to understanding the meaning of novel combinations of terms. Taking subClassOf as an example, it is not out of the question for a single class to be specified as subClassOf two other classes. What does this mean?

In an informal thesaurus setting, the meaning of such a construct is decided informally: What do we *want* such an expression to mean? Since we have a clear but informal notion of what *broader term* means, we can use that intuition to argue for a number of positions, including but not limited to, deciding that such a situation should not be allowed, to defining search behavior for all terms involved. When the meaning of a construct like *broader term* is defined informally, the interpretation of novel combinations must be resolved by consensus or authoritative proclamation.

---

[1]http://spinrdf.org/

OOP also faces the issue of deciding an appropriate interpretation for a single subclass of two distinct classes. The issue is known as *multiple inheritance,* and it is much discussed in OOP circles. Indeed, each OOP modeling system has a response to this issue, ranging from a refusal to allow it (C#), a distinction between different types of inheritance (*interface* vs. *implementation* inheritance, e.g., Java), to complex systems for defining such things (e.g., the Meta-Object Protocol of the Common Lisp Object System). Each of these provides an answer to the multiple inheritance question, and each is responsive to particular design considerations that are important for the respective programming language.

In an inference-based system like the Semantic Web, the answer to this question (for better or worse) is defined by the interaction of the basic inference patterns. How does multiple inheritance work in the RDF Schema Language? Just apply the rule twice. If A is `subClassOf` B and A is also `subClassOf` C, then any individual *x* that is a member of A will also be a member of B and of C. No discussion is needed, no design decisions. The meaning of `subClassOf`, in any context, is given elegant expression in a single simple rule: the type propagation rule. This feature of inference systems is particularly suited to a Semantic Web context, in which novel combinations of relationships are bound to occur as data from multiple sources are merged.

WHERE ARE THE SMARTS?

An inference-based system for describing the meaning of Semantic Web constructs is elegant and useful in a distributed setting, but how does it help us make our data more useful? For our application to behave differently, we will need a new capability in our deployment architecture, something that will respond to queries based not only on the triples that have been asserted but also on the triples that can be inferred based on the rules of inference. This architecture is shown in Figure 6.1, and it is very similar to the RDF query architecture shown in Figure 4.4.

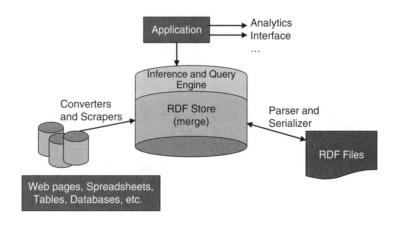

FIGURE 6.1

Semantic Web architecture with inferencing.

The novelty of this architecture is an inferencing capability that stands with the query component between the application and the RDF data store. The power of a query engine with inferencing capability is determined by the set of inferences that it supports. An RDFS inference query engine supports a small set of inferences defined in the RDFS standard; an OWL inference query engine supports the larger set of OWL inferences. (Note that there are alternative formulations where the data are preprocessed by an inferencing engine and then queried directly. We discuss this later in this chapter.)

EXAMPLE Simple RDFS Query

Suppose we have an inference engine that includes support for the type propagation rule working over an RDF store that contains only these two triples:

```
shop:Henleys rdfs:subClassOf shop:Shirts.
shop:ChamoisHenley rdf:type shop:Henleys.
```

Suppose we have a SPARQL triple pattern that we use to examine these triples, thus:

Ask:
```
SELECT ?item
WHERE {?x rdf:type shop:Shirts . }
```

In a plain RDF query situation, this pattern will match no triples because there is no triple with predicate rdf:type and object shop:Shirts. However, since the RDFS inference standard includes the type propagation rule just listed, with an RDFS inferencing query engine, the following single result will be returned:

Answer:

?item
Shop:ChamoisHenley

Asserted triples versus inferred triples

It is often convenient to think about inferencing and queries as separate processes, in which an inference engine produces all the possible inferred triples, based on a particular set of inference rules. Then, in a separate pass, an ordinary SPARQL query engine runs over the resulting augmented triple store. It then becomes meaningful to speak of *asserted triples* versus *inferred triples.*

Asserted triples, as the name suggests, are the triples that were asserted in the original RDF store. In the case where the store was populated by merging triples from many sources, all the triples are asserted. Inferred triples are the additional triples that are inferred by one of the inference rules that govern a particular inference engine. It is, of course, possible for the inference engine to infer a triple that has already been asserted. In this case, we still consider the triple to have been asserted. It is important to note that there is no logical distinction between inferred and asserted triples, the inference engine will draw exactly the same conclusions from an inferred triple as it would have done, had that same triple been asserted.

EXAMPLE Asserted versus Inferred Triples

Even with a single inference rule like the type propagation rule, we can show the distinction of asserted vs. inferred triples. Suppose we have the following triples in a triple store:

```
shop:Henleys rdfs:subClassOf shop:Shirts.
shop:Shirts rdfs:subClassOf shop:MensWear.
shop:Blouses rdfs:subClassOf shop:WomensWear.
shop:Oxfords rdfs:subClassOf shop:Shirts.
shop:Tshirts rdfs:subClassOf shop:Shirts.
shop:ChamoisHenley rdf:type shop:Henleys.
shop:ClassicOxford rdf:type shop:Oxfords.
shop:ClassicOxford rdf:type shop:Shirts.
shop:BikerT rdf:type shop:Tshirts.
shop:BikerT rdf:type shop:MensWear.
```

These triples are shown graphically in Figure 6.2.

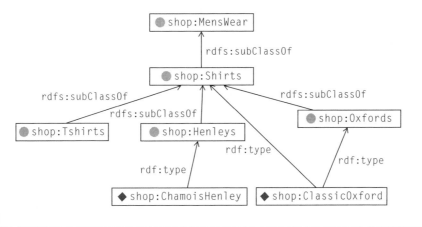

FIGURE 6.2

Asserted triples in the catalog model.

An inferencing query engine that enforces just the type propagation rule will draw the following inferences:

```
shop:ChamoisHenley rdf:type shop:Shirts.
shop:ChamoisHenley rdf:type shop:MensWear.
shop:ClassicOxford rdf:type shop:Shirts.
shop:ClassicOxford rdf:type shop:MensWear.
shop:BikerT rdf:type shop:Shirts.
shop:BikerT rdf:type shop:MensWear.
```

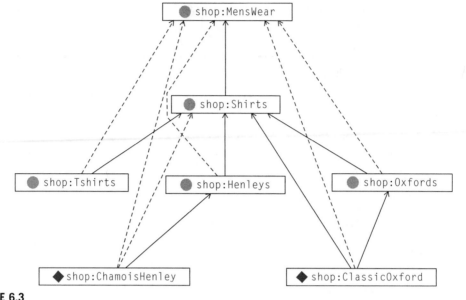

FIGURE 6.3

All triples in the catalog model. Inferred triples are shown as dashed lines.

Some of these triples were also asserted; the complete set of triples over which queries will take place is as follows, with inferred triples in italics:

```
shop:Henleys rdfs:subClassOf shop:Shirts.
shop:Shirts rdfs:subClassOf shop:MensWear.
shop:Blouses rdfs:subClassOf shop:WomensWear.
shop:Oxfords rdfs:subClassOf shop:Shirts.
shop:TShirts rdfs:subClassOf shop:Shirts.
shop:ChamoisHenley rdf:type shop:Henleys.
shop:ChamoisHenley rdf:type shop:Shirts.
shop:ChamoisHenley rdf:type shop:MensWear.
shop:ClassicOxford rdf:type shop:Oxfords.
shop:ClassicOxford rdf:type shop:Shirts.
shop:ClassicOxford rdf:type shop:MensWear.
shop:BikerT rdf:type shop:Tshirts.
shop:BikerT rdf:type shop:Shirts.
shop:BikerT rdf:type shop:MensWear.
```

All triples in the model, both asserted and inferred, are shown in Figure 6.3. We use the convention that asserted triples are printed with unbroken lines, and inferred triples are printed with dashed lines. This convention is used throughout the book.

The situation can become a bit more subtle when we begin to merge information from multiple sources in which each source itself is a system that includes an inference engine. Most RDF implementations provide a capability by which new triples can be asserted directly in the triple store. This makes it quite straightforward for an application to assert any or all inferred triples. If those triples are then serialized (say, in RDF/XML) and shared on the Web, another application could merge them with other sources and draw further inferences. In complex situations like this, the simple distinction of *asserted* versus *inferred* might be too coarse to be a useful description of what is happening in the system.

WHEN DOES INFERENCING HAPPEN?

The RDFS and OWL standards define what inferences are valid, given certain patterns of triples. But *when* does inferencing happen? Is inferencing done at all? Where and how are inferred triples stored, if at all? How many of them are there?

These questions are properly outside the range of the definitions of RDFS and OWL, but they are clearly important for any implementation that conforms to these standards. It should, therefore, come as no surprise that the answers to these questions can differ from one implementation to another. The simplest approach is to store all triples in a single store, regardless of whether they are asserted or inferred. As soon as a pattern is identified, any inferred triples are inserted into the store. We will call this *cached inferencing*, since all inferences are stored ("cached") with the data. This approach is quite simple to describe and implement but risks an explosion of triples in the triple store. At the other extreme, an implementation could instead never actually store any inferred triples in any persistent store at all. Inferencing is done in response to queries only. We will call this *just in time inferencing*, since the inferences are computed at the latest possible moment. The query responses are produced in such a way as to respect all the appropriate inferences, but no inferred triple is retained. This method risks duplicating inference work, but it is parsimonious in terms of persistent storage. These different approaches have an important impact in terms of change management. What happens if a data source changes—that is, a new triple is added to some data store or a triple is removed? A strategy that persistently saves inferences will have to decide which inferred triples must also be removed. This presents a difficult problem, since it is possible that there could be many ways for a triple to be inferred. Just because one inference has been undermined by the removal of a triple, does that mean that it is appropriate to remove that triple? An approach that recomputes all inferences whenever a query is made need not face this issue.

An important variant of "just in time" inferencing is where no explicit inferencing is done at all. We already saw, in our example about subclasses of Shirts, how a query could explicitly express what data it wanted, without relying on the inference semantics of the model at all. As we see in the next section, even in this case, where there is no explicit inferencing, the inference interpretation of a model is still important in organizing and understanding a semantic application.

Inferencing as specification

At the beginning of this chapter, we looked at a query to find all the Shirts in a catalog, explicitly tracing down the all `rdfs:subClassOf` links:

```
SELECT ?item
WHERE  {?class :subClassOf* :Shirts .
        ?item a ?class . }
```

This selection was done to support a search operation—"find me all the chamois Shirts." This query operates without any explicit reference to inference at all; it returns its answers without reference to inferred triples vs. asserted triples; it just processes the asserted data. But how do we know that the items returned by this query are Shirts?

This same question could be asked of a program in Java or C++ or even SQL—if we write a program to collect up the members of all the subclasses of Shirts (and their subclasses, and so on), do we know that all the things we have collected are Shirts? If we return one of these things as the result of a user search, can we be justified in thinking that it is itself a shirt? This suggests a role that a semantic model can play in the interpretation of data—it can tell us whether the queries we have written are correct. In this example, our model tells us that every Henley is a shirt, because the class Henleys is a subclass of the class Shirts. The same goes for Oxfords, and for any subclasses of Oxfords. The model, along with its formal semantics, guarantees that all the results of this query will indeed be shirts.

In this sense, the model is a specification. Any discussion about the appropriateness of a particular query can appeal to the model for arbitration—is this query consistent with the model? In this example, the model tells us that any result from this query will be a Shirt, so it is appropriate to treat them as such. When the model is written in a language for which there is a capability to do automated inferences (like RDFS, RDFS-Plus, or OWL), it becomes particularly useful—the specification is said to be *executable*. This means that we can run a program that will tell us exactly what the model means. In the example above where we showed asserted and inferred triples, we showed the results of just such a capability, resulting in a list of all the Shirts (of any type).

When building an application, we might decide to use a general-purpose inference capability, or we might decide to use an extended query (like the one shown here), or we might write a program in some other language. A specification (even an executable one) tells us what our program or query ought to do; it doesn't tell us how we should do it. Regardless of this implementation choice, the model plays a central role of justifying the query or program. If many people develop different systems (even using different technological approaches), the results they provide will be consistent, if they justify them all against the same model.

SUMMARY

RDF provides a way to represent data so that information from multiple sources can be brought together and treated as if they came from a single source. But when we want to use that data, the differences in those sources comes out. For instance, we'd like to be able to write a single query that can fetch related data from all the integrated data sources.

The Semantic Web provides an approach to this problem in the form of modeling languages in which the relationship between data sources can be described. A modeling construct's meaning is given by the pattern of inferences that can be drawn from it. Information integration can be achieved by invoking inferencing before or during the query process; a query returns not only the asserted data but also inferred information. This inferred information can draw on more than one data source.

We have seen how even very simple inferencing can provide value for data integration. But just exactly what kind of inferencing is needed? There isn't a single universal answer to this question. The

Semantic Web standards identify a number of different levels of expressivity, each supporting different inferences, and intended for different levels of sophistication of data integration over the Semantic Web.

In the following chapters, we will explore three particular inferencing levels. They differ only in terms of the inferences that each of the languages allow. RDFS (Chapter 6) is a recommendation defined and maintained by the W3C. It operates on a small number of inference rules that deal mostly with relating classes to subclasses and properties to classes. RDFS-PLUS (Chapter 7) is a mode that we have defined for this book. We have found a particular set of inference patterns to be helpful both pedagogically (as a gentle introduction to the more complex inference patterns of OWL) and practically (as a useful integration tool in its own right). RDFS-PLUS builds on top of RDFS to include constraints on properties and notions of equality. OWL (Chapters 9 and 10) is a recommendation defined and maintained by the W3C, which builds further to include rules for describing classes based on allowed values for properties. All of these standards use the notion of inferencing to describe the meaning of a model; they differ in the inferencing that they support.

Fundamental concepts

The following fundamental concepts were introduced in this chapter.

Inferencing—The process by which new triples are systematically added to a graph based on patterns in existing triples.

Asserted triples—The triples in a graph that were provided by some data source.

Inferred triples—Triples that were added to a model based on systematic inference patterns.

Inference rules—Systematic patterns defining which of the triples should be inferred.

Inference engine—A program that performs inferences according to some inference rules. It is often integrated with a query engine.

RDF schema

Just as Semantic Web modeling in RDF is about graphs, Semantic Web modeling in the RDF Schema Language (RDFS) is about sets. Some aspects of set membership can be modeled in RDF alone, as we have seen with the `rdf:type` built-in property. But RDF itself simply creates a graph structure to represent data. RDFS provides some guidelines about how to use this graph structure in a disciplined way. It provides a way to talk about the vocabulary that will be used in an RDF graph. Which individuals are related to one another, and how? How are the properties we use to define our individuals related to other sets of individuals and, indeed, to one another? RDFS provides a way for an

125

information modeler to express the answers to these sorts of questions as they pertain to particular data modeling and integration needs.

As such, RDFS is like other schema languages: It provides information about the ways in which we describe our data. But RDFS differs from other schema languages in important ways.

SCHEMA LANGUAGES AND THEIR FUNCTIONS

RDFS is the schema language for RDF. But what is a schema language in the first place? There are a number of successful schema languages for familiar technologies, but the role that each of these languages play in the management of information is closely tied to the particular language or system.

Let's consider document modeling systems as an example. For such a system, a schema language allows one to express the set of allowed formats for a document. For a given schema, it is possible to determine (often automatically) whether a particular document conforms to that schema. This is the major capability provided by XML Schema definitions. XML parsers can automatically determine whether a particular XML document conforms to a given schema.

Other schema languages help us to interpret particular data. For example, a database schema provides header and key information for tables in a relational database. There is neither anything in the table itself to indicate the meaning of the information in a particular column nor anything to indicate which column is to be used as an index for the table. This information is appropriately included in the database schema, since it does not change from one data record to the next.

For Object-Oriented Programming systems, the class structure plays an organizing role for information as well. But in object-oriented programming, the class diagram does more than describe data. It determines, according to the inheritance policy of the particular language, what methods are available for a particular instance and how they are implemented. This stands in stark contrast to relational databases and XML, in that it does not interpret information but instead provides a systematic way for someone to describe information and available transformations for that information.

Given this variety of understandings of how schema information can be used in different modeling paradigms, one might wonder whether calling something a schema language actually tells us anything at all! But there is something in common among all these notions of a schema. In all cases, the schema tells us something about the information that is expressed in the system. The schema is information about the data.

How then can we understand the notion of schema in RDF? What might we want to say about RDF data? And how might we want to say it? The key idea of the schema in RDF is that it should help provide some sense of *meaning* to the data. It accomplishes this by specifying semantics using inference patterns.

Relationship between schema and data

In most modeling systems, there is a clear division between the data and its schema. The schema for a relational database is not typically expressed in a table in the database; the object model of an object-oriented system is not expressed as objects, and an XML DTD is not a valid XML document.

But in many cases, modern versions of such systems do model the schema in the same form as the data; the meta-object protocol of Common Lisp and the introspection API of Java represent the object models as objects themselves. The XML Stylesheet Definition defines XML Styles in an XML language.

In the case of RDF, the schema language was defined in RDF from the very beginning. That is, all schema information in RDFS is defined with RDF triples. The relationship between "plain" resources in RDF and schema resources is made with triples, just like relationships between any other resources. This elegance of design makes it particularly easy to provide a formal description of the semantics of RDFS, simply by providing inference rules that work over patterns of triples. While this is good engineering practice (in some sense, the RDF standards committee learned a lesson from the issues that the XML standards had with DTDs), its significance goes well beyond its value as good engineering. In RDF, everything is expressed as triples. The meaning of asserted triples is expressed in new (inferred) triples. The structures that drive these inferences, that describe the meaning of our data, are also in triples. This means that this process can continue as far as it needs to; the schema information that provides context for information on the Semantic Web can itself be distributed on the Semantic Web.

We can see this in action by showing how a set is defined in RDFS. The basic construct for specifying a set in RDFS is called an `rdfs:Class`. Since RDFS is expressed in RDF, the way we express that something is a class is with a triple—in particular, a triple in which the predicate is `rdf:type`, and the object is `rdfs:Class`. Here are some examples that we will use in the following discussion:

```
:AllStarPlayer rdf:type rdfs:Class.
:MajorLeaguePlayer rdf:type rdfs:Class.
:Surgeon rdf:type rdfs:Class.
:Staff rdf:type rdfs:Class.
:Physician rdf:type rdfs:Class.
```

These are triples in RDF just like any other; the only way we know that they refer to the schema rather than the data is because of the use of the term in the `rdfs:` namespace, `rdfs:Class`. But what is new here? In Chapter 3, we already discussed the notion of `rdf:type`, which we used to specify that something was a member of a set. What do we gain by specifying explicitly that something is a set? We gain a description of the meaning of membership in a set. In RDF, the only "meaning" we had for set membership was given by the results of some query; `rdf:type` actually didn't behave any differently from any other (even user-defined) property. How can we specify what we *mean* by set membership? In RDFS, we express meaning through the mechanism of inference.

THE RDF SCHEMA LANGUAGE

RDFS "extends" RDF by introducing a set of distinguished resources into the language. This is similar to the way in which a traditional programming language can be extended by defining new language-defined keywords. But there is an important difference: In RDF, we already had the capability to use any resource in any triple (Anyone can say Anything about Any topic). So by identifying certain specific resources as "new keywords," we haven't actually extended the language at all! We have simply identified certain triples as having a special meaning, as defined by a standard.

How can we define the "meaning" of a distinguished resource? As we saw in Chapter 6, in RDFS, meaning is expressed by specifying inferences that can be drawn when the resource is used in a certain way. Throughout the rest of this section, whenever we introduce a new RDFS resource, we will answer the question "What does it mean?" with an answer of the form "In these circumstances (defined by some pattern of triples), you can add (infer) the following new triples." We already saw how to do this with the type propagation rule for `rdfs:subClassOf`; now we will demonstrate this principle using another of the most fundamental terms in RDFS: `rdfs:subPropertyOf`.

Relationship propagation through `rdfs:subPropertyOf`

The basic intuition behind the use of `rdfs:subPropertyOf` is that terminology includes verbs as well as nouns, and many of the same requirements for mapping nouns from one source to another will apply to relationships. Simple examples abound in ordinary parlance. The relationship *brother* is more specific than the relationship *sibling;* if someone is my brother, then he is also my sibling. This is formalized in RDFS for `rdfs:subPropertyOf` using an inference rule that is almost as simple as the one for `rdfs:subClassOf`.

```
CONSTRUCT {?x ?r ?y .}
WHERE {?x ?q ?y .
       ?q rdfs:subPropertyOf ?r }
```

That is, in any triple, we can replace the predicate with any property it is a `subPropertyOf`.

EXAMPLE Employment

A large firm engages a number of people in various capacities and has a variety of ways to administer these relationships. Some people are directly employed by the firm, whereas others are contractors. Among these contractors, some of them are directly contracted to the company on a freelance basis, others on a long-term retainer, and still others contract through an intermediate firm. All of these people could be said to work for the firm.

How can we model this situation in RDFS? First, we need to consider the inferences we wish to be able to draw and under what circumstances. There are a number of relationships that can hold between a person and the firm; we can call them `contractsTo`, `freeLancesTo`, `indirectlyContractsTo`, `isEmployedBy`, and `worksFor`.

If we assert any of these statements about some person, then we would like to infer that that person `worksFor` the firm. Furthermore, there are intermediate conclusions we can draw—for instance, both a freelancer and an indirect contractor contract to the firm and indeed work for the firm.

All these relationships can be expressed in RDFS using the `rdfs:subPropertyOf` relation:

```
:freeLancesTo rdfs:subPropertyOf contractsTo.
:indirectlyContractsTo rdfs:subPropertyOf contractsTo.
:isEmployedBy rdfs:subPropertyOf worksFor.
:contractsTo rdfs:subPropertyOf worksFor.
```

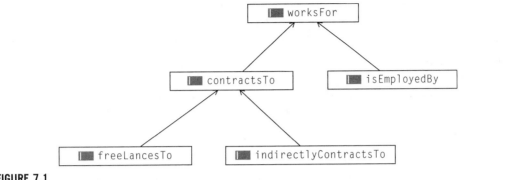

FIGURE 7.1

`rdfs:subPropertyOf` relations for workers in the firm.

The discussion will be easier to follow if we represent this as a diagram, where the arrows denote `rdfs:subPropertyOf` (see Figure 7.1).

To see what inferences can be drawn, we will need some instance data:

```
:Goldman :isEmployedBy :TheFirm.
:Spence :freeLancesTo :TheFirm.
:Long :indirectlyContractsTo :TheFirm.
```

The rule that defines the meaning of `rdfs:subPropertyOf` implies a new triple, replacing any subproperty with its superproperty. So, since

```
:isEmployedBy :rdfs:subPropertyOf :worksFor.
```

we can infer that

```
:Goldman :worksFor :TheFirm.
```

And because of the assertions about freelancing and indirect contracts, we can infer that

```
:Spence :contractsTo :TheFirm.
:Long contractsTo :TheFirm.
```

And finally, since, like asserted triples, inferred triples can be used to make further inferences, we can further infer that

```
:Spence :worksFor :TheFirm.
:Long :worksFor :TheFirm.
```

In general, `rdfs:subPropertyOf` allows a modeler to describe a hierarchy of related properties. Just as in class hierarchies, specific properties are at the bottom of the tree, and more general properties are higher up in the tree. Whenever any property in the tree holds between two entities, so does every property above it.

> The construct rdfs:subPropertyOf has no direct analog in object-oriented programming, where proper-
> ties are not first-class entities (i.e., they cannot be related to one another, independent of the class in which they are
> defined). For this reason, unlike the case of rdfs:subClassOf, object-oriented programmers have no conflict
> with a similar known concept. The only source of confusion is that subproperty diagrams like the preceding one are
> sometimes mistaken for class diagrams.

Typing data by usage—**rdfs:domain** and **rdfs:range**

We have seen how inferences around rdfs:subPropertyOf can be used to describe how two properties relate to each other. But when we describe the usage of terms in our data, we would also like to represent how a property is used relative to the defined classes. In particular, we might want to say that when a property is used, the triple subject comes from (i.e., has rdf:type) a certain class and that the object comes from some other type. These two stipulations are expressed in RDFS with the resources (keywords) rdfs:domain and rdfs:range, respectively.

In mathematics, the words *domain* and *range* are used to refer to how a function (or more generally, a relation) can be used. The domain of a function is the set of values for which it is defined, and the range is the set of values it can take. In Real Analysis, for instance, the relation *squareroot* has the positive numbers as the domain (since negative numbers don't have square roots in the reals), and all reals as the range (since there are both positive and negative square roots).

In RDFS, the properties rdfs:domain and rdfs:range have meanings inspired by the mathematical uses of these words. A property p can have an rdfs:domain and/or an rdfs:range. These are specified, as is everything in RDF, via triples:

```
:p rdfs:domain :D.
:p rdfs:range :R.
```

The informal interpretation of this is that the relation p relates values from the class D to values from the class R. D and R need not be disjoint, or even distinct.

The meaning of these terms is defined by the inferences that can be drawn from them. RDFS inferencing interprets domain with the inference rule:

```
CONSTRUCT {?x rdf:type ?D .}
WHERE {?P rdfs:domain ?D .
       ?x ?P ?y .}
```

Similarly, range is defined with the rule

```
CONSTRUCT {?y rdf:type ?D .}
WHERE {?P rdfs:range ?D .
       ?x ?P ?y .}
```

In RDFS, domain and range give some information about how the property P is to be used; domain refers to the subject of any triple that uses P as its predicate, and range refers to the object of any such triple. When we assert that property P has domain D (respectively, range R), we are saying that whenever we use the property P, we can infer that the subject (respectively object) of that triple is a member of the class D (respectively R). In short, domain and range tell us how P is to be used. Rather than signaling an error if P is used in a way that is apparently inconsistent with this declaration, RDFS will infer the necessary type information to bring P into compliance with its domain and range declarations.

In RDFS, there is no way to assert that a particular individual is not a member of a particular class (contrast with OWL, Chapter 12). In fact, in RDFS, there is no notion of an incorrect or inconsistent inference. This means that, unlike the case of XML Schema, an RDF Schema will never proclaim an input as invalid; it will simply infer appropriate type information. In this way, RDFS behaves much more like a database schema, which declares what joins are possible but makes no statement about the validity of the joined data.

Combination of domain and range with `rdfs:subClassOf`

So far, we have seen inference patterns for some resources in the *rdfs* namespace: `rdfs:domain`, `rdfs:range`, `rdfs:subPropertyOf`, and `rdfs:subClassOf`. We have seen how the inference patterns work on sample triples. But the inference patterns can also interact with one another in interesting ways. We can already see this happening with the three patterns we have seen so far. We will show the interaction between `rdfs:subClassOf` and `rdfs:domain` by starting with an example.

Suppose we have a very simple class tree that includes just two classes, Woman and Married-Woman, in the usual subclass relation:

```
:MarriedWoman rdfs:subClassOf :Woman.
```

Suppose we have a property called `hasMaidenName`, whose domain is `MarriedWoman`:

```
:hasMaidenName rdfs:domain :MarriedWoman.
```

Figure 7.2 shows how this looks in diagram form.

This unsurprising model holds some subtlety; let's examine closely what it says. If we assert the `hasMaidenName` of anything (even if we don't know that it is a Woman!), the rule for `rdfs:domain` allows us to infer that it is a `MarriedWoman`. So, for instance, if someone asserts

```
:Karen :hasMaidenName "Stephens".
```

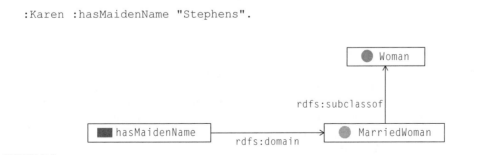

FIGURE 7.2

Domain and `subClassOf` triples for `hasMaidenName`.

We can infer

```
:Karen rdf:type :MarriedWoman.
```

But we can make further inferences based on the `rdfs:subClassOf` relationship between the classes—namely, that

```
:Karen rdf:type :Woman.
```

There was nothing in this example that was particular to `Karen`; in fact, if we learn of any resource at all that it has a `hasMaidenName`, then we will infer that it is a `Woman`. That is, we know that for any resource `X`, if we have a triple of the form

```
?X :hasMaidenName ?Y .
```

we can infer

```
?X rdf:type :Woman.
```

But this is exactly the definition of `rdfs:domain`; that is, we have just seen that

```
:hasMaidenName rdfs:domain :Woman.
```

This is a different way to use the definition of `rdfs:domain` from what we have encountered so far. Until now, we applied the inference pattern whenever a triple using `rdfs:domain` was asserted or inferred. Now we are inferring an `rdfs:domain` triple whenever we can prove that the inference pattern holds. That is, we view the inference pattern as the definition of what it means for `rdfs:domain` to hold.

We can generalize this result to form a new inference pattern as follows:

```
CONSTRUCT {?P rdfs:domain ?C .}
WHERE {?P rdfs:domain ?D .
       ?D rdfs:subClassof ?C .}
```

That is, whenever we specify the `rdfs:domain` of a property to be some class, we can also infer that the property also has any superclass as `rdfs:domain`. The same conclusion holds for `rdfs:range`, using the same argument.

These simple definitions of `domain` and `range` are actually quite aggressive; we can draw conclusions about the type of any element based simply on its use in a single triple whenever we have domain or range information about the predicate. As we shall see in later examples, this can result in some surprising inferences. The definitions of `domain` and `range` in RDFS are the most common problem areas for modelers with experience in another data modeling paradigm. It is unusual to have such a strong interpretation for very common concepts.

The interaction between `rdfs:domain` and `rdfs:subClassOf` can seem particularly counterintuitive when viewed in comparison to Object-Oriented Programming (OOP). One of the basic mechanisms for organizing code in OOP is called *inheritance*. There are a number of different schemes for defining inheritance, but they typically work by propagating information down the class tree; that is, something (e.g., a method or a variable) that is defined at one class is also available at its subclasses.

When they first begin working with RDFS, there is a tendency for OO programmers to expect inheritance to work the same way. This tendency results from an "obvious" mapping from RDFS to OOP in which an `rdfs:Class` corresponds to a Class in OOP, a property in RDFS corresponds to a variable in OOP, and in which the assertion

```
P rdfs:domain C.
```

corresponds to the definition of the variable corresponding to P being defined at class C. From this "obvious" mapping comes an expectation that these definitions should inherit in the same way that variable definitions inherit in OOP.

But in RDFS, there is no notion of inheritance per se; the only mechanism at work in RDFS is inference. The inference rule in RDFS that most closely corresponds to the OO notion of inheritance is the subclass propagation rule: that the members of a subclass are also members of a class. The ramifications of this rule for instance correspond to what one would expect from inheritance. Since an instance of a subclass is also an instance of the parent class, then anything we say about members of the parent class will necessarily hold for all instances of the subclass; this is consistent with usual notions of inheritance.

The interaction between `rdfs:domain` and `rdfs:subClassOf`, on the other hand, is more problematic. Using the "obvious" interpretation, we asserted that the variable `hasMaidenName` was defined at `MarriedWoman` and then inferred that it was defined at a class higher in the tree—namely, `Woman`. Seen from an OO point of view, this interaction seems like inheritance up the tree—in other words, just the opposite of what is normally expected of inheritance in OOP.

The fallacy in this conclusion comes from the "obvious" mapping of `rdfs:domain` as defining a variable relative to a class. In the Semantic Web, because of the AAA slogan, a property can be used anywhere, and it must be independent of any class. The property `hasMaidenName` was, by design, always available for any resource in the universe (including members of the class `Woman`); the assertion or inference of `rdfs:domain` made no change in that respect. That is, it is never accurate in the Semantic Web to say that a property is "defined for a class." A property is defined independently of any class, and the RDFS relations specify which inferences can be correctly made about it in particular contexts.

RDFS MODELING COMBINATIONS AND PATTERNS

The inference rules for RDFS are few in number and quite simple. Nevertheless, their effect can be quite subtle in the context of shared information in the Semantic Web. In this section, we outline a number of patterns of use of the basic RDFS features, illustrating each one with a simple example.

Set intersection

It is not uncommon for someone modeling in RDFS to ask whether some familiar notions from logic are available. "Can I model set intersection in RDFS?" is a common question. The technically correct answer to this question is simply "no." There is no explicit modeling construct in RDFS for set intersection (or for set union). However, when someone wants to model intersections (or unions), they don't always need to model them explicitly. They often only need certain particular inferences that are supported by these logical relations. Sometimes these inferences are indeed available in RDFS through particular design patterns that combine the familiar RDFS primitives in specific ways.

In the case of intersection in particular, one of the inferences someone might like to draw is that if a resource x is in C, then it is also in both A and B. Expressed formally, the relationship they are expressing is that $C \subseteq A \cap B$. This inference can be supported by making C a common subclass of both A and B, as follows:

```
:C rdfs:subClassOf :A.
:C rdfs:subClassOf :B.
```

How does this support an intersection-like conclusion? From the inference rule governing `rdfs:subClassOf`, it is evident that from the triple

```
?x rdf:type :C.
```

We can infer

```
?x rdf:type :B.
?x rdf:type :A.
```

as desired. Notice that we can only draw the inferences in one direction; from membership in C, we can infer membership in A and B. But from membership in A and B, we cannot infer membership in C. That is, we cannot express $A \cap B \subseteq C$. This is the sense in which RDFS cannot actually express set intersection; it can only approximate it by supporting the inferencing in one direction.

EXAMPLE Hospital Skills

Suppose we are describing the staff at a hospital. There are a number of different jobs and people who fill them, including nurses, doctors, surgeons, administrators, orderlies, volunteers, and so on. A very specialized role in the hospital is the surgeon. Among the things we know about surgeons is that they are members of the hospital staff. They are also qualified physicians. Logically, we would say that $Surgeon \subseteq Staff \cap Physician$—that is, *Surgeon* is a subset of those people who are both staff members and physicians.

Notice that we don't want to say that *every* staff physician is a surgeon, so the set inclusion goes only one way. From this statement, we want to be able to infer that if *Kildare* is a *Surgeon*, then he is also a member of the staff, and he is a physician. If we say

```
:Surgeon rdfs:subClassOf :Staff.
:Surgeon rdfs:subClassOf :Physician.
:Kildare rdf:type :Surgeon.
```

then we can infer that

```
:Kildare rdf:type :Staff.
:Kildare rdf:type :Physician.
```

We cannot make the inference the other way; that is, if we were to assert that *Kildare* is a *Physician* and member of the *Staff*, no RDFS rules are applicable, and no inferences are drawn. This is appropriate; consider the case in which *Kildare* is a psychiatrist. As such, he is both a member of the *Staff* and a *Physician*, but it is inappropriate to conclude that he must be a *Surgeon*. (OWL, Chapter 12, provides means for making it so that this conclusion would hold, but RDFS does not.)

Property intersection

In RDFS, properties are treated in a way analogous to the treatment of classes, and all the same operations and limitations apply. Even though it might seem unfamiliar to think of a property as a set, we can still use the set combination terms (intersection, union) to describe the functionality supported for properties. As was the case for Class intersections and unions, RDFS cannot express these things exactly, but it is possible to approximate these notions with judicious use of `subPropertyOf`.

One of the inferences we can express using `subPropertyOf` is that one property is an intersection of two others, $P \subseteq R \cap S$. That is, if we know that two resources x and y are related by property P,

```
?x :P ?y .
```

we want to be able to infer both

```
?x :R ?y .
?x :S ?y.
```

EXAMPLE Patients in Hospital Rooms

Suppose we are describing patients in a hospital. When a patient is assigned to a particular room, we can infer a number of things about the patient: We know that they are on the duty roster for that room and that their insurance will be billed for that room. How do we express that both of these inferences come from the single assignment of a patient to a room?

```
:lodgedIn rdfs:subPropertyOf :billedFor.
:lodgedIn rdfs:subPropertyOf :assignedTo.
```

Now if patient `Marcus` is `lodgedIn` Room101,

```
:Marcus :lodgedIn :Room101.
```

we can infer the billing and duty roster properties as well:

```
:Marcus :billedFor :Room101.
:Marcus :assignedTo :Room101.
```

Notice that we cannot make the inference in the other direction; that is, if we were to assert that `Marcus` is `billedFor` Room101 and `assignedTo` Room101, no RDFS rules are applicable, and no inferences can be drawn.

SET UNION

Using a pattern similar to the one we used for set intersection, we can also express certain things about set unions in RDFS. In particular, we can express that $A \cup B \subseteq C$. We do this by making C a common superclass of A and B, thus:

```
:A rdfs:subClassOf :C.
:B rdfs:subClassOf :C.
```

Any instance ?x that is a member of either A or B is inferred to be also a member of C; that is,

```
?x rdf:type :A.
```
or
```
?x rdf:type :B.
```
implies
```
?x rdf:type :C.
```

EXAMPLE All Stars

In determining the candidates for a season's All Stars, a league's rules could state that they will select among all the players who have been named Most Valuable Player (MVP), as well as among those who have been top scorers (TopScorer) in their league. We can model this in RDFS by making AllStarCandidate a common superclass of MVP and TopScorer as follows:

```
:MVP rdfs:subClassOf :AllStarCandidate.
:TopScorer rdfs:subClassOf :AllStarCandidate.
```

Now, if we know that Reilly was named MVP and Kaneda was a TopScorer:

```
:Reilly rdf:type :MVP.
:Kaneda rdf:type :TopScorer.
```

then we can infer that both of them are AllStarCandidates

```
:Reilly rdf:type :AllStarCandidate.
:Kaneda rdf:type :AllStarCandidate.
```

as desired. Notice that as in the case of intersection, we can only draw the inference in one direction—that is, we can infer that AllStarCandidate $\supseteq$ MVP $\cup$ TopScorer, but not the other way around.

In summary, we can use rdfs:subClassOf to represent statements about intersection and union as follows:

- $C \subseteq A \cap B$ (by making C rdfs:subClassOf both A and B)
- $C \supseteq A \cup B$ (by making both A and B rdfs:subClassOf C).

Property union

One can use rdfs:subPropertyOf to combine properties from different sources in a way that is analogous to the way in which rdfs:subClassOf can be used to combine classes as a union. If two different sources use properties P and Q in similar ways, then a single amalgamated property R can be defined with rdfs:subPropertyOf as follows:

```
:P rdfs:subPropertyOf :R .
:Q rdfs:subPropertyOf :R .
```

For any pair of resources x and y related by P or by Q

```
?x :P ?y .
```

or

```
?x :Q ?y .
```

we can infer that

```
?x :R ?y .
```

EXAMPLE Merging Library Records

Suppose one library has a table in which it keeps lists of patrons and the books they have borrowed, it uses a property called `borrows` to indicate that a patron has borrowed a book. Another library uses `checkedOut` to indicate the same relationship.

Just as in the case of classes, there are a number of ways to handle this situation. If we are sure that the two properties have exactly the same meaning, we can make one property equivalent to another with a creative use of `rdfs:subPropertyOf` as follows:

```
Library1:borrows rdfs:subPropertyOf Library2:checkedOut.
Library2:checkedOut rdfs:subPropertyOf Library1:borrows.
```

Then any relationship that is expressed by one library will be inferred to hold for the other. In such a case, both properties are essentially equivalent.

If we aren't sure that the two properties are used in exactly the same way, but we have an application that we do know wants to treat them as the same, then we use the union pattern to create a common superproperty of both, as follows:

```
Library1:borrows rdfs:subPropertyOf :hasPossession.
Library2:checkedOut rdfs:subPropertyOf :hasPossession.
```

Using these triples, all patrons and books from both libraries will be related by the property `has-Possession`, thus merging information from the two sources.

Property transfer

When modeling the relationship between information that comes from multiple sources, a common requirement is to state that if two entities are related by some relationship in one source, the same entities should be related by a corresponding relationship in the other source. This can be accomplished quite easily in RDFS with a single triple. That is, if we have a property P in one source and property Q in another source, and we wish to state that all uses of P should be considered as uses of Q, we can simply assert that

```
:P rdfs:subPropertyOf :Q.
```

Now, if we have any triple of the form

```
?x :P ?y .
```

then we can infer that

```
?x :Q ?y .
```

It may seem strange to have a design pattern that consists of a single triple, but this use of `rdfs:subPropertyOf` is so pervasive that it really merits being called out as a pattern in its own right.

EXAMPLE Terminology Reconciliation

There are a growing number of standard information representation schemes being published in RDFS form. Information that has been developed in advance of these standards (or in a silo away from them) needs to be retargeted to be compliant with the standard. This process can involve a costly and error-prone search-and-replace process through all the data sources. When the data are represented in RDF, there is often an easier option available, using the Property Transfer pattern.

As a particular example, the *Dublin Core* is a set of standard attributes used to describe bibliographic information for library systems. One of the most frequently used Dublin Core terms is `dc:creator`, which indicates an individual (person or organization) that is responsible for having created a published artifact.

Suppose that a particular legacy bibliography system uses the term *author* to denote the person who created a book. This has worked fine for this system because it was not intended to classify books that were created without an author, such as compilations (which instead have an editor).

How can we make this data conformant to the Dublin Core without performing a costly and error-prone process to copy-and-replace *author* with `dc:creator`? This can be achieved in RDFS with the single triple.

```
:author rdfs:subPropertyOf dc:creator.
```

Now any individual for which the author property has been defined will now have the same value defined for the (standard) `dc:creator` property. The work is done by the RDFS inference engine instead of by an off-line editing process. In particular, this means that legacy applications that are using the *author* property can continue to operate without modification, while newer, Dublin Core–compliant applications can use the inferred data to operate in a standard fashion.

CHALLENGES

Each of the preceding patterns demonstrates the utility of combining one or more RDFS constructs to achieve a particular modeling goal. In this section, we outline a number of modeling scenarios that can be addressed with these patterns and show how they can be applied to address these challenges.

Term reconciliation

One of the most common challenges in terminology management is the resolution of terms used by different agents who want to use their descriptions together in a single federated application. For example, suppose that one agent uses the word *analyst,* and another uses the word *researcher.* There are a number of relationships that can hold between these two usages; we will examine a number of common relations as a series of challenges.

CHALLENGE 5

How do we then enforce the assertion that any member of the one class will automatically be treated as a member of the other? There are a number of approaches to this situation, depending on the details of the situation. All of them can be implemented using the patterns we have identified so far.

Solution

Let's first take the case in which we determine that a particular term in one vocabulary is fully subsumed by a term in another. For example, we determine that a `researcher` is actually a special case of an `analyst`. How can we represent this fact in RDFS?

First, we examine the inferences we want RDFS to draw, given this information. If a researcher is a special case of an analyst, then all researchers are also analysts. We can express this sort of "IF/THEN" relationship with a single `rdfs:subClassOf` relationship, thus:

```
:Researcher rdfs:subClassOf :Analyst.
```

Now any resource that is a `Researcher`, such as

```
:Wenger rdf:type :Researcher.
```

will be inferred to be an `Analyst` as well:

```
:Wenger rdf:type :Analyst.
```

If the relationship happens to go the other way around (that is, all analysts are researchers), the `rdfs:subClassOf` triple can be reversed accordingly.

CHALLENGE 6

What if the relationship is more subtle? Suppose there is considerable semantic overlap between the two concepts `analyst` and `researcher`, but neither concept is defined in a sharp, formal way. It seems that there could be some analysts who are not researchers, and vice versa. Nevertheless, for the purposes of the federated application, we want to treat these two entities as the same. What can we do?

Solution

In such a case, we can use the union pattern outlined previously. We can define a new term (for the federated domain) that is not defined in either of the sources, such as `investigator`. Then we effectively define `investigator` as the union of `researcher` and `analyst`, using the common superproperty idiom:

```
:Analyst rdfs:subClassOf :Investigator.
:Researcher rdfs:subClassOf :Investigator.
```

Described this way, we have made no commitment to a direct relationship between `analyst` and `researcher`, but we have provided a federated handle for speaking of the general class of these entities.

CHALLENGE 7

At the other extreme, suppose that we determine that the two classes really are identical in every way—that these two terms really are just two words for the same thing. In terms of inference, we would like any member of one class to be a member of the other, and vice versa.

Solution

RDFS does not provide a primitive statement of class equivalence, but the same result can be achieved with creative use of `rdfs:subClassOf`:

```
:Analyst rdfs:subClassOf :Researcher.
:Researcher rdfs:subClassOf :Analyst.
```

This may seem a bit paradoxical, especially to someone who is accustomed to object-oriented programming, but the conclusions based on RDFS inferencing are clear. For example, if we know that

```
:Reilly rdf:type :Researcher.
:Kaneda rdf:type :Analyst.
```

then we can infer the other statements:

```
:Reilly rdf:type :Analyst.
:Kaneda rdf:type :Researcher.
```

In effect, the two `rdfs:subClassOf` triples together (or, indeed, any cycle of `rdfs:subClassOf triples`) assert the equivalence of the two classes.

Instance-level data integration

Suppose you have contributions to a single question coming from multiple sources. In the case where the question determines which instances are of interest, there is a simple way to integrate them using `rdfs:subClassOf`. We will give an example from a simplified military domain.

A Command-and-Control Mission Planner wants to determine where ordnance can be targeted or, more specifically, where it cannot be targeted. There are a number of different sources of information that contribute to this decision. One source provides a list of targets and their types, some of which must never be targeted (civilian facilities like churches, schools, and hospitals). Another source provides descriptions of airspaces, some of which are off-limits (e.g., politically defined no-fly zones). A target is determined to be off-limits if it is excluded on the grounds of either of these data sources.

CHALLENGE 8

Define a single class whose contents will include all the individuals from all of these data sources (and any new ones that are subsequently discovered).

Solution

The solution is to use the union construction to join together the two information sources into a single, federated class.

```
fc:CivilianFacility rdfs:subClassOf cc:OffLimitsTarget.
space:NoFlyZone rdfs:subClassOf cc:OffLimitsTarget.
```

Now any instance from either the facility descriptions or the airspace descriptions that have been identified as restricted will be inferred to have `cc:OffLimitsTarget`.

Readable labels with `rdfs:label`

Resources on the Semantic Web are specified by URIs, which provide a globally scoped unique identifier for the resource. But URIs are not particularly attractive or meaningful to people. RDFS provides a built-in property, `rdfs:label`, whose intended use is to provide a printable name for any resource. This provides a standard way for presentation engines (e.g., web pages or desktop applications) to display the print name of a resource.

Depending on the source of the RDF data that are being displayed, there might be another source for human-readable names for any resource. One solution would be to change the display agent to use a particular display property for each resource. A simpler solution can be done entirely using the semantics of RDFS, through a combination of the property union and property transfer patterns.

Suppose we have imported RDF information from an external form, such as a database or spreadsheet, there are two classes of individuals defined by the import: `Person` and `Movie`. For `Person`, a property called `personName` is defined that gives the name by which that person is professionally known. For `Movie`, the property called `movieTitle` gives the title under which the movie was released. Some sample data from this import might be as follows:

```
:Person1 :personName "James Dean".
:Person2 :personName "Elizabeth Taylor".
:Person3 :personName "Rock Hudson".
:Movie1 :movieTitle "Rebel Without a Cause".
:Movie2 :movieTitle "Giant".
:Movie3 :movieTitle "East of Eden".
```

CHALLENGE 9

We would like to use a generic display mechanism, which uses the standard property `rdfs:label` to display information about these people and movies. How can we use RDFS to achieve this?

Solution

The answer is to define each of these properties as subproperties of `rdfs:label` as follows:

```
:personName rdfs:subPropertyOf rdfs:label.
:movieTitle rdfs:subPropertyOf rdfs:label.
```

When the presentation engine queries for `rdfs:label` of any resource, by the rules of RDFS inferencing, it will find the value of `personName` or `movieTitle`, depending on which one is defined for a particular individual. There is no need for the presentation engine to include any code that understands the (domain-specific) distinction between `Person` and `Movie`.

Data typing based on use

Suppose a shipping company has a fleet of vessels that it manages. The fleet includes new vessels that are under construction, vessels that are being repaired, vessels that are currently in service, and vessels that have been retired from service. The information that the company keeps about its ships might include the information in Table 7.1.

The information in the table can be expressed in RDF triples in the manner outlined in Chapter 3. Each row corresponds to a resource of type `ship:Vessel`; triples express the information that appears in the body of the table, such as the following:

```
ship:Berengaria ship:maidenVoyage "June 16, 1913".
ship:QEII ship:nextDeparture "Mar 4, 2010".
```

In addition to the class `ship:Vessel`, we can have subclasses that correspond to the status of the ships, such as the following:

```
ship:DeployedVessel rdfs:subClassOf ship:Vessel.
ship:InServiceVessel rdfs:subClassOf ship:Vessel.
ship:OutOfServiceVessel rdfs:subClassOf ship:Vessel.
```

A `DeployedVessel` is one that has been deployed sometime in its lifetime; an `InServiceVessel` is one that is currently in service; and an `OutOfServiceVessel` is one that is currently out of service (for any reason, including retired ships and ships that have not been deployed).

Table 7.1 Ships

Name	Maiden Voyage	Next Departure	Decommission Date	Destruction Date	Commander
Berengaria	June 16, 1913	–	1938	–	Johnson
QEII	May 2, 1969	March 4, 2010	–	–	Warwick
Titanic	April 10, 1912	–	–	April 14, 1912	Smith
Constitution	July 22, 1798	January 12, 2009	–	–	Preble

CHALLENGE 10

How can we automatically classify each vessel into more specific subclasses, depending on the information we have about it in Table 7.1? For instance, if a vessel has had a maiden voyage, then it is a `ship:DeployedVessel`. If its next departure is set, then it is an `ship:InServiceVessel`. If it has a decommission date or a destruction date, then it is an `ship:OutOfServiceVessel`.

Solution

We can enforce these inferences using `rdfs:domain` as follows:

```
ship:maidenVoyage rdfs:domain ship:DeployedVessel.
ship:nextDeparture rdfs:domain ship:InServiceVessel.
ship:decommissionedDate rdfs:domain ship:OutOfServiceVessel.
ship:destructionDate rdfs:domain ship:OutOfServiceVessel.
```

The whole structure is shown in Figure 7.3. `Vessel` has three subclasses: `DeployedVessel`, `InServiceVessel`, and `OutOfServiceVessel`. Each of these is in the domain of one or more of the properties `maidenVoyage`, `nextDeparture`, `decommissionedDate`, and `destructionDate`, as shown in the preceding triples and in Figure 6.3. Four instances are shown; `maidenVoyage` is specified for all four of them, so all of them have been classified as `DeployedVessel`. `QEII` and `Constitution` have `nextDeparture` dates specified, so these two are classified as `InServiceVessel`. The remaining two vessels, `Titanic` and `Berengaria`, have specified `destructionDate` and `decommissionedDate`, respectively, and thus are classified as `OutOfServiceVessel`.

CHALLENGE 11

All of these inferences concern the subject of the rows, that is, the vessels themselves. It is also possible to draw inferences about the entities in the other table cells.

How can we express the fact that the commander of a ship has the rank of `Captain`?

Solution

We express ranks as classes, as follows:

```
ship:Captain rdfs:subClassOf ship:Officer.
ship:Commander rdfs:subClassOf ship:Officer.
ship:LieutenantCommander rdfs:subClassOf ship:Officer.
ship:Lieutenant rdfs:subClassOf ship:Officer. ship:Ensign
rdfs:subClassOf ship:Officer.
```

Now we can express the fact that a ship's commander has rank `Captain` with `rdfs:range`, as follows:

```
ship:hasCommander rdfs:range ship:Captain.
```

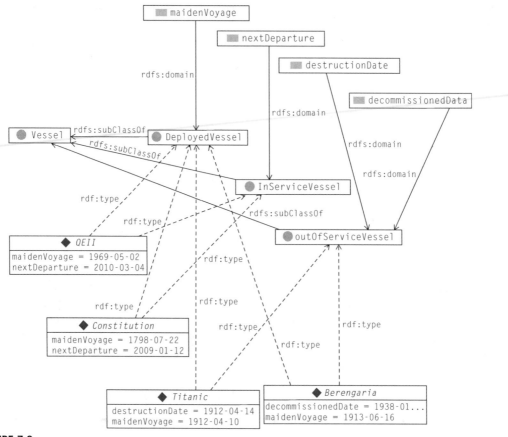

FIGURE 7.3

Inferring classes of vessels from the information known about them.

From the information in Table 7.1, we can infer that all of Johnson, Warwick, Smith, and Preble are members of the class ship:Captain. These inferences, as well as the triples that led to them, can be seen in Figure 7.4.

Filtering undefined data

A related challenge is to sort out individuals based on the information that is defined for them. The set of individuals for which a particular value is defined should be made available for future processing; those for which it is undefined should not be processed.

CHALLENGE 12

In the preceding example, the set of vessels for which nextDeparture is defined could be used as input to a scheduling system that plans group tours. Ships for which no nextDeparture is known should not be considered.

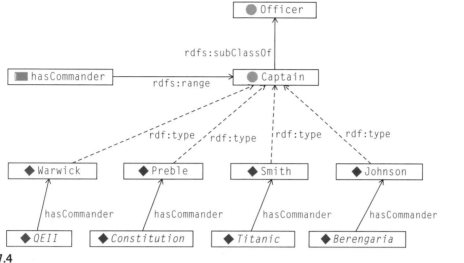

FIGURE 7.4

Inferring that the commanders of the ships have rank "Captain."

Solution

It is easy to define the set of vessels that have `nextDeparture` specified by using `rdfs:domain`. First, define a class of `DepartingVessels` that will have these vessels as its members. Then define this to be the domain of `nextDeparture`:

```
ship:DepartingVessel rdf:type rdfs:Class.
ship:nextDeparture rdfs:domain ship:DepartingVessel.
```

From Table 7.1, only the Constitution and the QEII are members of the class `ship:DepartingVessels` and can be used by a scheduling program (see Figure 7.5).

RDFS and knowledge discovery

The use of `rdfs:domain` and `rdfs:range` differs dramatically from similar notions in other modeling paradigms. Because of the inference-based semantics of RDFS (and OWL), domains and ranges are not used to validate information (as is the case, for example, in OO modeling and XML) but instead are used to determine new information based on old information. We have just seen how this unique aspect of `rdfs:domain` and `rdfs:range` support particular uses of filtering and classifying information.

These definitions are among the most difficult for beginning Semantic Web modelers to come to terms with. It is common for beginning modelers to find these tools clumsy and difficult to use. This difficulty can be ameliorated to some extent by understanding that RDFS in general, and `domain` and `range` in particular, are best understood as tools for knowledge discovery rather than knowledge description. On the Semantic Web, we don't know in advance how information from somewhere else

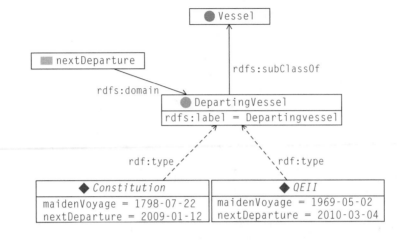

FIGURE 7.5

Ships with a `nextDeparture` specified are `DepartingVessels`.

on the Web should be interpreted in a new context. The RDFS definitions of `domain` and `range` allow us to discover new things about our data based on its use.

What does this mean for the skillful use of `domain` and `range` in RDFS? They are not to be used lightly—that is, merely as a way to bundle together several properties around a class. Filtering results such as those shown in these challenge problems are the result of the use of `domain` and `range`. Proper use of `domain` and `range` must take these results into account. Recommended use of `domain` and `range` goes one step further; its use is in one of these patterns, where some particular knowledge filtering or discovery pattern is intended. When used in this way (e.g., using `domain` to describe which of the ships are departing), it is guaranteed that the meaning of `domain` and `range` will be appropriate even in a web setting.

MODELING WITH DOMAINS AND RANGES

Although RDFS has considerable applicability in data amalgamation and the simplicity of its small number of axioms makes it compact and easy to implement, there are some confusions that arise even in very simple modeling situations when using RDFS.

Multiple domains/ranges

In our shipping example, we had two definitions for the `nextDeparture` domain:

```
ship:nextDeparture rdfs:domain DepartingVessel.
ship:nextDeparture rdfs:domain InServiceVessel.
```

What is the interpretation of these two statements? Is the `nextDeparture` domain `Departing-Vessel`, `InServiceVessel`, or both? What does this sort of construction mean?

The right way to understand what a statement or set of statements means in RDFS is to understand what inferences can be drawn from them. Let's consider the case of the `QEII`, for which we have the following asserted triples:

```
ship:QEII ship:maidenVoyage "May 2, 1969".
ship:QEII ship:nextDeparture "Mar 4, 2010".
ship:QEII ship:hasCommander Warwick.
```

The rules of inference for `rdfs:domain` allow us to draw the following conclusions:

```
ship:QEII rdf:type ship:DepartingVessel.
ship:QEII rdf:type ship:InServiceVessel.
```

Each of these conclusions is drawn from the definition of `rdfs:domain`, as applied, respectively, to each of the domain declarations just given. This behavior is not a result of a discussion of "what will happen when there are multiple domain statements?" but rather a simple logical conclusion based on the definition of `rdfs:domain`.

How can we interpret these results? Any vessel for which a `nextDeparture` is specified will be inferred to be a member (i.e., `rdf:type`) of both `DepartingVessel` and `InServiceVessel` classes. Effectively, any such vessel will be inferred to be in the *intersection* of the two classes specified in the domain statements. This is something that many people find counterintuitive, even though it is "correct" in RDFS.

In object-oriented modeling, when one asserts that a property (or field, or variable, or slot) is associated with a class (as is done by `rdfs:domain`), the intuition is that "it is now permissible to use this property to describe members of this class." If there are two such statements, then the intuitive interpretation is that "it is now permissible to use this property with members of either of these classes." Effectively, multiple domain declarations are interpreted in the sense of set union: You may now use this property to describe any item in the *union* of the two specified domains. For someone coming in with this sort of expectation, the *intersection* behavior of RDFS can be something of a surprise.

This interaction makes it necessary to exercise some care when modeling information with the expectation that it will be merged with other information. Let's suppose we have another modeling context in which a company is managing a team of traveling salespeople. Each salesperson has a schedule of business trips. Some of the triples that define this model are as follows:

```
sales:SalesPerson rdfs:subClassOf foaf:Person.
sales:sells rdfs:domain sales:SalesPerson.
sales:sells rdfs:range sales:ProductLine.
sales:nextDeparture rdfs:domain sales:SalesPerson.
```

That is, we have a sales force that covers certain `ProductLines`; each member travels on a regular basis, and it is useful for us to track the date of the next departure of any particular `SalesPerson`.

Suppose we were to merge the information for our sales force management with the schedules of the ocean liners. This merge becomes interesting if we map some of the items in one model to items in another. An obvious candidate for such a mapping is between `sales:nextDeparture` and `ship:nextDeparture`. Both refer to dates, and the intuition is that they specify the next departure date of something or someone. So a simple connection to make between the two models would be to link these two properties, such as the following:

```
sales:nextDeparture rdfs:subPropertyOf ship:nextDeparture.
ship:nextDeparture rdfs:subPropertyOf sales:nextDeparture.
```

using the mutual `subPropertyOf` pattern. The intuition here is that the two uses of `nextDeparture`, one for ships and the other for sales, are in fact the same.

But wait! Let's see what inferences are drawn from this merger. Suppose we have a triple that describes a member of the sales force:

```
sales:Johannes sales:nextDeparture "May 31, 2008".
```

and we already have the triple about the `QEII`:

```
ship:QEII ship:nextDeparture "Mar 4, 2010".
```

What inferences can we draw from these two triples? Using `rdfs:subPropertyOf` inferences first, then `rdfs:domain` inferences, and finally using the `rdfs:subClassOf` triple with `foaf:Person`, we get the following inferred triples:

```
sales:Johannes ship:nextDeparture "May 31, 2008".
ship:QEII sales:nextDeparture "Mar 4, 2010".
sales:Johannes rdf:type ship:DepartingVessel.
ship:QEII rdf:type sales:SalesPerson.
ship:QEII rdf:type foaf:Person.
```

These inferences start off innocently enough, but they become more and more counterintuitive as they go on, and eventually (when the `QEII` is classified as a `foaf:Person`) become completely outrageous (or perhaps dangerously misleading, especially given that the Monarch herself might actually be a `foaf:Person`, causing the inferences to confuse the Monarch with the ship named after her). The asserted triples, and the inferences that can be drawn from them, are shown in Figure 7.6.

It is easy to lay blame for this unfortunate behavior at the feet of the definition of `rdfs:domain`, but to do so would throw out the baby with the bathwater. The real issue in this example is that we have made a modeling error. The error resulted from the overzealous urge to jump to the conclusion that two properties should be mapped so closely to each other. The ramifications of using `subPropertyOf` (or any other RDFS construct) can be subtle and far-reaching.

In particular, when each of these models stated its respective domain and range statements about `sales:nextDeparture` and `ship:nextDeparture`, respectively, it was saying, "Whenever you see any individual described by `sales:nextDeparture` (resp. `ship:nextDeparture`), that individual is known to be of type `sales:SalesPerson` (resp. `ship:DepartingVessel`)." This is quite a strong statement, and it should be treated as such. In particular, it would be surprising if two properties defined so specifically would not have extreme ramifications when merged.

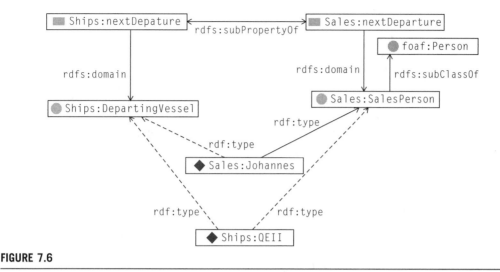

FIGURE 7.6

Inferences resulting from merging two notions of `nextDeparture`.

So what is the solution? Should we refrain from merging properties? This is hardly a solution in the spirit of the Semantic Web. Should we avoid making strong statements about properties? This will not help us to make useful models. Should we change the RDFS standard so we can't make these statements? This is a bit extreme, but as we shall see, OWL does provide some more subtle constructs for property definitions that allow for finer-grained modeling. Rather, the solution lies in understanding the source of the modeling error that is at the heart of this example: We should refrain from merging things, like the two notions of `nextDeparture`, whose meanings have important differences.

Using the idioms and patterns of RDFS shown in this chapter, there are more things we can do, depending on our motivation for the merger. In particular, we can still merge these two properties but without making such a strong statement about their equivalence.

If, for instance, we just want to merge the two notions of `nextDeparture` to drive a calendar application that shows all the departure dates for the sales force and the ocean liner fleet, then what we really want is a single property that will provide us the information we need (as we did in the property union pattern). Rather than mapping the properties from one domain to another, instead we map both properties to a third, domain-neutral property, thus:

```
ship:nextDeparture rdfs:subPropertyOf cal:nextDeparture.
sales:nextDeparture rdfs:subPropertyOf cal:nextDeparture.
```

Notice that the amalgamating property `cal:nextDeparture` doesn't need any domain information at all. After all, we don't need to make any (further) inferences about the types of the entities that it is used to describe. Now we can infer that

```
sales:Johannes cal:nextDeparture "May 31, 2008".
ship:QEII cal:nextDeparture "Mar 4, 2010".
```

A single calendar display, sorted by the property `cal:nextDeparture`, will show these two dates, but no further inference can be made. In particular, no inferences will be made about considering the `QEII` as a member of the sales force or `Johannes` as a sailing vessel.

What can we take from this example into our general Semantic Web modeling practice? Even with a small number of primitives, RDFS provides considerable subtlety for modeling relationships between different data sources. But with this power comes the ability to make subtle and misleading errors. The way to understand the meaning of modeling connections is by tracing the inferences. The ramifications of any modeling mapping can be worked through by following the simple inference rules of RDFS.

NONMODELING PROPERTIES IN RDFS

In addition to the properties described so far, RDFS also provides a handful of properties that have no defined inference semantics—that is, there are no inferences that derive from them. We already saw one example of such a property, `rdfs:label`. No inferences are drawn from `rdfs:label`, so in that sense it has no semantics. Nevertheless, it does by convention have an operational semantics in that it describes the ways in which display agents interact with the model.

Cross-referencing files: `rdfs:seeAlso`

Every resource in a Semantic Web model is specified by a URI that can also be dereferenced and used as a URL. In the case where this URL resolves to a real document, this provides a place where defining information about a resource can be stored.

In some contexts, it is useful to include some supplementary information about a resource for its use in a certain context. This is usually meant to be other documents that might help explain the entity—for example, we might include a pointer to a Wikipedia entry, or a pointer to related data (e.g., if the resource corresponds to a table from a database, the supplementary information could be the other tables from the same database) or even to another RDF or RDFS file that contains linked information. For such cases, `rdfs:seeAlso` provides a way to specify the web location of this supplementary information (i.e. it should be a URI, not a human-readable property). `rdfs:seeAlso` has no formal semantics, so the precise behavior of any processor when it encounters `rdfs:seeAlso` is not specified. A common behavior of tools that encounter `rdfs:seeAlso` links is to expose those links in a browser or application interface through which the RDFS document is being used.

Organizing vocabularies: `rdfs:isDefinedBy`

Just as `rdfs:seeAlso` can provide supplementary information about a resource, `rdfs:isDefinedBy` provides a link to the primary source of information about a resource. This allows modelers to specify where the definitional description of a resource can be found. `rdfs:isDefinedBy` is defined in RDF to be a `rdfs:subPropertyOf` of `rdfs:seeAlso`.

Model documentation: `rdfs:comment`

Just as in any computer language (modeling languages, markup languages, or programming languages), sometimes it is helpful if a document author can leave natural language comments about a model for future readers to see. Since RDFS is implemented entirely in RDF, the comment feature is also implemented in RDF. To make a comment on some part of a model, simply assert a triple using the property `rdfs:comment` as a predicate. For example:

```
sales:nextDeparture rdfs:comment "This indicates the next
        planned departure date for a salesperson."
```

SUMMARY

RDFS is the schema language for RDF; it describes constructs for types of objects (`Classes`), relating types to one another (`subClasses`), properties that describe objects (`Properties`), and relationships between them (`subProperty`). The Class system in RDFS includes a simple and elegant notion of inheritance, based on set inclusion; one class is a subclass of another means that instances of the one are also instances of the other.

The RDFS language benefits from the distributed nature of RDF by being expressed in RDF itself. All schema information (classes, subclasses, subproperties, domain, range, etc.) is expressed in RDF triples. In particular, this makes schema information, as well as data, subject to the AAA slogan: Anyone can say Anything about Any topic—even about the schema.

The semantics of RDFS is expressed through the mechanism of inferencing; that is, the meaning of any construct in RDFS is given by the inferences that can be inferred from it. For example, it is this simple but powerful mechanism for specifying semantics that allows for the short and elegant definition of subclass and subproperty.

RDFS also includes the constructs `rdfs:domain` and `rdfs:range` to describe the relationship between properties and classes. The meanings of these constructs are given by very simple rules, but these rules have subtle and far-reaching impact. The rules may be simple, but the statements are powerful.

Even with its small set of constructs and simple rules, RDFS allows for the resolution of a wide variety of integration issues. Whenever you might think of doing a global find-and-replace in a set of structured data, consider using `rdfs:subPropertyOf` or `rdfs:subClassOf` instead. It may seem trivial to say that one should merge only entities from multiple sources that don't have important differences. Using the inference mechanism of RDFS, we can determine just what happens when we do merge things and judge whether the results are desirable or dangerous. Although RDFS does not provide logical primitives like union and intersection, it is often possible to achieve desired inferences by using specific patterns of `subClassOf` and `subPropertyOf`. RDFS provides a framework through which information can flow; we can think of `subClassOf` and `subPropertyOf` as the IF/THEN facility of semantic modeling. This utility persists even when we move on to modeling in OWL. In fact, using `subClassOf` in this way provides a cornerstone of OWL modeling.

When used in careful combination, the constructs of RDFS are particularly effective at defining how differently structured information can be used together in a uniform way.

Fundamental concepts

The following fundamental concepts were introduced in this chapter.

rdfs:subClassOf—Relation between classes, that the members of one class are included in the members of the other.

rdfs:subPropertyOf—Relation between properties, that the pairs related by one property are included in the other.

rdfs:domain and *rdfs:range*—Description of a property that determines class membership of individuals related by that property.

Logical operations (Union, Intersection, etc.) in RDFS—RDFS constructs can be used to simulate certain logical combinations of sets and properties.

RDFS-Plus

RDFS provides a very limited set of inference capabilities that, as we have seen, have considerable utility in a Semantic Web setting for merging information from multiple sources. In this chapter, we take the first step toward the Web Ontology Language, OWL, in which more elaborate constraints on how information is to be merged can be specified. We have selected a particular set of OWL constructs to present at this stage. This set was selected to satisfy a number of goals:

- Pedagogically, these constructs constitute a gentle addition to the constructs that are already familiar from RDFS, increasing the power of the language without making a large conceptual leap from RDFS.
- Practically, we have found that this set of OWL constructs has considerable utility in the information integration projects we have done. In fact, it is much easier to find and describe case studies using RDFS-Plus this set of OWL constructs than it is to find case studies that use RDFS by itself.
- Computationally, this subset of OWL can be implemented using a wide variety of inferencing technologies, lessening the dependency between the Semantic Web and any particular technology.

153

For these reasons, we feel that this particular subset will have value beyond the pedagogical value in this book. We call this subset of OWL *RDFS-Plus,* because we see a trend among vendors of Semantic Web tools and Web applications designers for determining a subset of OWL that is at the same time useful and can be implemented quickly. We have identified this particular subset via an informal poll of cutting-edge vendors, and from our own experience with early adopters of Semantic Web technology.

Just as was the case for RDFS, RDFS-Plus is expressed entirely in RDF. The only distinction is that there are a number of resources, all in the namespace *owl.* The meaning of these resources is specified, as before, by the rules that govern the inferences that can be made from them. As we did for RDFS, we will specify the rules that govern the inferences using SPARQL CONSTRUCT queries.

In the case of RDFS, we saw how the actions of an inference engine could be used to combine various features of the schema language in novel ways. This trend will continue for RDFS-Plus, but as you might expect, the more constructs we have to begin with, the more opportunity we have for useful and novel combinations.

INVERSE

The names of many of the OWL constructs come from corresponding names in mathematics. Despite their mathematical names, they also have a more common, everyday interpretation. The idea owl:inverseOf is a prime example; if a relationship—say, hasParent—is interesting enough to mention in a model, then it's a good bet that another relationship—say, hasChild—is also interesting. Because of the evocative names hasParent and hasChild, you can guess the relationship between them, but of course the computer can't. The OWL construct owl:inverseOf makes the relationship between hasParent and hasChild explicit, and describes precisely what it means.

In mathematics, the inverse of a function f (usually written as f^{-1}) is the function that satisfies the property that if $f(x) = y$, then $f^{-1}(y) = x$. Similarly in OWL, the inverse of a property is another property that reverses its direction.

To be specific, we look at the meaning of owl:inverseOf. In OWL, as in RDFS, the meaning of any construct is given by the inferences that can be drawn from it. We can express the rule for owl:inverseOf in SPARQL as follows:

```
CONSTRUCT {?y ?q ?x}
WHERE {?p owl:inverseOf ?q .
       ?x ?p ?y . }
```

In the examples in the book, we have already seen a number of possibilities for inverses, though we haven't used them so far. In our Shakespeare examples, we have the triples

```
lit:Shakespeare lit:wrote lit:Macbeth.
lit:Macbeth lit:setIn geo:Scotland.
```

If, in addition to these triples, we also state some inverses, such as:

```
lit:wrote owl:inverseOf lit:writtenBy.
lit:settingFor owl:inverseOf lit:setIn.
```

then we can infer that

```
lit:Macbeth lit:writtenBy lit:Shakespeare.
geo:Scotland lit:settingFor lit:Macbeth.
```

Although the meaning of `owl:inverseOf` is not difficult to describe, what is the utility of such a construct in a modeling language? After all, the effect of `inverseOf` can be achieved just as easily by writing the query differently. For instance, if we want to know all the plays that are `setIn` Scotland, we can use the inverse property `settingFor` in our query pattern, such as

```
{geo:Scotland lit:settingfor?play.}
```

Because of the semantics of the inverse property, this will give us all plays that were `setIn` Scotland.

But we could have avoided the use of the inverse property and simply written the query as

```
{?play lit:setIn geo:Scotland.}
```

We get the same answers, and we don't need an extra construct in the modeling language.

While this is true, `owl:inverseOf` nevertheless does have considerable utility in modeling, based on how it can interact with other modeling constructs. In the next two challenges, we'll see how some earlier challenges can be extended using inverses.

CHALLENGE 2, CONTINUED: USING SPARQL TO TRANSFORM HIERARCHICAL DATA

In Chapter 5, we saw a Challenge problem to use SPARQL to transform hierarchical data. The original data was expressed using a variety of properties like `hasSon`, `hasMother`, `hasDaughter`, and `hasFather`. The response to the challenge involved a series of SPARQL queries to transform e.g., `hasMother` into `hasParent`. The queries that accomplished the transformations all had a very similar form, e.g.,

CONSTRUCT {?s :hasParent ?o}
WHERE {?s :hasMother ?o}

The transformation that this query accomplishes can also be represented in RDFS. This query says "whenever a triple uses `hasMother`, infer a similar triple with `hasParent`." This can be expressed in RDFS by relating the two properties together with `subPropertyOf`, thus:

```
:hasMother rdfs:subPropertyOf :hasParent .
```

When we combine this statement with the definition of `subPropertyOf`, we see that we come to the same conclusions—from every triple that uses `hasMother` we can infer a similar triple using `hasParent`.

Some of the queries included a bit of a twist on this pattern—for example, one query rectified uses of `hasSon` as follows:

CONSTRUCT {?s :hasParent ?o}
WHERE {?o :hasSon ?s}

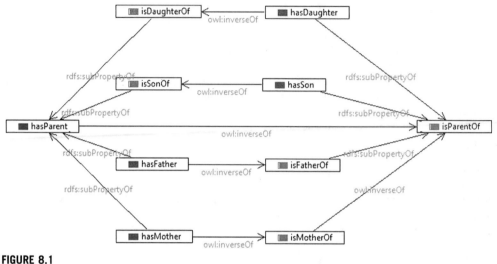

FIGURE 8.1

Display of family relationships, and how they are connected. The figure shows only the
`subPropertyOf` relationships, not the `inverseOf` relationships.

A simple `subPropertyOf` relationship can't capture the meaning of this query, because the order of the subject and object are reversed. We can't model this relationship in RDFS alone. But with the addition of `inverseOf`, we can do it. We will need to introduce a new property that is the inverse of `hasSon`. We'll call it `isSonOf`.

```
:isSonOf owl:inverseOf :hasSon .
:isSonOf rdfs:subPropertyOf :hasParent .
```

Using the definition of `subPropertyOf` from RDFS, and the definition of `inverseOf` from OWL, we get the same result as we did from the SPARQL query—from each triple that use `hasSon`, we can infer a new triple using `hasParent`, with the appropriate subject and object.

One advantage to representing these relationships in RDFS-Plus is that all the relationships among these properties are represented in a single model, and can even be displayed visually. If we define all the variations of sons, daughters, parents, etc., we can see them in a single display as shown in Figure 8.1.

This is a fairly common modeling pattern in RDFS-Plus, in which a hierarchy of properties is specified, along with a corresponding hierarchy of inverses.

Challenge: integrating data that do not want to be integrated

In the Property Union challenge, we had two properties, `borrows` and `checkedOut`. We were able to combine them under a single property by making them both `rdfs:subPropertyOf` the same parent property, `hasPosession`. We were fortunate that the two sources of data happened to link a `Patron` as the subject to a `Book` as the object (i.e., they had the same domain and range). Suppose instead that the second source was an index of books, and for each book there was a field specifying the patron the book was `signedTo` (i.e., the domain and range are reversed).

CHALLENGE 13

How can we merge `signedTo` and `borrows` in a way analogous to how we merged `borrows` and `checkedOut`, given that `signedTo` and `borrows` don't share good domains and ranges?

Solution

The solution involves a simple use of `owl:inverseOf` to specify two properties for which the domain and range do match, as required for the merge. We define a new property—say, `signedOut`—as the inverse of `signedTo`, as follows:

```
:signedTo owl:inverseOf :signedOut.
```

Now we can use the original Property Union pattern to merge `signedOut` and `borrows` into the single `hasPossession` property:

```
:signedOut rdfs:subPropertyOf :hasPossession.
:borrows rdfs:subPropertyOf :hasPossession.
```

So if we have some data expressed using `signedTo`, along with data expressed with `borrows`, as follows:

```
:Amit :borrows :MobyDick.
:Marie :borrows :Orlando.
:LeavesOfGrass :signedTo :Jim.
:WutheringHeights :signedTo :Yoshi.
```

then with the rule for `inverseOf`, we have the additional triples

```
:Jim :signedOut :LeavesOfGrass.
:Yoshi :signedOut :WutheringHeights.
```

and with `subPropertyOf`, we have

```
:Amit :hasPossession :MobyDick.
:Marie :hasPossession :Orlando.
:Jim :hasPossession :LeavesOfGrass.
:Yoshi :hasPossession :WutheringHeights.
```

as desired.

Solution (alternative)

There is a certain asymmetry in this solution; the choice to specify an inverse for `signedTo` rather than for `hasPossession` was somewhat arbitrary. Another solution that also uses `owl:inverseOf` and `rdfs:subPropertyOf` and is just as viable as the first is the following:

```
:signedTo :rdfs:subPropertyOf :possessedBy.
:borrows rdfs:subPropertyOf :hasPossession.
:possessedBy owl:inverseOf :hasPossession.
```

These statements use the same rules for `owl:inverseOf` and `rdfs:subPropertyOf` but in a different order, resulting in the same `hasPossession` triples. Which solution is better in what situations? How can we tell which to use?

If all we were concerned with was making sure that the inferences about `hasPossession` will be supported, then there would be no reason to prefer one solution over the other. But modeling in the Semantic Web is not just about supporting desired inferences but also about supporting reuse. What if someone else

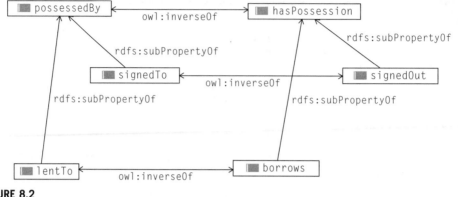

FIGURE 8.2

Systematic combination of `inverseOf` and `subPropertyOf`.

wants to use this model in a slightly different way? A future query is just as likely to be interested in `hasPossession` as `possessedBy`. Furthermore, we might in the future wish to combine `has Possession` (or `possessedBy`) with another property. For this reason, one might choose to use both solutions together by using both `inverseOf` and `subPropertyOf` in a systematic way—that is, by specifying inverses for every property, regardless of the `subPropertyOf` level. In this case, this results in

```
:signedTo owl:inverseOf :signedOut.
:signedTo rdfs:subPropertyOf :possessedBy.
:signedOut rdfs:subPropertyOf :hasPossession.
:lentTo owl:inverseOf :borrows.
:lentTo rdfs:subPropertyOf :possessedBy.
:borrows rdfs:subPropertyOf :hasPossession.
:possessedBy owl:inverseOf :hasPossession.
```

The systematicity of this structure can be more readily seen in Figure 8.2. The attentive reader might have one more concern about the systematicity of Figure 8.2—in particular, the selection of which properties are the subject of `owl:inverseOf` and which are the object (in the diagram, which ones go on the left or on the right of the diagram) is arbitrary. Shouldn't there be three more `owl:inverseOf` triples, pointing from right to left? Indeed, there should be, but there is no need to assert these triples, as we shall see in the next challenge.

Challenge: using the modeling language to extend the modeling language

It is not unusual for beginning modelers to look at the list of constructs defined in OWL and say, "There is a feature of the OWL language I would like to use that is very similar to the ones that are included. Why did they leave it out? I would prefer to build my model using a different set of primitives." In many cases, the extra language feature that they desire is actually already supported by OWL as a combination of other features. It is a simple matter of using these features in combination.

CHALLENGE 14

For example, RDFS allows you to specify that one class is a `subClassOf` another, but you might like to think of it the other way around (perhaps because of the structure of some legacy data you want to work with) and specify that something is `superClassOf` something else. That is, you want the parent class to be the subject of all the definitional triples. Using your own namespace `myowl:` for this desired relation, you would like to have the triples look like this:

```
:Food myowl:superClassOf :BakedGood;
      myowl:superClassOf :Confectionary;
      myowl:superClassOf :PackagedFood;
      myowl:superClassOf :PreparedFood;
      myowl:superClassOf :ProcessedFood.
```

If we instead use `rdfs:subClassOf`, all the triples go the other way around; *Food* will be the object of each triple, and all the types of *Food* will be the subjects.

Since OWL does not provide a `superClassOf` resource (or to speak more correctly, OWL does not define any inference rules that will provide any semantics for a `superClassOf` resource), what can we do?

Solution

What do we want `myowl:superClassOf` to mean? For every triple of the form

```
?P myowl:superClassOf ?Q.
```

we want to be able to infer that

```
?Q rdfs:subClassOf ?P.
```

This can be accomplished simply by declaring an inverse

```
myowl:superClassOf owl:inverseOf rdfs:subClassOf.
```

It is a simple application of the rule for `owl:inverseOf` to see that this accomplishes the desired effect. Nevertheless, this is not a solution that many beginning modelers think of. It seems to them that they have no right to modify or extend the meaning of the OWL language or to make statements about the OWL and RDFS resources (like `rdfs:subClassOf`). But remember the AAA slogan of RDF: *Anyone can say Anything about Any topic.* In particular, a modeler can say things about the resources defined in the standard.

In fact, we can take this slogan so far as to allow a modeler to say

```
rdfs:subClassOf owl:inverseOf rdfs:superClassOf.
```

This differs from the previous triple in that the subject is a resource in the (standard) RDFS namespace. The RDF slogan allows a modeler to say this, and indeed, there is nothing in the standards that will prevent it. However, referring to a resource in the RDFS namespace is likely to suggest to human readers of the model that this relationship is part of the RDFS standard. Since one purpose of a model is to communicate to other human beings, it is generally not a good idea to make statements that are likely to be misleading, so we do not endorse this practice.

Challenge: the marriage of Shakespeare

Consider a simple model about the marriage of Shakespeare—a model with only one triple.

```
bio:AnneHathaway bio:married lit:Shakespeare.
```

If we were to query this with the SPARQL query

```
SELECT ?who
WHERE  {?lit:Shakespeare bio:married ?who}
```

We would get no answer—Shakespeare married no one, despite our intuition that marriage is a two-way street. We would like to express this part of our understanding of how marriage works in a model.

CHALLENGE 15

How can we infer marriages in the reverse direction from which they are asserted?

Solution

We could do this by simply declaring bio:married to be its own inverse, thus:

```
bio:married owl:inverseOf bio:married.
```

Now any triple that used bio:married would automatically be inferred to hold in the other direction. In particular, if we asserted

```
bio:AnneHathaway bio:married lit:Shakespeare.
```

we could infer that

```
lit:Shakespeare bio:married bio:AnneHathaway.
```

This pattern of self-inverses is so common that it has been built into OWL using a special construct called owl:SymmetricProperty.

SYMMETRIC PROPERTIES

owl:inverseOf relates one property to another. The special case in which these two properties are the same (as was the case for bio:married for the Shakespeare example) is common enough that the OWL language provides a special name for it: owl:SymmetricProperty. Unlike owl:inverseOf, which is a property that relates two other properties, owl:SymmetricProperty is just an aspect of a single property and is expressed in OWL as a Class. We express that a property is symmetric in the same way as we express membership in any class—in other words:

```
:P rdf:type owl:SymmetricProperty.
```

As usual, we express the meaning of this statement in SPARQL:

```
CONSTRUCT {?p owl:inverseOf ?p. }
WHERE {?p a owl:SymmetricProperty . }
```

So in the case of the marriage of Shakespeare, we can simply assert that

```
bio:married rdf:type owl:SymmetricProperty.
```

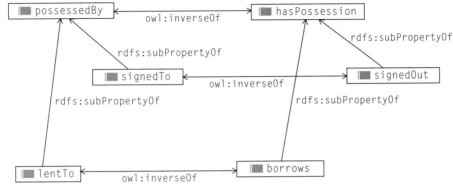

FIGURE 8.3

Systematic combination of `inverseOf` and `subPropertyOf`. Contrast this with Figure 8.2, with one-directional inverses.

Using OWL to extend OWL

As we describe more and more of the power of the OWL modeling language, there will be more and more opportunities to define at least some aspects of a new construct in terms of previously defined constructs. We can use this method to streamline our presentation of the OWL language. We have seen a need for this already in figure Figure 8.2, in which all of our inverses are expressed in one direction but we really need to have them go both ways, as shown in Figure 8.3.

We asserted the triples from left to right—namely:

```
:possessedBy owl:inverseOf :hasPossession.
:signedTo owl:inverseOf :signedOut.
:lentTo owl:inverseOf :borrows.
```

But we would like to be able to infer the triples from right to left—namely:

```
:hasPossession owl:inverseOf :possessedBy.
:signedOut owl:inverseOf :signedTo.
:borrows owl:inverseOf :lentTo.
```

CHALLENGE 16

How can we infer all of these triples without having to assert them?

Solution

Since we want `owl:inverseOf` to work in both directions, this can be done easily by asserting that `owl:inverseOf` is its own inverse, thus:

```
owl:inverseOf owl:inverseOf owl:inverseOf.
```

You might have done a double take when you read that `owl:inverseOf` is its own inverse. Fortunately, we now have a more readable and somewhat more understandable way to say this—namely:

```
owl:inverseOf rdf:type owl:SymmetricProperty.
```

In either case, we get the inferences we desire for Figure 8.3, in which the inverses point both ways. This also means that all the inferences in both directions will always be found.

TRANSITIVITY

In mathematics, a relation *R* is said to be *transitive* if *R(a,b)* and *R(b,c)* implies *R(a,c)*. The same idea is used for the OWL construct `owl:TransitiveProperty`. Just like `owl:SymmetricProperty`, `owl:TransitiveProperty` is a class of properties, so a model can assert that a property is a member of the class

```
:P rdf:type owl:TransitiveProperty.
```

The meaning of this is given by a somewhat more elaborate rule than we have seen so far in this chapter.

```
CONSTRUCT {?x ?p ?z .}
WHERE {?x ?p ?y .
       ?y ?p ?x .
       ?p a owl:TransitiveProperty . }
```

Notice that there is no need for even more elaborate rules like

```
CONSTRUCT {?a ?p ?d .}
WHERE {?a ?p ?b .
       ?b ?p ?c .
       ?c ?p ?d . }
```

since this conclusion can be reached by applying the simple rule over and over again.

Some typical examples of transitive properties include ancestor/descendant (if Victoria is an ancestor of Edward, and Edward is an ancestor of Elizabeth, then Victoria is an ancestor of Elizabeth) and geographical containment (if Osaka is in Japan, and Japan is in Asia, then Osaka is in Asia).

Challenge: relating parents to ancestors

A model of genealogy will typically include notions of parents as well as ancestors, and we'd like them to fit together. But parents are not transitive (my parents' parents are not my parents), whereas ancestors are.

CHALLENGE 17

How can we allow a model to maintain consistent ancestry information, given parentage information.

Solution

Start by defining the parent property to be a `subPropertyOf` the ancestor property, thus:

```
:hasParent rdfs:subPropertyOf :hasAncestor.
```

Then declare ancestor (only) to be a transitive property:

```
:hasAncestor rdf:type owl:TransitiveProperty.
```

Let's see how this works on some examples.

```
:Alexia :hasParent :WillemAlexander.
:WillemAlexander :hasParent :Beatrix.
:Beatrix :hasParent :Wilhelmina.
```

Because of the subPropertyOf relation between hasParent and hasAncestor and the fact that hasAncestor is a TransitiveProperty, we can infer that

```
:Alexia :hasAncestor :WillemAlexander.
:WillemAlexander :hasAncestor :Beatrix.
:Alexia :hasAncestor :Beatrix.
:WillemAlexander :hasAncestor :Wilhelmina.
:Alexia :hasAncestor :Wilhelmina.
```

Information about the heritage is integrated, regardless of whether it originated with hasParent or hasAncestor. Information about hasParent, on the other hand, is only available as it was directly asserted because it was not declared to be transitive. The results of this inference are shown in Figure 8.4.

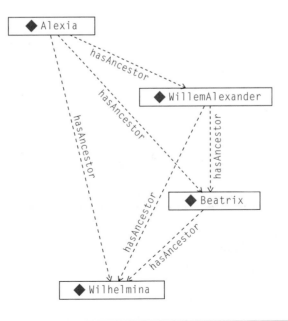

FIGURE 8.4

Inferences from transitive properties.

Challenge: layers of relationships

Sometimes it can be somewhat controversial whether a property is transitive or not. For instance, the relationship that is often expressed by the words "part of" in English is sometimes transitive (a piston is part of the engine, and the engine is part of the car; is the piston part of the car?) and sometimes not (Mick Jagger's thumb is part of Mick Jagger, and Mick Jagger is part of the Rolling Stones; is Mick Jagger's thumb part of the Rolling Stones?). In the spirit of anticipating possible uses of a model, it is worthwhile to support both points of view whenever there is any chance that controversy might arise.

CHALLENGE 18

How can we simultaneously maintain transitive and nontransitive versions of the `partOf` information?

Solution

We can define two versions of the `partOf` property in different namespaces (or with different names) with one a `subPropertyOf` the other, and with the superproperty declared as transitive:

```
dm:partOf rdfs:subPropertyOf gm:partOf.
gm:partOf rdf:type owl:TransitiveProperty.
```

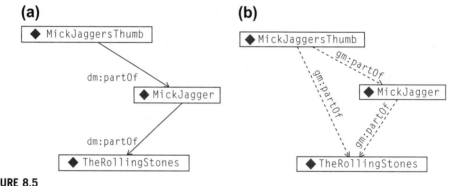

FIGURE 8.5

Different interpretations of `partOf`.

Depending on which interpretation of `partOf` any particular application needs, it can query the appropriate property. For those who prefer to think that Mick Jagger's thumb is not part of the Rolling Stones, the original `dm:partOf` property is useful. For those who instead consider that Mick Jagger's thumb is part of the Rolling Stones, the transitive superproperty `gm:partOf` is appropriate (see Figure 8.5)

Managing networks of dependencies

The same modeling patterns we have been using to manage relationships (like ancestry) or set containment (like part of) can be used just as well in a very different setting—namely, to manage networks of dependencies. In the series of challenges that follow, we will see how the familiar constructs of `rdfs:subPropertyOf`, `owl:inverseOf`, and `owl:TransitiveProperty` can be combined in novel ways to model important aspects of such networks.

A common application of this idea is in workflow management. In a complex working situation, a variety of tasks must be repeatedly performed in a set sequence. The idea of workflow management is that the sequence can be represented explicitly and the progress of each task tracked in that sequence. Why would someone want to model workflow in a Semantic Web? The answer is for the same reason one wants to put anything on the Web: so that parts of the workflow can be shared with others, encouraging reuse, review, and publication of work fragments.

Real workflow specifications are far too detailed to serve as examples in a book, so we will use a simple example to show how it works. Let's make some ice cream, using the following recipe:

Slice a vanilla bean lengthwise, and scrape the contents into 1 cup of heavy cream. Bring the mixture to a simmer, but do not boil. While the cream is heating, separate three eggs. Add 1/2 cup white sugar to the eggs and beat until fluffy. Gradually add the warm cream, beating constantly. Return the custard mixture to medium heat, and cook until mixture leaves a heavy coat on the back of

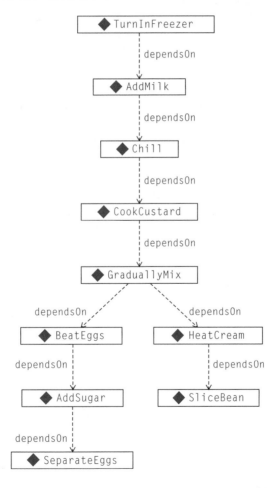

FIGURE 8.6

Dependencies for homemade ice cream.

a spatula. Chill well. Combine custard with 1 cup whole milk, and turn in ice cream freezer according to manufacturer's instructions.

First, let's use a property `dependsOn` to represent the dependencies between the steps and define its inverse `enables`, since each step enables the next in the correct execution of the workflow:

```
:dependsOn owl:inverseOf :enables.
```

Now we can define the dependency structure of the recipe steps:

```
:SliceBean :enables :HeatCream.
:SeparateEggs :enables :AddSugar.
:AddSugar :enables :BeatEggs
:BeatEggs :enables :GraduallyMix.
:HeatCream :enables :GraduallyMix.
:GraduallyMix :enables :CookCustard.
:CookCustard :enables :Chill.
:Chill :enables :AddMilk.
:AddMilk :enables :TurnInFreezer.
```

Because of the `inverseOf`, we can view these steps either in enabling order as asserted or in dependency order, as shown in Figure 8.6.

CHALLENGE 19

For any particular step in the process, we might want to know all the steps it depends on or all the steps that depend on it. How can we do this, using the patterns we already know?

Solution

We can use the `subPropertyOf/TransitiveProperty` pattern for each of `dependsOn` and `enables` as follows:

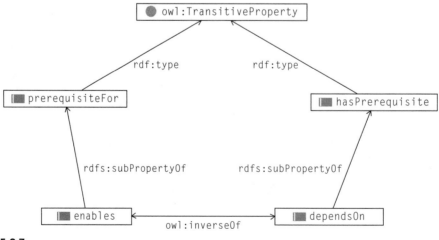

FIGURE 8.7

Transitive properties `hasPrerequisite` and `prerequisiteFor` defined in terms of `dependsOn` and `enables`.

```
:dependsOn rdfs:subPropertyOf :hasPrerequisite.
:hasPrerequisite rdf:type owl:TransitiveProperty.
:enables rdfs:subPropertyOf :prerequisiteFor.
:prerequisiteFor rdf:type owl:TransitiveProperty.
```

These relationships can be seen graphically in Figure 8.7.

From these triples, for instance, we can infer that `GraduallyMix` has five prerequisites—namely:

```
:GraduallyMix :hasPrerequisite :AddSugar;
        :hasPrerequisite :SeparateEggs;
        :hasPrerequisite :SliceBean;
        :hasPrerequisite :HeatCream;
        :hasPrerequisite :BeatEggs.
```

CHALLENGE 20

In a more realistic workflow management setting, we wouldn't just be managing a single process (corresponding to a single recipe). We would be managing several processes that interact in complex ways. We could even lose track of which steps are in the same procedure. Is there a way to find out, given a particular step, what the other steps in the same process are? In our recipe example, can we model the relationship between steps so that we can connect steps in the same recipe together?

Solution

First, we combine together both of our fundamental relationships (`enables` and `dependsOn`) as common `subPropertyOf` a single unifying property (`neighborStep`). We then, in turn, make that a `subPropertyOf` of a transitive property (`inSameRecipe`), shown here in Turtle and in Figure 8.8(a).

```
:dependsOn rdfs:subPropertyOf :neighborStep.
:enables rdfs:subPropertyOf :neighborStep.
:neighborStep rdfs:subPropertyOf :inSameRecipe.
:inSameRecipe rdf:type owl:TransitiveProperty.
```

What inferences can we draw from these triples for the instance `GraduallyMix`? Any directly related step (related by either `dependsOn` or `enables`) becomes a `neighborStep`, and any combination of neighbors is rolled up with `inSameRecipe`. A few selected inferences are shown here:

```
:GraduallyMix :neighborStep :BeatEggs;
            :neighborStep :HeatCream;
            :neighborStep :CookCustard.
            :CookCustard :neighborStep :Chill;
            :neighborStep :GraduallyMix.
:GraduallyMix :inSameRecipe :BeatEggs;
            :inSameRecipe :HeatCream;
            :inSameRecipe :CookCustard.
            :CookCustard :inSameRecipe :Chill;
            :inSameRecipe :GraduallyMix.
```
...

```
:GraduallyMix :inSameRecipe :AddMilk;
             :inSameRecipe :CookCustard;
             :inSameRecipe :TurnInFreezer;
             :inSameRecipe :AddSugar;
             :inSameRecipe :SeparateEggs;
             :inSameRecipe :SliceBean;
             :inSameRecipe :HeatCream;
             :inSameRecipe :GraduallyMix;
             :inSameRecipe :Chill;
             :inSameRecipe :BeatEggs.
```

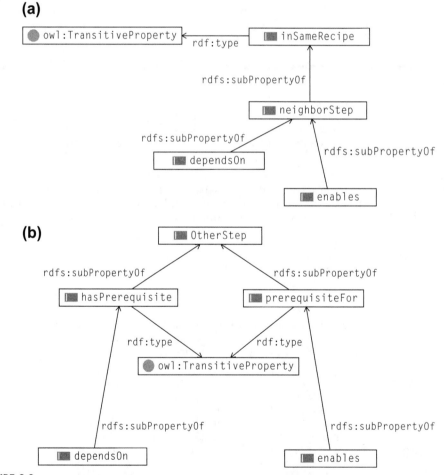

FIGURE 8.8

Contrast patterns for `inSameRecipe` (includes self) and `otherStep` (excludes self). Both patterns work from the same input properties `dependsOn` and `enables` but yield different results.

All the steps in this recipe have been gathered up with `inSameRecipe`, as desired. In fact, any two steps in this recipe will be related to one another by `inSameRecipe`, including relating each step to itself. In particular, the triple

```
:GraduallyMix :inSameRecipe :GraduallyMix.
```

has been inferred. Although this is, strictly speaking, correct (after all, indeed `GraduallyMix` is in the same recipe as `GraduallyMix`), it might not be what we actually wanted to know.

CHALLENGE 21

How can we define a property that will relate a recipe step only to the other steps in the same recipe?

Solution

Earlier we defined two properties, `hasPrerequisite` and `prerequisiteFor`, one looking "downstream" along the dependencies and one looking "upstream."

```
:dependsOn rdfs:subPropertyOf :hasPrerequisite.
:hasPrerequisite rdf:type owl:TransitiveProperty.
:enables rdfs:subPropertyOf :prerequisiteFor.
:prerequisiteFor rdf:type owl:TransitiveProperty.
```

If we join these two together under a common superproperty that is not transitive, we get the following:

```
:hasPrerequisite rdfs:subPropertyOf :otherStep.
:prerequisiteFor rdfs:subPropertyOf :otherStep.
```

These relationships are shown diagrammatically in Figure 8.8(b).

We track the inferences separately for each property. For `hasPrerequisite`, we have already seen that we can infer the following:

```
:GraduallyMix :hasPrerequisite :AddSugar;
      :hasPrerequisite :SeparateEggs;
      :hasPrerequisite :SliceBean;
      :hasPrerequisite :HeatCream;
      :hasPrerequisite :BeatEggs.
```

For `prerequisiteFor`, we get the following inferences:

```
:GraduallyMix :prerequisiteFor :AddMilk;
      :prerequisiteFor :CookCustard;
      :prerequisiteFor :TurnInFreezer;
      :prerequisiteFor :Chill.
```

Now, for `otherStep`, we get the combination of these two. Notice that neither list includes `GraduallyMix` itself, so it does not appear in this list either.

```
:GraduallyMix :otherStep :AddMilk;
      :otherStep :CookCustard;
      :otherStep :TurnInFreezer;
      :otherStep :AddSugar;
      :otherStep :SeparateEggs;
      :otherStep :SliceBean;
      :otherStep :HeatCream;
      :otherStep :Chill;
      :otherStep :BeatEggs.
```

Figure 8.8 shows the two patterns. For `inSameRecipe`, we have a single transitive property at the top of a `subPropertyOf` tree; both primitive properties (`enables` and `dependsOn`) are brought together, and any combinations of the resulting property (`neighborStep`) are chained together as a `TransitiveProperty` (`inSameRecipe`). For `otherStep`, the top-level property itself is not transitive but is a simple combination (via two `subPropertyOf` links) of two transitive properties (`hasPrerequisite` and `prerequisiteFor`). Inference for each of these transitive properties is done separately from the other, and the results combined (without any more transitive interaction). Hence, for `inSameRecipe`, the reflexive triples like

```
:GraduallyMix :inSameRecipe :GraduallyMix
```

are included, whereas for `otherStep`, they are not.

Another ramification of the difference between these two models has to do with whether or not they can "turn the corner" in Figure 8.6 and determine a relationship between, e.g., `BeatEggs` and `HeatCream`. The transitive structure of `inSameRecipe` allows this to happen, whereas for `otherStep` it does not; that is, we can infer

```
:BeatEggs :inSameRecipe :HeatCream
```

but not

```
:BeatEggs :otherStep :HeatCream .
```

EQUIVALENCE

RDF provides a global notion of identity that has validity across data sources; that global identity is the URI. This makes it possible to refer to a single entity in a distributed way. But when we want to merge information from multiple sources controlled by multiple stakeholders, it is not necessarily the case that any two stakeholders will use the same URI to refer to the same entity. Thus, in a federated information setting, it is useful to be able to stipulate that two URIs actually refer to the same entity. But there are different ways in which two entities can be the same. Some are more equal than others. RDFS-Plus provides a variety of notions of equivalence. As with other constructs in OWL, these different constructs are defined by the inferences they entail.

Equivalent classes

We previously used a simple idiom to express that one class had the same elements as another; in particular, we asserted two triples

```
:Analyst rdf:subClassOf :Researcher.
:Researcher rdf:subClassOf :Analyst.
```

to indicate that every *Analyst* is a *Researcher* and every *Researcher* is an *Analyst*. As we saw, the rule for `rdf:subClassOf` can be applied in each direction to support the necessary inferences to make every *Analyst* a *Researcher* and vice versa. When two classes are known to always have the same members, we say that the classes are *equivalent*. The preceding pattern allows us to express class equivalence in RDFS, if in a somewhat unintuitive way.

RDFS-Plus provides a more intuitive expression of class equivalence, using the construct `owl:equivalentClass`. A single triple expresses class equivalence in the obvious way:

```
:Analyst owl:equivalentClass :Researcher.
```

As with any other construct in RDFS or OWL, the precise meaning of `owl:equivalentClass` is given by the inferences that can be drawn, which we express in SPARQL:

```
CONSTRUCT {?r rdf:type ?b .}
WHERE {?a owl:equivalentClass ?b .
       ?r rdf:type ?a . }
```

So far, this is just the type propagation rule that we used to define the meaning of `rdf:subClassOf` in Chapter 7. But `owl:equivalentClass` has another rule as well:

```
CONSTRUCT {?r rdf:type ?a .}
WHERE {?a owl:equivalentClass ?b .
       ?r rdf:type ?b . }
```

That is, the two classes `?a` and `?b` have exactly the same members.

It seems a bit of a shame that something as simple as equivalence requires two rules to express, especially when the rules are so similar. In fact, this isn't necessary; if we observe that

```
owl:equivalentClass rdf:type owl:SymmetricProperty.
```

then there is no need for the second rule; we can infer it from the first rule and the symmetry of `equivalentClass`.

In fact, we don't actually need any rules at all; if we also assert that

```
owl:equivalentClass rdfs:subPropertyOf rdfs:subClassOf.
```

we can use the rules for `subPropertyOf` and `subClassOf` to infer everything about `equivalentClass`! Let's see how the rules for OWL, which we have already learned work for `owl:equivalentClass`, in the case of the *Analyst* and the *Researcher*.

From the rule about `rdfs:subClassOf` and the statement of equivalence of *Analyst* and *Researcher,* we can infer that

```
:Analyst rdfs:subClassOf :Researcher.
```

But since `owl:equivalentClass` is symmetric, we can also infer that

```
:Researcher owl:equivalentClass :Analyst.
```

and by applying the rule for `rdfs:subClassOf` once again, we get

```
:Researcher rdfs:subClassOf :Analyst.
```

That is, simply by applying what we already know about `rdfs:subClassOf` and `owl:SymmetricProperty`, we can infer both `rdfs:subClassOf` triples from the single `owl:equivalentClass` triple.

Notice that when two classes are equivalent, it only means that the two classes have the same members. Other properties of the classes are not shared; for example, each class keeps its own rdfs:label. This means that if these classes have been merged from two different applications, each of these applications will still display the class by the original print name; only the members of the class will change.

Equivalent properties

We have seen how to use rdfs:subPropertyOf to make two properties behave in the same way; the trick we used there was very similar to the double subClassOf trick. We use rdfs:subPropertyOf twice to indicate that two properties are equivalent.

```
:borrows rdfs:subPropertyOf :checkedOut.
:checkedOut rdfs:subPropertyOf :borrows.
```

RDFS-Plus also provides a more intuitive way to express property equivalence, using owl:equivalentProperty, as follows:

```
:borrows owl:equivalentProperty :checkedOut.
```

When two properties are equivalent, we expect that in any triple that uses one as a predicate, the other can be substituted—this is, we can define it in SPARQL with

```
CONSTRUCT {?a :checkedOut ?b . }
WHERE {?a :borrows ?b . }
```

and vice versa. We can accomplish this in a manner analogous to the method used for owl:equivalentClass. We define owl:equivalentProperty in terms of other RDFS-Plus constructs.

```
owl:equivalentProperty rdfs:subPropertyOf
rdfs:subPropertyOf.
owl:equivalentProperty rdf:type owl:SymmetricProperty.
```

Starting with the asserted equivalence of *borrows* and checkedOut, using these triples, and the rules for rdfs:subPropertyOf and owl:SymmetricProperty, we can infer that

```
:borrows rdfs:subPropertyOf checkedOut.
:checkedOut owl:equivalentProperty borrows.
:checkedOut rdfs:subPropertyOf borrows.
```

Once we have inferred that borrows and checkedOut are rdfs:subPropertyOf one another, we can make all the appropriate inferences.

When we express new constructs (like owl:equivalentProperty in this section) to constructs we already know (rdfs:subPropertyOf and owl:SymmetricProperty), we explicitly describe how the various parts of the language fit together. That is, rather than just noticing that the rule governing owl:equivalent Property is the same rule as the one that governs rdfs:subPropertyOf (except that it works both ways!), we can actually model these facts. By making owl: equivalentProperty a subproperty of rdfs:subProperty Of, we explicitly assert that they are governed by the same rule. By making owl: equivalentProperty an owl:SymmetricProperty, we assert the fact that this rule works in both directions. This makes the relationship between the parts of the OWL language explicit and, in fact, models them in OWL.

Same individuals

Class equivalence—that is, `owl:equivalentClass`—and property equivalence (`own:equivalentProperty`) provide intuitive ways to express relationships that were already expressible in RDFS. In this sense, neither of these constructs has increased the expressive power of RDFS-Plus beyond what was already available in RDFS. They has just made it easier to express and clearer to read. These constructs refer respectively to classes of things and the properties that relate them.

But when we are describing things in the world, we aren't only describing classes and properties; we are describing the things themselves. These are the members of the classes. We refer to these as *individuals*. We have encountered a number of individuals in our examples so far—Wenger the Analyst, Kildare the Surgeon, Kaneda the All-Star Player—and any number of things whose class membership has not been specified—Wales, The Firm, and *Moby Dick*. But remember the nonunique naming assumption: Often, our information comes from multiple sources that might not have done any coordination in their reference to individuals. How do we handle the situation in which we determine that two individuals that we originally thought of separately are in fact the same individual?

In RDFS-Plus, this is done with the single construct `owl:sameAs`. Our old friend William Shakespeare will provide us with an example of how `owl:sameAs` works. From Chapter 3, we have the following triples about the literary career of William Shakespeare:

```
lit:Shakespeare lit:wrote lit:AsYouLikeIt;
        lit:wrote lit:HenryV;
        lit:wrote lit:LovesLaboursLost;
        lit:wrote lit:MeasureForMeasure;
        lit:wrote lit:TwelfthNight;
        lit:wrote lit:WintersTale;
        lit:wrote lit:Hamlet;
        lit:wrote lit:Othello.
```

Suppose we have at our disposal information from the Stratford Parish Register, which lists the following information from some baptisms that occurred there. We will use `spr:` as the namespace identifier for URIs from the Stratford Parish Register.

```
spr:Gulielmus spr:hasFather spr:JohannesShakspere.
spr:Susanna spr:hasFather spr:WilliamShakspere.
spr:Hamnet spr:hasFather spr:WilliamShakspere.
spr:Judeth spr:hasFather spr:WilliamShakspere.
```

Suppose that our research determines that, indeed, the resources mentioned here as `spr:Gulielmus`, `spr:WilliamShakspere`, and `lit:Shakespeare` all refer to the same individual, so the answer to the question "Did Hamnet's father write *Hamlet*?" would be "yes." If we had known that all of these things refer to the same person in advance of having represented the Stratford Parish Register in RDF, we could have used the same URI (e.g., `lit:Shakespeare`) for each occurrence of the Bard. But we are living in the data wilderness, and now it is too late; the URIs from each data source have already been chosen. What is to be done?

First, let's think about how to pose the question "Did Hamnet's father write *Hamlet*?" We can write this as a graph pattern in SPARQL as follows:

```
{spr:Hamnet spr:hasFather?d.
 ?d lit:wrote lit:Hamlet.}
```

that is, we are looking for a single resource that links Hamnet to *Hamlet* via the two links `spr:hasFather` and `lit:wrote`.

In RDFS-Plus, we have the option of asserting the sameness of two resources. Let's start with just one:

```
spr:WilliamShakspere owl:sameAs lit:Shakespeare.
```

The meaning of this triple, as always in RDFS-Plus, is expressed by the inferences that can be drawn. The rule for `owl:sameAs` is quite intuitive; it says that if A `owl:sameAs` B, then in any triple where we see A, we can infer the same triple, with A replaced by B. So for our Shakespeare example, the inference is defined as

```
CONSTRUCT {lit:Shakespeare ?p ?o . }
WHERE {spr:WilliamShakespeare ?p ?o . }
```

Similarly,

```
CONSTRUCT {?s ?p lit:Shakespeare. }
WHERE {?s ?p spr:WilliamShakespeare. }
```

More generally, `owl:sameAs` is defined by three rules that can be expressed in SPARQL as

```
CONSTRUCT {?s ?p ?x. }
WHERE {?s ?p ?y.
       ?x owl:sameAs ?y .}
CONSTRUCT {?x ?p ?o. }
WHERE {?y ?p ?o .
       ?x owl:sameAs ?y .}
CONSTRUCT {?s ?x ?o. }
WHERE {?s ?y ?o .
       ?x owl:sameAs ?y .}
```

Also, as we did for `owl:equivalentClass` and `owl:equivalentProperty`, we assert that `owl:sameAs` is an `owl:SymmetricProperty`:

```
owl:sameAs rdf:type owl:SymmetricProperty.
```

Otherwise, we would need three more rules, with the `owl:sameAs` triples reversed. This allows us to infer that

```
lit:Shakespeare owl:sameAs spr:WilliamShakspere.
```

so that we can replace any occurrence of `lit:Shakespeare` with `spr:WilliamShakspere` as well.

Let's see how this works with the triples we know from literary history and the Register. We list all triples, with asserted triples in Roman and inferred triples in *italics*. Among the inferred triples, we begin by replacing `lit:Shakespeare` with `spr:WilliamShakspere`, then continue by replacing `spr:WilliamShakspere` with `lit:Shakespeare`:

```
lit:Shakespeare lit:wrote lit:AsYouLikeIt;
lit:wrote lit:HenryV;
lit:wrote lit:LovesLaboursLost;
lit:wrote lit:MeasureForMeasure;
lit:wrote lit:TwelfthNight;
lit:wrote lit:WintersTale;
lit:wrote lit:Hamlet;
lit:wrote lit:Othello.
spr:Gulielmus spr:hasFather spr:JohannesShakspere.
spr:Susanna spr:hasFather spr:WilliamShakspere.
spr:Hamnet spr:hasFather spr:WilliamShakspere.
spr:Judeth spr:hasFather spr:WilliamShakspere.
spr:WilliamShakspere
    lit:wrote lit:AsYouLikeIt;
    lit:wrote lit:HenryV;
    lit:wrote lit:LovesLaboursLost;
    lit:wrote lit:MeasureForMeasure;
    lit:wrote lit:TwelfthNight;
    lit:wrote lit:WintersTale;
    lit:wrote lit:Hamlet;
    lit:wrote lit:Othello.
spr:Susanna spr:hasFather lit:Shakespeare.
spr:Hamnet spr:hasFather lit:Shakespeare.
spr:Judeth spr:hasFather lit:Shakespeare.
```

Now the answer to the query "Did Hamnet's father write *Hamlet*?" is "yes," since there is a binding for the variable *?d* in the preceding SPARQL graph pattern. In fact, there are two possible bindings: *?d* = `lit:Shakespeare` and *?d* = `spr:Shakspere`.

Challenge: merging data from different databases

We have seen how to interpret information in a table as RDF triples. Each row in the table became a single individual, and each cell in the table became a triple. The subject of the triple is the individual corresponding to the row that the cell is in; the predicate is made up from the table name and the field name; and the object is the cell contents. Table 8.1 (from Table 3.10) shows 63 triples for the 7 fields and 9 rows. Let's look at just the triples having to do with the `Manufacture_Location`.

```
mfg:Product1 mfg:Product_Manufacture_Location Sacramento.
mfg:Product2 mfg:Product_Manufacture_Location Sacramento.
mfg:Product3 mfg:Product_Manufacture_Location Sacramento.
mfg:Product4 mfg:Product_Manufacture_Location Elizabeth.
mfg:Product5 mfg:Product_Manufacture_Location Elizabeth.
mfg:Product6 mfg:Product_Manufacture_Location Seoul.
mfg:Product7 mfg:Product_Manufacture_Location Hong Kong.
mfg:Product8 mfg:Product_Manufacture_Location Cleveland.
mfg:Product9 mfg:Product_Manufacture_Location Cleveland.
```

Table 8.1 Sample Tabular Data for Triples

			Product			
ID	Model Number	Division	Product Line	Manufacture Location	SKU	Available
1	ZX-3	Manufacturing Support	Paper Machine	Sacramento	FB3524	23
2	ZX-3P	Manufacturing Support	Paper Machine	Sacramento	KD5243	4
3	ZX-3S	Manufacturing Support	Paper Machine	Sacramento	IL4028	34
4	B-1430	Control Engineering	Feedback Line	Elizabeth	KS4520	23
5	B-1430X	Control Engineering	Feedback Line	Elizabeth	CL5934	14
6	B-1431	Control Engineering	Active Sensor	Seoul	KK3945	0
7	DBB-12	Accessories	Monitor	Hong Kong	ND5520	100
8	SP-1234	Safety	Safety Valve	Cleveland	HI4554	4
9	SPX-1234	Safety	Safety Valve	Cleveland	OP5333	14

Table 8.2 Sample Data: Parts and the Facilities Required to Produce Them

	Product	
ID	Model Number	Facility
1	B-1430	Assembly Center
2	B-1431	Assembly Center
3	M13-P	Assembly Center
4	ZX-3S	Assembly Center
5	ZX-3	Factory
6	TC-43	Factory
7	B-1430X	Machine Shop
8	SP-1234	Machine Shop
9	1180-M	Machine Shop

Suppose that another division in the company keeps its own table of the products with information that is useful for that division's business activities—namely, it describes the sort of facility that is required to produce the part. Table 8.2 shows some products and the facilities they require. Some of the products in Table 8.2 also appeared in Table 8.1, and some did not. It is not uncommon for different databases to overlap in such an inexact way.

CHALLENGE 22

Using the products that appear in both tables, how can we write a federated query that will cross-reference cities with the facilities that are required for the production that takes place there?

Solution
If these two tables had been in a single database, then there could have been a foreign-key reference from one table to the other, and we could have joined the two tables together. Since the tables come from two different databases,

there is no such common reference. This is typical of data found in the wilderness; no effort has been made to align data from different sources.

When we turn both tables into triples, the individuals corresponding to each row are assigned global identifiers. Suppose that we use the namespace `p:` for this second database; when we turn Table 8.2 into triples, we get 27 triples, for the 9 rows and 3 fields. The triples corresponding to the required facilities are as follows:

```
p:Product1 p:Product_Facility "Assembly Center".
p:Product2 p:Product_Facility "Assembly Center".
p:Product3 p:Product_Facility "Assembly Center".
p:Product4 p:Product_Facility "Assembly Center".
p:Product5 p:Product_Facility "Factory".
p:Product6 p:Product_Facility "Factory".
p:Product7 p:Product_Facility "Machine Shop".
p:Product8 p:Product_Facility "Machine Shop".
p:Product9 p:Product_Facility "Machine Shop".
```

Although we have global identifiers for individuals in these tables, those identifiers are not the same. For instance, `p:Product1` is the same as `mfg:Product4` (both correspond to model number B-1430). How can we cross-reference from one table to the other? The answer is to use a series of `owl:sameAs` triples, as follows:

```
p:Product1 owl:sameAs mfg:Product4.
p:Product2 owl:sameAs mfg:Product6.
p:Product4 owl:sameAs mfg:Product3.
p:Product5 owl:sameAs mfg:Product1.
p:Product7 owl:sameAs mfg:Product5.
p:Product8 owl:sameAs mfg:Product8.
```

Now if we match the following SPARQL graph pattern:

```
{?p p:Product_Facility ?facility.
 ?p mfg:Product_Manufacture_Location ?location.}
```

and display *?facility* and *?location,* we get the results in Table 8.3.

This solution has addressed the challenge for the particular data in the example, but the solution relied on the fact that we knew which product from one table matched with which product from another table. But `owl:sameAs` only solves part of the problem. In real data situations, in which the data in the tables change

Table 8.3 Locations Cross-Referenced with Facilities, Computed via Products

?location	?facility
Elizabeth	Assembly Center
Seoul	Assembly Center
Sacramento	Assembly Center
Sacramento	Factory
Elizabeth	Machine Shop
Cleveland	Machine Shop

frequently, it is not practical to assert all the `owl:sameAs` triples by hand. In the next section, we will see how RDFS-Plus provides a solution to the rest of the challenge.

COMPUTING SAMENESS—FUNCTIONAL PROPERTIES

Functional Properties in OWL get their name from a concept in mathematics, but like most of the OWL constructs, they have a natural interpretation in everyday life. A function property is one for which there can be just one value. Examples of such properties are quite common: `hasMother` (since a person has just one biological mother), `hasBirthplace` (someone was born in just one place), and `birthdate` (just one) are a few simple examples.

In mathematics, a *function* is a mapping that gives one value for any particular input, so x^2 is a function, since for any value of x, there is exactly one value for x^2. Another way to say this is that if $x = y$, then $x^2 = y^2$. To solve the previous challenge problem, we have to have constructs in RDFS-Plus that have this same sort of behavior; that is, we want to describe something as being able to refer to only a single value.

The next two constructs, `FunctionalProperty` and `InverseFunctionalProperty`, use this idea to determine when two resources refer to the same individual, thereby providing the OWL modeler with a means for describing how information from multiple sources are to be considered as a distributed web of information. These constructs provide an important semantic framework for using RDFS-Plus in the Semantic Web setting.

Functional properties

RDFS-Plus borrows the name *functional* to describe a property that, like a mathematical function, can only take one value for any particular individual. The precise details of the meaning of `owl:FunctionalProperty` is given, as usual, as an inference pattern expressed in SPARQL:

```
CONSTRUCT {?a owl:sameAs ?b . }
WHERE {?p rdf:type owl:FunctionalProperty .
       ?x ?p ?a .
       ?x ?p ?b . }
```

This definition of `owl:FunctionalProperty` is analogous to the mathematical situation in which we know that x^2 has a single unambiguous value. More precisely, if we know that $x^2 = a$ and $x^2 = b$, then we may conclude that $a = b$. In RDFS-Plus, this looks as follows, in which the first three triples are asserted and the fourth is inferred:

```
math:hasSquare rdf:type owl:FunctionalProperty.
:x math:hasSquare :A.
:x math:hasSquare :B.
:A owl:sameAs :B.
```

Functional properties are important in RDFS-Plus because they allow sameness to be inferred. For instance, suppose that in the Stratford Parish Registry we have an entry that tells us

```
lit:Shakespeare fam:hasFather bio:JohannesShakspere.
```

and that from Shakespeare's grave we learn that

```
lit:Shakespeare fam:hasFather bio:JohnShakespeare.
```

We would like to conclude that John and Johannes are in fact the same person. If we know from a background model of family relationships that

```
fam:hasFather rdf:type owl:FunctionalProperty.
```

then we can conclude, from the definition of `owl:FunctionalProperty`, that

```
bio:JohannesShakspere owl:sameAs bio:JohnShakespeare.
```

as desired.

Although `owl:FunctionalProperty` provides us with a means of concluding that two resources are the same, this is not the usual pattern for determining that two entities are the same in most real data. Much more common is the closely related notion of `owl:InverseFunctionalProperty`, which we treat next.

Inverse functional properties

Some people consider `owl:InverseFunctionalProperty` to be the most important modeling construct in RDFS-Plus, especially in situations in which a model is being used to manage data from multiple sources. Whether or not this is true, it is certainly true that it has the most difficult name with respect to its utility of any construct.

The name `owl:InverseFunctionalProperty` was chosen to be consistent with the closely related `owl:FunctionalProperty`, and in fact one can think of an `owl:Inverse FunctionalProperty` simply as the inverse of an `owl:Functional Property`. So if `math:hasSquare` is a functional property, then its inverse, `math: hasSquareRoot`, is an inverse functional property.

What exactly does this mean in terms of inferences that can be drawn? The rule looks very similar to the rule for `owl:FunctionalProperty`,

```
CONSTRUCT {?a owl:sameAs ?b . }
WHERE {?p rdf:type owl:InverseFunctionalProperty .
       ?a ?p ?x .
       ?b ?p ?x . }
```

For example, if we define a property `buriedAt` to be sufficiently specific that we cannot have two people buried at the same location, then we can declare it to be an `owl:Inverse FunctionalProperty`. If we were then to have two triples that assert

```
spr:Shakespere buriedAt:TrinityChancel.
lit:Shakespeare buriedAt:TrinityChancel.
```

then we could infer that

```
spr:Shakespere owl:sameAs lit:Shakespeare.
```

an `owl:InverseFunctionalProperty` plays a similar role as a key field in a relational database. A single value of the property cannot be shared by two entities, just as a key field may not be duplicated in more than one row. Unlike the case of a relational database, RDFS-Plus does not signal an error if two entities are found to share a value for an inverse functional property. Instead, RDFS-Plus infers that the two entities must be the same. Because of the nonunique naming assumption, we cannot tell that two entities are distinct just by looking at their URIs.

Examples of inverse functional properties are fairly commonplace; any identifying number (Social Security number, employee number, driver's license number, serial number, etc.) is an inverse functional property. In some cases, full names are inverse functional properties, though in most applications, name duplications (is it the same John Smith?) are common enough that full names are not inverse functional properties. In an application at the Boston Children's Hospital, it was necessary to find an inverse functional property that would uniquely identify a baby (since newborns don't always have their Social Security numbers assigned yet). The added catch was that it had to be a property that the mother was certain, or at least extremely likely, to remember. Although babies are born at any time of day in a busy hospital, it is sufficiently unusual for two babies to be born at exactly the same minute that time of birth could be used as an inverse functional property. And every mother was able to remember when her baby was born.

Now that we have inverse functional properties, we are able to continue the solution to the challenge. Previously, we merged information from two databases by matching the global URIs of individuals from two databases with the following series of `owl:sameAs` triples:

```
p:Product1 owl:sameAs mfg:Product4.
p:Product2 owl:sameAs mfg:Product6.
p:Product4 owl:sameAs mfg:Product3.
p:Product5 owl:sameAs mfg:Product1.
p:Product7 owl:sameAs mfg:Product5.
p:Product8 owl:sameAs mfg:Product8.
```

Once we had these triples, we were able to cross-reference cities with facilities, using products as an intermediary. But we had to create these triples by hand.

CHALLENGE 23

How can we infer the appropriate `owl:sameAs` triples from the data that have already been asserted?

Solution

The approach we will take to this challenge is to find an inverse functional property that is present in both data sets that we can use to bridge between them. When we examine Tables 8.1 and 8.2, we see that they both have a field called `ModelNo`, which refers to the identifying model number of the product. As is typical for such identifying numbers, if two products have the same model number, they are the same product. So we want to declare `ModelNo` to be an inverse functional property, thus:

```
mfg:Product_ModelNo rdf:type owl:InverseFunctionalProperty.
```

This almost works, but there is still a catch: Each database has its own `ModelNo` property. The one in this triple came from the database in Chapter 3; in this chapter, there is another property, `p:Product_ModelNo`. So it seems that we still have more integration to do. Fortunately, we already have the tool we need to do this; we simply have to assert that these two properties are equivalent, thus:

```
p:Product_ModelNo owl:equivalentProperty mfg:Product_ModelNo.
```

It really doesn't matter in which order we do any of these things. Since `owl:equivalent Property` is symmetric, we can write this triple with the subject and object reversed, and it will make no difference to the inferences.

Let's see how these inferences roll out. We begin with the asserted triples from both data sources and proceed with inferred triples:

```
p:Product1 p:Product_ModelNo "B-1430".
p:Product2 p:Product_ModelNo "B-1431".
p:Product3 p:Product_ModelNo "M13-P".
p:Product4 p:Product_ModelNo "ZX-3S".
p:Product5 p:Product_ModelNo "ZX-3".
p:Product6 p:Product_ModelNo "TC-43".
p:Product7 p:Product_ModelNo "B-1430X".
p:Product8 p:Product_ModelNo "SP-1234".
p:Product9 p:Product_ModelNo "1180-M".
mfg:Product1 mfg:Product_ModelNo "ZX-3".
mfg:Product2 mfg:Product_ModelNo "ZX-3P".
mfg:Product3 mfg:Product_ModelNo "ZX-3S".
mfg:Product4 mfg:Product_ModelNo "B-1430".
mfg:Product5 mfg:Product_ModelNo "B-1430X".
mfg:Product6 mfg:Product_ModelNo "B-1431".
mfg:Product7 mfg:Product_ModelNo "DBB-12".
mfg:Product8 mfg:Product_ModelNo "SP-1234".
mfg:Product9 mfg:Product_ModelNo "SPX-1234".
p:Product1 mfg:Product_ModelNo "B-1430".
p:Product2 mfg:Product_ModelNo "B-1431".
p:Product3 mfg:Product_ModelNo "M13-P".
p:Product4 mfg:Product_ModelNo "ZX-3S".
p:Product5 mfg:Product_ModelNo "ZX-3".
p:Product6 mfg:Product_ModelNo "TC-43".
p:Product7 mfg:Product_ModelNo "B-1430X".
p:Product8 mfg:Product_ModelNo "SP-1234".
p:Product9 mfg:Product_ModelNo "1180-M".
p:Product1 owl:sameAs mfg:Product4.
p:Product2 owl:sameAs mfg:Product6.
p:Product4 owl:sameAs mfg:Product3.
p:Product5 owl:sameAs mfg:Product1.
p:Product7 owl:sameAs mfg:Product5.
p:Product8 owl:sameAs mfg:Product8.
```

The last six triples are exactly the `owl:sameAs` triples that we needed to complete our challenge.

Although this use of `owl:InverseFunctionalProperty` works fine for an example like this, most real data integration situations rely on more elaborate notions of identity that include multiple properties as well as uncertainty (what about that one freak day when two babies were born the same minute and the same second at the same hospital?). This problem can often be solved by using combinations of OWL properties that we will explore later in this book, although a fully general solution remains a topic of research.

Combining functional and inverse functional properties

It is possible and often very useful for a single property to be both an `owl:FunctionalProperty` and an `owl:InverseFunctionalProperty`. When a property is in both of these classes, then it is effectively a *one-to-one* property; that is, for any one individual, there is exactly one value for the property, and vice versa. In the case of identification numbers, it is usually desirable that the property be one-to-one, as the following challenge illustrates.

CHALLENGE 24

Suppose we want to assign identification numbers to students at a university.

These numbers will be used to assign results of classes (grades), as well as billing information for the students. Clearly no two students should share an identification number, and neither should one student be allowed to have more than one identification number. How do we model this situation in RDFS-Plus?

Solution

Define a property `hasIdentityNo` that associates a number with each student so that its domain and range are defined by

```
:hasIdentityNo rdfs:domain :Student.
:hasIdentityNo rdfs:range xsd:Integer.
```

Furthermore, we can enforce the uniqueness properties by asserting that

```
:hasIdentityNo rdf:type owl:FunctionalProperty.
:hasIdentityNo rdf:type owl:InverseFunctionalProperty.
```

Now any two students who share an identity number must be the same (since it is Inverse Functional); furthermore, each student can have at most one identity number (since it is Functional).

To summarize, there are several ways we can use these properties:

Functional Only—`hasMother` is a functional property only. Someone has exactly one mother, but many people can share the same mother.

Inverse Functional Only—`hasDiary` is an inverse functional property only. A person may have many diaries, but it is the nature of a diary that it is not a collaborative effort; it is authored by one person only.

Both Functional and Inverse Functional—`taxID` is both inverse functional and functional, since we want there to be exactly one `taxID` for each person and exactly one person per `taxID`.

A FEW MORE CONSTRUCTS

RDFS-Plus provides a small extension to the vocabulary beyond RDFS, but these extensions greatly increase the scope of applicability of the language. In the preceding examples, we have seen how these new features interact with the features of RDFS to provide a richer modeling environment. The inclusion of `owl:inverseOf` combines with `rdfs:subClassOf` by allowing us to align properties that might not have been expressed in compatible ways in existing data schemas. The inclusion of `owl:TransitiveProperty` combines with `rdfs:subPropertyOf` in a number of novel combinations, as seen here, allowing us to model a variety of relationships among chains of individuals.

The most applicable extensions, from a Semantic Web perspective, are those that deal with sameness of different individuals. `sameAs`, `FunctionalProperty`, and `InverseFunctional Property` in particular provide the OWL modeler with a means for describing how information from multiple sources is to be merged in a distributed web of information.

OWL provides a few more distinctions that, although they do not provide any semantics to a model, provide some useful discipline and provide information that many editing tools can take advantage of when displaying models. For example, when displaying what value some property takes for some subject, should the GUI display be a link to another object or a widget for a particular data type? Tools that get this right seem intuitive and easy to use; tools that don't seem awkward. So OWL provides a way to describe properties that can help a tool sort this out. This is done in OWL by distinguishing between `owl:DatatypeProperty` and `owl:ObjectProperty`.

In RDF, a triple always has a resource as its subject and predicate, but it can have either another resource as object or it can have a data item of some XML data type. We have seen plentiful examples of both of these:

```
ship:QEII ship:maidenVoyage "May 2, 1969".
mfg:Product1 mfg:Product_SKU "FB3524".
:AnneHathaway bio:married lit:Shakespeare.
:GraduallyMix :inSameRecipe :BeatEggs.
spr:Susanna spr:hasFather spr:WilliamShakspere.
```

Most tools that deal with OWL at this time prefer to make the distinction. In this case, `ship: maidenVoyage` and `mfg:Product_SKU` are data type properties, while `bio:married`, `inSameRecipe`, and `spr:hasFather` are object properties. In triples, we say:

```
ship:maidenVoyage rdf:type owl:DatatypeProperty.
mfg:Product_SKU rdf:type owl:DatatypeProperty.
bio:married rdf:type owl:ObjectProperty.
inSameRecipe rdf:type owl:ObjectProperty.
spr:hasFather rdf:type owl:ObjectProperty.
```

Another distinction that is made in OWL is the difference between `rdfs:Class` and `owl:Class`.

In Chapter 7 we introduced the notion of `rdfs:Class` as the means by which schema information could be represented in RDF. Since that time, we have introduced a wide array of "schema-like" constructs like inverse, subproperty, transitivity, and so on. OWL also provides a special case of `rdfs:Class` called `owl:Class`. Since OWL is based on RDFS, it was an easy matter to make `owl:Class` backward compatible with `rdfs:Class` by saying that every member of `owl:Class` is also a member of `rdfs:Class`. This statement needn't be made in prose, since we can say it in RDFS. In particular, the OWL specification stipulates that

```
owl:Class rdfs:subClassOf rdfs:Class.
```

Most tools today insist that classes used in OWL models be declared as members of `owl:Class`. In this chapter, we have left these class declarations out, since this level of detail was not needed for the modeling examples we provided. Implicit in the examples in this chapter, are statements such as

```
:Food rdf:type owl:Class.
:BakedGood rdf:type owl:Class.
:Confectionary rdf:type owl:Class.
:PackagedFood rdf:type owl:Class.
:PreparedFood rdf:type owl:Class.
:ProcessedFood rdf:type owl:Class.
mfg:Product rdf:type owl:Class.
p:Product rdf:type owl:Class.
```

SUMMARY

The constructs in RDFS-Plus are a subset of the constructs in OWL. This subset provides considerable flexibility for modeling in the Semantic Web. In the next chapter, we will see some examples of how RDFS-Plus is used in some large-scale Semantic Web projects. A summary of the constructs in this set follow.

Fundamental concepts

The following fundamental concepts were introduced in this chapter.

rdfs:subClassOf—Members of subclass are also member of superclass.
rdfs:subPropertyOf—Relations described by subproperty also hold for superproperty.
rdfs:domain—The subject of a triple is classified into the domain of the predicate.
rdfs:range—The object of a triple is classified into the range of the predicate.

Annotation properties

rdfs:label—No inferential semantics, printable name.
rdfs:comment—No inferential semantics, information for readers of the model.

OWL features: equality

equivalentClass—Members of each class are also members of the other.
equivalentProperty—Relations that hold for each property also hold for the other.
sameAs—All statements about one instance hold for the other.

OWL features: property characteristics

inverseOf—Exchange subject and object.
TransitiveProperty—Chains of relationships collapse into a single relationship.

SymmetricProperty—A property that is its own inverse.
FunctionalProperty—Only one value allowed (as object).
InverseFunctionalProperty—Only one value allowed (as subject).
ObjectProperty—Property can have resource as object.
DatatypeProperty—Property can have data value as object.

Using RDFS-Plus in the wild

We have seen a number of examples of the use of RDFS-Plus modeling for merging information from multiple sources in a dynamic and flexible way. In this chapter, we describe two example uses of the RDFS-Plus constructs. Both of these applications of RDFS-Plus have attracted considerable user communities in their respective fields. Both of them also make essential use of the constructs in RDFS-Plus, though often in quite different ways. These are real modeling applications built by groups who originally had no technology commitment to RDF or OWL (though both were conceived as RDF applications).

In both cases, the projects are about setting up an infrastructure for a particular web community. The use of RDFS-Plus appears in the models that describe data in these communities, rather than in the everyday use in these communities. In this book, we are describing how modeling works in RDFS and OWL, so we focus on the community infrastructure of these projects.

The first application is part of a major US government effort called Data.gov (http://data.gov). Data.gov is an effort made by the US government to publish public information. There are hundreds of thousands of datasets in Data.gov, of which hundreds are made available in RDF, with many more being converted all the time. Data.gov is a great example of the data wilderness; the published data sets come from a wide variety of source formats and collection methodologies, resulting in idiosyncratic data representations. Data.gov shows how technologies like RDFS and SPARQL can be useful in dealing with this sort of data wilderness.

The second application is called FOAF, for "Friend of a Friend." FOAF is a project dedicated to creating and using machine-readable homepages that describe people, the links between them, and the things they create and do. It is based on RDF, but it originally made no commitment to RDFS or OWL.

FOAF was originally based on RDF because of the inherently distributed and weblike nature of the project requirements. As the project evolved, there was a need to describe the relationships between various resources in a formal way; this led it to RDFS and then on to RDFS-Plus.

In this chapter, we describe each of these efforts and show the use they make of the RDFS-Plus constructs we introduced in previous chapters.

OPEN GOVERNMENT DATA

In 2009, the US Government formalized a commitment to making public government data open and accessible, Prior to this time, it was typical for information to be published in the form of reports with "infographics," visualizations like pie charts and times lines, which could be printed and read by human beings, but were very difficult to process by computer. Data.gov makes hundreds of thousands of data sets available in a variety of machine-readable formats. The metadata for all of these data sets, and the content for more than 500 of them, were released as RDF in May 2010, and more are being converted now that RDF has become one of the approved government data formats.

In the United Kingdom, a similar site called Data.gov.uk (http://data.gov.uk) also releases many government data sets directly as RDF. The United Kingdom has done significant work in linking these data sets to by creating standard URIs for things such as schools and roadways, as well as for many government agencies and functions. Many other government organizations are also releasing data including not just that from nations, but also from cities, states, provinces, counties, tribal entities, etc. A number of NGOs, particularly the World Bank and several UN units, are also releasing such data. As of the end of 2010, the United States and the United Kingdom were the only ones directly releasing data as RDF, although third parties in countries around the world are now converting data from their governments to RDF and making it available on the Web.

These open government data resources are good examples of what Tim Berners-Lee calls "raw" data—machine-readable files from the wilderness released without any specific effort to make them applicable to a particular application. The advantage of "raw" data of this sort is that it can be reused in multiple applications created by multiple communities; but this requires some means of processing it. We will show an example of utilizing raw open government data by examining a particular US data set from Data.gov. This data set contains a listing of cases filed with the FHEO (Office of Fair Housing/ Equal Opportunity) about alleged violations of Title VIII of the Fair Housing Act. The act protects various minorities against certain kinds of discrimination in housing.

The FHEO data (Data.gov data set #1329) are available in many formats, including RDF. The information in this data set looks a lot like it came from a spreadsheet (which is not surprising, as it was originally released in Excel and only later converted to RDF); there are about 40,000 entries that look like this:

```
:entry1
      a          dgtwc:DataEntry ;
      :case_number "02-06-0270-8" ;
      :color   "0" ;
      :disability "1" ;
      :familial_status "0" ;
      :filed_cases "1" ;
      :filing_date "2/13/2006" ;
      :national_origin "0" ;
      :national_origin_hispanic "0" ;
      :race   "0" ;
      :race_asian "0" ;
      :race_asian_and_white "0" ;
      :race_black_and_white "0" ;
      :race_black_or_african_american "0" ;
      :race_hawaiian_or_pacific_islander "0" ;
      :race_native_american "0" ;
      :race_native_american_and_black "0" ;
      :race_native_american_and_white "0" ;
      :race_other_multi_racial "0" ;
      :race_white "0" ;
      :religion "0" ;
      :retaliation "0" ;
      :sex    "0" ;
      :violation_county "Kings County" ;
      :violation_state "New York" .
```

(We note that there is an ongoing discussion on the design of US government URIs and the representations for RDF conversions, the details above were based on the conversion status as of late 2010.)

Note that there are several triples all with the same subject (in this case, :entry1), and with the same predicates about the basis, filing date, and location of the discrimination complaint. The filing basis (e.g., race, religion, color, etc.) is expressed with the values "0" (to indicate a factor that is not a basis for the complaint) and "1" (to indicate a factor that is a basis for the complaint). This somewhat idiosyncratic way to express the basis for the complaint is not uncommon in the data wilderness; for example, it may have resulted from a data entry process in which a user could put a checkmark next to the basis for a report.

CHALLENGE 25: HOW CAN RDFS HELP US ORGANIZE AND PROCESS FHEO DATA?

Solution

A more flexible way to represent information of this sort is to define a class of complaints based on each factor, along with a class for complaints in general, like this:

```
FHEO:Asian rdfs:subClassOf FHEO:Complaint .
FHEO:AsianAndWhite rdfs:subClassOf FHEO:Complaint .
FHEO:Black rdfs:subClassOf FHEO:Complaint .
FHEO:BlackAndWhite rdfs:subClassOf FHEO:Complaint .
```

```
FHEO:Color rdfs:subClassOf FHEO:Complaint .
FHEO:Disability rdfs:subClassOf FHEO:Complaint .
FHEO:FamilialStatus rdfs:subClassOf FHEO:Complaint .
FHEO:NationalOrigin rdfs:subClassOf FHEO:Complaint .
FHEO:Hispanic rdfs:subClassOf FHEO:Complaint .
FHEO:HPI rdfs:subClassOf FHEO:Complaint .
FHEO:NA rdfs:subClassOf FHEO:Complaint .
FHEO:NABlack rdfs:subClassOf FHEO:Complaint .
FHEO:NAWhite rdfs:subClassOf FHEO:Complaint .
FHEO:Other rdfs:subClassOf FHEO:Complaint .
FHEO:Race rdfs:subClassOf FHEO:Complaint .
FHEO:Religion rdfs:subClassOf FHEO:Complaint .
FHEO:Retaliation rdfs:subClassOf FHEO:Complaint .
FHEO:Sex rdfs:subClassOf FHEO:Complaint .
FHEO:White rdfs:subClassOf FHEO:Complaint .
```

We can now express the status of :entry1 as a case of disability discrimination with the single triple.

```
:entry1 a FHEO:Disability .
```

Since FHEO:Disability is a subclass of FHEO:Complaint, we can infer from the type propagation rule that :entry1 is also a FHEO:Complaint.

Building a model of this sort lets us describe our complaints in a concise form, but it doesn't change our data—the data are still in the form of "1" and "0." How can we transform our data, so that all the entries with a "1" for the property:disability become members of the class :Disability, and those with a "1" entry for the property :race become members of the class :Race, etc.? Each of these is easy to accomplish with a SPARQL CONSTRUCT of the form.

```
CONSTRUCT {?e a :Disability}
WHERE {?e a dgtwc:DataEntry .
        ?e :disability "1" . }
```

We can define nineteen of these queries, one per legally identified discrimination factor. This will construct the triple

```
:entry1 a FHEO:Disability .
```

as desired.

SPARQL used in this way constitutes an inference method, just as RDFS and RDFS-Plus are inference methods. In contrast to RDFS and RDFS-Plus, SPARQL CONSTRUCT can be used to express highly customized rules about data. In this case, we used a SPARQL CONSTRUCT to define a rule relating the form in which we found the data, to the form we'd like it to be in.

Describing relationships in data

Now that we have a description of our data in classes, we can start to describe relationships in the data in RDFS. Let's take a look at some relationships in this data that we could express this way.

Consider the properties from the original data—things like :race, :national_origin, :religion, etc. But we also have properties like :race_asian, :race_white, :national_origin_hispanic. One might wonder if there is some relationship between these values—for instance, is it true that all cases listed under :race_asian are (or should be) listed under :race as well? If so, how should we represent this?

First, we can check the data to see if this is the case. Let's find out if there is any case that lists Asian as a basis that does not also list Race as a basis. In terms of classes, we want to find members of the class FHEO:Asian that are not also members of the class FHEO:Race. We can do this with an ASK query in SPARQL:

```
ASK
{?a a FHEO:Asian .
 UNSAID {?a a FHEO:Race}}
```

When we evaluate this query over the RDF version of data set 1329, we get the answer **false**; that is, every case of Asian bias is also a case of racial bias. We can express a relationship like this in RDFS (thereby expressing our opinion that this holds not just for the data we have observed, but for all data yet to come) with a single triple in RDFS:

```
FHEO:Asian rdfs:subClassOf FHEO:Race .
```

Similar comments apply to many of the relationships in this data. We can express them all in, as summarized in Figure 9.1.

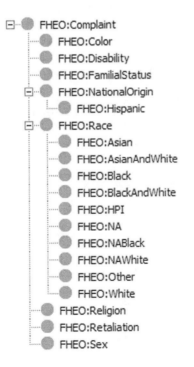

FIGURE 9.1

Relationships between types of FHEO complaint, sorted by discrinination basis.

We can verify this model against the current data, by using a SPARQL query that tests every-subclass of FHEO:Complaint, to see whether it has any members that are not also members of its own parent. This query uses many of the different SPARQL constructs discussed in Chapter 5:

```
SELECT (COUNT (?suball) AS ?total) (COUNT (?subonly) AS
?mismatch)   ?class ?parent
WHERE {
   ?class rdfs:subClassOf+ FHEO:Complaint .
   ?class rdfs:subClassOf ?parent .
   FILTER (?parent != FHEO:Complaint)
   {
    {?suball a ?class}
   UNION
    {?subonly a ?class .
     UNSAID{?subonly a ?parent}
    }
   }
 }
GROUP BY ?class   ?parent
```

This query finds the subclasses of FHEO:Complaint (leaving out the direct subclasses), and compares each one to its own parent. The comparison is done by finding all the complaints that are members of the subclass, regardless of what else they might be members of (*?suball*), and also all complaints that are members of the subclass but not members of the parent class (*?subonly*). Finally, it counts up the number of matches, sorted by *?class* and *?parent*. The result is given in Table 9.1. The results show that all the subclass relationships indeed hold in the current data.

Merging data with RDF and SPARQL

Data set #1329 includes more data about each complaint than just its type; it also includes information about the location of the complaint. The data aren't very precise—they only show it down to the level

Table 9.1 Results of SPARQL query, checking subClassOf relationships in the FHEO model against current data

Total	Mismatch	Class	Parent
3283	0	FHEO:Hispanic	FHEO:NationalOrigin
290	0	FHEO:Asian	FHEO:Race
33	0	FHEO:AsianAndWhite	FHEO:Race
11516	0	FHEO:Black	FHEO:Race
617	0	FHEO:BlackAndWhite	FHEO:Race
24	0	FHEO:HPI	FHEO:Race
216	0	FHEO:NA	FHEO:Race
62	0	FHEO:NABlack	FHEO:Race
37	0	FHEO:NAWhite	FHEO:Race
205	0	FHEO:Other	FHEO:Race
1148	0	FHEO:White	FHEO:Race

of one of the many hundreds of counties found in US states. But we can take advantage of linking this information to other data to find out where the events took place. The data is in the form

```
FHEOFiling:entry13459 a FHEO:FamilialStatus ;
    FHEO:violation_county "Los Angeles County" ;
    FHEO:violation_state "California" .
```

Suppose we have another data source that cross-references county names with their location (given by latitude and longitude, by street address, etc.). This sort of data is available from various address services (several of which will provide it in forms that can be displayed on Google map). To demonstrate how this works, we will use a data set at http://www.workingontologist.org/Examples/chapter9/counties. These data include information in the form

```
US:Los_Angeles_CountyCalifornia
    a US:County ;
    rdfs:label "Los Angeles County, California" ;
    geo:lat "34.3871821"^^xsd:float ;
    geo:long "-228.1122679"^^xsd:float .
```

We would like to be able to cross-reference our FHEO data with these data, to find out where the alleged incidents occurred. Once again, we can do this with SPARQL CONSTRUCT.

These two data sets (almost) align at the name of the county. The county geographical data are indexed by the full name of the county, including the name of the state (separated by a comma). The FHEO data include names of counties and names of states. We just need to adjust these two so that we can compare them.

We already saw in Chapter 5 how we can concatenate strings together in a SPARQL query. We can get the combined name of the county and state from a complaint with the query

```
SELECT (fn:concat (?county, ", ", ?state) AS ?countyname)
WHERE {
    ?complaint FHEOFiling:violation_county ?county .
    ?complaint FHEOFiling:violation_state ?state .
}
```

If we use this query as a subquery, we can use its results to guide the search for a county by *?countyname*.

```
SELECT ?county ?complaint ?lat ?long
WHERE {
    {SELECT (fn:concat (?county, ", ", ?state) AS ?countyname)
     WHERE {
         ?d FHEO:violation_county ?county .
         ?d FHEO:violation_state ?state .
     }
    }
    ?county rdfs:label ?countyname .
    ?county a US:County .
    ?county geo:lat ?lat .
    ?county geo:long ?long
}
```

This query gives us a cross-reference between complaints and the counties they occurred in. But the reason we did this cross-reference was so that we could get some geographical data from the second datasource, that wasn't in the first one; we get that information from the last two triples in the graph pattern.

We can take this example further, by sorting the results according to various criteria. For example, we might want to know how many complaints associated with a particular basis occurred in each county. The basis for a complaint is now just a class that it belongs to—so we can get that by finding the type of the complaint. We restrict the type to types of complaint.

```
SELECT ?type (COUNT (?complaint) AS ?severity) ?countyname ?lat ?long
WHERE {
        {SELECT ?type ?complaint (fn:concat (?county, ", ", ?state)
             AS ?countyname)
        WHERE {
             ?type rdfs:subClassOf+ FHEO:Complaint .
             ?complaint a ?type .
             ?complaint FHEO:violation_county ?county .
             ?complaint FHEO:violation_state ?state .
          }
        }
        ?c rdfs:label ?countyname .
        ?c a US:County .
        ?c geo:lat ?lat .
        ?c geo:long ?long .
    }
GROUP BY ?type ?countyname ?lat ?long
HAVING (?severity > 300)
```

This query combines many of the features of SPARQL from Chapter 5. Starting with the match of a complaint to a county, we also find the type of the complaint (limited only to types that are subclasses of FHEO:Complaint). Then, for each type/county name pair, we count the number of distinct complaints (as *?severity*). Finally, we sort by severity, keeping those results having more than 300 complaints. The results are shown in Table 9.2.

These results include enough information to drive an API for displaying things on the map. If we choose an icon with a different size and intensity for each basis and severity, then we can put these data on a map as shown in Figure 9.2.

Table 9.2 Results of query counting number of complaints per type and county

Type	Severity	Countyname	Lat	Long
Disability	322	New York County, New York	40.7834345	−73.9662495
Disability	579	Los Angeles County, California	34.3871821	−118.1122679
Disability	317	Maricopa County, Arizona	33.2917968	−112.4291464
Familial Status	378	Los Angeles County, California	34.3871821	−118.1122679
Race	431	Los Angeles County, California	34.3871821	−118.1122679
Race	322	Cook County, Illinois	41.7376587	−87.6975540
Race	339	Tarrant County, Texas	32.7732044	−97.3516558

This same method can be generalized to mash up more data sets. For example, any data set that uses county names is amenable to this same query. Mashing up multiple data sets is as easy as loading the new classes for the new data sets, and letting SPARQL do the rest. This approach is being used on US government data sets every day, providing insight into the otherwise unmanageable data.

DATA.GOV SUMMARY

The example mashup using data.gov shown here really represents only the tip of the iceberg of what has been done, and continues to be done, with open government data sets. A development community has generated a large number of applications using the RDF data from the United Kingdom, and in the United States researchers at Rensselaer Polytechnic Institute (RPI), have used this approach to produce a wide variety of applications using government data, several of which are highlighted on the official US data.gov page (See http://data.gov/semantic). The provisioning of government data as RDF makes it easy to mix and match data sets, producing visualizations, applications and reports that mashup information from multiple data sets or combine government data with other web data (Wikipedia, news articles, Google results, etc.), which would have been significantly harder and more expensive to do with pre-Semantic Web technologies.

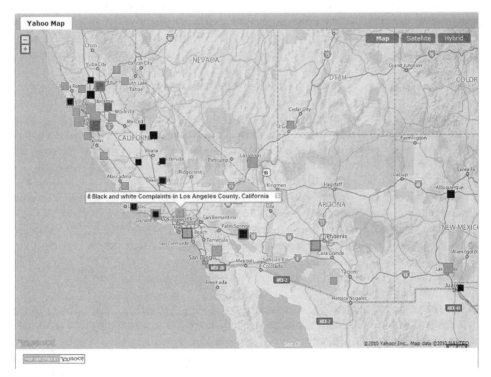

FIGURE 9.2

Map display of the data in Table 9.2.

SPARQL plays a key technological role in all of these mashups. SPARQL provides the analyst with a pattern matching tool for extracting just the necessary information to drive a report or a display. Many of the more advanced features of SPARQL (aggregates, filters, subqueries, UNIONS, etc.) are put to good use in these mashup applications. (The web site http://logd.tw.rpi.edu contains a number of demo mashups, each linked to a page which shows the specific SPARQL queries used in producing them.)

FOAF

FOAF (Friend of a Friend) is a format for supporting distributed descriptions of people and their relationships. The name Friend of a Friend is intended to evoke the fundamental relationship that holds in social networks; you have direct knowledge of your own friends, but only through your network can you access the friends of your friends. Though the FOAF project dates back to early in the year 2000, and thus predated many of the most popular social networking web sites like Friendster, LinkedIn, and Facebook, many of the issues that FOAF was designed to deal with are at the center of the discussion of the social network industry ten years later: privacy, ownership, and distribution of data. FOAF began with a simple observation: If we are to support social networks on the Web, individuals must be able to take control of their own data, host it as they please, manage it using whatever tools they please, but still interact with other users, regardless of the choices these other users make. The most successful social networking sites did not take these things into account at first; now issues of privacy and data ownership are hot topics for any social network. FOAF is also the basis of a number of growing "open social" efforts that aim to allow users to integrate their own information across the many social-networking sites and applications available on the Web.

FOAF works in the spirit of the AAA principle: Anyone can say Anything about Any topic. In the case of FOAF, the topics that anyone is usually saying things about are people. Other things that are commonly related to what we might want to say about people, such as Organizations (that people belong to), Projects (that people work on), Documents (that people have created or that describe them), and Images (that depict people), are also included in the core FOAF description. Information about a single person is likely to be distributed across the Web and represented in different forms. On their own web page, a person is likely to list basic information about interests, current projects, and some images. Further information will be available only on other pages; a photoset taken at a party or conference could include a picture that depicts a person who has not listed that photoset in her own web page. A conference organizer could include information about a paper that lists its authors, even if the authors themselves might not have listed the paper on their own web site. A laboratory or office might have a page that lists all of its members. FOAF leverages the distributed nature of RDF to provide a distributed representation of this information. Social networking sites have begun to make information available in FOAF for web-scale distribution.

Given that there are a number of social networking web sites available and that each one of them has a way to represent its members, information about them, and ways in which they are connected to one another, one could well ask why there is a need for yet another way to describe people and their social networks. The idea of FOAF is not to replace any of these systems but to provide a framework whereby this information can be distributed. Furthermore, using RDF, FOAF provides a framework that is extensible. Because Anyone can say Anything about Any topic, FOAF allows anyone to make novel statements about people, projects, and so on and to relate these statements to other statements already made.

FOAF leverages the AAA principle as well as the distributed and extensible nature of RDF in an essential way. At any point in time, FOAF is a work in progress. There are vocabulary terms in FOAF whose semantics are defined only by natural language descriptions in the FOAF "standard." Other terms have definitions defined in RDFS-Plus that relate them in a formal way to the rest of the description. FOAF is designed to grow in an organic fashion, starting with a few intuitive terms and focusing their semantics as they are used. There is no need to commit early on to a set vocabulary, since we can use RDFS-Plus to connect new vocabulary and old vocabulary, once we determine the desired relationship between them.

FOAF provides a small number of classes and properties as its starting point; these uses some of the basic constructs of RDFS-Plus to maintain consistency and to implement FOAF policies for information merging. FOAF is a fairly simple system for describing people, the things they create, and the projects they participate in. It is primarily organized around three classes: `foaf:Person`, `foaf:Group`, and `foaf:Document`.

People and agents

Although FOAF is primarily about people, some of the things we want to say about people are true of other things as well: groups, companies, and so forth. So a `foaf:Person` is defined as part of a compact hierarchy under the general grouping of `foaf:Agent`:

```
foaf:Person rdfs:subClassOf foaf:Agent.
foaf:Group rdfs:subClassOf foaf:Agent.
foaf:Organization rdfs:subClassOf foaf:Agent.
```

Many things we might say about a `foaf:Person` can hold for any `foaf:Agent`. In fact, FOAF is quite liberal in this regard; most of the properties we describe here for people hold for agents in general. Details of exactly which properties are used for which classes are available in the FOAF Vocabulary Specification at http://xmlns.com/foaf/0.1/.

Names in FOAF

Probably the most essential thing we know about a person is that person's name. FOAF provides a number of vocabulary terms to describe the name of a person. Even something as simple as a person's name can be quite complex. FOAF begins with a simple notion of name, which it sensibly calls `foaf:name`.

```
foaf:name rdfs:domain owl:Thing.
foaf:name rdfs:subPropertyOf rdfs:label.
```

That is, anything in the world can have a name (including a `foaf:Person`), and that name is also used as the printable label for that thing. For a `foaf:Person`, the name is typically the full name of the person, like "William Shakespeare" or "Anne Hathaway."

Although the full name of a person is quite useful, parts of a person's name are needed in some circumstances. `foaf:firstName`, `foaf:givenname`, `foaf:family_name`, and `foaf:surname` are four properties relating to names of people that are defined in FOAF. Each of them has an intuitive meaning, but there are no formal semantics; the meaning is given only in prose descriptions and by evolving conventions of use. As FOAF evolves, it will need to encompass different cultures and their use of names. Does the given name always come first? Is a family name always the surname? How do culture-specific names (for example, the "Christian name" that is still used in some cultures) relate to other names?

One of the advantages to basing FOAF on RDF is that it is not necessary to resolve all of these issues to begin the project of marking up data using the FOAF vocabulary. The strategy taken by FOAF is to begin by annotating a person's name while providing other naming vocabulary such as *surname, firstname, givenname,* and so on. Usage patterns will dictate which of these will turn out to be useful. If it turns out that, say, two properties are used in exactly the same way, then this observation can be cast by describing the relationship in OWL. For example:

```
foaf:surname owl:equivalentProperty foaf:family_name.
```

Nicknames and online names

Since FOAF is primarily used on the Web, it is expected that many of the people FOAF will be used to describe will be active in various Internet communities. For instance, it is likely that a FOAF Person will have a screen name on some online chat service. FOAF identifies `foaf:aimChatID`, `foaf:icqChatID`, `foaf:msnChatID`, and `foaf:yahooChatID` currently. In the spirit of extensibility of FOAF, new ID properties can be added on an as-needed basis. Although some part of the semantics of these properties is given by their natural language descriptions (which connect `foaf:yahooChatID` to the chat service Yahoo!), FOAF also makes a formal connection between these properties. In particular, all of them are subproperties of a single property, `foaf:nick`:

```
foaf:aimChatID rdfs:subPropertyOf foaf:nick.
foaf:icqChatID rdfs:subPropertyOf foaf:nick.
foaf:msnChatID rdfs:subPropertyOf foaf:nick.
foaf:yahooChatID rdfs:subPropertyOf foaf:nick.
foaf:jabberID rdfs:subPropertyOf foaf:nick.
```

Following the rules of `rdfs:subPropertyOf` from Chapter 6, this means that any `foaf:Person` who is active in chat spaces is likely to have multiple values for the property `foaf:nick`—that is, to have multiple nicknames. They can, of course, have further nicknames as well. For instance, when William Shakespeare became active in Internet chat rooms, from a FOAF point of view, all those screen names are also nicknames:

```
lit:Shakespeare foaf:aimChatID "Willie1564".
lit:Shakespeare foaf:msnChatID "TempestMan".
lit:Shakespeare foaf:nick "Willie1564".
lit:Shakespeare foaf:nick "TempestMan".
```

Of course, we can still assert a nickname for the poet and playwright, even if he doesn't use it as a screen name anywhere:

```
lit:Shakespeare foaf:nick "The Bard of Avon".
```

Online persona

The Internet provides a number of ways for a person to express himself, and FOAF is under constant revision to provide properties to describe these things. A person is likely to have an electronic mailbox, and FOAF provides a property `foaf:mbox` for this purpose. Many people maintain a number of web pages describing parts of their lives. Some have personal homepages, some have homepages at their workplace or school, and some may even have both. Even their workplaces can have homepages. FOAF uses the same strategy for these properties as it does for names: It provides a wide array of properties, defined informally (by natural language descriptions).

foaf:homepage—relates a person to their primary homepage. This property applies to anything in FOAF, not just to people.

foaf:workplaceHomepage—the homepage of the workplace of a person. Anything can have a homepage (even an employer), but only a `foaf:Person` can have a `workplaceHomepage`.

foaf:workInfoHomepage—the homepage of a person at their workplace. Such a page is usually hosted by a person's employer, but it is about the person's own work there.

foaf:schoolHomepage—the homepage of the school that a `foaf:Person` attended.

As the Internet provides new means of expression, FOAF keeps up:

foaf:weblog—the address of the weblog of a person.

All of these properties specify instances of the class `foaf:Document`—that is, a web page is a `foaf:Document`, a weblog is a `foaf:Document`, and so on.

Groups of people

One of the interesting things about people is the groups they belong to. FOAF provides a class called `foaf:Group` to define these groups. A group is connected to its members via a property called, appropriately enough, `foaf:member`. A `foaf:Group` is defined quite loosely; any grouping of people can be described this way. For instance, we could define a group called English Monarchy as follows:

```
:English_Monarchy
    a foaf:Group;
    foaf:name "English Monarchy";
    foaf:homepage "http://www.monarchy.com/";
    foaf:member :William_I, :Henry_I, :Henry_II,
        :Elizabeth_I, :Elizabeth_II.
```

A group in FOAF is an individual of type `foaf:Group`. As such, there are a number of properties that can describe it, like `foaf:name` (as we see here). In fact, a `foaf:Group` has a lot in common with a `foaf:Person`; it can have a chat ID, a nickname, an email box, a homepage, or even a blog.

It is also useful to consider the members of a group as instances of a class—that is, to relate the instance of `foaf:Group` to an `rdfs:Class`. For this purpose, FOAF provides a link from a group to a class, called `foaf:membershipClass`. Suppose that the membership class for `English_Monarchy` is called `Monarch`; this connection is expressed in FOAF with the triple.

```
:English_Monarchy foaf:membershipClass :Monarch.
```

The members of the group English_Monarchy all have type *Monarch:*

```
:William_I a:Monarch.
:Henry_I a:Monarch.
:Henry_II a:Monarch.
:Elizabeth_I a:Monarch.
:Elizabeth_II a:Monarch.
```

Ideally, all of these triples should be maintained automatically; that is, any individual of type Monarch should appear as a member of the group English_Monarchy and every member of the group English_Monarchy should have Monarch as a type. This stipulation is stated explicitly as part of the FOAF description. We will see in Chapter 11 how to use the capabilities of OWL to build a model from which we can infer these triples. The distinction between the instance English_Monarchy and the class Monarch is a subtle one: The class Monarch is a type in RDFS, and as such, it refers to schematic things about monarchs—property domains, subclasses, and so on. English_Monarchy, on the other hand, refers to the institution of the monarchy itself, which refers to things like this history of the monarchy, web pages and books about the monarchy, and so on.

In our examples so far, we have kept the world of classes separate from the world of instances. The only relationship between an instance and a class has been the rdf:type property. The intuition behind foaf:membershipClass is that it indicates a class, whose instances are exactly the same as the members of the group. The expression of this kind of relationship, in which we sometimes wish to view something as an instance (e.g., English_Monarchy, an instance of the class foaf:Group) and sometimes as a class (e.g., the class Monarch, representing all the instances that are foaf:member of that group), is an example of a practice called *metamodeling*. We will see more about metamodeling when we learn about the rest of the OWL language, and we will see how we can use metamodeling constructs in OWL to formalize the relationship between a foaf:Group and its foaf:membershipClass.

Things people make and do

Interesting people create things. They write books, publish web pages, create works of art, found companies, and start organizations. FOAF provides two properties to relate people to their creations: foaf:made and foaf:maker. They are inverses of one another, and they relate a foaf:Agent to an owl:Thing as follows:

```
foaf:made rdfs:domain foaf:Agent.
foaf:made rdfs:range owl:Thing.
foaf:maker rdfs:domain owl:Thing.
foaf:maker rdfs:range foaf:Agent.
foaf:made owl:inverseOf foaf:maker.
```

That is, anything in the describable universe is fair game for being made by some agent. Even another agent could have a foaf:maker!

If a person is an author, then he is likely to have publications to his credit. The property `foaf:publications` relates a `foaf:Person` to any `foaf:Document` published. Interestingly, FOAF does not specify that a person has `foaf:made` any of their `foaf:publications`. In the spirit of the AAA principle, if we were to decide to make such a statement, we could do so simply by saying

```
foaf:publications rdfs:subPropertyOf foaf:made.
```

Identity in FOAF

The main goal of FOAF is to apply the AAA principle to describing networks of people; anyone can contribute descriptions about anyone. But this leads to a problem: It is easy enough for me to describe myself; I can publish a document that says whatever I wish to make known. If someone else wants to contribute information about me (say, for example, that the publisher of this book wants to add the information that I am an author), how will that person refer to me? Or if I have several profiles on different sites that I would like to merge together, how can I link them to describe the one thing that is "me"? This is a key issue in social networking today—systems like OpenID provide naming services so that individuals can have a single identity that cuts across various social networks.

The RDF approach to this question is quite simple; RDF uses URIs to denote the things it describes; that means that I should have a URI that denotes me, and anyone who wants to make a comment about me can make it using that URI. This is a simple, elegant, and standard solution to this problem. This is the solution that OpenID uses, and, to some extent, every social network system uses; a user's screen name becomes a URI; no two users on the same system are allowed to have the same name, so the referent of a URI like http://www.facebook.com/#!/markzuckerberg is unambiguous.

But FOAF is a distributed social networking system—can we expect people to just make up a URI to refer to themselves? As social networking matures, this solution is becoming more and more viable; in fact, for many applications, a Facebook identity counts as a shared identity for many other social networks as well, making it into a sort of naming authority for the Web (as is OpenID). But widespread as these things are, they are still not ubiquitous—one can be a very active Internet citizen without having a Facebook account. Certainly in the days when FOAF was young, these naming authorities were not in widespread use. FOAF needed a way for people to refer to one another that would use some part of the Internet infrastructure that was already ubiquitous and familiar. Is there any identifying marker that everyone on the Internet already has and is already familiar with?

The clearest answer to this puzzle is email. Just about anyone who is described on the Web in any way at all has an email address. (Even in 2010, efforts like Webfinger take the same approach—they aim to take advantage of the ubiquity and familiarity of an email address to deal with identity on the social web). Email works quite well as an identification mechanism; it is quite rare that two people share the same email address. It is so rare that for the purposes of FOAF, email can serve as a unique identifier for people on the Web. Notice that it isn't a problem if someone has two or more email addresses or if some email address is valid only for a limited period of time. All FOAF requires of the email address is that another person doesn't share it (either simultaneously or later on).

202 CHAPTER 9 Using RDFS-Plus in the wild

We can express this constraint in plain language by saying simply that two people who share the same email address are in fact not two distinct people at all but instead are the same person. As we have already seen, RDFS-Plus has a way to formalize this relationship. When a property uniquely identifies an individual, we say that the property is an `owl:InverseFunctionalProperty`. So in FOAF, we can express the central role that `foaf:mbox` plays in identifying individuals with the single triple.

```
foaf:mbox rdf:type owl:InverseFunctionalProperty.
```

Once we identify `foaf:mbox` as an `owl:InverseFunctionalProperty`, we realize that a similar statement can be made about a number of the properties we use to describe people; it is unusual for two people to share a `yahooChatID` or an `aimChatID`. In fact, all of the following properties in FOAF are `owl:InverseFunctionalProperties`:

```
foaf:aimChatID rdf:type owl:InverseFunctionalProperty.
foaf:homepage rdf:type owl:InverseFunctionalProperty.
foaf:icqChatID rdf:type owl:InverseFunctionalProperty.
foaf:jabberID rdf:type owl:InverseFunctionalProperty.
foaf:mbox rdf:type owl:InverseFunctionalProperty.
foaf:msnChatID rdf:type
owl:InverseFunctionalProperty.foaf:yahooChatID rdf:type
owl:InverseFunctionalProperty.
```

Using the `foaf:mbox` (and similar properties) as identifiers of individuals solves the technical problem of identifying individuals by some preexisting identification, but it raises another problem: Publishing someone's email address is considered a violation of privacy, since email addresses (and chat IDs) can be used to pester or even attack someone by sending unwanted, offensive, or just bulky mail. So if we want to apply the AAA principle to William Shakespeare, and we know that he uses the email address Shakespeare@gmail.com, we can refer to him as "the person with email 'Shakespeare@gmail.com'" (using a blank node, as we did for Shakespeare's inspiration):

```
[foaf:mbox "Shakespeare@gmail.com "]
```

When we do this, we publish his email address in plain text for information vandals to steal and use. This isn't a very polite thing to do to someone we know and respect. For this reason, FOAF also offers an obfuscated version of `foaf:mbox`, called `foaf:mbox_sha1sum`. It indicates the result of applying a hashing function called SHA-1 to the email address. The SHA-1 function is publicly available but very difficult to reverse. To get the obfuscated string—f964f2dfd4784fe9d68a da960099e0b592e16a95—we apply the algorithm to Shakespeare's email address. Now we can refer to him using this value:

```
[foaf:mbox_sha1sum
"f964f2dfd4784fe9d68ada960099e0b592e16a95" ]
```

without compromising his privacy. Unfortunately, FOAF does not provide a standard way to obfuscate the other identifying properties such as `foaf:aimChatID`, `foaf:yahooChatID`, and so forth, although several proposals to update FOAF include these.

It's not what you know, it's who you know

The key to FOAF as a social networking system is the ability to link one person to another. FOAF provides a single, high-level property for this relationship, called `foaf:knows`. The idea behind `foaf:knows` is simple: One person knows another one, who knows more people, and so on, forming a network of people who know people. There isn't a lot of inferencing going on with `foaf:knows`; the only triples defined for it are

```
foaf:knows rdfs:domain foaf:Person.
foaf:knows rdfs:range foaf:Person.
```

that is, `foaf:knows` just links one `foaf:Person` to another.

The lack of inferencing over `foaf:knows` is by design; the `foaf:knows` design is intentionally vague, to indicate some relationship between people. Such a relationship could be concluded informally from other information—for instance, co-authors can usually be assumed to know one another. And while it is usual to think that if one person knows another that the relationship is mutual, the FOAF designers intentionally left out the assertion of `foaf:knows` as an `owl:SymmetricProperty`, since there might even be some disagreement about whether one person knows another. Despite its vague definition, `foaf:knows` provides the infrastructure for using FOAF for social networking, as it links one person to the next and then to the next and so on.

FACEBOOK'S OPEN GRAPH PROTOCOL

FOAF may have been around the longest, but the largest social network to date is Facebook. Facebook began life, as other social network sites did, as a world unto itself—things were in Facebook, or they weren't. Facebook didn't include Web pages that were outside its own network. One of the ways Facebook has addressed this was the 2010 adoption of the Open Graph Protocol (OGP), which allows it to integrate with other web sites in new ways.

The first and most obvious manifestation of the OGP is an extension of a Facebook facility called "like." Every Facebook resource has a distinctive button on it called "like"; when a user clicks that button, that page goes into their profile as something they like. Their contacts can see that they like this, and they can opt to receive any updates about the thing they "like." Facebook "like" is a very simple way for a user to customize their profile to reflect their own personality.

The problem with "like" was that you could only "like" a page on Facebook. If you read a news story at a major newspaper or saw a concert listing that you wanted to "like," there was no way to do it. The Facebook OGP expanded the coverage of Facebook to include pages that weren't already part of Facebook. The OGP in effect moved Facebook one step toward being a global linked data network. The linkages aren't profound—just people saying that they "like" something—but the OGP is an innovative move toward a linked web of data.

To make this work, Facebook had to make it easy for someone to put information on a web page—any web page—that would allow Facebook to treat this page as something someone could point to ("like") in the Facebook network. To make this happen, they had to overcome two obstacles: First, they needed a language in which web page authors could describe their pages to Facebook, and they needed a way for this information to be embedded in the web page itself. (Facebook has produced a number of different ways of putting "like" buttons on pages, not just OGP.)

The OGP model

The Facebook Open Graph Protocol includes a very simple model that allows web page authors to describe the multiple things their web pages describe, in such a way that someone could "like" them in Facebook. The sorts of things that someone might want to describe include Sports, Businesses (bars, restaurants, etc.), People (actors, musicians, authors, etc.), Places, Products, and Web sites. A non-normative version of the OGP model in RDFS simply lists about two dozen of these types of things one might want to describe in OGP.

OGP also defines a number of properties that one can use to describe the things one might like. There are properties that describe location (either with place names, like "Palo Alto, California," or with coordinates like latitude and longitude), properties for display purposes (like an image that depicts the thing), contact information (e.g., phone number, email, fax number), and identifiers (e.g., UPC, ISBN or URL). The OGP model doesn't map these properties to the classes, e.g., to say that it is a person or a business that has a phone number, or a book that has an ISBN number, etc. It simply provides the types (Classes) and properties.

OGP has been criticized for being insular and uncooperative because it did not adopt existing standards for all these things. FOAF already has properties for contacting and identifying people; the W3C already has a standard for geospatial models that includes properties for latitude and longitude. Other existing or emerging standards refer to just about any of the types or properties used by OGP. But OGP defined brand new ones. Doesn't this contribute to the confusion of the Web, having just one more standard?

It should be obvious to you by now that this criticism is based on a misunderstanding of the Semantic Web. The *Non-Unique Naming Assumption* admits that in a distributed system, this sort of thing will happen—different people will come up with new names for the same old things. We can't try to get everyone to agree to use the same names—there are legitimate reasons why they want their own names. In the case of Facebook, their user tests showed that content managers were not happy with having to remember names from multiple sources—to remember, for instance, that it was `foaf:mbox`, but `geo:lat` and `sioc:Site` etc.; they wanted their vocabulary all in a single namespace, so that they just had to remember a few dozen words, and they could describe their content.

The Semantic Web solution to this is to allow all of these models to coexist on the Web. We can have `og:email` (where "og:" is the namespace prefix for the OGP) alongside `foaf:mbox`, and `og:latitude` as well as `geo:lat`. The Semantic Web does not require that either of these systems prevail over the other; the two can coexist. OGP can keep its single namespace for content managers who don't want to be bothered with multiple names, while FOAF, the W3C, and any other organization can maintain their own models. Since everything is an RDF resource, we can specify how they relate using RDFS-Plus.

The OGP RDFS model expresses these relationships as follows:

```
og:latitude rdfs:seeAlso geo:lat .
og:email rdfs:seeAlso foaf:mbox .
```

We could find fault in this model's lack of specificity, using `rdfs:seeAlso` instead of something more expressive, like `owl:equivalentProperty` from RDFS-Plus. Using `owl:equivalentProperty` would make it clear that anything that FOAF calls an `mbox` is something that OGP would call an email, and vice versa. Using `rdfs:seeAlso` makes no such commitment—it simply indicates a resource in FOAF that we should look at, if we are interested in knowing more about `og:email`. But for the purposes of linking OGP with other ontologies, `rdfs:seeAlso` does what is needed.

Embedding OGP in a web page

A web page author can describe what their page is about using the simple OGP model, but they still have to publish that information somehow. The easiest way to do this is to embed the description right in the web page itself. This solution lets the web page author maintain a single page on a particular subject, putting all the necessary information into that page.

Facebook uses a simplified version of RDFa to encode OGP data in a web page. As with the vocabulary itself, user tests showed that embedding information in the web page had to be very simple. In particular, the web page author shouldn't have to face a lot of decisions about how to do it.

The solution was to put all the OGP data into HTML tags in the page header. For example, workingontologist.org, the web page for this book, has the following information in its header:

```
<meta property="og:type" content="book"/>
<meta property="og:url" content="http://www.workingontologist.com/"/>
<meta property="og:image"
      content="http://covers.elsevier.com/165_FW/9780123735560.jpg"/>
<meta property="og:site_name" content="Working Ontologist"/>
```

This tells Facebook that this site is about a book that it is called Working Ontologist, that it is available at the URL http://workingontologist.org/, and provides a link to a picture of the cover. All the words that begin with `og:` in this snippet are from the OGP model, as is the type "book." This provides Facebook all it needs to put a "like" button on the page, so that Facebook users can follow any updates that happen. We suggest you go to the web page right now, click on this button, and see what happens.

SUMMARY

OGP and FOAF demonstrate how fairly simple sets of modeling constructs can be used to create extensible, distributed information networks. They both take advantage of the distributed nature of RDF to allow extension to a network of information to be distributed across the Web.

FOAF takes something of an evolutionary approach to information extension. Many concepts have a broad number of terms (like the several variants of "name" that we examined). FOAF can be extended as new features are needed. For instance, `foaf:weblog` was not as important before blogging became fashionable, but has now surpassed the more classical `foaf:homepage` in importance.

OGP is arguably the most successful Semantic Web model ever; less than a year after its introduction, its use on the Web is becoming pervasive—as of late 2010 about 10–15% of the like buttons on the Web used the RDFa approach. With every Yahoo! shopping page, *New York Times* article, CNN news story, etc., having a "like" button, with at least four triples per button, it is difficult to estimate just how many RDF triples are generated from OGP use. Its success is certainly due in some degree to the enormous success of Facebook itself, but it is also due to the commitment to simplicity that the

Facebook OGP made in its design. OGP includes only a couple dozen simple types along with about the same number of properties.

OGP is also a clear example of the principles of the Semantic Web at work. There are already many number of models about social networking out there—FOAF being just one example. On the Web, we can't expect everyone to agree on any one of these. Different applications have differing needs. Facebook identified a strong need for simplicity, so it re-invented several notions already available in other places. But that doesn't mean that OGP creates just another impenetrable silo of information; even at its inception, its connection to these other systems was built-in to its model, in a machine-readable, queryable way. OGP, from the outset, is part of a network of descriptive metadata for entities in social networks.

Fundamental concepts

The following fundamental concepts were introduced in this chapter.

Data.gov—Project to make US government spending data available in RDF.

FOAF—Namespace for a system of representation of social network information; short for "friend of a friend."

Metamodeling—Generally speaking, the craft of building a model that describes another model. A specific example is the practice of representing a class in a model as an individual member of another class. FOAF does this explicitly with the `foaf:membershipClass` property that links an individual of type `foaf:Group` to the class of all members of the group.

RDFa—a system for embedding RDF data in a web page.

OGP—the Open Graph Protocol that lets Facebook users link to pages outside of Facebook.

SKOS—managing vocabularies with RDFS-Plus

SIMPLE KNOWLEDGE ORGANIZATION SYSTEM (SKOS)

SKOS (the Simple Knowledge Organization System) is a W3C Recommendation that provides a means for representing knowledge organization systems (including controlled vocabularies, thesauri, taxonomies, and folksonomies) in a distributed and linkable way. Knowledge Organization Systems have been around for a long time, most formally as part of Library Science, but means for representing and exchanging them in a computer network have not.

Given the existence of several thesaurus standards, one could well wonder why people found it necessary to create another one. The key differentiator between SKOS and existing thesaurus standards is its basis in the Semantic Web. Unlike existing standards, SKOS was designed from the start to allow modelers to create modular knowledge organizations that can be reused and referenced across the Web. SKOS was not designed to replace any thesaurus standard but in fact to augment them by bringing the distributed nature of the Semantic Web to thesauri and controlled vocabularies. Toward this end, it was also a design goal of SKOS that it be possible to map any thesaurus standards to SKOS in a fairly straightforward way.

As an example of using SKOS, for many years, the United Nations Food and Agriculture Organization has maintained a thesaurus called AGROVOC for organizing documents about agriculture. Figure 10.1 shows a sample from the SKOS publication of AGROVOC. The diagram shows six concepts, which are related to one another by various properties that are defined in the SKOS Core. Data properties are shown within the boxes corresponding to the concepts. As we shall see, each of these properties is defined in relation to other properties, so certain useful inferences can be made.

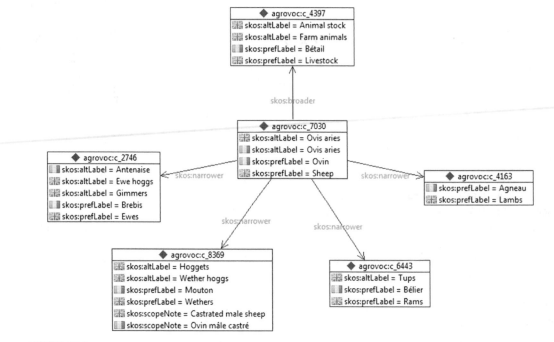

FIGURE 10.1

Sample concepts from AGROVOC.

The same information from Figure 10.1 is shown as triples in Turtle here:

```
agrovoc:c_4397
  a skos:Concept ;
  skos:prefLabel "Bétail"@fr , "Livestock"@en ;
  skos:altLabel "Animal stock"@en , "Farm animals"@en .

agrovoc:c_2746
  a skos:Concept ;
  skos:prefLabel "Brebis"@fr , "Ewes"@en  ;
  skos:altLabel "Gimmers"@en , "Antenaise"@fr , "Ewe hoggs"@en .

agrovoc:c_4163
  a skos:Concept ;
  skos:prefLabel "Agneau"@fr , "Lambs"@en .

agrovoc:c_6443
  a skos:Concept ;
  skos:prefLabel "Bélier"@fr , "Rams"@en ;
  skos:altLabel "Tups"@en .
```

```
agrovoc:c_8369
  a skos:Concept ;
  skos:prefLabel "Wethers"@en , "Mouton"@fr ;
  skos:altLabel "Wether hoggs"@en , "Hoggets"@en ;
  skos:scopeNote "Ovin mâle castré"@fr , "Castrated male
sheep"@en .

agrovoc:c_7030
  a skos:Concept ;
  skos:prefLabel "Sheep"@en , "Ovin"@fr ;
  skos:altLabel "Ovis aries"@en , "Ovis aries"@fr ;
  skos:broader agrovoc:c_4397 ;
  skos:narrower agrovoc:c_2746, agrovoc:c_6443, agrovoc:c_8369,
agrovoc:c_4163 .
```

First, let's look at internationalization. SKOS is maintained by the UN in several languages, including English and French; each concept has labels in multiple languages. None of these languages can take precedence over any other—so the UN uses numbers instead of names as the basis of the URI's for resources in AGROVOC. The human readable names are given as strings associated with the concepts in a variety of ways. Strings in Turtle optionally include a language tag (taken from the XML standard) to indicate the language they are written in—in this fragment, we have retained labels in English ("en") and French ("fr").

Next, let's look more closely at those strings, and how labels are managed in SKOS. As we have seen before, there is already a label resource defined in RDFS: `rdfs:label`. Although `rdfs:label` has no formal semantics defined (that is, there are no inferences that concern `rdfs:label`), it does have the informal meaning that it is something that can be used as the printable or human readable name of a resource. SKOS provides a more detailed notion of a concept's label, in accordance with usual thesaurus practice. In particular, it defines three different kinds of labels: a preferred label, an alternative label, and a hidden label. These are defined in SKOS with the following triples:

```
skos:prefLabel
    a rdf:Property;
    rdfs:label "preferred label"@en;
    rdfs:subPropertyOf rdfs:label.
skos:altLabel
    a rdf:Property;
    rdfs:label "alternative label"@en;
    rdfs:subPropertyOf rdfs:label.
skos:hiddenLabel
    a rdf:Property;
    rdfs:label "hidden label"@en;
    rdfs:subPropertyOf rdfs:label.
```

The SKOS definition includes a number of other triples defining these properties, but we will concentrate on these for this description.

Notice that each property has an `rdfs:label`, which provides a human readable version of the name of each resource. Furthermore, each of these properties is declared to be of type `rdf:Property`. Finally, each of these is declared to be a subproperty of `rdfs:label`. What does this mean in terms of RDFS-Plus?

As we have already seen, `rdfs:subPropertyOf` propagates triples from the subproperty to the superproperty. In the first case, from any triple using `skos:prefLabel` as a predicate, we can infer the same triple with `rdfs:label` as a predicate instead. The same is true for `skos:altLabel` and `skos:hiddenLabel`; in particular, in our AGROVOC example, we can infer (among many others) the following triples:

```
agrovoc:c_7030 rdfs:label "Sheep"@en .
agrovoc:c_7030 rdfs:label "Ovin"@fr .
```

That is, every SKOS label shows up as an `rdfs:label`. In AGROVOC, more than one value for `rdfs:label` can be inferred. This is perfectly legal in RDFS-Plus (after all, `rdfs:label` is not an `owl:FunctionalProperty`), even though it is a challenge to know how to display such a resource, if it has multiple print names.

SKOS uses this same pattern for many of the properties it defines; for each of them, the sort of inference it supports is similar. So for the seven documentation properties in SKOS, six of them are subproperties of the seventh, thus:

```
skos:definition rdfs:subPropertyOf skos:note.
skos:scopeNote rdfs:subPropertyOf skos:note.
skos:example rdfs:subPropertyOf skos:note.
skos:historyNote rdfs:subPropertyOf skos:note.
skos:editorialNote rdfs:subPropertyOf skos:note.
skos:changeNote rdfs:subPropertyOf skos:note.
```

SEMANTIC RELATIONS IN SKOS

SKOS defines several "*semantic relations*," properties that relate concepts to one another, corresponding to familiar terms like *broader, narrower,* and *related* from thesaurus standards. But SKOS includes subtle variants of these properties, and models their relationships to one another. Figure 10.2 shows the semantic relations in SKOS, and how they are related.

The most familiar relations in this diagram are `skos:broader`, `skos:narrower`, and `skos:related`, which correspond to familiar thesaurus relations BT, NT, and RT, respectively. Two of them, `skos:broader` and `skos:narrower` (which are mutual inverses), are subproperties of transitive properties, `skos:broaderTransitive` and `skos:narrowerTransitive` (see Chapter 8 for Mutual Inverses), respectively. This is a familiar pattern we have seen already in Challenges 17 and 18 in Chapter 8. In those challenges, we maintained consistent versions of a relationship, one transitive and one not transitive (or, more accurately speaking, not necessarily transitive). These challenges defined a simple design pattern to solve this problem, in which one property (not defined to be transitive) is a subproperty of another that is defined to be transitive. We see two occurrences of this pattern in the SKOS property tree, once each for broader and narrower.

Let's see how these uses of the transitive superproperty pattern, along with the inverses in the SKOS property tree, work together in the AGROVOC thesaurus.

First, since `skos:narrower` is an inverse of `skos:broader`, we can make the following inferences about AGROVOC concepts in Figure 10.1.

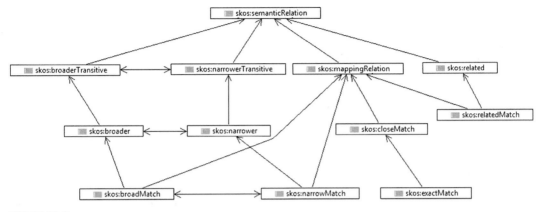

FIGURE 10.2

SKOS structure of Semantic Relations. Single arrows in the diagram refer to `rdfs:subPropertyOf` relationships; double arrows are `owl:inverseOf` relationships.

```
agrovoc:c_4397 skos:narrower agrovoc:c_7030 .
agrovoc:c_2746 skos:broader agrovoc:c_7030 .
agrovoc:c_4163 skos:broader agrovoc:c_7030 .
agrovoc:c_6443 skos:broader agrovoc:c_7030 .
agrovoc:c_8369 skos:broader agrovoc:c_7030 .
```

Furthermore, since `skos:narrower` and `skos:broader` are subproperties of `skos:narrowerTransitive` and `skos:broaderTransitivec`, respectively, we can infer that these things are also related with the transitive versions of broader and narrower:

```
agrovoc:c_4397 skos:narrowerTransitive agrovoc:c_7030 .
agrovoc:c_2746 skos:broaderTransitive agrovoc:c_7030 .
agrovoc:c_4163 skos:broaderTransitive agrovoc:c_7030 .
agrovoc:c_6443 skos:broaderTransitive agrovoc:c_7030 .
agrovoc:c_8369 skos:broaderTransitive agrovoc:c_7030 .
agrovoc:c_7030 skos:narrowerTransitive agrovoc:c_4397.
agrovoc:c_7030 skos:broaderTransitive agrovoc:c_2746 .
agrovoc:c_7030 skos:broaderTransitive agrovoc:c_4163.
agrovoc:c_7030 skos:broaderTransitive agrovoc:c_6443.
agrovoc:c_7030 skos:broaderTransitive agrovoc:c_8369.
```

and that every concept in this sample is `narrowerTransitive` than the item at the "top" of the tree, `agrovoc:c_4397` ("Livestock"):

```
agrovoc:c_4397 skos:narrowerTransitive agrovoc:c_7030.
agrovoc:c_4397 skos:narrowerTransitive agrovoc:c_2746.
agrovoc:c_4397 skos:narrowerTransitive agrovoc:c_4163.
agrovoc:c_4397 skos:narrowerTransitive agrovoc:c_6443.
agrovoc:c_4397 skos:narrowerTransitive agrovoc:c_7030.
```

Similar triples can be inferred (swapping subject for object, as usual) for the inverse property, `skos:broaderTransitive`.

In the case of `skos:related`, it is not defined as `owl:TransitiveProperty`, so we cannot make inferences about chains of related items. Thus, in AGROVOC, Meat is related to Meat Animals is related to Turtles is related to Aquatic Animals is related to Mollusca is related to Mother of Pearl, but it isn't a surprise that Meat isn't related to Mother of Pearl. However, `skos:related` is an `owl:SymmetricProperty` which means that since "Mother of Pearl" (`c_4951`) is related to "Decorative uses" (`c_2149`), that `c_2149` is related to `c_4951`.

Meaning of semantic relations

It is no accident that there is a considerable similarity between the definitions in SKOS of `skos:narrower` and `skos:broader` and the definition of `rdfs:subClassOf` and `superClassOf` (which is not defined in the RDFS standard). These pairs of properties are intended for modeling hierarchies. In both cases, it is desirable that the hierarchies could be traversed either "upward" or "downward." In both cases, transitivity of the relationship is important. In the case of RDF, the transitive nature of `subClassof` is represented directly. SKOS uses a more sophisticated model, in which the user of the model can decide if they want to use a transitive notion of broader or narrower, or not.

There is one definition for `subClassOf` that has no corresponding condition in SKOS. In RDFS, the type propagation rule holds.

```
CONSTRUCT {?x rdf:type ?C}
WHERE {?x rdf:type ?B.
       ?B rdfs:subClassOf ?C . }
```

Because of this rule, there is no confusion about the interpretation of `rdfs:subClassOf`. This rule makes it clear that C has more members (or at least, just as many) as B; that is, C is the more encompassing of the two classes.

Since we have no such rule in SKOS, there is the possibility for confusion; when we say

```
agrovoc:c_7030 skos:broader agrovoc:c_4397.
```

should we read this (in English) as "`c_7030` (Sheep) has broader term `c_4397` (Livestock)," or should we read it as "`c_4397` (Livestock) is broader than `c_7030` (Sheep)"? There is nothing in the formal SKOS model to tell us which is which. The relationship is expressed informally in the annotations on `skos:broader` and `skos:narrower`; that is, the labels "has broader" and "has narrower" respectively indicate that the former interpretation is the intended one—Sheep has broader term Livestock. It is important to keep this in mind when reading the SKOS examples that follow in this book, where we will see triples like

```
:Sheep skos:broader :Livestock.
```

For many people, this interpretation of `broader` is backward from what they expect.

If there were an inference-based definition of the semantics of `skos:broader` (as there is, for example, for `rdfs:subClassOf`), then the intended direction of this statement would be explicit.

There would be no need to rely on the interpretation of examples (like this one for `Sheep` and `Livestock`) to communicate which way the terms are intended to be used.

SKOS and linked vocabularies

One of the main advantages of SKOS is that it allows vocabularies to be linked. Controlled vocabularies and thesauri predate the age of the computer. Many vocabularies were developed before there was any idea of representing them on a computing platform, not to mention in a networked setting. Vocabularies with this sort of heritage have been developed to be stand-alone vocabularies, providing their own viewpoint on what words to use to describe some domain.

In a world of computer networks, it is now common for vocabularies to interact. A collection of content organized using one vocabulary is presented to the same audience as a collection using another vocabulary. The vocabularies themselves become linked information resources.

SKOS is uniquely suited for this purpose. Since SKOS is represented in RDF, every term has a unique identifier (its URI), which can be referenced on the Web. This makes it possible to make statements about how a term in one vocabulary relates to a term in another.

SKOS provides a handful of matching properties exactly for this purpose:

```
skos:exactMatch
skos:narrowMatch
skos:broadMatch
skos:closeMatch
```

The relationship between these properties and other SKOS properties is shown in Figure 10.2.

The idea of these mapping relations is that we can express relationships between terms in different vocabularies. We have already seen the AGROVOC concept c_7030 ("Sheep"). In the United States, the National Agriculture Library (NAL) has its own vocabulary, that includes a term `NAL:38846` ("sheep"). What is the relationship between these two concepts? On the face of it, we might suspect them to be the same. We can express this as

```
NAL:38846 skos:exactMatch AGROVOC:c_7030 .
```

The property `skos:exactMatch` doesn't have any inference-based semantics. To be more precise, there are no triples that we can infer from an `exactMatch` that will help us to understand what it means. It does, however, have a conventional meaning, that the two terms can be used interchangeably across a wide range of information retrieval applications.

While we might believe that these two terms are interchangeable, someone else might disagree, and believe that the USDA has a more specific notion of sheep than the United Nations does. This situation can also be expressed in SKOS, as

```
NAL:38846 skos:broadMatch AGROVOC:c_7030 .
```

Someone else might not be willing to make such a commitment, and instead only believes that the two variants of the word "sheep" can be used interchangeably in a few information retrieval settings. They can express this in SKOS by saying

```
NAL:38846 skos:closeMatch AGROVOC:c_7030 .
```

Finally, someone might want to relate a term in one vocabulary to another, but not want to imply that they are referring to the same thing. For instance, someone might want to record the fact that the NAL concept for "mutton" (`NAL:51747`) is related to the AGROVOC notion of "Sheep." There is no implication that these are the same thing, but there is some relationship. When searching for content about mutton, it makes sense for an information retrieval system to notify the searcher that there could be relevant content indexed under Sheep. This can be said in SKOS as

```
NAL:51747 skos:relatedMatch AGROVOC:c_7030 .
```

Unlike the meanings of words like `subClassOf`, `sameAs`, `inverseOf`, etc., in RDFS-Plus, the meanings of the words in SKOS have much less inference-based semantics. Their meaning is largely conventional, referring to how they should be treated by an information retrieval system.

But the SKOS standard is not mute about how these terms relate to one another, and in fact SKOS uses RDFS-Plus to define those relationships. As we have seen in Figure 10.2, these properties participate in an elaborate `subProperty` structure. We have already seen how this structure relates `skos:broader` to `skos:broaderTransitive`. It also relates the matching properties to one another, and to the other SKOS properties.

In particular, we might wonder when we should use `skos:broadMatch` and when we should just use `skos:broader`. Informally, `broadMatch` is intended when mapping one vocabulary to another; we are stating that two terms that were defined separately are, nevertheless, related. But will we miss out on something, if we don't also state that they are related by `skos:broader`?

A quick look at Figure 10.2 can put our worries to rest. We see from the figure that

```
skos:broadMatch rdfs:subPropertyOf skos:broader .
```

This makes the situation clear—when we assert that a term has a `broadMatch` with another term, we have also implied that it is simply broader. The SKOS model makes it clear that we may infer that all our matches are also related by `skos:broader`. In short, we aren't missing out on anything by simply using `broadMatch`.

Similar comments apply to `closeMatch` and `exactMatch`; if we were to assert that the NAL notion of Sheep is an `exactMatch` to the AGROVOC notion of Sheep, we could also infer that they are also a `closeMatch`; this is because (again, as shown in Figure 10.2),

```
skos:exactMatch rdfs:subPropertyOf skos:closeMatch .
```

In particular, if an information retrieval system were to use `skos:closeMatch` as a means by which it determined which terms to cross-reference, it would catch all the exact matches as well.

CONCEPT SCHEMES

SKOS includes the notion of a *Concept Scheme*. A concept scheme is a largely informal collection of concepts, corresponding roughly to a particular thesaurus or knowledge organization system. While concept schemes have little formal definition, they are useful for conveying the intention of the publisher of one or more thesauri. Common practice for using concept schemes is mixed. Some authorities (e.g., AGROVOC) publish their whole vocabulary as a single concept scheme. Others (e.g., the Library of Congress) publish each of their vocabularies using a separate concept scheme corresponding in part to different licensing controls on the different vocabularies. The National Agriculture Library uses several concept schemes, one for each highest-level heading.

A concept scheme can be seen as a set of concepts. There are no conditions that membership in a concept scheme be related in any way to the semantic relations, `skos:broader`, `skos:narrower`, or `skos:related`; a concept can be in one concept scheme while its broader and narrower concepts are in another. Concepts are related to a concept scheme by the properties `skos:inScheme`, `skos:hasTopConcept`, and `skos:topConceptOf`.

Concepts in a concept scheme are related to the scheme using `skos:inScheme`. So the two concepts `NAL:38846` ("sheep") and `AGROVOC:c_7030` ("Sheep") we used in an earlier example are in a different concept scheme, as follows:

```
AGROVOC:c_7030 skos:inScheme <http://www.fao.org/aos/agrovoc>.
NAL:38846 skos:inScheme NAL:S .
```

We, of course, knew that these concepts were maintained by different authorities because of their differing URIs. The explicit statement of inclusion in a concept scheme makes this relationship explicit and queryable with SPARQL.

A concept scheme can also have one or more distinguished concepts called *Top Concepts*. The semantic relations `skos:broader` and `skos:narrower` define a tree structure of concepts. It is possible to find the top of such a tree structure with a SPARQL query, but it is convenient to indicate it with a special property. This is the purpose of `skos:hasTopConcept` and `skos:topConceptOf`. Two triples describe the relationship between top concepts and other members of a concept scheme:

```
skos:topConceptOf rdfs:subPropertyOf skos:inScheme .
skos:topConceptOf owl:inverseOf skos:hasTopConcept .
```

As a result of these two triples, the top concept of a scheme must also be in that scheme, and the properties `topConceptOf` and `hasTopConcept` are inverses.

Managing SKOS concept schemes

Common practice for using these properties is varied; some vocabularies don't use them at all (leaving membership in the concept scheme implicit). Others use `inScheme` but make no indication of top concepts. Among those that indicate top concepts, some use `hasTopConcept` and others use `topConceptOf`.

All of these practices are acceptable according to the SKOS standard, but having so many acceptable practices, while making the job of the thesaurus writer easy, makes it more difficult for the consumer of a vocabulary to find his or her way around. In a move toward normalizing thesaurus presentation in SKOS, we will offer the following recommended practice for using concept schemes:

1. Align concept schemes to your own governance practice. In particular, use one concept scheme per vocabulary that is controlled by a single work process.
2. Propagate membership in concept schemes across `skos:broader` and `skos:narrower`. That is, the inference given by the following SPARQL CONSTRUCT should be valid:

```
CONSTRUCT {?c skos:inScheme ?S }
WHERE   {?a skos:inScheme ?S .
         ?a skos:broader ?c .}
```

A similar rule holds for `skos:narrower`.

3. Use `skos:broadMatch` (resp. `skos:narrowMatch`, `skos:exactMatch`, `skos:closeMatch`) only to map concepts that are in different concept schemes.
4. Indicate the top of all `skos:broader` trees with `skos:hasTopConcept`. Do not indicate any concepts internal to the tree as top concepts.
5. Keep the number of top concepts in any single concept scheme small (i.e., fewer than a half dozen)

These guidelines are intended to provide some coherence to SKOS presentation, but are not normative in any way. They are motivated by experiences made while reading vocabularies prepared by a variety of authorities. While there may be good reasons to break any of these rules, keeping to them ensures that thesaurus presentations are not surprising (e.g., keeping concepts in a single scheme together in the same broader/narrower tree), and that it is easy for someone searching a vocabulary to know where to start (by indicating the top concept). Some of them are just common sense (e.g., not indicating internal nodes as "top" concepts), while others are somewhat arbitrary (e.g., why stipulate `hasTopConcept` instead of `topConceptOf?`).

The existence of concept schemes provides an example of the motivation for having the property `skos:exactMatch`, even in light of the extant and very similar property `owl:sameAs`. The semantics of `owl:sameAs` state that any two resources that are `sameAs` one another are interchangeable in every statement. This means that if two concepts were `sameAs` one another, then they would necessarily be in the same concept scheme. Since concept schemes reflect authority and work process, this is clearly not appropriate. The property `exactMatch` makes much less commitment to interchangeability of concepts, indicating only that one concept act like the other in information retrieval settings.

SKOS INTEGRITY

While many things in SKOS are not formally defined by inferences it does include a number of integrity conditions that can be applied to any SKOS model to verify that it conforms to the standard. These conditions are normative, in that a model that violates them cannot be said to be conformant to the standard. There are 46 such conditions on the core SKOS ontology. We will not cover all of them in this book, but by examining a few of them, we hope to convey the basic idea of how SKOS is intended to be used.

Many of the constraints can be (and are) expressed in RDFS. In fact, all of the relationships shown in Figure 10.2 are part of the SKOS constraints, along with domain/range information such as:

```
skos:inScheme rdfs:range skos:ConceptScheme .
skos:semanticRelation rdfs:domain skos:Concept.
skos:semanticRelation rdfs:range skos:Concept.
```

That is, if something is in a scheme, then the thing it is in a `skos:ConceptScheme`. Any two things related by any semantic relation (that includes `broader`, `narrower`, `related`, and all the matching relations) are both members of the class `skos:Concept`.

Other constraints are most easily represented in SPARQL. We can use an ASK query to specify Boolean conditions in SPARQL; thus we can specify a condition that evaluates as *true* if there is a violation of the constraint. For instance, one constraint says that a resource has no more than one value of `skos:prefLabel` per language tag. This can be expressed in SPARQL as

```
ASK
WHERE  {?c skos:prefLabel ?l1 .
        ?c skos:prefLabel ?l2 .
        FILTER (lang (?l1) = lang (?l2))
        FILTER (?l1 != ?l2)
}
```

This query uses the function `lang (?x)` that returns the language tag for a string ("en" for English, "fr" for French, and so on). If the language tag matches for two different strings (i.e., they don't match), then we have a violation of the constraint.

Certain properties are constrained to be disjoint, e.g., `skos:related` and `skos:broaderTransitive`. That is, if two concepts are related, one cannot have the other as a broader term. This can be expressed in SPARQL as

```
ASK
WHERE  {?a skos:related ?b .
        ?a skos:broader* ?b }
```

That is, it is a violation if ?a and ?b are related, and one is broader (transitive) than the other.

In general, the integrity constraints in SKOS guarantee that a vocabulary is orderly, in a manner conducive to its use (and re-use) in information retrieval settings. It wouldn't do for a single concept to have two preferred labels in the same language, and once you know that one concept is broader than another, there is no need to shortcut this by making them related concepts as well.

SKOS IN ACTION

SKOS is a great example of what we have in mind when we call something "a model on the Semantic Web"; it models particular standards for how to represent thesauri in a Web-oriented way that encourages linking and reuse. We have seen what this model says about terms and concepts in a thesaurus and how they can relate to one another. But how is SKOS itself being used? What do we gain by representing a thesaurus in SKOS?

Utilization of the SKOS standard has grown dramatically since the W3C made it a Recommendation (second version in 2008). In addition to AGROVOC and the US National Agriculture library, many large-scale thesauri have been published in SKOS, including the Library of Congress Subject Headings, the West Key Numbering System, and EUROVOC, as well as a multitude of smaller scale vocabularies.

What has driven the popularity of SKOS? There are a number of factors involved.

First is its simplicity. The initial "S" in SKOS stands for "Simple," and the committee succeeded in large part in making it simple. This means that vocabularies represented in just about any other vocabulary system can be translated to SKOS without a lot of effort. The basic SKOS relationships (broader, narrower, related) and classes (Concept, ConceptScheme) do a good job of capturing what is essential in vocabularies.

Second is the ease with which a vocabulary can be transformed from other systems into SKOS. For the most part, if it is possible to query an existing vocabulary for broader, narrower, and related terms, then the vocabulary can be converted directly into SKOS. Simply record the outcome of that query as a triple:

```
?narrow skos:broader ?broad .
```

The simplicity of this process has enabled a cottage industry of SKOS conversions. It is not uncommon to see vocabularies that have been traditionally presented in spreadsheets, XML, databases and other storage formats published in SKOS.

A closely related factor is that until SKOS, there was no *de jure* standard way to represent a vocabulary in digital form. This is a surprising state of affairs, brought about in part by the dominance of many proprietary digital vocabulary forms, and the failure of non-proprietary forms to gain the stamp of approval of a major standards body. While there are many thesaurus standards supported by groups like ISO and NISO, these standards did not include normative recommendations for how to store a thesaurus in digital form.

The final factor is more subtle. Translation of a vocabulary into SKOS involves selecting a globally unique identifier for each concept. In practice, this is not a difficult thing to do (most thesauri already have some locally unique identifier anyway; e.g., the West Key Numbering System has its key numbers; the Library of Congress Subject Headings have their own identifiers). But translation into SKOS turns these locally unique identifiers into *globally* unique identifiers. This provides a great advantage when relating vocabularies to one another. As organizations merge and as information is published on a worldwide scale, it becomes more and more necessary to be able to link one vocabulary to another. This Web-enabled aspect of vocabulary management is something that older thesaurus standards (developed pre-Web) were not designed to support.

The case of AGROVOC and the NAL vocabulary illustrates this advantage. Shortly after the introduction of SKOS, the United Nations pursued a project to map these two thesauri together. The project needed a representation that would allow for terms from the two sources to be distinguished from one another. For example, the AGROVOC word for "Groundwater" and the NAL word for "groundwater" must be managed separately, but it also must be possible to represent the relationship between them. The point of the project was to compare and manage proposed relationships between them—is the AGROVOC notion of "Groundwater" the same as the NAL notion of "groundwater"? Or is it broader? Or narrower? Or just closely related? Whatever conclusion tone proposes, it is necessary to be able to talk about the AGROVOC term and the NAL term in the same statement. The translation of terms into URIs makes it possible to relate these things with a single triple, e.g.,

```
NAL:11571 skos:broadMatch AGROVOC:c_3391 .
```

SUMMARY

SKOS demonstrates how a fairly simple set of modeling constructs can be used to create extensible, distributed information networks. SKOS takes advantage of the distributed nature of RDF to allow extension to a network of information to be distributed across the web. It relies on the inferencing structure of RDFS-Plus to add completeness to their information structure.

SKOS vocabularies provide a cornerstone for linking information on the web. In order for two information sources to integrate, they have to have some common ground. Controlled vocabularies are the best candidate for such common ground. Publishing vocabularies in SKOS allows the concepts they define to be referenced on a global scale.

Controlled vocabularies are everywhere—not just in high-profile places like the United Nations or the Library of Congress. Anything that has a standard, official name can be used in a controlled vocabulary. Names of universities, stock symbols of companies, place names, names of months, all of these things are controlled vocabularies. Many of them have been published in SKOS, and many more are under way.

Fundamental concepts

The following fundamental concepts were introduced in this chapter.

Controlled Vocabulary—A set of terms providing common reference for linked information systems.

SKOS—Namespace for a system of representation for information management. SKOS stands for "Simple Knowledge Organization System."

AGROVOC—The United Nations agriculture vocabulary, see http://aims.fao.org/website/AGROVOC-Thesaurus.

NAL—the National Agriculture Library, see http://agclass.nal.usda.gov/.

Basic OWL

In previous chapters, we saw how RDFS-Plus as a modeling system provides considerable support for distributed information and federation of information. Simple constructs in RDFS-Plus can be combined in various ways to match properties, classes, and individuals. In the previous chapter, we saw this utility applied to knowledge organization (SKOS). In this chapter, we present the modeling capabilities of OWL that go beyond RDFS-Plus.

The OWL Recommendation is now in version 2.0, which extends the capabilities of OWL 1.0 with a number of new modeling constructs, but does not change the fundamental principles of how OWL works. Most of the modeling patterns in this book are valid in both OWL 1.0 as well as OWL 2.0; when something is specifically only available in OWL 2.0, we will indicate it explicitly.

We begin our presentation of OWL with a treatment of `owl:Restriction`. This single construct enhances the representational power of OWL by allowing us to describe classes in terms of other things we have already modeled. As we shall see, this opens up whole new vistas in modeling capabilities.

RESTRICTIONS

Suppose we have defined in RDFS a class we call `Base ballTeam`, with a particular subclass called `MajorLeagueTeam`, and another class we call `BaseballPlayer`. The roster for any particular season would be represented as a property `playsFor` that relates a `BaseballPlayer` to a `BaseballTeam`. Certain players are special in that they play for a `MajorLeagueTeam`. We'd like to define that class and call it `MajorLeaguePlayer` (presented here as Major League Players, to avoid confusion). If we are interested in the fiscal side of baseball, we could also be interested in the class of Agents who represent Major League Players, and then the bank accounts controlled by the Agents who represent Major League Players and so on.

One of the great powers of the Semantic Web is that information that has been specified by one person in one context can be reused either by that person or by others in different contexts. There is no expectation that the same source who defined the roster of players will be the one that defines the role of the agents or of the bank accounts. If we want to use information from multiple sources together, we need a way to express concepts from one context in terms of concepts from the other. In OWL, this is achieved by having a facility with which we can describe new classes in terms of classes that have already been defined. This facility can also be used to model more complex constructs than the ones we've discussed so far.

We have already seen how to define simple classes and relationships between them in RDFS and OWL, but none of the constructs we have seen so far can create descriptions of the sort we want in our Major League Baseball Player example. This is done in OWL using a language construct called a `Restriction`.

Consider the case of a `MajorLeaguePlayer`. We informally defined a `MajorLeague Player` as someone who plays on a `MajorLeagueTeam`. The intuition behind the name `Restriction` is that membership in the class `MajorLeaguePlayer` is restricted to those things that play for a `MajorLeagueTeam`. Since a `Restriction` is a special case of a `Class`, we will sometimes refer to a `Restriction` as a *Restriction Class* just to make that point clear.

More generally, a `Restriction` in OWL is a `Class` defined by describing the individuals it contains. This simple idea forms the basis for extension of models in OWL: If you can describe a set of individuals in terms of known classes, then you can use that description to define a new class. Since this new class is now also an existing class, it can be used to describe individuals for inclusion in a new class, and so on. We will return to the baseball player example later in this chapter, but first we need to learn more about the use of restriction classes.

EXAMPLE Questions and Answers

To start with, we will use a running example of managing questions and answers, as if we were modeling a quiz, examination, or questionnaire. This is a fairly simple area that nevertheless illustrates a wide variety of uses of restriction classes in OWL.

Informally, a questionnaire consists of a number of questions, each of which has a number of possible answers. A question includes string data for the text of the question, whereas an answer includes string data for the text of the answer. In contrast to a quiz or examination, there are typically no "right" answers in a questionnaire. In questionnaires, quizzes, and examinations, the selection of certain answers may preclude the posing of other questions.

This basic structure for questionnaires can be represented by classes and properties in OWL. Any particular questionnaire is then represented by a set of individual questions, answers, and concepts and particular relationships between them.

The basic schema for the questionnaire is as follows and is shown diagrammatically in Figure 11.1. Throughout the example, we will use the namespace *q:* to refer to elements that relate to question-naires in general, and the namespace *d:* to refer to the elements of the particular example questionnaire.

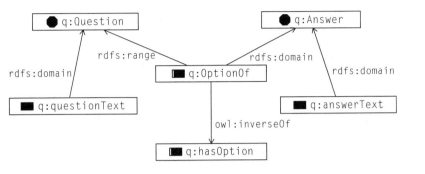

FIGURE 11.1

Question, answer, and the properties that describe them.

```
q:Answer a owl:Class.
q:Question a owl:Class.
q:optionOf a owl:ObjectProperty;
   rdfs:domain q:Answer;
   rdfs:range q:Question;
   owl:inverseOf q:hasOption.
q:hasOption a owl:ObjectProperty.
q:answerText a owl:DatatypeProperty;
   rdfs:domain q:Answer;
   rdfs:range xsd:string.
q:questionText a owl:FunctionalProperty,
                 owl:DatatypeProperty;
   rdfs:domain q:Question;
   rdfs:range xsd:string.
```

A particular questionnaire will have questions and answers. For now, we will start with a simple questionnaire that might be part of the screening for the helpdesk of a cable television and Internet provider:

- What system are you having trouble with?
  - Possible answers (3): Cable TV, High-Speed Internet, Both
- What television symptom(s) are you seeing?
  - Possible answers (4): No Picture, No Sound, Tiling, Bad Reception.

This is shown as follows and graphically in Figure 11.2.

```
d:WhatProblem a q:Question;
   q:hasOption d:STV, d:SInternet, d:SBoth;
   q:questionText "What system are you having trouble
   with?".
d:STV a q:Answer;
   q:answerText "Cable TV".
d:SInternet a q:Answer;
   q:answerText "High-speed Internet".
d:SBoth a q:Answer;
```

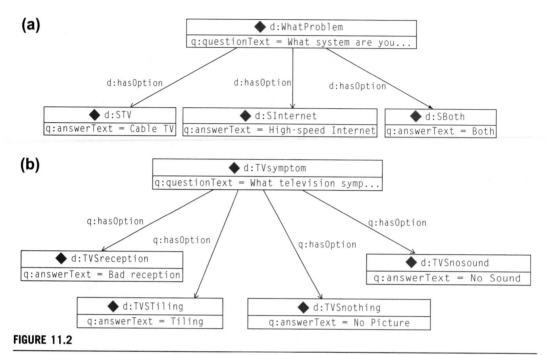

FIGURE 11.2

Some particular questions and their answers.

```
    q:answerText "Both".
d:TVsymptom a q:Question;
    q:questionText "What television symptoms are you
    having?";
    q:hasOption d:TVSnothing, d:TVSnosound, d:TVStiling,
               d:TVSreception.
d:TVSnothing a q:Answer;
    q:answerText "No Picture".
d:TVSnosound a q:Answer;
    q:answerText "No Sound".

d:TVStiling a q:Answer;
    q:answerText "Tiling".
d:TVSreception a q:Answer;
    q:answerText "Bad reception".
```

Consider an application for managing a questionnaire in a web portal. This application performs a query against this combined data to determine what question(s) to ask next. Then for each question, it presents the text of the question itself and the text of each answer, with a select widget (e.g., radio button) next to it. We haven't yet defined enough information for such an application to work, and we have made no provisions to determine which questions to ask before any others or how to record answers to the questions. We start with the latter.

We first define a new property `hasSelectedOption`, a subproperty of `hasOption`:

```
q:hasSelectedOption a owl:ObjectProperty;
                    rdfs:subPropertyOf q:hasOption.
```

When the user who is taking a questionnaire answers a question, a new triple will be entered to indicate that a particular option for that question has been selected. That is, if the user selects "Cable TV" from the options of the first question `d:WhatProblem`, then the application will add the triple

```
d:WhatProblem q:hasSelectedOption d:STV.
```

to the triple store. Notice that there is no need to remove any triples from the triple store; the original `d:hasOption` relationship between `d:WhatProblem` and `d:STV` still holds. As we develop the example, the model will provide ever-increasing guidance for how the selection of questions will be done.

Adding "restrictions"

The language construct in OWL for creating new class descriptions based on descriptions of the prospective members of a class is called the *restriction* (`owl:Restriction`). An `owl:Restriction` is a special kind of class (i.e., `owl:Restriction` is an `rdfs:subClassOf owl:Class`). A restriction is a class that is defined by a description of its members in terms of existing properties and classes.

In OWL, as in RDF, the AAA slogan holds: Anyone can say Anything about Any topic. Hence, the class of all things in owl (`owl:Thing`) is unrestricted. A `Restriction` is defined by providing some description that limits (or restricts) the kinds of things that can be said about a member of the class. So if we have a property `orbitsAround`, it is perfectly legitimate to say that anything `orbitsAround` anything else. If we restrict the value of `orbitsAround` by saying that its object must be `TheSun`, then we have defined the class of all things that orbit around the sun (i.e., our solar system).

Kinds of restrictions

OWL provides a number of kinds of restrictions, three of which are `owl:allValuesFrom`, `owl:someValuesFrom`, and `owl:hasValue`. Each describes how the new class is constrained by the possible asserted values of properties.

Additionally, a restriction class in OWL is defined by the keyword `owl:onProperty`. This specifies what property is to be used in the definition of the restriction class. For example, the restriction defining the objects that orbit around the sun will use `owl:onProperty orbitsAround`, whereas the restriction defining major league players will use `owl:onProperty playsFor`.

A restriction is a special kind of a class, so it has individual members just like any class. Membership in a restriction class must satisfy the conditions specified by the kind of restriction (`owl:allValuesFrom`, `owl:someValuesFrom`, or `owl:hasValue`), as well as the `onProperty` specification.

owl:someValuesFrom

`owl:someValuesFrom` is used to produce a restriction of the form "All individuals for which at least one value of the property `P` comes from class `C`." In other words, one could define the class

AllStarPlayer as "All individuals for which at least one value of the property playsFor comes from the class AllStarTeam." This is what the restriction looks like:

```
[a owl:Restriction;
   owl:onProperty :playsFor;
   owl:someValuesFrom :AllStarTeam]
```

Notice the use of the [...] notation. As a reminder from Chapter 3, this refers to an anonymous node (a bnode) described by the properties listed here; that is, this refers to a single bnode, which is the subject of three triples, one per line (separated by semicolons).

The restriction class defined in this way refers to exactly the class of individuals that satisfy these conditions on playsFor and AllStarTeam. In particular, if an individual actually has some value from the class AllStarTeam for the property playsFor, then it is a member of this restriction class. Note that this restriction class, unlike those we've learned about in earlier chapters, has no specific name associated with it. It is defined by the properties of the restriction (i.e., restrictions on the members of the class) and thus it is sometimes referred to in the literature as an "unnamed class."

EXAMPLE Answered Questions

In the questionnaire example, we addressed the issue of recording answers to questions by defining a property hasOption that relates a question to answer options and a subproperty hasSelectedOption to indicate those answers that have been selected by the individual who is taking the questionnaire. Now we want to address the problem of selecting which question to ask.

There are a number of considerations that go into such a selection, but one of them is that (under most circumstances) we do not want to ask a question for which we already have an answer. This suggests a class of questions that have already been answered. We will define the set of AnsweredQuestions in terms of the properties we have already defined. Informally, an answered question is any question that has a selected option.

An answered question is one that has some value from the class *Answer* for the property hasSelectedOption. This can be defined as follows:

```
q:AnsweredQuestion owl:equivalentClass
[a owl:Restriction;
            owl:onProperty q:hasSelectedOption;
            owl:someValuesFrom q:Answer ].
```

Since

```
d:WhatProblem q:hasSelectedOption d:STV.
```

and

```
d:STV a q:Answer.
```

are asserted triples, the individual d:WhatProblem satisfies the conditions defined by the restriction class. That is, there is at least one value (someValue) for the property hasSelectedOption that is in the class `Answer`. Individuals that satisfy the conditions specified by a restriction class are inferred to be members of it. This inference can be represented as follows:

```
d:WhatProblem a [a owl:Restriction;
                 owl:onProperty q:hasSelectedOption;
                 owl:someValuesFrom q:Answer]
```

and, thus, according to the semantics of `equivalentClass`,

```
d:WhatProblem a q:AnsweredQuestion.
```

These definitions and inferences are shown in Figure 11.3.

owl:allValuesFrom

`owl:allValuesFrom` is used to produce a restriction class of the form "the individuals for which all values of the property P come from class C." This restriction looks like the following:

```
[a owl:Restriction;
   owl:onProperty P;
   owl:allValuesFrom C]
```

The restriction class defined in this way refers to exactly the class of individuals that satisfy these conditions on P and C. If an individual x is a member of this `allValuesFrom` restriction, a number of conclusions can follow, one for each triple describing x with property P. In particular, every value of property P for individual x is inferred to be in class C. So, if individual `MyFavoriteAllStarTeam` (a member of the class `BaseballTeam`) is a member of the restriction class defined by `owl:onProperty hasPlayer` and

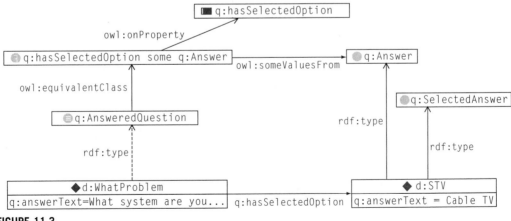

FIGURE 11.3

Definition of q:AnsweredQuestion and the resulting inferences for d:WhatProblem. Since d:WhatProblem has something (d:STV) of type q:Answer on property q:hasSelectedOption, it is inferred (*dotted line*) to be a member of AnsweredQuestion.

owl:allValuesFrom StarPlayer, then every player on MyFavoriteAllStarTeam is a StarPlayer. So, if MyFavoriteAllStarTeam hasPlayer Kaneda and MyFavoriteAllStarTeam hasPlayer Gonzales, then both Kaneda and Gonzales must be of type StarPlayer.

There is a subtle difference between someValuesFrom and allValuesFrom. Since someValuesFrom is defined as a restriction class such that there is at least one member of a class with a particular property, then it implies that there must be such a member. On the other hand, allValuesFrom technically means "if there are any members, then they all must have this property." This latter does not imply that there are any members. This will be more important in later chapters.

EXAMPLE Question Dependencies

In our questionnaire example, we might want to ask certain questions only after particular answers have been given. To accomplish this, we begin by defining the class of all selected answers, based on the property hasSelectedOption we have already defined. We can borrow a technique from Chapter 7 to do this. First, we define a class for the selected answers:

```
q:SelectedAnswer a owl:Class;
    rdfs:subClassOf q:Answer.
```

We want to ensure that any option that has been selected will appear in this class. This can be done easily by asserting that

```
q:hasSelectedOption rdfs:range q:SelectedAnswer.
```

This ensures that any value V that appears as the object of a triple of the form

```
? q:hasSelectedOption V.
```

is a member of the class SelectedAnswer. In particular, since we have asserted that

```
d:WhatProblem q:hasSelectedOption d:STV.
```

we can infer that

```
d:STV a q:SelectedAnswer.
```

Now that we have defined the class of selected answers, we describe the questions that can be asked only after those answers have been given. We introduce a new class called EnabledQuestion; only questions that also have type EnabledQuestion are actually available to be asked:

```
q:EnabledQuestion a owl:Class.
```

When an answer is selected, we want to infer that certain dependent questions become members of EnabledQuestion. This can be done with a restriction, owl:allValuesFrom.

To begin, each answer potentially makes certain questions available for asking. We define a property called enablesCandidate for this relationship. In particular, we say that an answer enables a question if selecting that answer causes the system to consider that question as a candidate for the next question to ask:

```
q:enablesCandidate a owl:ObjectProperty;
            rdfs:domain q:Answer;
              rdfs:range q:Question.
```

In our example, we only want to ask a question about television problems if the answer to the first question indicates that there is a television problem:

```
d:STV q:enablesCandidate d:TVsymptom.
d:SBoth q:enablesCandidate d:TVsymptom.
```

That is, if the answer to the first question, "What system are you having trouble with?," is either "Cable TV" or "Both," then we want to be able to ask the question "What television symptoms are you having?"

The following owl:allValuesFrom restriction does just that: It defines the class of things all of whose values for d:enablesCandidate come from the class d:EnabledQuestion:

```
[a owl:Restriction;
   owl:onProperty q:enablesCandidate;
   owl:allValuesFrom q:EnabledQuestion]
```

Which answers should enforce this property? We only want this for the answers that have been selected. How do we determine which answers have been selected? So far, we only have the property hasSelectedOption to indicate them. That is, for any member of SelectedAnswer, we want it to also be a member of this restriction class. This is exactly what the relation rdfs:subClassOf does for us:

```
q:SelectedAnswer rdfs:subClassOf
   [a owl:Restriction;
      owl:onProperty q:enablesCandidate;
      owl:allValuesFrom q:EnabledQuestion].
```

That is, a selected answer is a subclass of the unnamed restriction class.

Let's watch how this works, step by step. When the user selects the answer "Cable TV" for the first question, the type of d:STV is asserted to be SelectedAnswer, like the preceding.

```
d:STV a q:SelectedAnswer.
```

However, because of the rdfs:subClassOf relation, d:STV is a member of the restriction class, that is, it has the restriction as its type:

```
d:STV a
   [a owl:Restriction;
      owl:onProperty q:enablesCandidate;
      owl:allValuesFrom q:EnabledQuestion].
```

Any individual who is a member of this restriction necessarily satisfies the `allValuesFrom` condition; that is, any individual that it is related to by `d:enablesCandidate` must be a member of `d:EnabledQuestion`. Since

```
d:STV q:enablesCandidate d:TVsymptom.
```

we can infer that

d:TVsymptom a q:EnabledQuestion.

as desired. Finally, since we have also asserted the same information for the answer `d:SBoth`,

```
d:SBoth q:enablesCandidate d:TVsymptom.
```

We can see this inference and the triples that led to it in Figure 11.4. Restrictions are shown in the figures using a shorthand called the *Manchester Syntax* (named after its development at the University of Manchester). The shorthand summarizes a restriction using the keywords `all`, `some`, and `value` to indicate the restriction types `owl:allValuesFrom`, `owl:someValuesFrom`, and

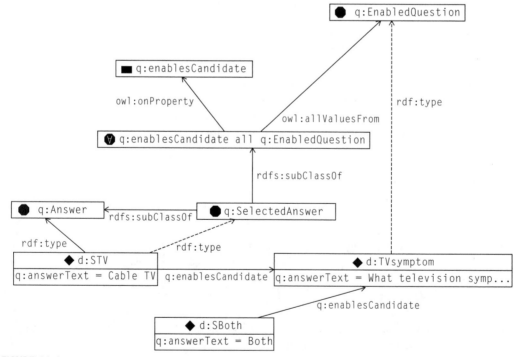

FIGURE 11.4

`d:STV enablesCandidate TVSymptom`, but it is also a member of a restriction on the property `enablesCandidate`, stipulating that all values must come from the class `q:EnabledQuestion`. We can therefore infer that `d:TVSymptom` has type `q:EnabledQuestion`.

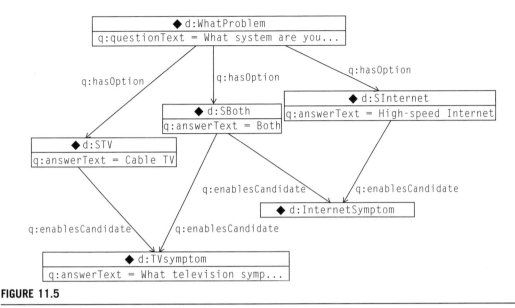

FIGURE 11.5

Questions and the answers that enable them.

`owl:hasValue`, respectively. The restriction property (indicated in triples by `owl:onProperty`) is printed before the keyword, and the target class (or individual, in the case of `owl:hasValue`) is printed after the keyword. We see an example of an `owl:allValuesFrom` restriction in Figure 11.4. It is important to note that this is only a shorthand; all the information needed for inferences is expressed in RDF triples.

Since `SBoth` also enables the candidate `TVSymptom`, the same conclusion will be drawn if the user answers "Both" to the first question. If we were to extend the example with another question about Internet symptoms `d:InternetSymptom`, then we could express all the dependencies in this short questionnaire as follows:

```
d:STV q:enablesCandidate d:TVsymptom.
d:SBoth q:enablesCandidate d:TVsymptom.
d:SBoth q:enablesCandidate d:InternetSymptom.
d:SInternet q:enablesCandidate d:InternetSymptom.
```

The dependency tree is shown graphically in Figure 11.5.

EXAMPLE Prerequisites

In the previous example, we supposed that when we answered one question, it made all of its dependent questions eligible for asking. Another way questions are related to one another in a questionnaire is a prerequisite. If a question has a number of prerequisites, all of them must be answered appropriately for the question to be eligible.

Consider the following triples that define a section of a questionnaire:

```
d:NeighborsToo a q:Question;
     q:hasOption d:NTY, d:NTN, d:NTDK;
     q:questionText "Are other customers in your building
     also experiencing problems?".
d:NTY a q:Answer;
     q:answerText "Yes, my neighbors are experiencing the
     same problem.".
d:NTN a q:Answer;
     q:answerText "No, my neighbors are not experiencing
     the same problem.".
d:NTDK a q:Answer;
     q:answerText "I don't know.".
```

This question makes sense only if the current customer lives in a building with other customers and is experiencing a technical problem. That is, this question depends on the answers to two more questions, shown following. The answer to the first question (d:othersinbuilding) should be d:OYes, and the answer to the second question (d:whatissue) should be d:PTech:

```
d:othersinbuilding
          a q:Question;
          q:hasOption d:ONo, d:OYes;
          q:questionText
              "Do you live in a multi-unit dwelling with
          other customers?".
d:OYes a q:Answer;
          q:answerText "Yes.".
d:ONo a q:Answer;
          q:answerText "No.".
d:whatIssue
          a q:Question;
          q:hasOption d:PBilling, d:PNew, d:PCancel,
          d:PTech;
          q:questionText
              "What can customer service help you with
          today?".
d:PBilling a q:Answer;
              q:answerText "Billing question.".
d:PNew a q:Answer;
              q:answerText "New account".
d:PCancel a q:Answer;
              q:answerText "Cancel account".
d:PTech a q:Answer;
              q:answerText "Technical difficulty".
```

A graphic version of these questions can be seen in Figure 11.6.

(a)

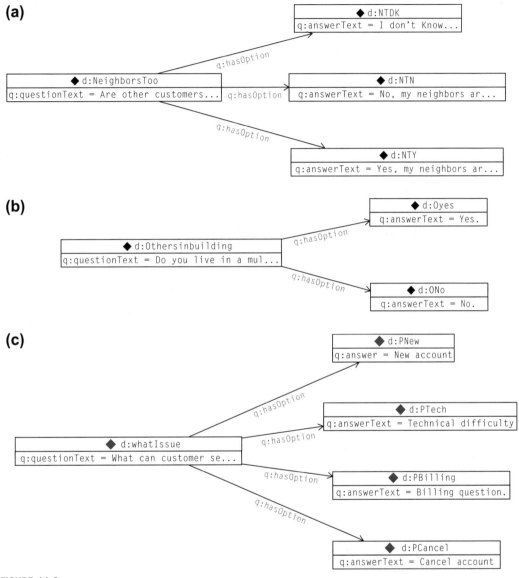

FIGURE 11.6

Questions about neighbors have two prerequisite questions.

CHALLENGE 26

How can we model the relationship between `d:NeighborsToo`, `d:whatIssue`, and `d:othersinbuilding` so that we will only ask `d:NeighborsToo` when we have appropriate answers to both `d:whatIssue` and `d:othersinbuilding`?

We introduce a new property `q:hasPrerequisite` that will relate a question to its prerequisites:

```
q:hasPrerequisite
   rdfs:domain q:Question;
   rdfs:range q:Answer.
```

We can indicate the relationship between the questions using this property:

```
d:NeighborsToo q:hasPrerequisite d:PTech, d:OYes.
```

This prerequisite structure is shown in graphical form in Figure 11.7.

Now we want to say that we will infer something is a `d:EnabledQuestion` if all of its prerequisite answers are selected. We begin by asserting that

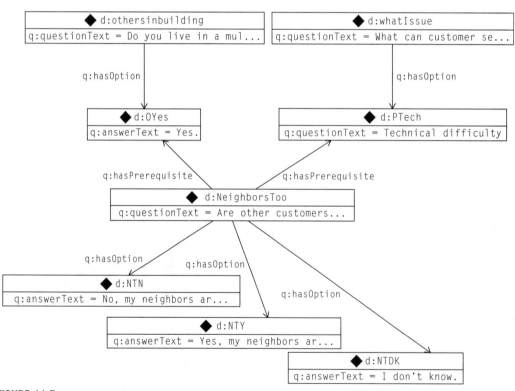

FIGURE 11.7

Some questions and their prerequisites.

```
[a owl:Restriction;
   owl:onProperty q:hasPrerequisite;
   owl:allValuesFrom q:SelectedAnswer]
      rdfs:subClassOf q:EnabledQuestion.
```

Notice that we can use the restriction class just as we could any other class in OWL, so in this case we have said that the restriction is a subclass of another class. Any question that satisfies the restriction will be inferred to be a member of d:EnabledQuestion by this subclass relation. But how can we infer that something satisfies this restriction?

For an individual ?x to satisfy this restriction, we must know that every time there is a triple of the form

```
?x hasPrerequisite ?y.
```

?y must be a member of the class d:SelectedAnswer. But by the Open World assumption, we don't know if there might be another triple of this form for which ?y is not a member of d:SelectedAnswer. Given the Open World assumption, how can we ever know that all prerequisites have been met?

The rest of this challenge will have to wait until we discuss the various methods by which we can (partially) close the world in OWL. The basic idea is that if we can say how many prerequisites a question has, then we can know when all of them have been selected. If we know that a question has only one prerequisite, and we find one that it is satisfied, then it must be the one. If we know that a question has no prerequisites at all, then we can determine that it is an EnabledQuestion without having to check for any SelectedAnswers at all.

owl:hasValue

The third kind of restriction in OWL is called owl:hasValue. As in the other two restrictions, it acts on a particular property as specified by owl:onProperty. It is used to produce a restriction whose description is of the form "All individuals that have the value A for the property P" and looks as follows:

```
[a owl:Restriction;
   owl:onProperty P;
   owl:hasValue A]
```

Formally, the hasValue restriction is just a special case of the someValuesFrom restriction, in which the class C happens to be a singleton set {A}.

Although it is "just" a special case, owl:hasValue has been identified in the OWL standard in its own right because it is a very common and useful modeling form. It effectively turns specific instance descriptions into class descriptions. For example, "The set of all planets orbiting the sun" and "The set of all baseball teams in Japan" are defined using hasValue restrictions.

EXAMPLE Priority Questions

Suppose that in our questionnaire, we assign priority levels to our questions. First we define a class of priority levels and particular individuals that define the priorities in the questionnaire:

```
q:PriorityLevel a owl:Class.
q:High a q:PriorityLevel.
q:Medium a q:PriorityLevel.
q:Low a q:PriorityLevel.
```

Then we define a property that we will use to specify the priority level of a question:

```
q:hasPriority
        rdfs:range q:PriorityLevel.
```

We have defined the range of q:hasPriority but not its domain. After all, we might want to set priorities for any number of different sorts of things, not just questions. We can use owl:hasValue to define the class of high-priority items:

```
q:HighPriorityItem owl:equivalentClass
[a owl:Restriction;
        owl:onProperty q:hasPriority;
        owl:hasValue q:High].
```

These triples are shown graphically in Figure 11.8. Note that where before we defined subclasses and superclasses of a restriction class, here we use owl:equivalentClass to specify that these classes are the same. So we have created a named class (q:HighPriorityItem) that is the same as the unnamed restriction class, and we can use this named class if we want to make other assertions or to further restrict the class.

We can describe Medium and Low priority questions in the same manner:

```
q:MediumPriorityItem owl:equivalentClass
[a owl:Restriction;
        owl:onProperty q:hasPriority;
        owl:hasValue q:Medium ].
q:LowPriorityItem owl:equivalentClass
[a owl:Restriction;
        owl:onProperty q:hasPriority;
        owl:hasValue q:Low ].
```

If we assert the priority level of a question, such as the following:

```
d:WhatProblem q:hasPriority q:High.
d:InternetSymptom q:hasPriority q:Low.
```

then we can infer the membership of these questions in their respective classes:

```
d:WhatProblem a q:HighPriorityItem.
d:InternetSymptom a q:LowPriorityItem.
```

We can also use owl:hasValue to work "the other way around." Suppose we assert that d:TVsymptom is in the class HighPriorityItem:

```
d:TVsymptom a q:HighPriorityItem.
```

Then by the semantics of owl:equivalentClass, we can infer that d:TVsymptom is a member of the restriction class and must be bound by its stipulations. Thus, we can infer that

```
d:TVsymptom q:hasPriority q:High.
```

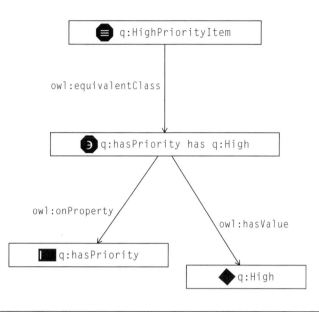

FIGURE 11.8

Definition of a `HighPriorityItem` as anything that has value `High` for the `hasPriority` property.

Notice that there is no stipulation in this definition to say that a `HighPriorityItem` must be a question; after all, we might set priorities for things other than questions. The only way we know that `d:TVsymptom` is a `q:Question` is that we already asserted that fact. In the next chapter, we will see how to use set operations to make definitions that combine restrictions with other classes.

CHALLENGE PROBLEMS

As we saw in the previous examples, the class constructors in OWL can be combined in a wide variety of powerful ways. In this section, we present a series of challenges that can be addressed using these OWL constructs. Often the application of the construct is quite simple; however, we have chosen these challenge problems because of their relevance to modeling problems that we have seen in real modeling projects.

Local restriction of ranges

We have already seen how `rdfs:domain` and `rdfs:range` can be used to classify data according to how it is used. But in more elaborate modeling situations, a finer granularity of domain and range inferences is needed. Consider the following example of describing a vegetarian diet:

```
:Person a owl:Class.
:Food a owl:Class.
:eats rdfs:domain :Person.
:eats rdfs:range :Food.
```

From these triples and the following instance data

```
:Maverick :eats :Steak.
```

we can conclude two things:

```
:Maverick a:Person.
:Steak a:Food.
```

The former is implied by the domain information, and the latter by the range information.

Suppose we want to define a variety of diets in more detail. What would this mean? First, let's suppose that we have a particular kind of person, called a Vegetarian, and the kind of food that a Vegetarian eats, which we will call simply VegetarianFood, as subclasses of Person and Food, respectively:

```
:Vegetarian a owl:Class;
   rdfs:subClassOf :Person.
:VegetarianFood a owl:Class;
   rdfs:subClassOf :Food.
```

Suppose further that we say

```
:Jen a:Vegetarian;
   :eats :Marzipan.
```

We would like to be able to infer that

```
:Marzipan a:VegetarianFood.
```

but not make the corresponding inference for Maverick's steak until someone asserts that he, too, is a vegetarian.

CHALLENGE 27

It is tempting to represent this with more domain and range statements—thus:

```
:eats rdfs:domain :Vegetarian.
:eats rdfs:range :VegetarianFood.
```

But given the meaning of rdfs:domain and rdfs:range, we can draw inferences from these triples that we do not intend. In particular, we can infer

```
:Maverick a :Vegetarian.
:Steak a :VegetarianFood.
```

which would come as a surprise both to Maverick and the vegetarians of the world.

How can the relationship between vegetarians and vegetarian food be correctly modeled with the use of the owl:Restriction?

Solution

We can define the set of things that only eat VegetarianFood using a restriction, owl:allValuesFrom; we can then assert that any Vegetarian satisfies this condition using rdfs:subClassOf. Together, it looks like this:

```
:Vegetarian rdfs:subClassOf
   [a owl:Restriction;
      owl:onProperty :eats;
      owl:allValuesFrom :VegetarianFood].
```

Let's see how it works. Since

```
:Jen a:Vegetarian.
```

we can conclude that

```
:Jen a [a owl:Restriction;
   owl:onProperty :eats;
      owl:allValuesFrom :VegetarianFood].
```

Combined with the fact that

```
:Jen :eats :Marzipan.
```

we can conclude that

```
:Marzipan a:VegetarianFood.
```

as desired. How does `Maverick` fare now? We won't say that he is a `Vegetarian` but only, as we have stated already, that he is a `Person`. That's where the inference ends; there is no stated relationship between `Maverick` and `Vegetarian`, so there is nothing on which to base an inference. Maverick's steak remains simply a `Food`, not a `VegetarianFood`.

The entire model and inferences are shown in Figure 11.9.

Challenge: filtering data based on explicit type

We have seen how tabular data can be used in RDF by considering each row to be an individual, the column names as properties, and the values in the table as values. We saw sample data in Table 3.12, which we repeat on page 240 as Table 11.1. Some sample triples from these data are shown in Table 11.2.

Each row from the original table appears in Table 11.2 as an individual in the RDF version. Each of these individuals has the same type—namely, `mfg:Product`—from the name of the table. These data include only a limited number of possible values for the "`Product_Line`" field, and they are known in advance (e.g., "Paper machine," "Feedback line," "Safety Valve," etc.).

A more elaborate way to import this information would be to still have one individual per row in the original table but to have rows with different types depending on the value of the Product Line column. For example, the following triples (among others) would be imported:

```
mfg:Product1 rdf:type ns:Paper_machine.
mfg:Product4 rdf:type ns:Feedback_line.
mfg:Product7 rdf:type ns:Monitor.
mfg:Product9 rdf:type ns:SafetyValve.
```

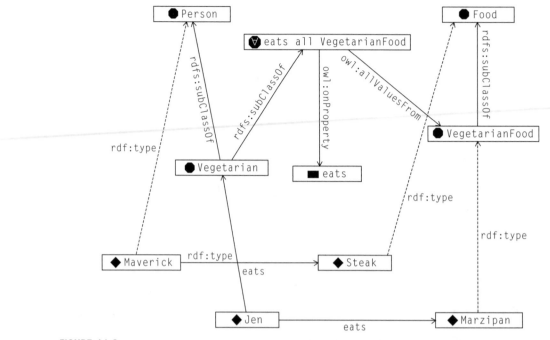

FIGURE 11.9

Definition of a vegetarian as a restriction on what the person eats.

Table 11.1 Typical Tabular Data for RDF Import						
Product						
ID	Model Number	Division	Product Line	Manufacture Location	SKU	Available
1	ZX-3	Manufacturing support	Paper machine	Sacramento	FB3524	23
2	ZX-3P	Manufacturing support	Paper machine	Sacramento	KD5243	4
3	ZX-3S	Manufacturing support	Paper machine	Sacramento	IL4028	34
4	B-1430	Control engineering	Feedback line	Elizabeth	KS4520	23
5	B-1430X	Control engineering	Feedback line	Elizabeth	CL5934	14
6	B-1431	Control engineering	Active sensor	Seoul	KK3945	0
7	DBB-12	Accessories	Monitor	Hong Kong	ND5520	100
8	SP-1234	Safety	Safety valve	Cleveland	HI4554	4
9	SPX-1234	Safety	Safety valve	Cleveland	OP5333	14

Table 11.2 Sample Triples

Subject	Predicate	Object
mfg:Product1	rdf:type	mfg:Product
mfg:Product1	mfg:Product_ID	1
mfg:Product1	mfg:Product_ModelNo	ZX-3
mfg:Product1	mfg:Product_Division	Manufacturing support
mfg:Product1	mfg:Product_Product_Line	Paper machine
mfg:Product1	mfg:Product_Manufacture_Location	Sacramento
mfg:Product1	mfg:Product_SKU	FB3524
mfg:Product1	mfg:Product_Available	23
mfg:Product2	rdf:type	mfg:Product
mfg:Product2	mfg:Product_ID	2
mfg:Product2	mfg:Product_ModelNo	ZX-3P
mfg:Product2	mfg:Product_Division	Manufacturing support
mfg:Product2	mfg:Product_Product_Line	Paper machine
mfg:Product2	mfg:Product_Manufacture_Location	Sacramento
mfg:Product2	mfg:Product_SKU	KD5243
mfg:Product2	mfg:Proudct_Available	4
mfg:Product3	rdf:type	mfg:Product
mfg:Product4	rdf:type	mfg:Product
mfg:Product5	rdf:type	mfg:Product …

This is a common situation when actually importing information from a table. It is quite common for type information to appear as a particular column in the table. If we use a single method for importing tables, all the rows become individuals of the same type. A software-intensive solution would be to write a more elaborate import mechanism that allows a user to specify which column should specify the type. A model-based solution would use a model in OWL and an inference engine to solve the same problem.

CHALLENGE 28

Build a model in OWL so we can infer the type information for each individual, based on the value in the "Product Line" field but using just the simple imported triples described in Chapter 3.

Solution

Since the classes of which the rows will be members (i.e., the product lines) are already known, we first define those classes:

```
ns:Paper_Machine rdf:type owl:Class.
ns:Feedback_Line rdf:type owl:Class.
ns:Active_Sensor rdf:type owl:Class.
ns:Monitor rdf:type owl:Class.
ns:Safety_Valve rdf:type owl:Class.
```

Each of these classes must include just those individuals with the appropriate value for the property mfg:Product_Product_Line. The class constructor that achieves this uses an owl:hasValue restriction, as follows:

```
ns:Paper_Machine owl:equivalentClass
    [a owl:Restriction;
        owl:onProperty mfg:Product_Product_Line
        owl:hasValue "Paper machine"].

ns:Feedback_Line owl:equivalentClass
    [a owl:Restriction;
        owl:onProperty mfg:Product_Product_Line
        owl:hasValue "Feedback line"].

ns:Active_Sensor owl:equivalentClass
    [a owl:Restriction;
        owl:onProperty mfg:Product_Product_Line
        owl:hasValue "Active sensor"].

ns:Monitor owl:equivalentClass
    [a owl:Restriction;
        owl:onProperty mfg:Product_Product_Line
        owl:hasValue "Monitor"].

ns:Safety_Valve owl:equivalentClass
    [a owl:Restriction;
        owl:onProperty mfg:Product_Product_Line
        owl:hasValue "Safety Valve"].
```

Each of these definitions draws inferences as desired. Consider mfg:Product1 ("ZX-3"), for which the triple

```
mfg:Product1 mfg:Product_Product_Line "Paper machine".
```

has been imported from the table. The first triple ensures that mfg:Product1 satisfies the conditions of the restriction for Paper_Machine. Hence,

```
mfg:Product1 rdf:type [a owl:Restriction;
        owl:onProperty mfg:Product_Product_Line
        owl:hasValue "Paper machine" ].
```

can be inferred. Since this restriction is equivalent to the definition for mfg:Paper_Machine, we have

```
mfg:Product1 rdf:type mfg:Paper_Machine.
```

as desired.

Furthermore, this definition maintains coherence of the data, even if it came from a source other than the imported table. Suppose that a new product is defined according to the following RDF:

```
os:ProductA rdf:type mfg:Paper_Machine.
```

The semantics of owl:equivalentClass means that all members of mfg:Paper_ Machine are also members of the restriction. In particular,

```
os:ProductA rdf:type [a owl:Restriction;
               owl:onProperty mfg:Product_Product_Line
               owl:hasValue "Paper Machine" ].
```

Finally, because of the semantics of the restriction, we can infer

```
os:ProductA mfg:Product_Product_Line "Paper Machine".
```

The end result of this construct is that regardless of how product information is brought into the system, it is represented both in terms of `rdf:type` and `mfg:Product_Product_Line` consistently.

CHALLENGE 29: Relating Classes and Individuals

OWL and RDFS provide considerable modeling power when talking about classes. In RDFS, we can say that all the members of one class are members of another. In OWL, we can say things about all the members of a class—for example, that they all have the value "Paper_Machine" on the property `Product_Product_Line`. We can use these powerful ways to relate classes to one another to describe individuals as well. When we combine these together, we can express rules about how individuals relate to one another.

We will consider an example from software system management. Suppose we have a policy that says that all of our desktop applications must conform to a particular piece of legislation, the Americans with Disabilities Act of 1990. How can we express this in RDFS and OWL?

Figure 11.10 shows the model graphically. First we define the set of desktop applications. A desktop application is something that runs on the desktop—so we model this with a restriction on the property `runsOn`, that it has the value `Desktop`. This is shown in the top of the figure. This is a typical pattern for relating a set of things to an individual; we defined the set of things that run on the desktop to the individual desktop using a single `hasValue` restriction.

In the bottom of the figure, we use this pattern again, but this time we relate the set of applications that comply with the Americans with Disabilities Act of 1990 (ADA90) with the ADA90 itself, again using a `hasValue` restriction.

By building these classes in this way, we can use the modeling power of OWL and RDFS to express more complex relationship. How do we say that all the desktop applications must conform to the ADA90? We see this in the middle of the diagram—we make one restriction a subset of the other. The figure shows a sample inference—The desktop supports MSExcel, which means that MSExcel runs on the desktop (since these two properties are inverses). This, in turn, means that MSExcel is a desktop application. But we have asserted that

```
:DesktopApplication rdfs:subClassOf :ConformantApplication .
```

This means that MSExcel must also be a conformant application. But conformant applications conform to the ADA90; as a member of this class, MSExcel must conform to this as well. This means that we can infer

```
:MSExcel :conformsTo :ADA90 .
```

This usage of `owl:hasValue` is so important that we view it as a design pattern, and give it a name—the *Class-Individual Mirror* pattern. The implementation of the pattern is simple—it is a single `hasValue` restriction on some property. The interpretation of it is that we are describing the relationship of an individual to a set—this is the set of all things that relate to this individual in a certain way. We will see the importance of this pattern for metamodeling in Chapter 15.

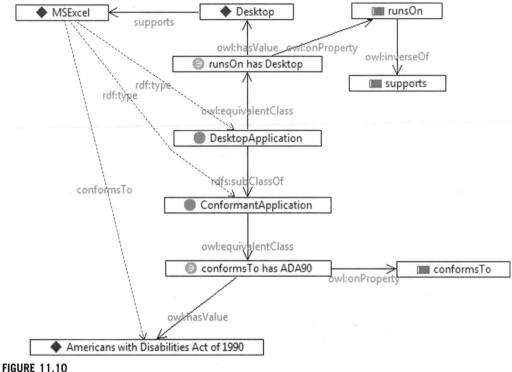

FIGURE 11.10

The Americans with Disabilities Act of 1990 as expressed in RDFS and OWL.

Challenge: relationship transfer in FOAF

When mapping from one model to another, or even when specifying how one part of a model relates to another, it is not uncommon to make a statement of the form "Everything related to A by property p should also be related to B but by property q." Some examples are "Everyone who plays for the All Star team is governed by the league's contract" and "Every work in the *Collected Works of Shakespeare* was written by Shakespeare." We refer to this kind of mapping as `relationship transfer`, since it involves transferring individuals in a relationship with one entity to another relationship with another entity. This situation arises in FOAF with groups of people. Recall that FOAF provides two ways to describe members of a group: the `foaf:member` relation, which relates an individual member G of `foaf:Group` to the individuals who are in that group, and that same group G, which is related to an `owl:Class` by the `foaf:membershipClass` property. We take an example from the life of Shakespeare to illustrate this.

Suppose we define a `foaf:Group` for `Shakespeares_Children`, as follows:

```
b:Shakespeares_Children
a foaf:Group;
   foaf:name "Shakespeare's Children";
   foaf:member b:Susanna, b:Judith, b:Hamnet;
   foaf:membershipClass b:ChildOfShakespeare.
```

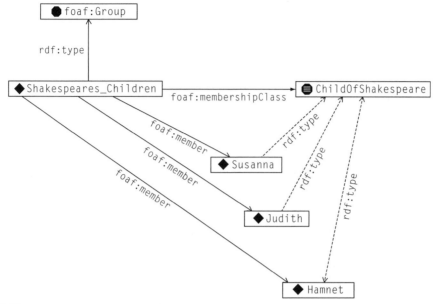

FIGURE 11.11

Inferences based on *membershipClass* in FOAF. FOAF specifies that the following rule should hold.

```
b:ChildOfShakespeare a owl:Class.
IF
   b:Shakespeares_Children foaf:member ?x
THEN
?x rdfs:type b:ChildOfShakespeare.
```

Figure 11.11 shows graphically the result of this rule in the case of Shakespeare's family. The fine lines represent asserted triples, and the three bold lines represent the triples that are to be inferred.

CHALLENGE 30

How can we get the inferences shown in Figure 11.11 by using only the constructs from OWL (i.e., without special-purpose rules)?

Solution

The solution parallels the solution for relationship transfer in SKOS, but in this case, the relationship we are transferring to is rdf:type. We begin as we did in that example—by defining an inverse of foaf:member:

```
b:memberOf owl:inverseOf foaf:member.
```

Now we can define `ChildOfShakespeare` to be (equivalent to) the class of all individuals who are `b:memberOf b:Shakespeares_Children`, using an `owl:hasValue` restriction:

```
b:ChildOfShakespeare
   a owl:Class;
   rdfs:label "Child of Shakespeare";
   owl:equivalentClass
      [a owl:Restriction;
       owl:hasValue b:Shakespeares_Children;
       owl:onProperty b:memberOf
      ].
```

Let's follow the progression of Shakespeare's children through this inference. From Figure 11.11, we begin with three triples:

```
b:Shakespeares_Children foaf:member b:Hamnet.
b:Shakespeares_Children foaf:member b:Judith.
b:Shakespeares_Children foaf:member b:Susanna.
```

By the semantics of `owl:inverseOf`, we can infer

```
b:Hamnet b:memberOf b:Shakespeares_Children.
b:Judith b:memberOf b:Shakespeares_Children.
b:Susanna b:memberOf b:Shakespeares_Children.
```

Therefore, all three are also members of the restriction defined previously, so we can conclude that

```
b:Hamnet rdf:type b:ChildOfShakespeare.
b:Judith rdf:type b:ChildOfShakespeare.
b:Susanna rdf:type b:ChildOfShakespeare.
```

Following similar reasoning, we can also turn this inference around backward; if we instead assert that

```
b:Hamnet rdf:type b:ChildOfShakespeare.
b:Judith rdf:type b:ChildOfShakespeare.
b:Susanna rdf:type b:ChildOfShakespeare.
```

we can infer that

```
b:Shakespeares_Children foaf:member b:Hamnet.
b:Shakespeares_Children foaf:member b:Judith.
b:Shakespeares_Children foaf:member b:Susanna.
```

ALTERNATIVE DESCRIPTIONS OF RESTRICTIONS

In this book, we describe OWL and its semantics with respect to the interpretation of OWL as RDF triples as defined in the W3C OWL documents. Other characterizations have been used during the history of OWL and even appear in user interfaces of some tools. Each characterization uses its own vocabulary to describe exactly the same things. In this section we review some of the most common languages you will encounter when discussing OWL restrictions and classes, and we also provide a recommendation for best-practice terminology.

The semantics of `rdfs:subClassOf` and `owl:equivalentClass` are quite easy to characterize in terms of the inferences that hold

```
X rdfs:subClassOf Y.
```

can be understood as a simple IF/THEN relation; if something is a member of X, then it is also a member of Y.

```
X owl:equivalentClass Y.
```

can be understood as an IF and only IF relation, that is two IF/THEN relations, one going each way; if something is a member of X, then it is also a member of Y, and vice versa.

These relations remain unchanged in the case where X and/or Y are restrictions. We can see these relationships with examples taken from the solar system. Consider two classes: one is a named class `SolarBody`, which we'll call class A for purposes of this discussion. The other is the unnamed class defined by a restriction `onProperty` orbits that it `hasValue TheSun`, which we'll call class B. We can say that all solar bodies orbit the sun by asserting

```
A rdfs:subClassOf B.
```

In other words, if something is a solar body, then it orbits the sun.

Other terms are used in the literature for this situation. For example, it is sometimes described by saying that "orbiting the sun is a necessary condition for `SolarBody`." The intuition behind this description is that if you know that something is a `SolarBody`, then it is necessarily the case that it orbits the sun. Since such a description of the class `SolarBody` describes the class but does not provide a complete characterization of it (that is, you cannot determine from this description that something is a member of `SolarBody`), then this situation is also sometimes denoted by saying that "orbiting the sun is a `partial` definition for the class `SolarBody`."

If, on the other hand, we say that solar bodies are the same as the set of things that orbit the sun, we can express this in OWL compactly as

```
A owl:equivalentClass B.
```

Now we can make inferences in both directions: If something orbits the sun, then it is a `SolarBody`, and if it is a `SolarBody`, then it orbits the sun. This situation is sometimes characterized by saying that "orbiting the sun is a *necessary and sufficient* condition for `SolarBody`." The intuition behind this description is that if you know something is a `SolarBody`, then it is necessarily the case that it orbits the sun. But furthermore, if you want to determine that something is a `SolarBody`, it is sufficient to establish that it orbits the sun. Furthermore, since such a description does fully characterize the class `SolarBody`, this situation is also sometimes denoted by saying that "orbiting the sun is a `complete` definition for the class `SolarBody`."

Finally, if we say that all things that orbit the sun are solar bodies, we can express this compactly in OWL as

```
B rdfs:subClassOf A.
```

That is, if something orbits the sun, then it is a `SolarBody`. Given the usage of the words *necessary* and *sufficient,* one could be excused for believing that in this situation one would say that "orbiting the sun is a *sufficient condition* for `SolarBody`." However, it is not common practice to use the word *sufficient* in this way. Despite the obvious utility of such a statement from a modeling perspective and its simplicity in terms of OWL (it is no more complex than a *partial* or *complete* definition), there is no term corresponding to *partial* or *complete* for this situation.

Because of the incomplete and inconsistent way the words *partial, complete, sufficient,* and *necessary* have been traditionally used to describe OWL, we strongly discourage their use and recommend instead the simpler and consistent use of the OWL terms `rdfs:subClassOf` and `owl:equivalentClass`.

SUMMARY

A key functionality of OWL is the ability to define restriction classes. The unnamed classes are defined based on restrictions on the values for particular properties of the class. Using this mechanism, OWL can be used to model situations in which the members of a particular class must have certain properties. In RDFS, the domain and range restrictions can allow us to make inferences about all the members of a class (such as `playsFor` relating a baseball player to a team). In OWL, one can use restriction statements to differentiate the case between something that applies to all members of a class versus some members, and even to insist on a particular value for a specific property of all members of a class.

When restrictions are used in combination with the constructs of RDFS (especially `rdfs:subPropertyOf` and `rdfs:subClassOf`), and when they are cascaded with one another (restrictions referring to other restrictions), they can be used to model complex relationships between properties, classes, and individuals. The advantage of modeling relationships in this way (over informal specification) is that interactions of multiple specifications can be understood and even processed automatically.

OWL also provides other kinds of restrictions that can be placed on the members of a class using other kinds of `onProperty` restrictions. We discuss these in the next chapter.

Fundamental concepts

The following fundamental concepts were introduced in this chapter.

>*owl:Restriction*—The building block in OWL that describes classes by restricting the values allowed for certain properties.
>*owl:hasValue*—A type of restriction that refers to a single value for a property.
>*owl:someValuesFrom*—A type of restriction that refers to a set from which some value for a property must come.
>*owl:allValuesFrom*—A type of restriction that refers to a set from which all values for a property must come.
>*owl:onProperty*—A link from a restriction to the property it restricts.

Counting and sets in OWL

Restrictions provide a concise way to describe a class of individuals in terms of the properties we know that describe the individuals themselves. As we saw in the previous chapter, we can use this construct to define notions like *Vegetarian* (describing someone in terms of the type of food that they eat), to sift information from a table (describing something according to a value of one property), and to manage groups of people or terms (describe something based on its membership in a group). The restrictions defined in Chapter 11 are powerful methods for defining classes of individuals.

   In this chapter, we see that OWL augments this capability with a full set theory language, including intersections, unions, and complements. These can be used to combine restrictions together (e.g., the set of planets that go around the sun *and* have at least one moon) or to combine the classes we use to define restrictions (a *Vegetarian* is someone who eats food that is *not Meat*). This combination provides a potent system for making very detailed descriptions of information.

OWL also includes restrictions that refer to *cardinalities*—that is, referring to the number of distinct values for a particular property some individual has. So we can describe "the set of planets that have at least three moons" or "the teams that contain more than one all-star player." Reasoning with cardinalities in OWL is surprisingly subtle. Perhaps we shouldn't be surprised that it is difficult to count how many distinct things there are when one thing might have more than one name (i.e., more than one URI), and we never know when someone might tell us about a new thing we didn't know about before. These are the main reasons why cardinality inferencing in OWL is quite conservative in the conclusions it can draw.

UNIONS AND INTERSECTIONS

We begin with the basic logical combinations, which are familiar from set theory. OWL provides a facility for defining new classes as unions and intersections of previously defined classes. All set operations can be used on any class definition at all in OWL, including named classes and restrictions. This allows OWL to express a wide variety of combinations of classes and conditions. The semantics for the constructors as one would expect, matching the set operations of the same name.

Syntactically, they use the list constructs of RDF, as follows:

```
U1 a owl:Class;
   owl:unionOf (ns:A ns:B...).
I1 a owl:Class;
   owl:intersectionOf (ns:A ns:B...).
```

The union of two or more classes includes the members of all those classes combined; the intersection includes the members that belong to every one of the classes.

The intersection of two (or more) classes is a new class; this can be represented in OWL/RDF by either naming that class (as just shown) or by defining an anonymous class (an individual of type owl:Class), which is defined to be the intersection of other classes using the property owl:intersectionOf (likewise owl:unionOf). An anonymous class of this sort can be used again in a model by naming using owl:equivalentClass, as follows:

```
bb:MajorLeagueBaseballPlayer owl:equivalentClass
   [a owl:Class;
      owl:intersectionOf
   (bb:MajorLeagueMember bb:Player bb:BaseballEmployee)].
```

Although the semantics of intersectionOf and unionOf are straightforward, they have a particular application to Semantic Web modeling when used in conjunction with restrictions.

Natural language descriptions of restrictions often have a notion of intersection built in. "All planets orbiting the sun" is actually the intersection of all things that orbit the sun (hasValue restriction) and all planets. The set of major league baseball players is the intersection of the things that play on a major league team (someValuesFrom restriction) and baseball players. Intersections work just as well on restrictions as they do on named classes; we can define these things directly using intersections:

```
:SolarPlanet a owl:Class;
   owl:intersectionOf (
      :Planet
      [a owl:Restriction;
       owl:onProperty :orbits;
       owl:hasValue :TheSun
   ]).
:MajorLeagueBaseballPlayer a owl:Class;
   owl:intersectionOf (
      :BaseballPlayer
      [a owl:Restriction;
       owl:onProperty :playsFor;
       owl:someValuesFrom :MajorLeagueTeam
   ]).
```

EXAMPLE High-Priority Candidate Questions

In the previous chapter, we defined a class of candidate questions based on dependencies of selected answers, and we defined priorities for the questions themselves. We will use the set constructors to combine these two to form a class of candidate questions of a particular priority. An application that asks questions and records answers using this construct would only ask high-priority questions that have been enabled by answers given so far.

First, let's revisit the description of `SelectedAnswer` that classifies dependent questions as `EnabledQuestion`:

```
q:SelectedAnswer rdfs:subClassOf
   [a owl:Restriction;
    owl:onProperty q:enablesCandidate;
    owl:allValuesFrom q:EnabledQuestion].
```

We now want to define a class of questions that we are ready to ask, based on two criteria: First, if they have been enabled by the description above and, second, if they are high priority. This is done with an `intersectionOf` contstructor:

```
q:CandidateQuestion owl:equivalentClass
   [a owl:Class;
    owl:intersectionOf
        (q:EnabledQuestion q:HighPriorityQuestion)].
```

With this description of `q:CandidateQuestion`, only questions with value `q:High` for the property `q:hasPriority` can become candidates.

Alternately, we could make a more relaxed description for candidate questions that include medium-priority questions:

```
q:CandidateQuestion owl:equivalentClass
   [a owl:intersectionOf
       (q:EnabledQuestion
         [a owl:unionOf
            (q:HighPriorityQuestion
              q:MediumPriorityQuestion)])].
```

Closing the world

A key to understanding how set operations and counting works in OWL is the impact of the *Open World Assumption*. Not only does it make counting difficult, but even the notion of set complement is subtle when you assume that a new fact can be discovered at any time. Who's to say that something isn't a member of a class when the very next statement might assert that it actually is? Fortunately, there are ways in OWL to assert that certain parts of the world are closed; in such situations, inferences having to do with complements or counting become much clearer.

Consider, for example, the following bit of dialogue:

RIMBAUD: I saw a James Dean movie last night.
ROCKY: Was it Giant?
RIMBAUD: No.
ROCKY: Was it East of Eden?
RIMBAUD: No.
ROCKY: James Dean only made three movies; it must have been Rebel Without a Cause.
RIMBAUD: Yes, it was.

This sort of inference relies on the fact that James Dean made only three movies. In light of the open world assumption, how can we make such a claim? After all, in an open world, someone could come along at any time and tell us about a fourth James Dean movie. We will use the example of James Dean's movies to illustrate how OWL provides a controlled means for modeling closed aspects of the world.

Enumerating sets with `owl:oneOf`

In the James Dean example, it wasn't necessary that we reject the open world assumption completely. We simply needed to know that for a particular class (James Dean movies), all of its members are known. When one is in a position to enumerate the members of a class, a number of inferences can follow.

OWL allows us to enumerate the members of a class using a construct called `owl:oneOf`, as shown here:

```
ss:SolarPlanet rdf:type owl:Class;
  owl:oneOf (ss:Mercury ss:Venus ss:Earth ss:Mars
             ss:Jupiter ss:Saturn ss:Uranus ss:Neptune).
```

The class `SolarPlanet` is related via the property `owl:oneOf` to a list of the members of the class. Informally, the meaning of this is that the class `SolarPlanet` contains these eight individuals and no others. `owl:oneOf` places a limit on the AAA slogan. When we say that a class is made up of exactly these items, nobody else can say that there is another distinct item that is a member of that class. Thus, `owl:oneOf` should be used with care and only in situations in which the definition of the class is not likely to change—or at least not change very often. In the case of the solar planets, this didn't change for 50 years. We can probably expect that it won't change again for quite a while.

Although `owl:oneOf` places a limitation on the AAA slogan and Open World assumption, it places no limitation on the Nonunique Naming assumption. That is, `owl:oneOf` makes no claim about whether, say, Mercury might be the same as Venus.

When combined with `owl:someValuesFrom`, `owl:oneOf` provides a generalization of `owl:hasValue`. Whereas `owl:hasValue` specifies a single value that a property can take, `owl:someValuesFrom` combined with `owl:oneOf` specifies a distinct set of values that a property can take.

CHALLENGE 31

In the dialogue with Rimbaud, Rocky used the fact that James Dean made only three movies to help determine what movie Rimbaud had seen. How do we represent this in OWL?

Solution

Since James Dean has been dead for more than 50 years, it seems a sad but safe bet that he won't be making any more movies. We can therefore express the class of James Dean movies using `owl:oneOf` as follows:

```
:JamesDeanMovie a owl:Class;
    owl:oneOf (:Giant :EastOfEden :Rebel).
```

Informally, this states that the class `JamesDeanMovie` is made up of only `Giant`, `EastOfEden`, and `Rebel`. What is the formal meaning of `owl:oneOf`? As usual, we define the meaning of a construct in terms of the inferences that can be drawn from it. In the case of `owl:oneOf`, there are a number of inferences that we can draw.

First, we can infer that each instance listed in `owl:oneOf` is indeed a member of the class. From our assertion about `:JamesDeanMovie`, we can infer that each of these things is a James Dean movie:

```
:Giant rdf:type :JamesDeanMovie.
:EastOfEden rdf:type :JamesDeanMovie.
:Rebel rdf:type :JamesDeanMovie.
```

The meaning of `owl:oneOf` goes further than simply asserting the members of a class; it also asserts that these are the *only* members of this class. In terms of inferences, this means that if we assert that some new thing is a member of the class, then it must be `owl:sameAs` one of the members listed in the `owl:oneOf` list. In our James Dean example, if someone were to introduce a new member of the class—say:

```
:RimbaudsMovie rdf:type :JamesDeanMovie.
```

then we can infer that Rebel must be `owl:sameAs` one of the other movies already mentioned.

This inference differs from the inferences that we have seen so far. Up to this point, we were able to express inferences in terms of new triples that can be inferred. In this case, the inference tells us that *some* triple from a small set holds, but we don't know which one. We can't assert any new triples, and we can't respond to a query any differently.

How do we turn this kind of inference into something from which we assert a triple? If we compare where we are now with the conversation between Rocky and Rimbaud, we are right at the point where Rocky has heard from Rimbaud that he saw a James Dean movie. Rocky doesn't know which movie he has seen, but because of his background knowledge, he knows that it was one of three movies. How does Rocky proceed? He eliminates candidates until he can conclude which one it is. To do this in OWL, we must be able to say that some individual is *not* the same as another.

Differentiating individuals with `owl:differentFrom`

There's an old joke about the three major influences on the price of a piece of real estate: location, location, and location. The joke is, of course, that when you promised to name three influences, any reasonable listener expects you to give three *different* influences. Because of the *nonunique naming assumption* in the Semantic Web, we have to be explicit about these things and name things that are, in fact, different from one another. OWL provides `owl:differentFrom` for this. Its use is quite simple: To assert that one resource is different from another requires a single triple:

```
ss:Earth owl:differentFrom ss:Mars.
```

Informally, this triple means that we can rely on the fact that `ss:Earth` and `ss:Mars` refer to different resources when making arguments by counting or by elimination. Formally, `owl:differentFrom` supports a number of inferences when used in conjunction with other constructs like `owl:cardinality` and `owl:oneOf`, as we shall see.

CHALLENGE 32

Use OWL to model the dialogue between Rocky and Rimbaud so that OWL can draw the same inference that Rocky did—namely, that Rimbaud saw *Rebel Without a Cause*.

Solution
At the beginning of the dialogue, Rocky knows that the movie Rimbaud saw was one of the three movies: `EastOfEden`, `Giant`, or `Rebel`. We have already shown how to represent this using `owl:oneOf`. But he doesn't know which one. He can make a guess: Perhaps it was `Giant`. If he is right, we can simply assert that

```
:RimbaudsMovie owl:sameAs :Giant.
```

But what if (as was the case in the dialogue) he was wrong, and Rimbaud didn't see `Giant`? We express this in OWL, using `owl:differentFrom`, as follows:

```
:RimbaudsMovie owl:differentFrom :Giant.
```

This narrows things down a bit, but we still don't know whether Rimbaud saw *East of Eden* or *Rebel Without a Cause*. So Rocky tries again: Was the movie *East of Eden?* When the answer is negative, we have another `owl:different From` triple:

```
:RimbaudsMovie owl:differentFrom :EastOfEden.
```

Now we are in the position that Rocky was in at the end of the dialogue; we know that there are just three James Dean movies, and we know that Rimbaud did not see *Giant* or *East of Eden*. Just as Rocky was able to conclude that Rimbaud saw *Rebel Without a Cause*, the semantics of `owl:oneOf` and `owl:differentFrom` allow us to infer that

```
:RimbaudsMovie owl:sameAs :Rebel.
```

We can see these assertions and the inference in Figure 12.1.

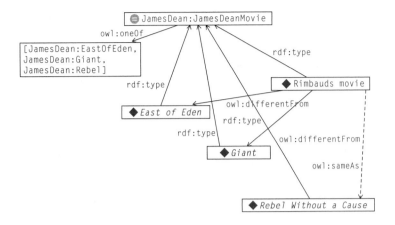

FIGURE 12.1

Rimbauld's movie is neither *Giant* nor *East of Eden*, so we infer that it is *Rebel Without a Cause*.

DIFFERENTIATING MULTIPLE INDIVIDUALS

The nonunique naming assumption allowed us to use a new resource—RimbaudsMovie—to stand in for an indeterminate movie. With appropriate use of modeling constructs, we were able to get inferences about which movie it actually was, using owl:sameAs to indicate the answer. The nonunique naming assumption applies to all resources. For instance, even though we intuitively know that ss:Earth and ss:Mars do not refer to the same thing, we need to state that in our model. We did this before using owl:differentFrom. We also want to say that ss:Earth is different from ss:Jupiter and ss:Venus, ss:Venus is different from ss:Mars, and so on.

To simplify the specification of lists of items, all of which are different from one another, OWL provides owl:AllDifferent and owl:distinctMembers—two constructs. Using these, we will specify that a list of individuals is distinct from one another. The list of items is specified as an RDF list. We specify that this list should be treated as a set of mutually different individuals by referring to it in a triple using owl:distinctMembers as a predicate. The domain of owl:distinctMembers is owl:AllDifferent.

It is customary for the subject of an owl:distinctMembers triple to be a bnode, so the statement that all eight planets are mutually distinct would be expressed in N3 as

```
[a owl:AllDifferent;
 owl:distinctMembers (ss:Mercury
                       ss:Venus
                       ss:Earth
                       ss:Mars
                       ss:Jupiter
                       ss:Saturn
                       ss:Uranus
                       ss:Neptune)].
```

Formally, this is the same as asserting the 28 `owl:differentFrom` triples, one for each pair of individuals in the list. In the case of James Dean's movies, we can assert that the three movies are distinct in the same way:

```
[a owl:AllDifferent;
 owl:distinctMembers (:EastOfEden
                       :Giant
                       :Rebel)].
```

The view of this bit of N3 in terms of triples is shown in Figure 12.2. The movies are referenced in an RDF list (using `rdf:first` and `rdf:rest` to chain the entities together). For longer lists (like the planets), the chain continues for each entity in the list.

Earlier we saw that the class `JamesDeanMovie` was defined using `owl:oneOf` to indicate that these are the only James Dean movies in existence. Now we have gone on to say that additionally these three movies are distinct. It is quite common to use `owl:oneOf` and `owl:AllDifferent` together in this way to say that a class is made up of an enumerated list of distinct elements.

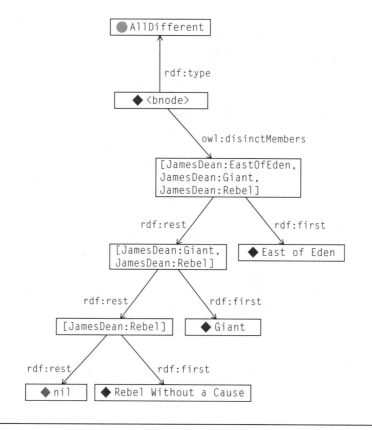

FIGURE 12.2

Using `owl:AllDifferent` and `owl:distinctMembers` to indicate that the three James Dean movies are distinct. The movies are referred to in an RDF list.

CARDINALITY

So far, we have seen restrictions that define classes based on the presence of certain values for given properties. OWL allows a much finer-grained way to define classes, based on the number of distinct values a property takes. Such a restriction is called a *cardinality restriction*. This seemingly simple idea turns out to have surprising subtlety when modeling in OWL. Cardinality restrictions allow us to express constraints on the number of individuals that can be related to a member of the restriction class. For example, a baseball team has exactly nine (distinct) players. A person has two (biological) parents. Cardinality restrictions can be used to define sets of particular interest, like the set of one-act plays or the set of books that are printed in more than one volume.

The syntax for a cardinality restriction is similar to that for the other restrictions we have already seen. Here is the restriction that defines the class of things that have exactly nine players:

```
[a owl:Restriction;
 owl:onProperty :hasPlayer;
 owl:cardinality 9]
```

Of course, instead of 9, we could have any nonnegative integer. We can also use cardinality restrictions to specify upper and lower bounds:

```
[a owl:Restriction;
 owl:onProperty :hasPlayer;
 owl:minCardinality 10]
```
and

```
[a owl:Restriction;
 owl:onProperty :hasPlayer;
 owl:maxCardinality 2]
```

These specify the set of things that have at least 10 players and at most 2 players, respectively. Specifying that the `owl:cardinality` is restricted to n is the same as saying that both the `owl:minCardinality` and `owl:maxCardinality` are restricted to the same value n. Cardinality refers to the number of *distinct* values a property has; it therefore interacts closely with the nonunique naming assumption and `owl:differentFrom`.

The semantics of cardinality restrictions are similar to those of other restrictions. If we can prove that an individual has exactly (respectively at least, at most) n distinct values for the property P, then it is a member of the corresponding `owl:cardinality` (respectively `owl:minCardinality`, `owl:maxCardinality`) restriction. So a rugby union team (with 15 players) and a soccer team (with 11) are both members of the restriction class with minimum `cardinality 10`; a bridge team (with two players) is not, though it is a member of the restriction class with max cardinality 2.

Similarly, if we assert that something is a member of an `owl:cardinality` restriction, then it must have exactly *n* distinct values for the property P. So if we define a baseball team to be a subclass of the restriction class with exact `cardinality 9`, we can conclude that a baseball team has exactly nine (distinct) players. Similar conclusions follow from restrictions on minimum and maximum cardinality. We will demonstrate the use of cardinality restrictions through a series of challenge problems based on the James Dean example.

CHALLENGE 33

Rocky and Rimbaud continue their conversation.

> RIMBAUD: *Do you own any James Dean movies?*
> ROCKY: *They are the only ones I own.*
> RIMBAUD: *Then I guess you don't own very many movies! No more than three.*

Model these facts in OWL so that Rimbaud's conclusion follows from the OWL semantics.

Solution

First we model Rocky's statement that he owns only James Dean movies. We will need a property called ownsMovie to indicate that someone owns a movie:

```
:ownsMovie a owl:ObjectProperty.
```

In OWL, we make general statements about an individual by asserting that the individual is a member of a restriction class. So we can say that Rocky owns only James Dean movies by using the owl:allValuesFrom restriction from Chapter 9:

```
:JamesDeanExclusive owl:equivalentClass
   [a owl:Restriction;
    owl:onProperty :ownsMovie;
    owl:allValuesFrom :JamesDeanMovie].
:Rocky a:JamesDeanExclusive.
```

Rocky is a member of the class JamesDeanExclusive, which is the class of things for which all the values of ownsMovie come from the class JamesDeanMovie.

How can we model Rimbaud's conclusion? We define the class of things that don't own many movies (where by "not many," we mean at most three) as follows:

```
:FewMovieOwner owl:equivalentClass
   [a owl:Restriction;
    owl:onProperty:ownsMovie;
    owl:maxCardinality 3].
```

Now Rimbaud's conclusion can be formulated as a triple:

```
:Rocky a:FewMovieOwner.
```

This triple can be inferred from the model because all the values of the property ownsMovie for Rocky come from the class JamesDeanMovie, and there are only three of them, and they are all distinct, so Rocky can own at most three movies. This inference is shown in Figure 12.3.

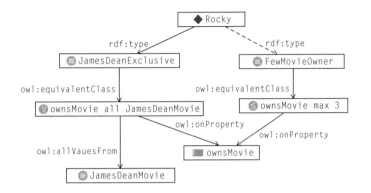

FIGURE 12.3

We asserted that Rocky is a `JamesDeanExclusive`; we infer that he owns only a few movies.

CHALLENGE 34

Model this situation and conclusion in OWL.

> RIMBAUD: *How many movies do you own, then?*
> ROCKY: *Three.*
> RIMBAUD: *That's all of them; so you must own the one I saw last night,* Rebel Without a Cause.

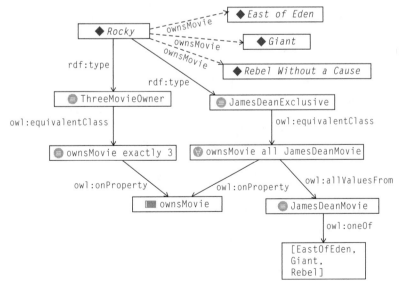

FIGURE 12.4

Rocky owns three movies, and he owns only James Dean movies, so he must own each of them.

Solution

We assert that Rocky owns exactly three movies by asserting that he is a member of an `owl:cardinality` restriction class for "the set of things that own exactly three movies":

```
:ThreeMovieOwner owl:equivalentClass
   [a owl:Restriction;
    owl:onProperty :ownsMovie;
    owl:cardinality 3].
:Rocky a:ThreeMovieOwner.
```

Since Rocky owns exactly three distinct movies, and all of his movies are members of `JamesDeanMovie`, and there are just three different `JamesDeanMovies`, he must own each of them. In particular, we can infer

```
:Rocky :ownsMovie :Rebel.
```

These assertions and inferences can be seen in Figure 12.4.

Qualified cardinality (OWL 2.0)

Cardinality restrictions in OWL allow us to say how many distinct values a property can have for any given subject. Other restrictions tell us about the classes of which those values can or must be members. But these restrictions work independently of one another; we cannot say how many values from a particular class a particular subject can have. A simple example of qualified cardinality is a model of a hand: A hand has five fingers, one of which is a thumb.

Qualified cardinalities may seem like a needless modeling detail, and, in fact, a large number of models get by quite fine without them. But models that want to take advantage of detailed cardinality information often find themselves in need of such detailed modeling. This happens especially when modeling the structure of complex objects.

For example, when modeling an automobile, it might be useful to say that a properly equipped automobile includes five tires, four of which must be regular road-worthy tires and a fifth that is a designated spare tire which might not have all the properties of a regular tire. Structural models of this sort often make extensive use of qualified cardinalities. Qualified cardinalities also will require syntactic extensions to OWL; in this case, however, they do work within the decidability constraints of OWL DL and thus they are likely to be added in a future version of OWL.

In our James Dean example, we can make use of qualified cardinality to say that while a movie can have any number of stars, a James Dean movie must have exactly one star who is James Dean. This is accomplished with a slight generalization of the form for cardinality:

```
:JamesDeanMovie rdfs:subClassOf
    [ a owl:Restriction ;
      owl:onClass :JDPerson ;
      owl:onProperty :stars ;
      owl:qualifiedCardinality "1"^^xsd:nonNegativeInteger
    ] .
    :JDPerson a owl:Class ; owl:oneOf (:JamesDean) .
```

JDPerson is the singleton class that includes only James Dean; the qualified cardinality restriction looks just like a cardinality restriction, but includes the reference (via owl:onClass) to :JDPerson. The same conditions from non-unique naming and the open world assumption hold for qualified cardinalities as for any others; in this example, we could infer that

  :EastOfEden :stars :JamesDean .

This is because :EastOfEden is a James Dean movie, and hence stars exactly one member of the class :JDPerson. There is only one member of that class, so :EastOfEden must star him. The qualified cardinality restrictions include all of the variants of normal cardinality restrictions, that is, owl:maxQualifiedCardinality and owl:minQualifiedCardinality.

Small cardinality limits

OWL provides the facility to use any natural number as a cardinality. We have seen how this provides an inference engine with the information needed to determine membership in a class based on counting the number of distinct individuals that satisfy some condition. The particular restrictions of cardinalities to the small numbers 0 and 1 have special modeling utility.

minCardinality 1: The restriction of the minCardinality to 1 indicates the set of individuals for which some value for the specified property is required. The Restriction onProperty ownsMovie minCardinality 1 explicitly specifies the set of individuals who own at least one movie.

maxCardinality 1: The restriction of maxCardinalilty to 1 specifies that a value is unique (but need not exist). The restriction onProperty ownsMovie maxCardinality 1 explicitly specifies the set of individuals who own at most one movie—in other words, they have limited themselves to a single movie.

minCardinality 0: The restriction of the minCardinality to 0 describes a set of individuals for which the presence of a value for the onProperty is optional. In the semantics of OWL, this is superfluous (since properties are always optional anyway), but the explicit assertion that something is optional can be useful for model readability. The restriction onProperty ownsMovie minCardinality 0 explicitly specifies the set of individuals for which owning a movie is optional.

maxCardinality 0: The restriction of the maxCardinality to 0 indicates the set of individuals for which no value for the specified property is allowed. The restriction onProperty ownsMovie maxCardinality 0 explicitly specifies the set of individuals who own no movies.

These four special cases of cardinality are closely related. minCardinality 1 and maxCardinality 0 form a partition of minCardinality 0; that is, minCardinality 1 and maxCardinality 0 are disjoint from one another, they are both subclasses of minCardinality 0, and together (minCardinality 1 union maxCardinality 0) they make up all of minCardinality 0 (which is equivalent to owl:Thing, the class of all individuals).

SET COMPLEMENT

The complement of a set is the set of all things not in that set. The same definition applies to classes in OWL. The complement of a class is another class whose members are all the things not in the complemented class. Since a complement applies to a single class, we can define it using a single triple:

```
ex:ClassA owl:complementOf ex:ClassB.
```

Although set complements seem quite straightforward, they can easily be misused, and OWL (like any formal system) can be quite unforgiving in such situations.

For example, we might be tempted to say that minor league players are the complement of major league players (asserting that there are just these two types of players and that nobody can be both).

```
bb:MinorLeaguePlayer owl:complementOf bb:MajorLeaguePlayer.
```

From this description, all of the players who are not bb:MajorLeaguePlayers will be included in bb:MinorLeaguePlayer. However, the complement class includes everything that is not in the referred class, so in addition to hopeful rookies, the class bb:MinorLeaguePlayer includes managers, fans, and indeed anything else in the universe, like movies or planets.

To avoid such a situation, common practice is not to refer to complementary classes directly. Instead, it is common practice to combine complement with intersection.

```
bb:MinorLeaguePlayer owl:intersectionOf
    ([ a owl:Class;
       owl:complementOf bb:MajorLeaguePlayer]
    bb:Player).
```

That is, a MinorLeaguePlayer is a player who is not a MajorLeaguePlayer.

Thus, members of bb:MinorLeaguePlayer include only members of the class bb:Player but does not include players that are included in bb:MajorLeaguePlayer. This is much closer to the natural meaning suggested by the name. This definition makes use of a bnode to specify an anonymous class. There is no need to name the class that is the complement of bb:MajorLeaguePlayer, so it is specified anonymously using the bnode notation "[a owl:Class...]."

CHALLENGE 35

Rocky's friend Paul joins in the discussion.

> PAUL: *Are you talking about James Dean? I love him! I have all his movies.*
> RIMBAUD: *But you aren't obsessive, are you? I mean, you have other movies, too, don't you?*
> ROCKY: *I'm not obsessive!*
> PAUL: *Of course, I have some movies that aren't James Dean movies.*
> ROCKY: *You must have at least four movies then!*

Model this situation and conclusion in OWL.

Solution

For this challenge, we need to have an inverse for `ownsMovie`:

```
:ownedBy owl:inverseOf :ownsMovie.
```

We can define the class of all the movies that Paul owns as follows:

```
:PaulsMovie a owl:Class;
   owl:intersectionOf
       ([ a owl:Restriction;
           owl:onProperty :ownedBy;
           owl:hasValue :Paul]
           :Movie).
```

Paul says that he owns every James Dean movie—that is, every `JamesDeanMovie` is a `PaulsMovie` (but possibly not vice versa), so we assert

```
:JamesDeanMovie rdfs:subClassOf :PaulsMovie.
```

Paul claims to own other movies, too. We can express that by saying

```
:Paul a [a owl:Restriction;
       owl:onProperty :ownsMovie;
       owl:someValuesFrom
           [owl:complementOf :JamesDeanMovie]].
```

Let's look at this one in some detail.

```
[owl:complementOf :JamesDeanMovie]
```

is an anonymous class (bnode) that includes everything that is not a James Dean movie.

```
[a owl:Restriction;
 owl:onProperty :ownsMovie;
 owl:someValuesFrom [owl:complementOf :JamesDeanMovie]]
```

is an anonymous class (bnode) of all the things that have some value for `ownsMovie` that isn't a James Dean movie. We claim that Paul is such a thing.

Finally, we define the class of people who own four or more movies, using

```
owl:minCardinality.
     :ManyMovieOwner
     owl:equivalentClass
  [a owl:Restriction;
   owl:onProperty :ownsMovie;
   owl:minCardinality 4].
```

Now, Paul owns all of James Dean's movies (all three of them) and at least one that isn't a James Dean movie. That makes (at least) four in all; so we can infer that *Paul* qualifies as a member of `ManyMovieOwner`.

```
:Paul rdf:type :ManyMovieOwner.
```

These assertions and conclusion can be seen in Figure 12.5.

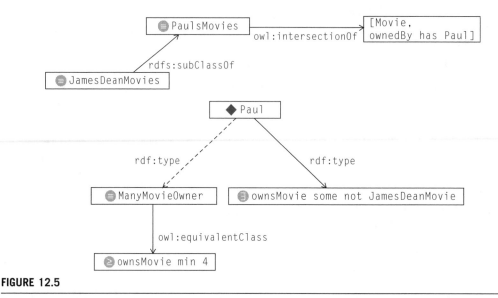

FIGURE 12.5

Paul owns every James Dean movie, and he owns some others, so he owns at least four movies.

DISJOINT SETS

We have seen how we can use `owl:complementOf` to describe the class that includes all the individuals that are not in some class. A related idea is that two sets have no individual in common. When this happens, we say that the sets are *disjoint,* and we represent this situation in OWL using `owl:disjointWith`, as follows:

```
:Man owl:disjointWith :Woman.
:Meat owl:disjointWith :Fruit.
:Fish owl:disjointWith :Fowl.
```

For any members of disjoint classes, we can infer that they are `owl:differentFrom` one another—for instance, we might assert that

```
:Irene a:Woman.
:Ralph a:Man.
```

we can infer that

```
:Irene owl:differentFrom :Ralph.
```

This simple idea can have powerful ramifications when combined with other constructs in OWL, as we can see in the following challenge problems.

CHALLENGE 36

Our moviegoers continue their conversation:

> PAUL: *I am a big movie fan. Not only do I own all the James Dean movies, but I also have movies with Judy Garland, Tom Cruise, Dame Judi Dench, and Antonio Banderas!*
> ROCKY: *You must own at least seven movies!*
> PAUL: *How do you know that?*
> ROCKY: *Because none of those people played in movies together!*

Model this situation and conclusion in OWL.

Solution

How do we express, in OWL, that Paul owns a Judy Garland movie? We assert that Paul is a member of the class of things that own Judy Garland movies. Thus, the statements that Paul has made about the movies he owns can be modeled in OWL using an `owl:someValuesFrom` restriction for each one:

```
:Paul a [a owl:Restriction;
          owl:onProperty :ownsMovie;
          owl:someValuesFrom :JudyGarlandMovie].
:Paul a [a owl:Restriction;
          owl:onProperty :ownsMovie;
          owl:someValuesFrom :JudiDenchMovie].
:Paul a [ a owl:Restriction;
          owl:onProperty :ownsMovie;
          owl:someValuesFrom :TomCruiseMovie].
:Paul a [ a owl:Restriction;
          owl:onProperty :ownsMovie;
          owl:someValuesFrom :AntonioBanderasMovie].
```

We can define the set of people who own seven or more movies using `owl:minCardinality`:

```
:SevenMovieOwner a owl:Restriction;
                 owl:onProperty ownsMovie;
                 owl:minCardinality 7.
```

How do we know that Paul is a member of this class? As Rocky points out in the dialogue, we don't know until we know that all the sets of movies he mentioned are disjoint. That is, we need to know

```
JamesDeanMovie owl:disjointWith JudyGarlandMovie.
JamesDeanMovie owl:disjointWith TomCruiseMovie.
JamesDeanMovie owl:disjointWith JudiDenchMovie.
JamesDeanMovie owl:disjointWith AntonioBanderasMovie.
JudyGarlandMovie owl:disjointWith TomCruiseMovie.
JudyGarlandMovie owl:disjointWith JudiDenchMovie.
JudyGarlandMovie owl:disjointWith AntonioBanderasMovie.
TomCruiseMovie owl:disjointWith JudiDenchMovie.
TomCruiseMovie owl:disjointWith AntonioBanderasMovie.
JudiDenchMovie owl:disjointWith AntonioBanderasMovie.
```

Now we know that Paul has three James Dean movies and at least one movie from each of the other actors named here. Furthermore, none of these movies appears twice, since all of the sets are disjoint. An inference engine can confirm that Rocky is justified in counting to seven movies, and

```
:Paul a :SevenMovieOwner.
```

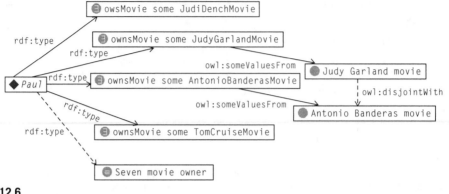

FIGURE 12.6

Paul owns three James Dean movies (Figure 12.5), plus one each from other actors, making seven (or more) in total.

These assertions and inferences can be seen in Figure 12.6.

Notice how `owl:someValuesFrom` interacts with cardinality; each restriction of `someValuesFrom` guarantees the existence of one value for the specified property. When these values are known to be distinct, we can count (at least) one per `someValuesFrom` restriction.

Just as we had `owl:AllDifferent` as a way to specify that several individuals are mutually distinct, we could have something like `owl:AllDisjoint` to indicate that a set of classes is mutually disjoint. As it happens, the OWL standard did not include such a construct, though some proposals for extensions to OWL include such a facility.

PREREQUISITES REVISITED

We have already explored how prerequisites can be modeled in OWL using `owl:allValuesFrom`. At that point, we had a problem with the Open World Assumption—namely, how can we tell that all prerequisites have been satisfied if we have to assume that someone can come along and set new prerequisites at any time? We'll use prerequisites to demonstrate a number of ways we can close the world.

As a reminder from Chapter 11, we modeled the fact that something that has all its prerequisites satisfied (i.e., selected) is an `EnabledQuestion` as follows:

```
q:hasPrerequisite a owl:ObjectProperty.
  [a owl:Restriction;
   owl:onProperty hasPrerequisite;
   owl:allValuesFrom q:SelectedAnswer]
     rdfs:subClassOf q:EnabledQuestion.
```

If something satisfies the restriction (all its values are members of `SelectedAnswer`), then it is also a member of `EnabledQuestion`.

No prerequisites

Let's start with the simple situation in which we know that there are no prerequisites at all. If something has no prerequisites, then there are no conditions to be checked, so it should be an EnabledQuestion. How can we know that something has no prerequisites?

We can assert the number of distinct values that an individual has for some property by using the cardinality restrictions. In particular, if we say that

```
c:WhatProblem a [a owl:Restriction;
                 owl:onProperty q:hasPrerequisite;
                 owl:cardinality 0].
```

Then we know that there are no triples of the form

```
c:WhatProblem q:hasPrerequisite?.
```

That is, WhatProblem has no prerequisites. Therefore it satisfies the restriction

```
c:WhatProblem a [a owl:Restriction;
                 owl:onProperty hasPrerequisite;
                 owl:allValuesFrom q:SelectedAnswer ].
```

hence

```
c:WhatProblem a q:EnabledQuestion.
```

The interpretation of owl:allValuesFrom in such a situation—that is, when we know that there are no values from the indicated class (or even no values at all!) can be a bit confusing. If there are no values at all, how can all of them be members of some class? The correct way to think about owl:allValuesFrom is as something that sets prerequisites, regardless of the name of the restricted property. Let's take a simple example: If a person has no children, then all of his or her children are boys.

First we define the set of people all of whose children are boys, with an allValuesFrom restriction:

```
:ParentOfBoysOnly owl:equivalentClass
   [a owl:Restriction;
    owl:onProperty :hasChild;
    owl:allValuesFrom :Boy].
```

How do we decide about membership in this class? Each triple with predicate hasChild places a prerequisite for its subject to be a member of the class. So the triple

```
:ElizabethII :hasChild :Charles.
```

places a prerequisite for ElizabethII to be a member of ParentOfBoysOnly—namely, that Charles must be a Boy. In this case, the prerequisite is satisfied.

But even though this prerequisite is satisfied, we still can't infer that ElizabethII is a member of ParentOfBoysOnly. In order to make such an inference, *all* prerequisites must be satisfied. Because of the Open World Assumption, there might be more facts about Elizabeth that we weren't aware of, that is, there might be more prerequisites we have to satisfy. In particular, if we come to learn that

```
:ElizabethII :hasChild :Anne.
```

we will have a prerequisite that isn't satisfied, so we won't be able to infer that `ElizabethII` is a member of `ParentOfBoysOnly`. The Open World Assumption means that there might always be another prerequisite that we didn't know about.

In general, it is difficult to infer that someone is a member of a class like `ParentOfBoysOnly`, which is defined as an `allValuesFrom` restriction. How can we ever know, in the face of the Open World Assumption, that all prerequisites have been satisfied? One way is if we assert that there is none. For instance, Elizabeth's ancestor, `ElizabethI`, was famous for having died childless. We can assert this in OWL by asserting her membership in a restriction class of `cardinality 0`, thus:

```
:ElizabethI a [a owl:Restriction;
              owl:onProperty :hasChild;
              owl:cardinality 0].
```

Now we know that there are no prerequisites on `ElizabethI`, so we can infer

```
:ElizabethI a :ParentOfBoysOnly.
```

We effectively used the cardinality restriction to close the world, at least in the case of Elizabeth's children.

Many people find this result counterintuitive—that someone with no children would have all of their children be boys. This conclusion is much more intuitive if you think of `owl:allValuesFrom` as working with prerequisites; it is intuitive to say that something that has no prerequisites is satisfied. In the semantics of OWL, this is the appropriate interpretation of `owl:allValuesFrom`.

Counting prerequisites

Another way to determine that something has satisfied all of its prerequisites is to count how many of them there are. Just as we have done with counting James Dean movies, we can count prerequisites. Suppose we know that something has exactly one prerequisite:

```
c:TvSymptom a [a owl:Restriction;
              owl:onProperty hasPrerequisite;
              owl:cardinality 1 ].
```

and that, furthermore, we actually know one prerequisite, and its type:

```
c:TvSymptom q: hasPrerequisite d:STV.
d:STV a q:SelectedAnswer.
```

We know that one of the prerequisites is a member of the class q:SelectedAnswer. We also know that there aren't any others (since the cardinality says there is just one of them). So we know that all of the prerequisites are members of the class q:SelectedAnswer:

```
c:TVSymptom a [a owl:Restriction;
               owl:onProperty hasPrerequisite;
               owl:allValuesFrom q:SelectedAnswer].
```

Just as in the James Dean examples, we can make inferences from larger counts if we know that all the entities are different. If we know, for example, that

```
c:TVTurnedOn a [a owl:Restriction;
                owl:onProperty hasPrerequisite;
                owl:cardinality 2].
c:TVTurnedOn q:hasPrerequisite c:TVSnothing.
c:TVTurnedOn q:hasPrerequisite c:STVSnosound.
c:TVSnothing owl:differentFrom c:STVSnosound.
c:TVSnothing a q:SelectedAnswer.
c:STVSnosound a q:SelectedAnswer.
```

we can infer that

```
c:TVTurnedOn a [a owl:Restriction;
                owl:onProperty hasPrerequisite;
                owl:allValuesFrom q:SelectedAnswer].
```

since there are only two prerequisites, and we know which two they are.

Guarantees of existence

The issue of prerequisites revealed a subtlety in the interpretation of owl:allValuesFrom—namely, that the membership of an individual A in an allValuesFrom restriction on property P does not guarantee that any triple of the form

```
A P ?.
```

exists at all. What should be the corresponding situation in the case of someValuesFrom? That is, if we say that an individual A is a member of a restriction onProperty P someValuesFrom another class C, should we insist that there is some triple of this form?

```
A P ?.
```

The interpretation of someValuesFrom is that we do know that there is a pair of triples of the form

```
A P X.
X rdf:type C.
```

Evidently, if we have both of these triples, then we certainly have a triple of the desired form. That is, in contrast to `allValuesFrom`, `someValuesFrom` does guarantee that some value is given for the specified property.

The case for `hasValue` is even more evident than that for `someValuesFrom`. Not only does `hasValue` guarantee that there is such a triple, but it even specifies exactly what it is. That is, if A is a member of the restriction `onProperty P hasValue X`, we can infer the triple

```
A P X .
```

CONTRADICTIONS

CHALLENGE 37

Model this situation and conclusion in OWL.

> ROCKY: *You're a Judy Garland fan? I have a couple of her movies, too!*
> RIMBAUD: *Wait a minute! That can't be right! You said that you own only James Dean movies,*
> *and now you say you have a Judy Garland movie. They weren't in any movie together!*

Solution

This solution requires us to introduce a new aspect of inferencing in OWL. The simplest form of inferencing we have seen was where we inferred new triples based on asserted ones. With the more advanced notions beyond RDFS-Plus, we saw how some inferences could not themselves be represented as triples but could result in new triples when combined with other assertions. But in this example, there are no new triples to be inferred at all.

Rimbaud does not make any new assertions about Rocky. Instead, he brings into question the validity of something that Rocky has asserted. In OWL terms, we say that Rimbaud has found a *contradiction* in what Rocky has said.

In this case, the contradiction arose because Rocky has made the following statements:

```
:JamesDeanExclusive owl:equivalentClass
   [a owl:Restriction;
    owl:onProperty :ownsMovie;
    owl:allValuesFrom :JamesDeanMovie].
:Rockya JamesDeanExclusive.
:Rocky a [a owl:Restriction;
          owl:onProperty :ownsMovie;
          owl:someValuesFrom :JudyGarlandMovie].
:JudyGarlandMovie owl:disjointWith :JamesDeanMovie.
```

The `owl:someValuesFrom` restriction guarantees that Rocky owns some Judy Garland movie (though we don't know which one), and the `owl:allValuesFrom` restriction tells us that this movie must also be a James Dean movie. Although such a movie would have undoubtedly been very popular, unfortunately we also know from the `owl:disjointWith` triple that there is no such movie; somewhere in this model there is a contradiction.

These assertions are shown in Figure 12.7; no inferences are shown, since the model contains a contradiction.

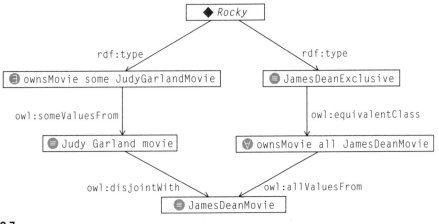

FIGURE 12.7

All of Rocky's films are James Dean films, but some of them are Judy Garland films.

The OWL semantics can tell us that there is a contradiction in this example, but it cannot tell us which assertion is wrong. The validity of an assertion has nothing to do with the OWL standard or its semantics; it has to do with the domain that is being modeled. Did Rocky lie about owning only James Dean movies? Or is he lying now about owning Judy Garland movies? Or, perhaps we are mistaken, and there is a Judy Garland/James Dean collaboration out there that nobody knows about (that is, we were mistaken when we said that these two classes were disjoint). There is no way to know which of these statements is incorrect. But OWL can tell us that their combination results in a contradiction.

The notion of contradiction gets to the heart of what we mean by modeling. A model is a description of the world and can be mistaken; that is, the model may not actually correspond to the actual state of affairs. The tools that surround OWL models help us to determine the nature of our models. If they are logically inconsistent, then we know that either our model is defective or our understanding of how it relates to the world is mistaken.

UNSATISFIABLE CLASSES

A contradiction arises when the assertions that have been made simply cannot all be true. There is a fundamental disagreement in the asserted statements. A similar situation can arise when we define a class in an inconsistent way. A slight variation on the previous example shows how this can happen. First, suppose we define the class of people who own Judy Garland movies that Rocky claims to be a member of:

```
:JudyGarlandMovieOwner owl:equivalentClass
   [a owl:Restriction;
   owl:onProperty :ownsMovie;
   owl:someValuesFrom :JudyGarlandMovie].
```

Now, instead of claiming that Rocky is a member of both this class and `JamesDeanExclusive`, let's define the class of such people:

```
:JDJG owl:intersectionOf
   (:JudyGarlandMovieOwner :JamesDeanExclusive).
```

Rocky has claimed to be a member of this class; this claim led to a contradiction.

We can define this class without asserting that Rocky is a member of it. Although this does not lead to a contradiction, the same argument that showed that Rocky cannot (consistently) be a member of this class can be used to show that *nothing* can be a member of this class, or that this class is empty. When we can prove that a class is empty, we say that the class itself is *unsatisfiable*. Although a contradiction indicates that some statement in the model is in conflict with others, an unsatisfiable class simply means that there can be no individuals who are members of that class. Of course, if we go on to assert that some individual is a member of an unsatisfiable class (as Rocky did, when he claimed to be a member of *JDJG*), and then the model contains a contradiction.

Figure 12.8 shows these assertions and the conclusions that follow. *JDJG* is a subclass of both `JudyGarlandMovieOwner` and `JamesDeanExclusive`, since it is defined as the intersection of these two classes. But it is also inferred to be subclass of `owl:Nothing`. This indicates in OWL that it can have no members, since `owl:Nothing` is the class that corresponds to the empty set.

Propagation of unsatisfiable classes

Once a model contains an unsatisfiable class, it is easy for other class definitions to be unsatisfiable as well. Here are a few of the simpler ways in which this can happen:

subclass: A subclass of an unsatisfiable class is itself unsatisfiable. If the subclass could (without contradiction) have an individual member, then so could the superclass.

someValuesFrom: A restriction (on any property) with `owl:someValuesFrom` an unsatisfiable class is itself unsatisfiable, since `owl:someValuesFrom` requires that there be some value that the property can indicate.

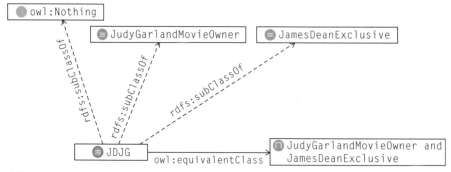

FIGURE 12.8

JDJG is the intersection of people who only own James Dean movies and people who own Judy Garland movies.

domain and range: If a property has an unsatisfiable `domain` or `range`, then the property becomes basically unusable. Any `someValuesFrom` restriction on that property is unsatisfiable. If any triple is asserted using that property as predicate, then the model results in a contradiction.

intersection of disjoints: The `owl:intersectionOf` two disjoint classes is unsatisfiable. The intersection of any class with an unsatisfiable class is unsatisfiable.

Some operations do not propagate unsatisfiable classes; the union of an unsatisfiable class and another class can be satisfiable. A restriction `owl:allValuesFrom` an unsatisfiable class can still be satisfiable (but none of its members can have any value for the property specified by `owl:onProperty` in the restriction).

These rules seem intuitive enough in isolation; their usefulness in modeling comes in during analysis of the results of an inference engine. Many inference engines will report on unsatisfiable classes, but in the face of several such classes, it can be difficult to tell just what is going on. Although some engines have tools to assist the modeler in tracking this, the use of these tools requires some understanding of how unsatisfiable classes can arise. This short list is not exhaustive, but it covers most of the common cases.

INFERRING CLASS RELATIONSHIPS

In the previous discussion, most of the inferences we drew were about individuals: Wenger is an Analyst, Jupiter is a Solar Planet, Kaneda is a Star Player, or Shakespeare married Anne Hathaway. In this chapter, we have begun to draw conclusions about classes—for example, *JDJG* is unsatisfiable. OWL allows us to draw a wide range of conclusions about classes. We can, in some circumstances, infer that one class is a subclass of another or that a class is the domain (or range) of a property. There are countless possibilities for how this can happen, but there are a few common patterns that are worth calling out. We'll return to our descriptions of baseball teams for examples:

Intersection and subclass: The intersection of two (or more) classes is a subclass of each intersected class. If `AllStarBaseballTeam` is the intersection of `AllStarTeam` and `BaseballTeam`, then it is also `rdfs:subClassOf` each of those classes.

Union and subclass: The union of two (or more) classes is a superclass of each united class. If `JBallTeam` is the union of `PacificLeagueTeam` and `CentralLeagueTeam`, then `PacificLeagueTeam` and `CentralLeagueTeam` are both `rdfs:subClassOf` `JBallTeam`.

Complement and subclass: Complement reverses the order of subclass. For example, if `AllStarBaseballTeam` is a subclass of `BaseballTeam`, then the complement of `BaseballTeam` is a subclass of the complement of `AllStarBaseballTeam`.

Subclass propagation through restriction: The subclass relationships propagate through restrictions. If `AllStarBaseballTeam` is a subclass of `BaseballTeam`, then the restriction (on any property—say, `playsFor`) `owl:allValuesFrom` `AllStarBaseballTeam` is a subclass of the restriction (on the same property `playsFor`) `owl:allValuesFrom` `BaseballTeam`. If we call the first restriction `AllStarBaseballPlayer` and the second restriction `BaseballPlayer` (both are reasonable names for these restrictions), then this pattern says that `AllStarBaseballPlayer` is a subclass of `BaseballPlayer`. The same propagation principle holds for any property and also for `owl:someValuesFrom`. If

AllStarBaseballTeam is a subclass of BaseballTeam, then the restriction on property playsFor some values from AllStarBaseballTeam is a subclass of the restriction on property playsFor some values from BaseballTeam.

***hasValue, someValuesFrom*, and *subClassOf*:** Propagation for owl:has Value works a bit differently from the way it works for owl:allValuesFrom or owl:someValuesFrom, since owl:hasValue refers to an individual, not a class. Suppose that the individual TokyoGiants is a member of class BaseballTeam; the restriction on property playsFor owl:hasValue TokyoGiants is a subclass of the restriction on property playsFor owl:someValuesFrom BaseballTeam.

Relative cardinalities: Subclass relations between cardinality restrictions arise from the usual rules of arithmetic on whole numbers. For example, if a ViableBaseballTeam must have at least nine players on its roster (owl:minCardinality9), and a FullBaseballTeam has exactly 10 players on the roster (owl:cardinality10), then FullBaseballTeam is a subclass of ViableBaseballTeam.

***owl:someValuesFrom* and *owl:minCardinality*:** If we say that something has some value from a particular class, then we can infer that it has at least one such value. So if BaseballTeam has some pitcher (i.e., BaseballTeam is a subclass of the restriction owl:onProperty hasPlayer owl:someValuesFrom Pitcher), we can infer that it has at least one pitcher (i.e., BaseballTeam is a subclass of the restriction owl:onProperty hasPlayer owl:minCardinality 1). Note that the same conclusion does not hold for owl:allValuesFrom; in short, someValuesFrom guarantees that there is some value; allValuesFrom makes no such guarantee.

The ability in OWL to infer class relationships is a severe departure from Object-Oriented modeling. In OO modeling, the class structure forms the backbone of the model's organization. All instances are created as members of some class, and their behavior is specified by the class structure. Changes to the class structure have far-reaching impact on the behavior of the system. In OWL, it is possible for the class structure to change as more information is learned about classes or individuals.

These aspects of OWL are not the result of whimsical decisions on the part of the OWL designers; they are a direct consequences of the basic assumptions about the Web—that is, the AAA slogan, the Open World nature of the Web, and the fact that names on the Web are not unique. A strict data model (like an object model) is useful when there is top-down governance of the system (as is the case when building a software system), but it doesn't work in an open, free system like the Web. Our understanding of the structure of knowledge will change as we discover more things— we cannot escape that! OWL at least provides a consistent and systematic way to understand those changes.

The logic underlying OWL goes beyond these propagation rules and encompasses inferences about subclasses regarding cardinalities. The technical details of the logic are beyond the scope of this book. In short, any class relationship that can be proven to hold, based on the semantics of restrictions, unions, intersections, and so on, will be inferred. The propagation patterns presented here don't cover all the possible class relationship inferences, but they are the most common patterns that appear in semantic models.

The ability in OWL to infer class relationships enables a style of modeling in which subclass relationships are rarely asserted directly. Instead, relationships between classes are described in terms

---

Table 12.1 Overview of Entities in the Baseball Model

AllStarBaseballPlayer	≡ playsFor **some** AllStarBaseballTeam
AllStarBaseballTeam	≡ BaseballTeam ∩ AllStarTeam
AllStarPlayer	≡ playsFor **some** AllStarTeam
AllStarTeam	⊆ Employs **some** AllStarPlayer
BaseballPlayer	≡ playsFor **some** BaseballTeam
BaseballTeam	⊆ Employs **some** BaseballPlayer
JBallTeam	≡ PacificLeagueTeam ∪ CentralLeagueTeam
	⊆ BaseballTeam
CarpPlayer	≡ playsFor **hasValue** Carp (the Carp is the name of the baseball team from Hiroshima)
CentralLeagueTeam	≡ **oneOf** Carp, Giants, BayStars, Tigers, Dragons, Swallows
PacificLeagueTeam	≡ **oneOf** Lions, Hawks, Fighters, BlueWave, Buffaloes, Marines
Player	**domain of** playsFor
Team	**range of** playsFor
playsFor	**inverse of** Employs

---

of unions, intersections, complements, and restrictions, and the inference engine determines the class structure. If more information is learned about a particular class or individual, then more class structure can be inferred. Subclass relationships are asserted only in that the members of one class are included in another.

The baseball model demonstrates this principle at work—we summarize the statements about baseball players and their teams in Table 12.1.

In Table 12.1, we write ≡ if the class in the left column is defined as equivalent to the expression in the right column, and ⊆ if the class is a subclass of the expression in the right column. Notice that the only direct subclass assertion (i.e., one class is a subclass of another) is for JBallTeam, which is asserted to be a subclass of BaseballTeam. All other assertions in the model either refer to logical combinations (intersections or unions) or to restrictions. Thus, the class tree as asserted is shown in Figure 12.9.

We can infer a number of subclass relationships from the definitions of the model in Table 12.1 and the subclass inferencing patterns we have seen.

- Since AllStarBaseballTeam is the intersection of BaseballTeam and AllStarTeam, then AllStarBaseballTeam is a subclass of BaseballTeam and AllStarTeam.
- Both AllStarBaseballPlayer and AllStarPlayer are someValuesFrom restrictions on the same property, playsFor, referencing AllStarBaseballTeam and AllStarTeam, respectively. The fact that AllStarBaseballTeam is a subclass of AllStarTeam can be propagated, so we can infer that AllStarBaseballPlayer is a subclass of AllStarPlayer. Similar reasoning allows us to infer that AllStarBaseballPlayer is a subclass of BaseballPlayer.
- Since JBallTeam is the union of PacificLeagueTeam and CentralLeagueTeam, we can conclude that PacificLeagueTeam and CentralLeagueTeam are subclasses of JBallTeam.

FIGURE 12.9

Class tree for the baseball ontology, as asserted.

- Since the Hiroshima Carp is a `CentralLeague` team, it is also a `JBallTeam` and thus a `BaseballTeam`. A `CarpPlayer` is a `hasValue` restriction on the `Carp`; thus, we can infer that `CarpPlayer` is a subclass of `BaseballPlayer`.
- The domain of `playsFor` is also used to make class inferences. Since `AllStarPlayer` is equivalent to the `someValuesFrom` restriction `onProperty playsFor`, any individual member of `AllStarPlayer playsFor` some team. But the domain of `playsFor` is `Player`, so that individual must also be a `Player`. We have just shown that any `AllStarPlayer` must be a `Player`; thus, `AllStarPlayer` is a subclass of `Player`.
- Even the range information gets into the act; since an `AllStarTeam` *employs* some `AllStarPlayer`, and since `employs` is the inverse of `playsFor`, that means that some person `playsFor` any `AllStarTeam`. But the range of `playsFor` is `Team`, so `AllStarTeam` must be a `Team`, as well.

We can see the inferred class structure in Figure 12.10. Notice that every class is involved in some class inferencing pattern so that in contrast to the asserted model, the inferred model has considerable depth to its class tree.

REASONING WITH INDIVIDUALS AND WITH CLASSES

From an RDF perspective, inferencing about individuals and inferencing about classes is very similar. In both cases, new triples are added to the model based on the triples that were asserted. From a modeling perspective, the two kinds of reasoning are very different. One of them draws specific conclusions about individuals in a data stream, while the other draws general conclusions about classes of individuals. These two kinds of reasoning are sometimes called A-box reasoning (for individuals)

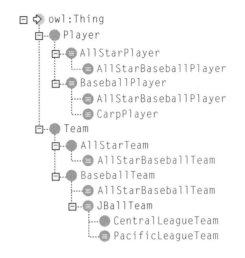

FIGURE 12.10

Inferred structure of the baseball model.

and T-box reasoning (for classes). The curious names A-box and T-box are historical and no longer have any relevance.

The utility of reasoning about individuals in a Semantic Web context is clear, and we have seen a number of examples of it throughout this book. We inferred things about the wife of Shakespeare, which movies belong to which people, and what terms are broader than others. All of these things are examples of reasoning about an individual. Information specified in one information source is transformed according to a model for use in another context. Mappings from one context to the next are specified using constructs like `rdfs:subClassOf`, `rdfs:subPropertyOf`, and various `owl:Restrictions`. Data can then be transformed and processed according to these models and the inferences specified in the RDFS and OWL standards for each of them.

The utility of reasoning about classes is more subtle. It can take place in the absence of any data at all! Class reasoning determines the relationships between classes of individuals. It determines how data are related in general. In advance of seeing any data about the Pacific League, we can determine that any team in that league is a baseball team. There is no need to process all the particular teams, or indeed any of them. We can guarantee that this is the case. Even if new teams join the league, we know that this will still be true. In this sense, class reasoning is similar to a compilation of the model. Whereas individual reasoning processes particular data items as input, Class reasoning determines general relationships among data and records those relationships with `rdfs:subClassOf`, `rdfs:subPropertyOf`, `rdfs:domain`, or `rdfs:range`. Once these general relationships have been inferred, processing of individual data can be done much more easily.

When we use individual and class reasoning together in a single system, we have a powerful system that smoothly integrates general reasoning with specific data transformations. This allows us to smoothly manage information based on whatever information we come across, generic or specific.

SUMMARY

At each level of our exposition of the Semantic Web languages from RDF to RDFS to the various levels of OWL, we have introduced new notions of how to understand a model. For RDF, the fundamental aspect of the model had to do with data sharing and federation. RDF answers the question "How do I get all the information I know about a single thing in one place?" For RDFS, we introduced the notion of inference, answering the question "Given that I know certain things about my data, what else can I figure out?" RDFS-Plus and the basic use of OWL gave us more comprehensive capabilities to infer new information from old. As we move on to the advanced features OWL, we are still working within the paradigm of inferencing as the source of meaning of our models, but we expand the sort of inferencing we can make to include inferences not just about our data but also about the model itself.

Up to this point, we could, for the most part, ignore the ramifications of the Open World Assumption of the Semantic Web. With the advanced constructs of OWL, where we can draw conclusions based on arguments of enumeration and elimination (as well as arguments based on properties and types, as we did with RDFS and RDFS-Plus), the impact of the open world becomes more apparent.

Armed with the concepts and constructs OWL from this chapter, we are now in a position to examine some more comprehensive OWL models. We can see how a modeler can use the constructs of OWL to describe how data from different sources will be federated on the Semantic Web. Just as we saw for RDFS-Plus, a model can mediate information from sources that have not yet been examined. Advanced OWL provides more powerful and complete ways to make this happen.

Fundamental concepts

The following fundamental concepts were introduced in this chapter.

owl:unionOf, owl:intersectionOf, owl:complementOf—Basic set operations applied to classes. Each of these is used to create a new class, based on the specified set operation applied to one or more defined classes.

Open World Assumption—This idea was introduced in Chapter 1, but strategies for closing the world for certain purposes were introduced here.

owl:oneOf—Specifies that a class consists just of the listed members.

owl:differentFrom—Specifies that one individual is not owl:sameAs another. This is particularly useful when making counting arguments.

owl:disjointWith—Specifies that two classes cannot share a member. This is often used as a sort of wholesale version of owl:differentFrom.

owl:cardinality, owl:minCardinality, owl:maxCardinality—Cardinality specifies information about the number of distinct values for some property. Combined with owl:oneOf, owl:differentFrom, owl:disjointWith, and so on, it can be the basis of inferences based on counting the number of values for a property.

Contradiction—With the advanced constructs of OWL, it is possible for a model to express a contradiction—that is, for a model to be logically inconsistent.

Satisfiability (unsatisfiability)—With the advanced constructs of OWL, it is possible to infer that a class can have no members, so such a class is *unsatisfiable*.

Ontologies on the Web—putting it all together

CHAPTER OUTLINE

A comprehensive listing of ontologies in the wild is impossible, just as a complete listing of all web pages is impossible. New ontologies and open data sets on the Semantic Web are showing up every day. In Chapter 9, we got a glimpse of the data sets that make up the data.gov project, and we saw how data based on FOAF and OGP are scattered all over the Web. In selecting ontologies for this chapter, we had to leave some favorite projects behind.

We ended up with three examples. These examples were chosen for this chapter because of their advanced use modeling features beyond RDFS-Plus, and how widespread their impact has been.

The first is called *Good Relations* (*GR* for short). GR allows businesses to make very detailed descriptions of their offerings on the marketplace. GR is similar to the OGP model described in Chapter 9 in that it provides a controlled vocabulary that can be used by Web content providers to mark up web pages. It differs from OGP in that it has a great deal more structure—business offerings come in all shapes and sizes and have a lot of details describing them.

The second is called *Quantities/Units/Dimensions/Types*, or *QUDT* for short. It addresses an obvious problem that must be solved in any attempt to align quantitative data, that is, data from multiple sources will be expressed in different units. In order to integrate data, it is necessary to be able to determine whether two quantities are commensurate (that's where the dimensions come in), and if so, how to convert from one system to another (that's where the units come in).

The third ontology is actually a whole collection of ontologies that are collectively known as the *Open Biological and Biomedical Ontologies* (*OBO*). As the name implies, this is a set of ontologies about biological and biomedical information. In contrast to Good Relations, which is a small vocabulary for describing information on the Web, OBO includes massive amounts of data about biomedicine and biology, including genome information, catalogs of known cancer genes, and biochemistry data.

THE GOOD RELATIONS ONTOLOGY

The Good Relations ontology (GR) was developed by Martin Hepp of the E-Business and Web Science Research Group at the Universitaet der Bundeswehr Muenchen. Like OGP, it has been used to annotate a large number of web pages. Within a year of its release, already tens of thousands of web pages were annotated in RDFa using GR. These annotations have been used by search engines (Yahoo! and Google, in particular) for Search Engine Optimization; the more completely a product can be described, the more highly it can be trusted to be an appropriate match for a search engine query. The use of GR for annotating product web pages at Best Buy and overstock.com resulted in web pages that were ranked more highly in search results than much more established pages. But Good Relations can do more than simply give pages a higher rank— Google uses Good Relations data to enhance the information it gives about a product in response to a search. Figure 13.1 shows search results for a product, with and without Good Relations markup. The page with Good Relations markup provides much more information to lead a potential buyer to the product.

How does GR allow someone to make such detailed descriptions of their business? While GR is relatively simple (in comparison, say, to OBO), there is more to it than can be covered in this case study. The interested reader is encouraged to see more of the GR at http://purl.org/goodrelations/ for a full and current description of the ontology. We will cover just enough of the GR ontology to see how it is used to describe products for Search Engine Optimization.

Hepp Research Personal SCSI Controller Card
The Hepp Research Personal SCSI is a 16-bit add-on card that allows attaching up to seven SCSI devices to...
www.heppresearch.com/commercecollator - Cached - Similar

Hepp Research Personal SCSI Controller Card
✭✭✭✭✭ 99 reviews - $99.99 - in stock
The Hepp Research Personal SCSI is a 16-bit add-on card that allows attaching up to seven SCSI devices to your computer. Designed in 1991 by Martin Hepp, the maker of the GoodRelations vocabulary for e-commerce.
www.heppresearch.com/commercecollator - Cached - Similar

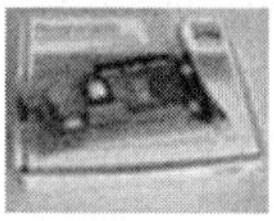

FIGURE 13.1

Google search results for the same product, without (top) and with (bottom) GR markup.

GR provides a way to express that a company is making an offer of a product or a service. This is expressed in three classes in GR:

```
gr:BusinessEntity a owl:Class .
gr:Offering a owl:Class .
gr:ProductOrService a owl:Class .
gr:offers
        a owl:ObjectProperty ;
        rdfs:domain gr:BusinessEntity ;
        rdfs:range gr:Offering .
gr:includes
        a owl:ObjectProperty ;
        rdfs:domain gr:Offering ;
        rdfs:range gr:ProductOrService .
```

This provides the basic framework of how a business offering is described in GR. GR provides many ways to enhance a description of an offering, based on these three things. We'll illustrate how this works with a real example of a business that uses GR and RDFa on its web site to enhance Search Engine Optimization.

EXAMPLE Plush Beauty Bar

The Plush Beauty Bar in West Hollywood has used RDFa to mark up its web site, http://plushbeautybar.com/, using the Good Relations ontology. We will use their markup as an example of the use of GR. The particular information in this example is for educational purposes only, and does not correspond to any real offerings by the Plush Beauty Bar. In this exposition, we will use the namespace prefix plush: for all resources defined by Plush Beauty Bar.

The Plush description begins with the business entity itself, the PlushBeautyBar. It offers several services, including a basic manicure (shiny buff or polish):

```
plush:Business a gr:BusinessEntity ;
    gr:offers plush:Offering_1 ;
    gr:offers plush:Offering_2 ;
    gr:offers plush:Offering_3 .
plush:Offering_1 rdfs:label "NAIL SERVICES (shiny buff or polish)" .
```

GR allows Plush to specify what kind of client they are advertising to—is this a Business-to-Business shop or a Business-to-Consumer shop? A nail salon is of course the latter—they are selling to individuals who want to buy a service. GR includes a property called gr:eligibleCustomerTypes for this. Its range is a class called BusinessEntityType, that includes a handful of predefined business entities that Plush can choose from:

```
gr:eligibleCustomerType a owl:ObjectProperty ;
        rdfs:domain gr:Offering ;
        rdfs:range gr:BusinessEntityType .
gr:Business a gr:BusinessEntityType .
gr:Enduser a gr:BusinessEntityType .
gr:PublicInstitution a gr:BusinessEntityType .
gr:Reseller a gr:BusinessEntityType .
```

Plush expresses its desired end customer as a selection from these business entity types:

```
plush:Offering_1 gr:eligibleCustomerType gr:Enduser .
```

In a similar fashion, GR provides predefined classes of business functions, payment methods, delivery methods, warranty scopes, etc., along with corresponding properties. Plus uses some of these to describe its offering as well:

```
plush:Offering_1
    gr:acceptedPaymentMethods
        gr:Cash , gr:Discover , gr:VISA , gr:MasterCard;
    gr:hasBusinessFunction gr:ProvideService .
```

Plush's services come at a price, of course, and GR allows Plush to describe these, as well. This poses a modeling problem—if we were to define a property called, say, :cost, that related an offering to a number, we could specify the amount of the price, but in business we need to know more about the cost than just the number, we need to know currency as well. This means that we have to put some more information on the cost relationship between the offering and its price. This is an example of *reification* from Chapter 3, and GR solves it by defining a class called a UnitPriceSpecification for the full description of a price. We'll see how Plush uses this to describe the price of their manicure:

```
plush:Offering_1 gr:hasPriceSpecification plush:PriceSpec_1 .
plush:PriceSpec_1 a gr:UnitPriceSpecification ;
    gr:hasCurrency "USD""^^xsd:string ;
    gr:hasCurrencyValue "19"^^xsd:float ;
    gr:hasUnitOfMeasurement "C62" .
```

This says that the manicure offering has a price, which is $19 (US). The unit of measure is worth looking at, since units of measure play a key role in commerce. GR uses the United Nations standard called UNECE for referring to measurement units; "C62" is the unit for "by the job." If instead Plush were charging by the hour, the unit would be the UNECE unit for hour, "HUR."

This offering is for a particular service; we have seen the price, the methods of payment, the kinds of customer, but we haven't yet talked about the service itself. An offering can include several services, but in this case, the offering includes just one—the basic manicure. This is stated simply as:

```
plush:Offering_1 gr:includes plush:Service_1 .
plush:Service_1 a gr:ProductOrService ;
    rdfs:label "NAIL SERVICES: Manicure" .
```

The information Plush expresses about its manicure offering is shown in Figure 13.2.

We can query this structure of this sort to answer questions like, "Show me the services for individual customers (i.e., end users) that cost less than $20" with SPARQL as follows:

```
SELECT ?service
WHERE  {?o a gr:Offering ;
           gr:eligibleCustomerTypes gr:EndUser ;
           gr:includes ?s ;
           gr:hasPriceSpecification ?ps .
       ?ps gr:hasCurrencyValue ?v;
           gr:hasCurrency "USD" .
       ?s rdfs:label ?service .
       FILTER (?v < 20)
       }
```

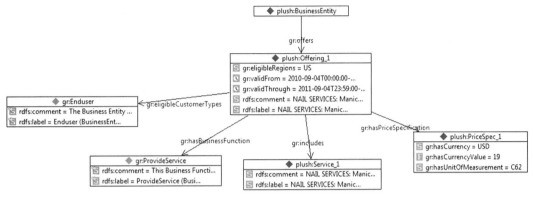

FIGURE 13.2

Information about Plush's manicure offering, shown in graph form.

The results will list all the services in that price range; a regular search engine can filter those based on keywords, to focus on the particular service desired.

INFERENCING IN THE GOOD RELATIONS ONTOLOGY

Suppose that in addition to its manicure services, Plush were to offer a massage service, priced by the hour. If we wanted to describe a one-and-a-half-hour massage session, the notion of `includes` would have to be reified, just as we did for the price. GR provides a means to do this, by introducing the notion of a `TypeAndQuantityNode`:

```
plush:Offering_2 a gr:Offering ;
     gr:includesObject plush:Quantity_2 .
plush:Quantity_2 a gr:TypeAndQuantityNode ;
     gr:typeOfGood plush:Service_2 ;
     gr:hasUnitOfMeasurement "HUR" ;
     gr:amountOfThisGood  "1.5"^^xsd:float .
plush:Service_2 a gr:ProductOrService ;
     rdfs:label "Relaxing Massage" .
```

This model differs from the description of the manicure in two ways; first, it includes the intermediate entity `Quantity_1` that allows us to make multiple statements about the massage service; in particular, that it lasts for 1.5 hours. The second difference is that the property used to connect the offering to the (reified) service description is `includesObject` (whereas it was `includes` in the manicure example). This is how GR indicates the reified relationship, by using the property `includesObject` to indicate the service.

This method for representing services by the hour (or any other good that is sold in some units) is expressive and consistent, but it does pose a problem when it comes to querying a Good Relations data set. If we represent massages as we have done here, and manicures as we did in the previous example, we can't query both structures using just the query we used for manicures—we will need a query that knows how to work with both ways of representing services.

One solution to this would be to retire the simple representation of services—the one that uses the predicate `includes`, that we used for the manicure—in favor of the more expressive representation using `includesObject`. This is certainly possible—we could represent the manicure as being a service, measured "by the job," i.e., unit "C62," where the amount is 1. Then the manicure representation would look like

```
plush:Offering_1 a gr:Offering ;
    gr:includesObject plush:Quantity_1 .
plush:Quantity_1 a gr:TypeAndQuantityNode ;
    gr:typeOfGood plush:Service_1 ;
    gr:hasUnitOfMeasurement "C62" ;
    gr:amountOfThisGood = "1" .
plush:Service_1 a gr:ProductOrService ;
    rdfs:label "NAIL SERVICES: Manicure " .
```

But this is a lot of work to go through, in comparison to the much simpler representation we are already using, i.e.,

```
plush:Offering_1 gr:includes plus:Service_1 .
```

Do we really have to abandon this simple representation, and go for the more complex one?

Good Relations includes a number of "Optional Axioms"—these are rules that apply to the Good Relations ontology, but are not expressed in the OWL representation of Good Relations. They are described on the Good Relations web site both in plain English, as well as in SPARQL.[1] One of these rules is designed exactly for this case. A simplified version of the rule can be expressed in SPARQL as

```
CONSTRUCT {
?o gr:includesObject _:n .
_:n rdf:type gr:TypeAndQuantityNode.
_:n gr:amountOfThisGood "1.0"^^xsd:float.
_:n gr:hasUnitOfMeasurement "C62"^^xsd:string.
_:n gr:typeOfGood ?p.}
WHERE
{
?o rdf:type gr:Offering.
?o gr:includes ?p. }
```

That is, if an offering `gr:includes` something, then construct a `TypeAndQuantityNode` with units "C62" ("by the job") and amount 1—building in the reified structure. Figure 13.3 shows the result of constructing these triples for the manicure example.

---

[1]http://www.ebusiness-unibw.org/wiki/GoodRelationsOptionalAxiomsAndLinks

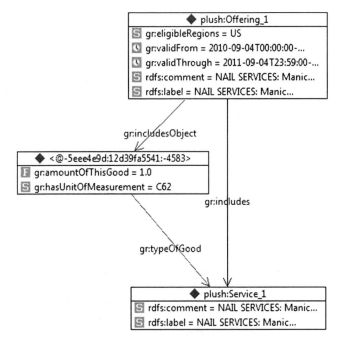

FIGURE 13.3

Offering_1 after inferencing; the reified object has been constructed from the asserted includes triple.

COMPOSING FILES

The Optional Axioms of Good Relations are not represented as part of the published GR ontology. The reason for this is that most of the optional axioms cannot be expressed in OWL, and the GR authors want GR to be an OWL ontology. But these rules can be expressed in languages that go beyond OWL. We want to leave the published GR ontology "pure" OWL, while having the non-OWL parts in another file. Most software languages have features for managing modularity of this sort, and OWL is no exception; it has language features for modularizing semantic models. These language features have no semantics for the model (they allow no new triples to be inferred), but they help us, as humans, to organize a model in a modular way.

owl:Ontology

OWL provides a built-in class whose members correspond to modular parts of a semantic model. It is customary for the URI of an *Ontology* to correspond to the URL of the file on the Web where the ontology is stored. This makes use of a slightly different syntax in Turtle than we have used so far. It is possible to spell out a URI by enclosing it in angle brackets:

```
<http://www.workingontologist.com/Examples/ch14/shakespeare.owl>
    a owl:Ontology.
```

Unlike the other constructs in OWL, the meaning of membership in `owl:Ontology` is not given by inference. In fact, one could say that it has no formal meaning at all. Informally, a member of `owl:Ontology` corresponds to a set of RDF triples. The set of triples such a resource corresponds to can be found by de-referencing its URI (as a URL), which is expected (informally) to resolve to an RDF data set (e.g., an RDF file). Formally, there is no connection in the model between an instance of `owl:Ontology` and the triples to which it corresponds.

Although such an individual has no significance from the point of view of model semantics, it can be quite useful when specifying modularity of semantic models. The primary way to specify modularity is with the property `owl:imports`.

owl:imports

This is a property that connects two instances of the class `owl:Ontology`. Just as is the case with `owl:Ontology` itself, no inferences are drawn based on `owl:imports`. But the meaning in terms of modularity of models is clear: When any system loads triples from the file corresponding to an instance of `owl:Ontology`, it can also find any file corresponding to an imported ontology and load that as well. This load can, in turn, trigger further imports, which trigger further loads, and so on. There is no need to worry about the situation in which there is a circuit of imports (e.g., GR imports OGP imports FOAF imports GR). A simple policy of taking no action when a file is imported for a second time will guarantee that no vicious loops will occur. The resulting set of triples is the union of all triples in all imported files.

In the case of GR, we can separate its rules out into a separate file, and have that file import the GR ontology. If someone just wants the "pure OWL" GR ontology, they can import it from its base URI, http://purl.org/goodrelations/v1. If someone else wants the GR ontology together with its (non-OWL) rules, they can import http://WorkingOntologist.org/Examples/Chapter13/GROptionalAxioms, which expresses these rules in a non-OWL rules language called SPIN, found at spinrdf.org.

```
<http://WorkingOntologist.org/Examples/Chapter13/GROptional Axioms>
      rdf:type owl:Ontology ;
      owl:imports <http://purl.org/goodrelations/v1> ;
      owl:imports <http://spinrdf.org/spin> .
```

SPIN is a very simple, SPARQL-based rules language that works by linking classes in an ontology to SPARQL CONSTRUCT queries. To express one of the optional axioms in SPIN, we simply assert a triple that relates a query to the relevant class. The axiom we saw in the previous section applied to offerings, so we associate the query that defines the rule with the `gr:Offering` class as follows:

```
gr:Offering spin:rule
      "CONSTRUCT {
        ?o gr:includesObject _:n .
        _:n rdf:type gr:TypeAndQuantityNode.
        _:n gr:amountOfThisGood "1.0"^^xsd:float.
        _:n gr:hasUnitOfMeasurement "C62"^^xsd:string.
        _:n gr:typeOfGood ?p.}
      WHERE
      {
        ?o rdf:type gr:Offering.
        ?o gr:includes ?p. } "
```

In this example, we have represented the query associated with `gr:Offering` as a string; SPIN also includes a way to represent the query in RDF that is often more convenient for storage, but is not as convenient for reading in a book. Associating a rule (in the form of a `CONSTRUCT` query) with a class allows us to specify the scope of each of the rules, and to express them in a familiar language. Like Good Relations itself, there is a lot more to SPIN, and the interested reader is referred to http://spinrdf.org/.

SUMMARY

The Good Relations ontology provides a way in which Web content providers can mark up their web pages to describe business offerings. Like OGP, its designers have made a commitment to simplicity. But as GR is more ambitious than OGP, it provides a good deal more sophistication in the model for providing structured descriptions of goods and services. GR both provides standards of reference for describing business entities (like `gr:EndUser` and `gr:ProvideService`), as well as referring to other standards (like the UN/CEFACT codes for units of measure). As such, it is a good Semantic Web citizen, providing linkages to familiar vocabularies as well as contributing its own.

To date, Good Relations has been used for Search Engine Optimization, with considerable impact. But the real value to having structured data is to support true semantic search, whereby a customer can be very specific about what they are searching for, and have some confidence that if it exists, then it can be found. Good Relations has made great strides in this direction, by achieving structured markup in tens of thousands of sites.

QUANTITIES, UNITS, AND DIMENSIONS

As part of the Constellation Program, NASA developed an ontology to deal with units of measure. The utility of controlling references to units in science and engineering has been understood for centuries, and there are several standard systems of units; there is the US Customary set of units (with things like miles, feet, and degrees Fahrenheit), the international system ("SI") that includes meters, kilograms, and Kelvins. NASA built an ontology of Quantities, Units, and Dimensions (QUDT)[2] to capture and manage this information.

What is the purpose of such an ontology? In contrast to OGP and Good Relations, which provide vocabularies that assist web page developers in marking up their pages, QUDT cuts across many domains. It was designed for science and engineering, but it has applicability in any setting where information can be expressed in different units. We have already seen an application for units in the Good Relations ontology—it is important to know how a service is measured—by the hour, by the minute, or by the job.

QUDT serves three major purposes in the Semantic Web. First, it provides a global reference for units. If one information source says that some product is measured in pounds, and another source

---

[2]QUDT also includes information about Types, which is beyond the scope of this treatment.

says that its service is provided in pounds, how do we know that they are making reference to the same notion of pound (there is more than one)? QUDT provides a URI for the notion of pound (with information to distinguish it from other units with the same common name), so that such references can be made unambiguously. QUDT is not alone in providing this service; as we have already seen with Good Relations, UN/CEFACT also provides a canonical set of codes for unambiguously identifying units. QUDT connects to the UN/CEFACT codes with the property `qudt:uneceCommonCode`.

The second purpose that QUDT serves is to provide conversion services. If two information sources provide information in terms of pounds, and we use something like UN/CEFACT or QUDT to determine that they are the same notion of pound, then we can compare the offerings. But what if one of them offers a product measured in pounds, and the other in kilograms? There are a few things that have to happen before we can compare the offerings. First, we have to understand whether it is even possible to compare pounds and kilograms (are they "commensurate" values). If they are, then we need to convert values from one unit to the other. QUDT offers both of these services. These services are useful in science and engineering settings, but also in more common settings like the commercial applications of Good Relations.

The third purpose that QUDT serves is mostly focused on engineering settings, where it is often important to verify the dimensions of certain quantities. One way to check for errors in a formula is to check the dimensions of the components of a formula; only quantities with the same dimensions may be added to one another or compared to one another; for example, it makes no sense to add kilograms and centimeters or to compare seconds to feet. A simple check for correct dimensions can turn up errors, even in quite complex formulas. QUDT includes a comprehensive model of dimensions, cross-referenced with units, which enables dimension-based calculations. The simplest application of this facility is for units conversion—it makes no sense to convert from one unit to another, if the units don't have the same dimension. The formula to convert from meters to feet, $1m = 3.28$ ft, can be checked for dimensional correctness—do meters and feet have the same dimension? Yes, they do; both are measures of length.

We will explore just enough of the QUDT ontology to show how it supports these three functions. The QUDT ontology supports this functionality through a careful separation of Quantities, Units, and Dimensions. In some sense, there is nothing new about this separation; treatment of these things has been ongoing in science and engineering for centuries. QUDT makes it referenceable on the Web and actionable. Further information about QUDT can be found at its web site, QUDT.org.

A *Quantity* is some measurable property. A *Quantity Kind* is, appropriately enough, the kind of thing one can measure—familiar quantity kinds are length, time, mass, and force, etc. A *Unit* is a standard of measurement for a particular quantity kind. A foot is a unit for measuring length; a second is a unit for measuring time. It is common to have several units for a single kind; feet, inches, kilometers, Angstroms, light-years, and furlongs are all measures for length.

QUDT uses the Local Restriction of Range pattern described in Chapter 11; that is, it uses `owl:allValuesFrom` to restrict the possible values for a property. The relationship between `qudt:Unit` and `qudt:QuantityKind` is called `qudt:quantityKind` (note the naming convention; `qudt:quantityKind` begins with a lower-case letter, and hence is a property; `qudt:QuantityKind` begins with an upper-case letter and is a class). The restriction on this relationship is defined as

```
qudt:Unit a owl:Class ;
     rdfs:subClassOf
          [ a owl:Restriction ;
            owl:allValuesFrom qudt:QuantityKind ;
            owl:onProperty qudt:quantityKind
          ] .
qudt:quantityKind a owl:ObjectProperty .
qudt:QuantityKind a owl:Class .
```

As an example of units and quantity, let's have a look at feet and length:

```
vocab-units:Foot a qudt:Unit ;
     qudt:quantityKind vocab-quantities:Length .
```

As an example of units and quantity, let's have a look at feet and length:

```
vocab-units:Foot a qudt:Unit ;
     qudt:quantityKind vocab-quantities:Length .
```

Following along as in the example of this pattern from Chapter 11, from these triples we can infer that

```
vocab-quantities:Length a qudt:QuantityKind .
```

QUDT includes a comprehensive list of units and quantities from many fields of science, including mechanics, thermodynamics, chemistry, informatics, and biology. It organizes its namespaces in a modular way—as we saw in this example, resources that describe how units work (like the resources `qudt:QuantityKind` and `qudt:Unit`) are in the `qudt:` namespace, while particular quantities and units (like `vocab-quantities:Length` and `vocab-units:Foot`) are in namespaces whose names begin with `vocab-`. These resources are so named because together they form controlled vocabularies; one for quantities and one for units. These resources resolve the first function of the QUDT vocabulary, that is, they provide unambiguous reference URIs for all the units and quantities in QUDT.

CONVERTING UNITS WITH QUDT

QUDT includes information that can be used to convert measurements from one unit to another. This is a workhorse for merging quantitative information on the Semantic Web. Conversions can be within the same system of units (meters to kilometers, seconds to hours, feet to miles) or crossing between systems (miles to kilometers, degrees Fahrenheit to degrees Centigrade). In order for such a conversion to make sense, the units must be *commensurate*—that is, they measure the same kind of thing. Miles and kilometers are both measurements of length, so it makes sense to consider a conversion between the two. Seconds and degrees Fahrenheit do not measure the same thing; it is not meaningful to convert from one to another.

Usually we can tell if two units are commensurate if they measure the same quantity kind, but in some cases, certain different quantity kinds are in fact commensurate. These are important situations, in that they usually reflect a deep connection between different scientific domains. For example, the law of Conservation of Energy states that energy is preserved in an interaction—but energy can take many forms, including thermal energy (heat), potential energy, kinetic energy, and others. Measurements of all these kinds are commensurate. QUDT represents this situation with a tree structure using a property called `qudt:generalization`. In particular,

```
vocab-quantities:KineticEnergy
    qudt:generalization vocab-quantities:EnergyAndWork .
vocab-quantities:PotentialEnergy
    qudt:generalization vocab-quantities:EnergyAndWork .
vocab-quantities:ThermalEnergy
    qudt:generalization vocab-quantities:EnergyAndWork .
```

This means that we can query for whether two units are commensurate with the following SPARQL query:

```
ASK WHERE {
    ?arg1 qudt:quantityKind ?kind1 .
    ?arg2 qudt:quantityKind ?kind2 .
    ?kind1 qudt:generalization* ?kind .
    ?kind2 qudt:generalization* ?kind .
}
```

That is, ?arg1 and ?arg2 are commensurate, if their associated quantity kinds are related to a common ancestor in the `qudt:generalization` tree. Recall that `qudt:generalization*` will match zero or more repeated occurrences of `qudt:generalization`, so that if *?kind1* and *?kind2* are the same thing (e.g,. Length), they will match; this means that the query will return **true** for *?arg1* bound to `vocab-units:Foot` and *?arg2* bound to `vocab-units:Meters`. It will also return **true** for `vocab-quantities:PotentialEnergy` and `vocab-quantities:ThermalEnergy`, because they both have a common generalization, `vocab-quantities:EnergyAndWork`.

Once we have determined that two units are commensurate, we can set about converting measurements in one unit to the other. Each unit includes two properties—`qudt:conversionMultiplier` and `qudt:conversionOffset`. As their names suggest, these provide conversion multipliers and offsets for each unit. For each dimension, there is a base unit for which the multiplier is 1 and the offset 0. It isn't important to know what the base unit is, in order to convert from one unit to the other. For example, to convert ten kilometers to miles, we can use the query

```
SELECT  (((((10.0 * ?M1) + ?O1) - ?O2) / ?M2) AS ?value)
WHERE {
    unit:Kilometer qudt:conversionMultiplier ?M1 ;
        qudt:conversionOffset ?O1 .
    unit:MileInternational qudt:conversionMultiplier ?M2 ;
        qudt:conversionOffset ?O2 .
}
```

Answer: 6.2137119223733395

QUDT includes over five hundred conversion factors, enabling thousands of such conversions.

Using QUDT conversions

We can express these conversions in a SPARQL query, but this isn't available as an inference. That is, if we have some quantity specified in miles, we can't always count on an inference engine to express that value in kilometers. Calculations of this sort are the sort of things that one usually puts into an application program. SPIN is an example of how to do this. SPIN is a proposal for a way to work with SPARQL in a programmatic way. Earlier in Chapter 6 we saw how SPIN could be used to attach queries to an ontology. Here we see another application of SPIN. The query we used to convert kilometers to miles required us to put the information about the conversion into the query; the number to be converted (10.0), the source unit (kilometer), and the target unit (mile). If we want to do another conversion, we would need another query, very similar in form, but with a different measurement and different designations of units. Far more convenient would be to parameterize the query, making it effectively into a function definition. The generalized query, using variables *?arg1*, *?arg2*, etc., for the function arguments, looks like

```
SELECT  (((((?arg1 * ?M1) + ?O1) - ?O2) / ?M2) AS ?value)
WHERE {
    ?arg2 qudt:conversionMultiplier ?M1 ;
        qudt:conversionOffset ?O1 .
    ?arg3 qudt:conversionMultiplier ?M2 ;
        qudt:conversionOffset ?O2 .
}
```

SPIN allows such queries to be given names, which themselves are resources in RDF. If we give this query the name `qudtspin:convert`, then we could write the 10 kilometer query simply as

```
SELECT  (qudtspin:convert(10.0, unit:Kilometer, unit:MileInternational)
        AS ?value)
WHERE {}
```

The function call to `qudtspin:convert` is doing all the work—there is nothing in the WHERE clause to match at all!

The conversion of 32 degrees Fahrenheit to Centigrade looks very similar:

```
SELECT  (qudtspin:convert(32.0, unit:DegreeFahrenheit, unit:DegreeCelsius)
        AS ?value)
WHERE {}
```
Answer: 0.0

CHALLENGE 38: COMPARISON SHOPPING WITH GOOD RELATIONS

Now that we can use QUDT to convert values from one unit to another, we can apply this to Good Relations data for purposes of comparison shopping.

At the end of the Good Relations section, we had an example of a massage service. Let's add some pricing information to it—a single one-and-a-half-hour session costs US$80.00.

```
plush:Offering_2 a gr:Offering ;
    gr:hasPriceSpecification plush:PriceSpec_2 ;
    gr:includesObject plush:Quantity_2 .
plush:Quantity_2 a gr:TypeAndQuantityNode ;
    gr:typeOfGood plush:Service_2 ;
    gr:hasUnitOfMeasurement "HUR" ;
    gr:amountOfThisGood  "1.5"^^xsd:float .
plush:Service_2 a gr:ProductOrService ;
    rdfs:label "Relaxing Massage" .
plush:PriceSpec_2 a gr:UnitPriceSpecification ;
    gr:hasCurrency "USD"^^xsd:string ;
    gr:hasCurrencyValue "80.00"^^xsd:float .
```

Down the street from Plush, a competing day spa has its own offer—a fifteen-minute chair massage, for the busy person-on-the-go:

```
dayspa:Offering_3 a gr:Offering ;
    gr:hasPriceSpecification dayspa:PriceSpec_3 ;
    gr:includesObject dayspa:Quantity_3 .
dayspa:Quantity_3 a gr:TypeAndQuantityNode ;
    gr:typeOfGood dayspa:Service_3 ;
    gr:hasUnitOfMeasurement "MIN"^^xsd:string ;
    gr:amountOfThisGood  "15"^^xsd:float .
dayspa:Service_3 a gr:ProductOrService ;
    rdfs:label "Chair Massage" .
dayspa:PriceSpec_3 a gr:UnitPriceSpecification ;
    gr:hasCurrency "USD"^^xsd:string ;
    gr:hasCurrencyValue "15.00"^^xsd:float .
```

Suppose we want to compare these two offerings in terms of their price per minute of services. All the information is there—one of them costs $15 for 15 minutes, the other is $80 for an hour and a half. But to make the comparison, we have to convert the amounts into the same units.

We can do this by combining Good Relations with QUDT. First, we want to query the Good Relations data to find out all the things we need to know to make the comparison. We can do this simply by generalizing the common data form into a query:

```
SELECT *
WHERE {
?offering a gr:Offering ;
    gr:hasPriceSpecification ?pricespec;
    gr:includesObject ?quantity .
?quantity a gr:TypeAndQuantityNode ;
    gr:typeOfGood ?service ;
    gr:hasUnitOfMeasurement ?UNunit ;
    gr:amountOfThisGood  ?amt .
?service  a gr:ProductOrService ;
    rdfs:label ?servicename .
?pricespec
    a gr:UnitPriceSpecification ;
     gr:hasCurrency ?currency ;
     gr:hasCurrencyValue ?price .
}
```

The graph pattern (the part after the keyword WHERE) corresponds line per line to the data, with all the values that the two examples don't have in common turned into variables. We have chosen names for the variables that indicate their role in the graph; for example, *?pricespec* is a `UnitPriceSpecification`; *?UNunit* is the designator for the units, using the United Nations UNECE standard (as is common practice with Good Relations).

We want to be able to use the conversion capabilities of QUDT on this information, so we need to link our Good Relations results to QUDT. The linkage point is, of course, the units. But Good Relations doesn't reference QUDT units directly—it references UNECE units. Fortunately, QUDT also references the UNECE units, with a property called `qudt:uneceCommonCode`. We can get the QUDT units by matching a triple using this property:

```
?qudtunit qudt:uneceCommonCode ?UNunit .
```

Now we are in a position to compute a comparable cost rate in price per minute. The choice of "minutes" here is somewhat arbitrary—we could have as easily chosen any other time unit, like seconds or hours. Now that we know what units (*?qudtunit*) the amount (*?amt*) is in, we can convert it to minutes using `qudtspin:convert`:

```
qudtspin:convert (?amt, ?qudtunit, unit:MinuteTime)
```

We can compute the cost per minute by dividing *?price* by this. The final query is

```
SELECT ?servicename ?currency
      ((?price/qudtspin:convert(?amt, ?qudtunit,
                              unit:MinuteTime))AS ?cost_per_min )
WHERE {
?offering a gr:Offering ;
     gr:hasPriceSpecification ?pricespec;
     gr:includesObject ?quantity .
?quantity a gr:TypeAndQuantityNode ;
     gr:typeOfGood ?service ;
     gr:hasUnitOfMeasurement ?UNunit ;
     gr:amountOfThisGood  ?amt .
?service   a gr:ProductOrService ;
     rdfs:label ?servicename .
?pricespec
     a gr:UnitPriceSpecification ;
     gr:hasCurrency ?currency ;
     gr:hasCurrencyValue ?price .
?qudtunit qudt:uneceCommonCode ?UNunit   .
} ORDER BY ( ?cost_per_min )
```

Answer:

servicename	currency	cost_per_min
Relaxing Massage	USD	0.88
Chair Massage	USD	1.0

We have given the quotient of price per minute the name *?cost_per_min*, and sorted from lowest cost to highest. The result shows that the Relaxing Massage is the better value per minute.

This example shows a number of features of the role that models play in linking data sources. The structure of the Good Relations ontology gave us a consistent way to represent offerings, prices, amounts, and units of competing businesses. QUDT provides useful services (units conversions) for computations over these data. But as often happens in the data wilderness, these two models were not designed to connect. In particular, the Good Relations model does not use QUDT as its unambiguous reference for units. Fortunately, there is a common reference shared by QUDT and Good Relations—namely, the United Nations UNECE unit names standard. Since they both share a reference to UNECE, the connection can be made (with a single triple in the graph pattern!). The result is a price comparison based on published information, from a single query over the combined data sets.

DIMENSION CHECKING IN QUDT

There are a lot of services that an engineer or scientist could ask of a system of units; many of these go by the name *dimensional analysis*. Whole books have been written on the subject; we can barely scratch the surface of this topic here (therefore, see the Further Reading section at the conclusion of the book). We will illustrate enough of the QUDT ontology to show how it can support certain basic operations in dimensional analysis.

The basic idea of dimensional analysis is that a quantity has a signature that tells how it relates to basic quantities like length, time, and mass. QUDT defines eight base quantities of this sort, but in this exposition, we will focus on these three. A compound quantity has a signature in these basic quantities. For example, the compound quantity velocity is defined as a ratio between distance and time; this means that its signature in terms of length, time, and mass is length/time. The signature can be written as a vector, with one vector component for each base unit, and the magnitude of the vector in that component being the exponent of the base quantity in the formula for the compound quantity. If we write our vectors in the order [length, mass, time] then the vector for velocity is $[1, 0, -1]$. The vector for any base quantity will have magnitude 1 in exactly one place; so the vector for mass is $[0, 1, 0]$. Acceleration is given as a quotient of velocity by time; so its vector is $[1, 0, -2]$.

This vector is called the *dimensionality* of a compound unit. These vectors can be used to check the validity of a scientific or engineering formula. For example, one of the basic laws of motion is given by the formula $F = ma$, or Force equals the product of mass times acceleration. Only quantities with identical dimensionality can be meaningfully compared, so this formula makes sense only if the dimensionality of Force is the same as the dimensionality of the product of mass and acceleration. The dimensionality of Force is given by the expression ml/t^2, that is, mass times length divided by time twice. The dimensionality of acceleration is given as l/t^2, or length divided by time twice, and mass is given simply by m. So we can check the dimensionality of $F = ma$ by replacing each term with its dimensions, i.e., $ml/t^2 = m \cdot (l/t^2)$. Since the dimensions on both sides are the same, the formula has been verified to pass the test of dimensionality. It is important to note that this kind of simple dimensional analysis can uncover certain formulas that are incorrect; a correct dimensional analysis does not guarantee that the formula doesn't have some other problems with it.

In terms of dimension vectors, we can do the same calculation using vectors. The dimension vector for Force is $[1, 1, -2]$. The vector for mass is $[0, 1, 0]$ and the vector for acceleration is $[1, 0, -2]$. The formula is verified if the vectors add up; that is, if the vector for mass plus the vector for acceleration

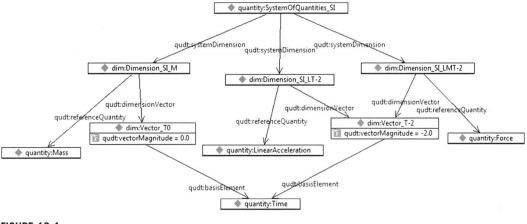

FIGURE 13.4

Dimensional structure in QUDT to support analysis of $F = ma$ (time dimension)

equals the vector for force. We add vectors element by element, and verify that indeed $[0, 1, 0] +$ $[1, 0, -2] = [1, 1, -2]$, verifying that the dimensions of the formula are identical.

QUDT supports dimensional analysis by representing over 200 dimensions, cross-referenced with corresponding quantities. Figure 13.4 shows the structure in QUDT needed to support this sort of analysis. We will go through each piece in turn.

First, there is the System of Quantities. QUDT includes eight different systems of quantities, including the standard international ("metric") system (SI, shown in the figure) as well as several variants of the CGS (centimeter-gram-second) and the US Customary system (with inches, yards, miles, pounds, etc.). A system of quantities defines the dimensions that can be measured in that system. Each system typically has dozens of dimensions associated with it. In the figure, we see three dimensions associated with the SI system of quantities—one for mass (`Dimension_SI_M`), one for length over time twice (`Dimension_SI_LT-2`) and one for length times mass over time twice (`Dimension_SI_LMT-2`). The naming convention for these dimensions includes the name of the system (SI) followed by the dimensions in the order length, mass, time, each followed by a number indicating the exponent for that dimension. These names are not used by any query mechanism—they are only used for humans to read the dimension names.

Since the names are only there for humans to read, if we want to query for the dimension vector for any of these, we need to represent their dimensional vectors in triples. This is shown in Figure 13.5 for `Dimension_SI_LMT-2`; for each of the three basis vectors, there is a one-dimensional vector. The magnitude of the vector is given by the property `vectorMagnitude` (its value is a floating point number, since fractional exponents are possible for certain units). The base quantity itself (mass, length, time) is given by the property `baseElement`.

We can see all of this come together in Figure 13-5 for the time dimension; we have our three quantities, `Mass`, `LinearAcceleration` and `Force`. Each of these is referenced by a particular dimension expression – m for mass, l/t^2 for linear acceleration, and ml/t^2 for force. Each of these, in turn, is related to several base vectors. The figure shows the vector for time, with coefficient zero for mass (since the vector for mass has a zero in the *time* place), coefficient -2 for linear acceleration

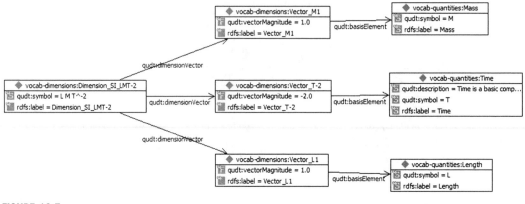

FIGURE 13.5

QUDT dimensional breakdown of ml/t^2

(since the vector for linear acceleration has a -2 in the *time* place), and also a coefficient -2 for force (since the vector for force also has a -2 in the *time* place). From the information in Figure 13.4, we are in a position to verify (for the *time* dimension, anyway) that the formula $F = ma$ is correct from a dimensional point of view, by noticing that the time coefficient for mass (0) plus that for linear acceleration (-2) equals the coefficient for force (-2); $0 + (-2) = -2$.

How can we write a SPARQL query to verify this calculation? First, let's have a look at some of the information from Figure 13.4 rendered verbatim in Turtle:

```
quantity:SystemOfQuantities_SI qudt:systemDimension dim:Dimension_SI_M .
dim:Dimension_SI_M qudt:referenceQuantity quantity:Mass .
dim:Dimension_SI_M  qudt:dimensionVector dim:Vector_T0 .
dim:Vector_T0 qudt:vectorMagnitude "0.0"^^xsd:float .
dim:Vector_T0 qudt:basisElement quantity:Time .
```

We can use these triples to form a query that will tell us the magnitude of the time dimension for the quantity mass by putting in variables at the appropriate places:

```
SELECT ?MassMagnitude
WHERE {
  quantity:SystemOfQuantities_SI qudt:systemDimension ?dim .
  ?dim qudt:referenceQuantity quantity:Mass .
  ?dim  qudt:dimensionVector ?vector .
  ?vector qudt:vectorMagnitude ?MassMagnitude .
  ?vector qudt:basisElement quantity:Time .
}
```
Answer: 0.0

We can verify the correctness of the dimensionality of $F = ma$ by repeating this pattern three times, once each for mass, acceleration and force. If we filter with the formula (`?MassMagnitude + ?AccMagnitude != ?ForceMagnitude`), we will eliminate those dimensions for which the vectors don't add up.

If we replace `quantity:Time` with another variable (*?base*), we can repeat this calculation for every vector base. We will need to list out those bases; QUDT provides this list as the class `qudt:VectorBase`. Finally, the dimension analysis matches exactly if there is no dimension for which it fails. We accomplish this in SPARQL by putting the check for a failure into a subquery, and then checking for no failures using the SPARQL keyword NOT EXISTS. If there does not exist a failure, then the query returns true. The complete query that checks the dimensions of $F = ma$ is shown here. It returns **true**, since the dimensions do check out.

```
ASK WHERE
{
  NOT EXISTS {
    SELECT *
    WHERE { ?base a qudt:VectorBase .
        quantity:SystemOfQuantities_SI qudt:systemDimension ?dim1 .
        ?dim1 qudt:referenceQuantity quantity:Mass .
        ?dim1  qudt:dimensionVector ?vector1 .
        ?vector1 qudt:vectorMagnitude ?MassMagnitude .
        ?vector1 qudt:basisElement ?base .
        quantity:SystemOfQuantities_SI qudt:systemDimension ?dim2 .
        ?dim2 qudt:referenceQuantity quantity:LinearAcceleration .
        ?dim2  qudt:dimensionVector ?vector2 .
        ?vector2 qudt:vectorMagnitude ?AccMagnitude .
        ?vector2 qudt:basisElement ?base.
        quantity:SystemOfQuantities_SI qudt:systemDimension ?dim3 .
        ?dim3 qudt:referenceQuantity quantity:Force .
        ?dim3  qudt:dimensionVector ?vector3 .
        ?vector3 qudt:vectorMagnitude ?ForceMagnitude .
        ?vector3 qudt:basisElement ?base.
    FILTER (?MassMagnitude + ?AccMagnitude != ?ForceMagnitude)
    } } }
```

The real test of a query like this is to try it on formulas that do not check out. Indeed, if we replace e.g,. Mass with Time or Force with Energy in this query, the result is false, since those dimensions do not add up.

While it is easy enough to build up a query like this from identical pieces, reading and maintaining them can become unwieldy. Since large parts of the query are repetitive, this is a great opportunity to define the repeating parts as SPIN functions. It is beyond the scope of this book to work out all the dimensional analysis queries using SPIN—but the same approach used to generate this query has been used to create SPIN functions for checking the dimensionality of formulas. Details of this approach can be found at http://qudt.org/.

SUMMARY

QUDT is an elaborate ontology, but not a very large one. It includes a few dozen classes and several hundred units, quantities, and vectors. But it expresses subtle distinctions that are important for providing services with units. It accomplishes the three major goals we laid out at the beginning of this section; it provides a global reference (URI) for comprehensive systems of units, it provides a means for converting from any unit to any commensurate unit, and it provides enough information to perform dimensional analysis on any of over 200 units that it defines. It accomplishes this with a careful separation of entities—quantities, units and dimensions, as well as a comprehensive catalog of information about the conventional units used throughout history and around the world.

BIOLOGICAL ONTOLOGIES

Ontologies in one form or another have been a mainstay of biological and life sciences for decades (one could even say for centuries). In recent years, there has been an explosion of biological information, along with a corresponding interest in ontologies to help organize that information. In this "in the wild" study, we make no attempt to provide a comprehensive catalog of biological ontologies. We will instead concentrate by example on the modeling aspects of biomedical ontologies and their use in the Semantic Web.

Just as was the case with QUDT, the biological ontologies serve many purposes on the Semantic Web. First, they provide unambiguous references to biological concepts. This is particularly important when there are tens of thousands of relevant concepts, including information about genes, diseases, chemicals, and organisms, etc. Having unambiguous names of this sort is essential for organizing information generated in different laboratories. Unambiguous terms of this sort are essential for locating publications—if a researcher suspects something interesting about a particular gene, indexing the vast corpus of biological publications for appropriate material is considerably enhanced by unambiguous names.

A closely related function has to do with the observation that in any global endeavor, many people will have already come up with naming schemes for these things—there are already multiple naming schemes for proteins, chemicals, and other biological entities. A key role of many of the biological ontologies is to provide a sort of Rosetta Stone to link these vocabularies together. The Semantic Web is a particularly suitable infrastructure for this sort of interoperation of vocabularies.

A more involved use of a biological ontology is for solving elaborate search problems, where the search relies on massive amounts of detailed knowledge about a technical domain (like chemistry, genomics, and proteomics). This places much more stringent requirements on an ontology. Many of the ontologies published today have sufficient detail to satisfy these requirements.

In this exposition, we will use an ontology called the *Chemical Entities of Biological Interest* (*CHEBI*, for short). CHEBI is being developed and maintained by the European Bioinformatics Institute, and contains information about over 20,000 chemical compounds. It is published as part of the Open Biological and Biomedical Ontologies Foundry (OBO Foundry), a sort of wiki space for collecting science-based ontologies. The OBO Foundry publishes ontologies in a number of forms including OWL. OBO Foundry OWL ontologies use certain ontology design patterns that we will examine in detail.

CHEBI AS UNAMBIGUOUS REFERENCE

CHEBI provides a URI identifier for every chemical it defines, and hence serves as a global reference for those chemicals. But CHEBI is not the only resource that identifies chemicals—many other resources do this as well. These other resources do not necessarily share CHEBI's focus on chemicals of biological interest, but there is still considerable overlap. For this reason, CHEBI includes several cross-references for each chemical it defines. For example, the herbicide glyphosate (better known by its trade name, Roundup) is represented in CHEBI as

```
chebi:CHEBI_27744
        rdfs:label "glyphosate"@en ;
        oboInOwl:hasDbXref
                [ a        oboInOwl:DbXref ;
                  rdfs:label "ChemIDplus:1071-83-6"
                ] ;
        oboInOwl:hasDbXref
                [ a        oboInOwl:DbXref ;
                  rdfs:label "KEGG_COMPOUND:1071-83-6"
                ] ;
        oboInOwl:hasDbXref
                [ a        oboInOwl:DbXref ;
                  rdfs:label "Beilstein:2045054"
                ] ;
        oboInOwl:hasDbXref
                [ a        oboInOwl:DbXref ;
                  rdfs:label "MSDchem:GPJ"
                ] ;
        oboInOwl:hasDbXref
                [ a        oboInOwl:DbXref ;
                  rdfs:label "Gmelin:279222"
                ] .
```

Glyphosate has identifying number 27744 in CHEBI, which is actually represented as the URI Chebi:CHEBI_27744. Every entity in CHEBI is assigned a number like this. While this policy makes the URIs difficult to read, it makes them easier to use in a multi-lingual setting or, as in this case, in a setting in which multiple names could be preferred by different groups. In defining cross-references to other chemical identification systems, CHEBI makes ample use of *reification* (Chapter 3). Each cross-reference is an individual member of the class oboInOwl:DbXref, with a label that indicates the details of the reference. In the example, we see references to several other authorities, with names given in the references (ChemIDPlus, Kegg, etc.). The DbXref is reified to allow other information to accompany the cross reference as available, e.g., a pointer to the governing body, effective dates, etc. This structure allows CHEBI to act as a sort of translation service among these other resources, for the chemicals that it describes.

CHEBI FOR COMPLEX SEARCH

A good deal of the complexity of the CHEBI ontology lies in the connections between the chemicals. It is typical of OBO ontologies to include complex interrelationships between the entities they define. CHEBI makes a particularly good pedagogical example of OBO style because of its relatively small size (only 20,000 concepts) and the small number of relationships between the chemicals it records.

Using our example chemical glyphosate, the fact that it is an herbicide is represented in CHEBI as

```
chebi:CHEBI_24527
        a owl:Class ;
        rdfs:label "herbicide"@en .
chebi:CHEBI_27744
        a owl:Class ;
        rdfs:label "glyphosate"@en ;
        rdfs:subClassOf
                [ a owl:Restriction ;
                  owl:onProperty obo:has_role ;
                  owl:someValuesFrom chebi:CHEBI_24527
                ] ;
```

The first thing to notice in this style of modeling is that every concept is represented in OWL as an `owl:Class`; the chemical "glyphosate" (`Chebi:CHEBI_27744`) as well as the role "herbicide" (`Chebi:CHEBI_24527`) are both classes. These two classes are related to one another as shown; *glyphosate* is a subclass of an `owl:Restriction` (as defined in Chapter 11), where that restriction is on the property `obo:has_role`, and stipulates that this property takes at least one value from (`owl:someValuesFrom`) the class *herbicide*. Notice that the property `obo:has_role` comes from OBO namespace; OBO Foundry defines dozens of properties that are useful for describing biological entities. CHEBI uses less than a dozen of them that have relevance to its domain of biochemistry. In addition to `obo:has_role` seen in this example, CHEBI uses `obo:has_part` (for constituent chemicals), and several chemistry-specific properties like `obo:is_conjugate_acid_of`, `obo:is_conjugate_base_of`, and `obo:has_parent_hydride`. The pattern we see here with "has role" and "herbicide" is repeated in CHEBI about 12,000 times, to relate various chemicals to their components, conjugate acids and bases, parent hydrides, etc. This pattern is typical of OBO ontologies and is used thousands of times in OBO Foundry.

Since this pattern is being used to reflect the fact that glyphosate has the role of herbicide, one might well wonder why this wasn't represented simply with a single triple

```
chebi:CHEBI_27733 obo:has_role chebi:CHEBI_24527 .
```

As usual, the answer to a question like this lies in the inferencing. What inferences can we draw from this pattern?

To see the answer to this, we need to view glyphosate in a larger context. Figure 13.6 shows some of the context of glyphosate in CHEBI.

CHEBI goes into considerable detail about classifications of chemicals. We see in this figure the information about glyphosate's role as an herbicide (center). It is a subclass of a restriction on the property *has role* that takes some value from the class *herbicide*. But we have further context about *herbicide*, in particular that it is a subclass of *pesticide*. We also see that *glyphosate* is a subclass, through a long chain of intermediaries, of two more restrictions, which stipulate that for *has part* it takes some value from *phosphorus*, and that for *has parent hydride*, it takes some value from *ammonia*.

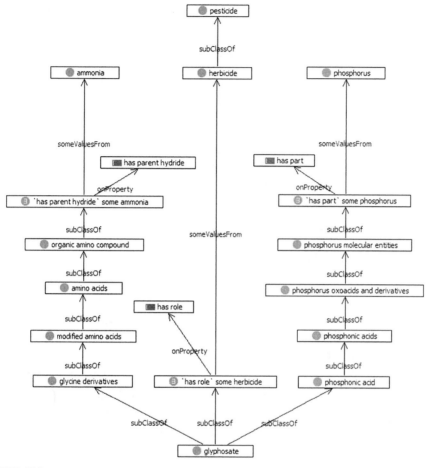

FIGURE 13.6

Excerpt from CHEBI, showing information about glyphosate. All concepts are shown with labels (e.g., "glyphosate") instead of CHEBI URIs (e.g., `Chebi:CHEBI:27744`).

Given these facts, we can use the inference mechanism of OWL to answer some useful questions. Suppose we are interested in pesticides containing phosphorus that have ammonia as a parent hydride. Figure 13.6, along with an understanding of the meaning of the modeling words `rdfs:subClassOf`, `owl:someValuesFrom`, and `owl:onProperty` tells us that glyphosate is such a chemical. But how, specifically, can we find this (or any other such chemical), based on this model?

First, we define (in OWL) the class of things we are seeking, that is, the intersection of things that have role pesticide, have part phosphorus, and have parent hydride ammonia. This is done with an intersection of three restrictions. (In RDF, we have to use the CHEBI URIs to refer to concepts; for reference, we have included the corresponding names of the concepts pesticide, ammonia and phosphorus in comments indicate with a hash (#) on each line where they occur.) Here's how that looks:

```
:MyChemical a owl:Class ;
    rdfs:label "My chemical" ;
    owl:intersectionOf (
        [ a owl:Restriction ;
          owl:onProperty obo:has_role ;
          owl:someValuesFrom chebi:CHEBI_25944 ] # pesticide
        [ a owl:Restriction ;
          owl:onProperty obo:has_parent_hydride ;
          owl:someValuesFrom chebi:CHEBI_16134 ] # ammonia
        [ a owl:Restriction ;
          owl:onProperty obo:has_part ;
          owl:someValuesFrom chebi:CHEBI_28659 ] # phosphorus
    ) .
```

Now if we run OWL inferences, we infer that

```
chebi:CHEBI_27733 rdfs:subclassOf :MyChemical .
```

That is, *glyphosate* is a match for the given specifications. The OWL semantics took care of all the complexity of Figure 13.6, including the chain of named classes that *glyphosate* is a subclass of, as well as the subclass chain between its stated role *herbicide* and the required role *pesticide*. The definition of the requirements didn't include any reference to any of these things—that was included in the CHEBI model and the OWL semantics.

It is also worth noting what inferences we **cannot** draw from the CHEBI model as shown in Figure 13.6. If, for example, we have a sample chemical in our lab, and our experiments show that it contains phosphorus as a part, and has ammonia as a parent hydride, this allows us to infer its membership in the two corresponding restrictions at the top of Figure 13.6. But this does not allow us to infer anything about the relationship of our sample to *glyphosate*. CHEBI is useful for searching for chemicals among those classified within it, not for identifying samples.

These examples provide some motivation for why the authors of CHEBI chose to define the herbicide role of *glyophosate* as a relationship between classes using `someValuesFrom`, rather than simply stating it as an explicit fact in a single triple.

```
chebi:CHEBI_27733 obo:has_role chebi:CHEBI_24527 .
```

By modeling this relationship with classes and `someValuesFrom`, they embedded the class *glyphosate* in a more comprehensive model that includes relevant facts, for example, facts about the relations between pesticides and herbicides. This allows the model (along with the OWL semantics) to do a lot of the work of question answering (for certain questions) about the entities in the model. The model encodes information in a way that a human questioner need not be aware of.

CHALLENGE 39: EXPRESSING CHEBI IN SKOS

The power of a model like CHEBI to respond flexibly to queries like this one comes at a price—the model itself is complex; for example, the relationship between *glyphosate* and *herbicide* is given by a pattern including a particular kind of restriction. Earlier, we asked why this couldn't have been represented simply with a single triple

```
chebi:CHEBI_27733 obo:has_role chebi:CHEBI_24527 .
```

In this challenge, we will examine how CHEBI could be represented in SKOS, and how we could satisfy the same information extraction needs outlined above, using that representation.

In the case of CHEBI, it is a simple matter to convert all the information about subclasses and restrictions into SKOS following this line of reasoning. Each class in CHEBI becomes a SKOS concept, each `rdfs:subClassOf` relationship becomes `skos:broader`, and each `owl:someValuesFrom` restriction becomes a direct reference. Figure 13.7 shows the same information from Figure 13-6, but transformed into SKOS in this way.

In many ways, Figure 13.7 is simpler than Figure 13.6; the fact that glyphosate has role herbicide is represented as a single triple, as is the fact that an organic amino compound has parent hydride ammonia. The inclusion relationships that were expressed as `subClassof` are now expressed as `broader`. But how would we query this structure to find an answer to the same question we asked earlier—"find the pesticides containing phosphorus that have ammonia as a parent hydride"? We can find these using SPARQL as follows:

```
SELECT ?result
WHERE {
    ?result skos:broader* ?concept1 .
    ?concept1 obo:has_parent_hydride ?concept2 .
    ?concept2 skos:broader* chebi:CHEBI_16134 . # ammonia
    ?result skos:broader* ?concept3 .
    ?concept3 obo:has_part ?concept4 .
    ?concept4 skos:broader* chebi:CHEBI_28659 . # phosphorus
    ?result skos:broader* ?concept5 .
    ?concept5 obo:has_role ?concept6 .
    ?concept6 skos:broader* chebi:CHEBI_25944 . # pesticide
}
```

This gives the same result as the OWL inference, namely that *glyphosate* satisfies all of these criteria. The representation is simpler, but the query is more complex. In particular, the query writer must take responsibility for all of the transitive relationships, using `skos:broader*` at each point, and making sure that it appears at every point in the query. This is a common trade-off in representation—does the model do more work, with a more involved representation, or does the query do more work, matching the correct information? The contrast between the OWL version of CHEBI and the SKOS version shows this; in OWL, certain queries can be done very easily, allowing the structure of the model to do all the work. But the structure is less suited to other queries ("Identify this sample"). The model does more of the work for the queries it was designed for, but its increased complexity can make other applications more complex.

The transformation from OWL into SKOS shown here was straightforward, because CHEBI uses a single pattern (using `owl:someValuesFrom`) to relate one concept to another. Some models use more complex pattern in OWL to relate concepts. For instance, one of the OBO Foundry ontologies is a thesaurus of cancer entities maintained by the National Cancer Institute (NCI). The NCI thesaurus includes disease descriptions (with far too much technical detail to include here) in which a disease is characterized by several syndromes—that is, a particular disease is indicated by a certain set of symptoms or another set of symptoms or another set of symptoms and so on. Complicated combinations of unions and intersections can be done in OWL in a standard way; the translation to SKOS of such things is not straightforward. An OWL inference engine will treat all such definitions in a consistent and correct manner.

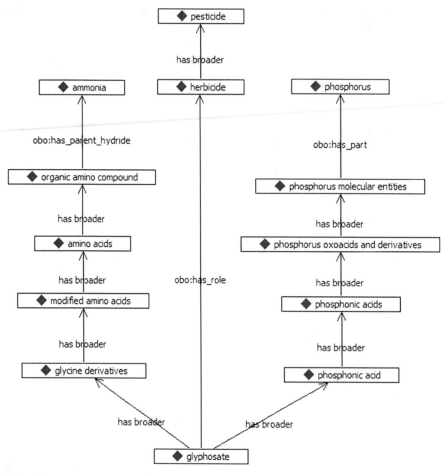

FIGURE 13.7

CHEBI concepts from Figure 13.6 shown in SKOS. The standard SKOS property `skos:broader` is shown here as "has broader."

SUMMARY

The three ontologies discussed in this chapter, Good Relations, QUDT, and OBO Foundry ontologies, cover the spectrum from ontologies that include almost no data at all (Good Relations) to ontologies that include very large amounts of richly interconnected data (OBO). They all supply, to varying extents, the basic capabilities of the Semantic Web of sharing information in a coherent way across multiple systems.

Good Relations is the smallest of the ontologies described here. Its main goal in the Semantic Web is to provide a framework in which information can be shared—a vocabulary that different suppliers can use to describe their offerings. The data in Good Relations aren't in the ontology at all; it is distributed across the Web. OBO Foundry ontologies, in contrast, are much, much larger, and include large amounts of data about biology, medicine, life sciences, etc. There are complex questions that can be answered, using OBO as a data resource. QUDT sits in the middle; it contains a good deal of data (conversion factors, relationships between dimensions and units, etc.), but its main purpose is to provide connection between other data sets; two data sources that both use Good Relations might still fail to be interoperable because of mismatch of units; QUDT provides enhanced interoperability in these cases. All three of these ontologies play the basic role in the Semantic Web of providing globally unambiguous names for standard entities—they differ only in the details of how these relationships can be used.

Fundamental concepts

The following fundamental concepts were introduced in this chapter.

`owl:imports`—Allows one ontology to refer explicitly to another. Triples from the imported ontology are available for inferencing in the importing ontology.

Ontology Design Patterns—Repeated modeling idioms that provide coherence and unity to a large model.

Good Relations—Ontology for representing and sharing information about commerce on the Web.

QUDT—Quantities, Units, Dimensions Types. Ontology of engineering units

OBO—Open Biological and Biomedical Ontologies. A collection of ontologies with relevance to the life sciences.

CHEBI—Chemical of Biological Interests. An example ontology from OBO relating to biochemistry.

Good and bad modeling practices

14

CHAPTER OUTLINE

In preceding chapters, we reviewed the constructs from RDF, RDFS, and OWL that go into a good model. We provided examples of successful models from a number of different backgrounds. Even after reaching this point, the prospect of creating a new model from scratch can seem daunting. Where should you begin? How do you tell a good model from a bad one?

Unlike the examples in the previous chapters, many of the examples in this chapter should not be used as templates or examples of good practice in building your own models. We indicate these examples with the label "antipattern" to indicate patterns that should not be emulated in your models.

GETTING STARTED

Often the first step of a journey is the most difficult one. How can you start the construction of a useful semantic model? Broadly speaking, there are three ways to get started, and the first comes directly from the nature of a web. Why build something if it is already available on the Web? One of the easiest ways to begin a modeling project is to find models on the Web that suit your needs. The second way is to leverage information assets that already have value for your organization.

It is not uncommon for an organization to have schemas, controlled vocabularies, thesauri, or other information organization artifacts that can provide an excellent source of vetted information for a semantic model. The third way is to engineer a model from scratch. In this case, certain standard engineering practices apply, including the development of requirements definitions and test cases.

Regardless of the manner in which a model was acquired, you must answer this question: Is this model, or some part of it, useful for my purposes? This poses two issues for the modeler: How do I express my intended purpose for a model? How do I determine whether a model satisfies some purpose?

Know what you want

How can we express our intentions for the purpose of a model? In the case where we are engineering a model from scratch, we can express requirements for the model we are creating. One common practice for semantic models usually starts with the notion of "competency questions." Begin the modeling process by determining what questions the model will need to answer. Then construct the model so that these questions can be answered, and, to the extent possible, model no further than necessary to answer them.

Although competency questions provide a reasonable start for specifying the purpose of a model, they have some limitations in the context of modeling in the Semantic Web. The first drawback is that for models that have been found on the Web, or for other information artifacts that we have used as a basis for a new model, competency questions typically will not have been provided. It is not uncommon for a modeler to find themselves in a position of determining what a model can do, based simply on an examination of the model.

A more serious limitation stems from the observation that a model in the Semantic Web goes beyond the usual role of an engineered artifact with system requirements. On the Semantic Web, it is expected that a model will be merged with other information, often from unanticipated sources. This means that the design of a semantic model must not only respond to known requirements (represented with competency questions) but also express a range of variation that anticipates to some extent the organization of the information with which it might be merged.

Although this seems like an impossible task (and in its full generality, of course, it is impossible to anticipate all the uses to which a model might be applied), there are some simple applications of it, in light of the other guidelines. You model `ShakespeareanWork` as a class not only when you have a corresponding competency question (e.g., "What are the works of Shakespeare?") but also whenever you anticipate that someone else might be interested in that competency question. You model `ShakespeareanWork` as a subclass of `ElizabethanWork` not just in the case when you have a competency question of that form (e.g., "What are all the kinds of Elizabethan works?") but also if you anticipate that someone might be interested in Shakespearean works and someone else might be interested in Elizabethan works, and you want the answers to both questions to be consistent (i.e., each `ShakespeareanWork` is also an `ElizabethanWork`).

This idea gets to the crux of how modeling in the Semantic Web differs from many other engineering modeling practices. Not only do you have to model for a particular engineering setting but for a variety of anticipated settings, as well. We have already seen examples of how this acts as a driving force behind our models in the wild. OBO ontologies are structured as they are, not primarily because a single stakeholder needs to understand the organization of the terminology of the life sciences, but because members of a community of stakeholders with different goals need answers to a variety of questions, which must all be answered consistently.

Say what you mean, mean what you say

The March Hare in *Alice in Wonderland* challenged Alice to say what she means and mean what she says. This is good advice for anyone building a model as well; the model is a set of statements that we ought to stand behind, and a modeling language gives us a way to make those statements. When we make a statement, we should mean it. If we have something to say, we should find a way to express it in a modeling language. We can only do this, if we have a way of knowing what statements in a modeling language mean. It is fine to talk about stakeholders, variation, and competency questions, but even when we do have a specific understanding of the intent of a model, how can we even determine whether the model, as constructed, meets that intention?

We can appeal to the intuition behind the names of classes and properties, but this is problematic for a number of reasons. First is the issue known as "wishful naming." Just because someone has named a class `ElizabethanWork` doesn't mean that it will contain all or even any works that might deserve that name. Second is the issue of precision. Just what did the modeler mean by `ElizabethanWork`? Is it a work created *by* Queen Elizabeth or one that was created during her reign? Or perhaps it is a work created by one of a number of prominent literary figures (the `ElizabethanAuthors`), whose names we can list once and for all. To determine whether a model satisfies some intent, we need an objective way to know what a model means and, in the case of competency questions, how a model can answer questions.

There are two ways a Semantic Web model answers questions. The first is comparable to the way a database answers questions: by having the appropriate data indexed in a way that can be directly accessed to answer the question. If we answer the question "What are the Elizabethan literary works?" this way, we would do so by having a class called, say, `ElizabethanWork` and maintain a list of works as members of that class.

This method for answering questions is fundamental to data management; at some point, we have to trust that we have some data that are correct or that are at least correct enough for our purposes. The special challenge of semantic modeling comes when we need to model for variability. How do we make sure that our answer to the question "What are the Shakespearean works?" is consistent with the answer to "What are the Elizabethan works?" (and how does this relate to the answer to the question "Who are the Elizabethan authors?"). This brings us to the second way a semantic model can answer questions: through the use of inferencing.

We can determine a model's answer to a particular question (or query) through an analysis of inferencing. What triples can we infer based on the triples that have already been asserted? This gives us more power to say what we mean and mean what we say. What do I mean when I refer to a `ShakespeareanWork`? If I mean that every `ShakespeareanWork` is an `ElizabethanWork`, then I should say that `ShakespeareanWork` is a subclass of `ElizabethanWork`. If furthermore I mean that an `ElizabethanWork` is one that was created or performed by an `ElizabethanAuthor` and that `Shakespeare` is one of these authors, then I say by building a model that entails the corresponding inferences (e.g., using `owl:someValuesFrom`). Inferencing is the way I can tell whether what I have said is what I mean—do the inferences the model entrails reflect the relationships between concepts that I mean to express?

MODELING FOR REUSE

One of the principal drivers in the creation of a semantic model is that it will be used by someone other than its designer in a new context that was not fully anticipated. If you are designing a model, you must consider the challenges the people using your model might face. How can you make this job easier for them?

Insightful names versus wishful names

When you are reusing a model that you found on the Web, you'd like to know the intent of the various components of the model (classes, properties, individuals). The support that a model provides for question answering is given formally by the inferences that the model entails. As far as an inference engine is concerned, entities in the model could have any name at all, like *G0001* or *Node97*. But names of this sort are of little help when perusing a model to determine whether it can satisfy your own goals. Putting the shoe on the other foot, when you build a model, you are also selecting names for those who will want to link to your model and need to know what is in it, as well as for those, including yourself at a later date, who may have to maintain or extend the model. There's a fine line between good naming and wishful thinking, but keeping in mind that your model will be "read" by others is always good practice.

A closely related issue to naming is the use of annotations like `rdfs:label`, `rdfs:comment`, and `rdfs:seeAlso`. Even if you choose a name for a resource that you understand, and even one that is understood by the community you participate in, there could well be another community who will find that usage meaningless or even misleading. We have seen an example of this before with `skos:broader`. For someone with a background in thesaurus management, it is understood that `skos:broader` is used to connect a narrow term to a broader term, such as:

```
:cheese skos:broader :dairy.
```

That is, `skos:broader` should be read as "has broader term." Other readers might expect this to be read "cheese is broader than dairy," and they would either be confused by the use of `skos:broader` or, worse, would misuse it in their own models. Judicious use of `rdfs:label` can alleviate this issue, as follows:

```
skos:broader rdfs:label "has broader".
```

In addition to the selection of meaningful names and quality naming, some simple conventions can contribute to the understandability of a model. The conventions listed next have grown up as de facto standard ways to name entities on the Semantic Web and are followed by the W3C itself as well as throughout this book.

Name resources in CamelCase: `CamelCase` is the name given to the style of naming in which multiword names are written without any spaces but with each word written in uppercase. We see this convention in action in W3C names like `rdfs:subClassOf` and `owl:InverseFunctionalProperty`.

Start class names with capital letters: We see this convention in the W3C class names `owl:Restriction` and `owl:Class`.

Start property names with lowercase letters: We see this convention in the W3C property names `rdfs:subClassOf` and `owl:inverseOf`. Notice that except for the first letter, these names are written in `CamelCase`.

Start individual names with capital letters: We see this convention at work in the `lit:Shakespeare` and `ship:Berengaria` examples in this book.

Name classes with singular nouns: We see this convention in the W3C class names `owl:DatatypeProperty` and `owl:SymmetricProperty` and in the examples in this book: `lit:Playwright`.

Keeping track of classes and individuals

One of the greatest challenges when designing a semantic model is determining when something should be modeled as a class and when it should be modeled as an individual. This issue arises especially when considering a model for reuse because of the distributed nature of a semantic model. Since a semantic model must respond to competency questions coming from different stakeholders, it is quite possible that one work practice has a tradition of considering something to be a class, whereas another is accustomed to thinking of it as an instance.

As a simple example, consider the idea of an endangered species. For the field zoologists who are tracking the number of breeding pairs in the world (and in cases where the numbers are very small, give them all names), the species is a class whose members are the individual animals they are tracking. For the administrator in the federal agency that lists endangered species, the species is an instance to be put in a list (i.e., asserted as a member of the class of endangered species) or removed from that list. The designer of a single model who wants to answer competency questions from both of these stakeholder communities is faced with something of a challenge. This situation can often be modeled effectively using the Class-Individual Mirror pattern in Chapter 11.

Another source of difficulty arises from the flexibility of human language when talking about classes and instances. We can say that Shakespeare is an Elizabethan author or that a poem is a literary work. In the first sentence, we are probably talking about the individual called Shakespeare and his membership in a particular class of authors. In the second, we are probably talking about how one class of things (poems) relates to another (literary works). Both of these sentences use the words "is *a(n)*" to describe these very different sorts of relationships. In natural languages, we don't have to be specific about which relationships we mean. This is a drawback of using competency questions in natural language: The question "What are the types of literary works?" could be interpreted as a request for the individuals who are members of the class `LiteraryWork`, or it could be asking for the subclasses (types) of the class `LiteraryWork`. Either way of modeling this could be considered a response to the question.

Although there is no hard and fast rule for determining whether something should be modeled as an instance or a class, some general guidelines can help organize the process. The first is based on the simple observation that classes can be seen as sets of instances. If something is modeled as a class, then there should at least be a possibility that the class might have instances. If you cannot imagine what instances would be members of a proposed class, then it is a strong indication that it should not be modeled as a class at all. For example, according to this guideline it is unlikely that we should use a class to refer to the literary figure known as Shakespeare. After all, given that we usually understand that we are talking about a unique literary figure, what could possibly be the instances of the class `Shakespeare`? If there is none, then `Shakespeare` should properly be modeled as an instance.

If you can imagine instances for the class, it is a good idea to name the class in such a way that the nature of those instances is clear. There are some classes having to do with Shakespeare that one might want to define. For example, the works of the bard, including 38 plays, 254 sonnets, 5 long poems, and so on could be a class of interest to some stakeholder. In such a case, the name of the class should not simply be `Shakespeare` but instead something like `ShakespeareanWork`. Considerable confusion can be avoided in the design phase by first determining what is to be modeled (the bard himself, his works, his family, etc.), then deciding if this should be a class or an instance, and then finally selecting a name that reflects this decision.

The second guideline has to do with the properties that describe the thing to be modeled. Do you know (or could you know) specific values for those properties or just in general that there is some value? For instance, we know in general that a play has an author, a first performance date, and one or more protagonists, but we know specifically about *The Tempest* that it was written by William Shakespeare, was performed in 1611, and has the protagonist Prospero. In this case, *The Tempest* should be modeled as an instance, and *Play* should be modeled as a class. Furthermore, *The Tempest* is a member of that class.

Model testing

Once we have assembled a model—either from designed components, reused components, or components translated from some other source—how can we test it? In the case where we have competency questions, we can start by making sure it answers those. More important, in the distributed setting of the Semantic Web, we can determine (by analyzing the inferences that the model entails) whether it maintains consistent answers to possible competency questions from multiple sources. We can also determine test cases for the model. This is particularly important when reusing a model. How does the model perform (i.e., what inferences can we draw from it?) when it is faced with information that is not explicitly in the scope of its design? In the analysis to follow, we will refer generally to *model tests*—ways you can determine if the model satisfies its intent.

COMMON MODELING ERRORS

In light of the AAA slogan (Anybody can say Anything about Any topic), we can't say that anything is really a modeling error. In our experience teaching modeling to scientists, engineers, content managers, and project managers, we have come across a handful of modeling practices that may be counterproductive for the reuse goals of a semantic model. We can't say that the models are strictly erroneous, but we can say that they do not accomplish the desired goals of sharing information about a structured domain with other stakeholders.

We have seen each of the antipatterns described in the following in a number of models. Here, we describe each one in turn and outline its drawbacks in terms of the modeling guidelines just given. We have given each of them a pejorative (and a rather fanciful) name as a reminder that these are antipatterns—common pitfalls of beginning modelers. Whenever possible, we will also indicate good practices that can replace the antipattern, depending on a variety of possible desired intents for the model.

Rampant classism (antipattern)

A common reaction to the difficult distinction between classes and instances is simply to define everything as a class. This solution is encouraged by most modeling tools, since the creation of classes is usually the first primitive operation that a user learns. The temptation is to begin by creating a class with the name of an important, central concept and then extend it by creating more classes whose names indicate concepts that are related to the original. This practice is also common when a model has been created by automatic means from some other knowledge organization source, like a thesaurus. A thesaurus makes much less commitment about the relationship between terms than does a semantic model between classes or between classes and individuals.

As an example, someone modeling Shakespeare and his works might begin by defining a class called `Shakespeare` and classes called `Plays`, `Poems`, `Poets`, `Playwrights`, and `TheTempest`. Then, define a property (an `owl:ObjectProperty`) called `wrote` and assert that Shakespeare wrote all of these things by asserting triples like the following:

```
:Playwrights :wrote :Plays.
:Poets :wrote :Poems.
:Shakespeare :wrote :Plays.
:ModernPlays rdfs:subClassOf :Plays.
:ElizabethanPlays rdfs:subClassOf :Plays.
:Shakespeare :wrote :TheTempest.
:Shakespeare :wrote :Poems.
```

and perhaps even

```
:TheTempest rdfs:subClassOf :Plays.
```

This seems to makes sense because, after all, `TheTempest` will show up next to `Plays` in just about any ontology display tool. The resulting model is shown in Figure 14.1.

Given the AAA slogan, we really can't say that anything in this set of triples is "wrong." After all, anyone can assert these triples. But we can start by noting that it does not follow the simple syntactic conventions in that the class names are plurals.

This model reflects a style typical of beginning modelers. The triples seem to translate into a sensible sentence in English: "Shakespeare wrote poems"; "Shakespeare wrote *The Tempest*." If you render `rdfs:subClassOf` in English as is *a,* then you have "*The Tempest* is a plays," which aside from the plural at the end, is a reasonable sentence in English. How can we evaluate whether this model satisfies the intent of the modeler or of someone who might want to reuse this model? We'll consider some tests that can tell us what this model might be useful for.

Let's start with some simple competency questions. This model can certainly answer questions of the form "Who wrote *The Tempest?*" The answer is available directly in the model. It can also answer questions like "What type of thing writes plays? What type of thing writes poems?" Again, these answers are represented directly in the model.

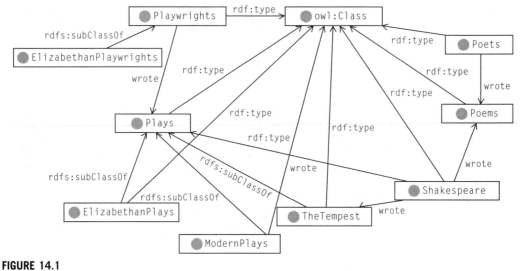

FIGURE 14.1

Sample model displaying rampant classism. Every node in this model has `rdf:type owl:Class`.

Suppose we want to go beyond mere questions and evaluate how the model organizes different points of view. It seems on the face of it that a model like this should be able to make sure that the answer to a question like "What type of thing wrote Elizabethan plays?" would at the very least include the class of playwrights, since playwrights are things that wrote plays and Elizabethan plays are plays. Can this model support this condition? Let's look at the relevant triples and see what inferences can be drawn:

```
:Playwrights a owl:Class;
   :wrote :Plays.
:ElizabethanPlays rdfs:subClassOf :Plays.
```

None of the inference patterns we have learned for OWL or RDFS applies here. In particular, there is *no* inference of the form

```
:Playwrights :wrote :ElizabethanPlays.
```

Another test criterion that this model might be expected to pass is whether it can distinguish between plays and types of plays. We do have some plays and types of plays in this model: *The Tempest* is a play, and Elizabethan play and modern play are types of plays. The model cannot distinguish between these two cases. Any query that returns *The Tempest* (as a play) will also return modern plays. Any query that returns Elizabethan play (as a type of play) will also return *The Tempest*. The model has not made enough distinctions to be responsive to this criterion.

If we think about these statements in terms of the interpretation of classes as sets, none of these results should come as a surprise. In this model, playwrights and plays are sets. The statement

"Playwrights wrote plays" makes no statements about individual playwrights or plays; it makes a statement about the sets.

But sets don't write anything, whereas playwrights and poets do. This statement, when made about sets, is nonsense. The OWL inference semantics bear this out: The statement has no meaning, so no inferences can be drawn. `TheTempest` is modeled here as a class, even though there is no way to imagine what its instances might be; it is a play, not a set. Plays are written by people (and have opening dates, etc.), sets do not.

Similar comments can be made about a statement like "Poets wrote poems." If triples like:

```
:Poets :wrote :Poems.
```

aren't meaningful, how should we render the intuition reflected by the sentence "Poets wrote poems"? This consideration goes beyond the simple sort of specification that we can get from competency questions. We could respond to questions like "Which people are poets?" or "Which things are poems?" with any model that includes these two classes. If we want the answers to these two questions to have some sort of consistency between them, then we have to decide just what relationship between *poems* and *poets* we want to represent.

We might want to enforce the condition "If someone is a poet, and he wrote something, then it is a poem." When we consider the statement in this form, it makes more sense (and a more readable model) if we follow the convention that names classes with singular nouns ("a poet," "a poem") rather than plurals (poets, poems).

We have already seen an example of how to represent a statement of this form. If something is an `AllStarTeam`, then all of its players are members of `StarPlayer`. Following that example, we can represent this same thing about poets and poems as follows:

```
:Poet rdfs:subClassOf [a owl:Restriction;
                       owl:onProperty :wrote;
                       owl:allValuesFrom :Poem].
```

If we specify an instance of *poet*—say, *Homer*—and something he wrote—say, *The Iliad*—then we can infer that *The Iliad* is a *poem,* thus:

```
:Homer :wrote :TheIliad.
:Homer a :Poet.
:TheIliad a :Poem.
```

This definition may work fine for Homer, but what happens if we press the boundaries of the model a bit and see what inferences it can make about someone like Shakespeare:

```
:Shakespeare :wrote :TheTempest.
:Shakespeare a :Poet.
:TheTempest a :Poem.
```

The conclusion that *The Tempest* is a poem is unexpected. Since it is common for poets to write things that don't happen to be poems, probably this isn't what we really mean by *"Poets wrote poems."* This is an example of a powerful method for determining the scope of applicability of a model. If you can devise a test that might challenge some of the assumptions in the model (in this case, the assumption that nobody can be both a poet and a playwright), then you can determine something about its boundaries.

What other results might we expect from the statement "Poets wrote poems"? We might expect that if someone is a *poet,* then they must have written at least one *poem.* (We have already seen a number of examples of this using `owl:someValuesFrom`.) In this case, this definition looks like this:

```
:Poet rdfs:subClassOf [a owl:Restriction;
                       owl:onProperty :wrote;
                       owl:someValuesFrom :Poem].
```

The inferences we can draw from this statement are subtle. For instance, from the following fact about *Homer*

```
:Homer a :Poet.
```

we can infer that he wrote something that is a *poem,* though we can't necessarily identify what it is.

When we say, "Poets wrote poems," we might expect something even stronger: that having written a *poem* is exactly what it means to be a *poet.* Not only does being a poet mean that you have written a *poem,* but also, if you have written a *poem,* then you are a poet. We can make inferences of this sort by using `owl:equivalentClass` as follows:

```
:Poet owl:equivalentClass [a owl:Restriction;
                           owl:onProperty :wrote;
                           owl:someValuesFrom :Poem].
```

Now we can infer that Homer is a poet from the poem that he wrote

```
:Homer :wrote :TheIliad.
:TheIliad a :Poem.
:Homer a :Poet.
```

In general, linking one class to another with an object property (as in *Poets wrote poems* in this example) does not support any inferences at all. There is no inference that propagates properties associated with a class to its instances, or to its subclasses, or to its superclasses. The only inferences that apply to object properties are those (like the inferences having to do with `rdfs:domain` and `rdfs:range`, or inferences from an `owl:Restriction`) that assume that the subject and object (*Shakespeare* and *poems* in this case) are instances, not classes.

This illustrates a powerful feature of OWL as a modeling language. The constructs of OWL make very specific statements about what the model means, based on the inference standard. A sentence like "Poets wrote poems" may have some ambiguity in natural language, but the representation in OWL is much more specific. The modeler has to decide just what they mean by a statement like "Poets wrote poems," but OWL allows these distinctions to be represented in a clear way.

Exclusivity (antipattern)

The rules of RDFS inferencing say that the members of a subclass are necessarily members of a superclass. The fallacy of exclusivity is to assume that the only candidates for membership in a subclass are those things that are already known to be members of the superclass.

Let's take a simple example. Suppose we have a class called *City* and a subclass called OceanPort, to indicate a particular kind of city

```
:OceanPort rdfs:subClassOf :City.
```

We might have a number of members of the class City, for example:

```
:Paris a :City.
:Zurich a :City.
:SanDiego a :City.
```

According to the AAA assumption, any of these entities could be an OceanPort, as could any other entity we know about—even things we don't yet know are cities, like New York or Rio de Janeiro. In fact, since Anyone can say Anything about Any topic, someone might assert that France or The Moon is an OceanPort. From the semantics of RDFS, we would then infer that France or The Moon are cities.

In a model that commits the error of exclusivity, we assume that because OceanPort is a subclass of City, the only candidates for OceanPort are those things we know to be cities, which so far are just Paris, Zurich, and San Diego. To see how the exclusivity fallacy causes modeling problems, let's suppose we are interested in answering the question "What are the cities that connect to an ocean?" We could propose a model to respond to this competency question as follows:

```
:OceanPort rdfs:subClassof :City.
:OceanPort owl:equivalentClass
        [a owl:Restriction;
        owl:onProperty :connectsTo;
        owl:someValuesFrom :Ocean].
```

These triples are shown graphically in Figure 14.2.

This model commits the fallacy of exclusivity; if we assume that only cities can be ocean ports, then we can answer the question by querying the members of the class OceanPort. But let's push the boundaries of this model. What inferences does it draw from some boundary instances that might violate some assumptions in the model? In particular, what if we consider

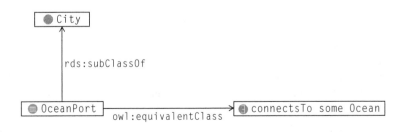

FIGURE 14.2

Erroneous definition of OceanPort as a city that connects to an Ocean.

something that is not a city but still connects to an ocean? Suppose we have the following facts in our data set:

```
:Zurich :connectsTo :RiverLimmat.
:Zurich :locatedIn :Switzerland.
:Switzerland :borders :France.
:Paris :connectsTo :LaSeine.
:Paris :locatedIn :France.
:France :connectsTo :Mediterranean.
:France :connectsTo :AtlanticOcean.
:SanDiego :connectsTo :PacificOcean.
:AtlanticOcean a :Ocean.
:PacificOcean a :Ocean.
```

and so on.

From what we know about `SanDiego` and the `PacificOcean`, we can conclude that `SanDiego` is an `OceanPort`, as expected

```
:SanDiego :connectsTo :PacificOcean.
:PacificOcean a :Ocean.
:SanDiego a :OceanPort.
```

Furthermore, since

```
:OceanPort rdfs:subClassOf :City.
```

we can conclude that

```
:SanDiego a :City.
```

So far, so good, but let's see what happens when we look at *France*.

```
:France :connectsTo :AtlanticOcean.
:AtlanticOcean a :Ocean
```

Therefore, we can conclude that

```
:France a :OceanPort.
```

and furthermore,

```
:France a :City.
```

This is not what we intended by this model, and it does not respond correctly to the question. The flaw in this inference came because of the assumption that only things known to be cities can be ocean ports, but according to the AAA assumption, anything can be an ocean port unless we say otherwise.

This fallacy is more a violation of the AAA slogan than any consideration of subclassing itself. The fallacy stems from assumptions that are valid in other modeling paradigms. For many modeling systems (like object-oriented programming systems, library catalogs, product taxonomies, etc.) a large part of the modeling process is the way items are placed into classes. This process is usually done by hand and is called *categorization* or *cataloging*. The usual way to think about such a system is that something is placed intentionally into a class because someone made a decision that it belongs there.

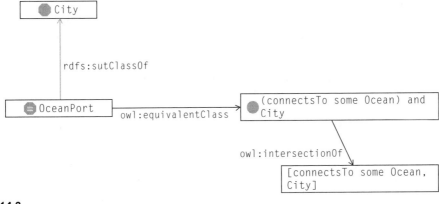

FIGURE 14.3

Correct model for an OceanPort as a *City* that also connects to an *Ocean*.

The interpretation of a subclass in this situation is that it is a refinement of the class. If someone wants to make a more specific characterization of some item, then they can catalog it into a subclass instead of a class.

If this construct does not correctly answer this competency question, what model will? We want something to become a member of OceanPort just if it is both a City and it connects to an Ocean. We do this with an *intersection* as shown in Figure 14.3.

Now that we have defined an OceanPort as the intersection of City and a restriction, we can infer that OceanPort is a subclass of City. Furthermore, only individuals that are known to be cities are candidates for membership in OceanPort, so anomalies like the previous one for *France* cannot happen.

The Class Exclusivity fallacy is a common error for anyone who has experience with any of a number of different modeling paradigms. Semantic Web modeling takes the AAA assumption more seriously than any other common modeling system. Fortunately, the error is easily remedied by using the intersection pattern shown in Figure 14.3.

Objectification (antipattern)

One common source of modeling errors is attempting to build a Semantic Web model that has the same meaning and behavior as an object system. Object systems, however, are not intended to work in the context of the three Semantic Web assumptions: AAA, Open World, and Nonunique Naming. In many cases, these differences in assumptions about the modeling context result in basic clashes of modeling interpretation.

A fundamental example of this kind of clash can be found in examining the role of a class in a model. In object modeling, a class is basically a template from which an instance is stamped. It makes little or no sense to speak of multiple classes (stamped out of two templates?) or of having a property that isn't in the class (where do you put it if there wasn't a slot in the template for it?).

In Semantic Web models, the AAA and the Open World assumptions are incompatible with this notion of a class. Properties in Semantic Web models exist independently of any class, and because of the AAA slogan, they can be used to describe any individual at all, regardless of which classes it belongs to. Classes are seen as sets, so membership in multiple classes is commonplace.

Let's consider a simple but illustrative example of how the intent of an object model is incompatible with modeling in the Semantic Web. Suppose an object model is intended to reflect the notion that a person has exactly two parents who are also people. These are the requirements an object model must satisfy:

1. A value for the property `hasParent` can be specified only for members of the `Person` class.
2. We will recognize as a mistake the situation in which only one value for `hasParent` is specified for a single person.
3. We recognize as a mistake the situation in which more than two values for `hasParent` are specified for a single person.

Before we even look at an OWL model that attempts to satisfy these conditions, we can make some observations about the requirements themselves. In particular, many of these requirements are at odds with the fundamental assumptions of Semantic Web modeling, as described by the AAA, Open World, and Nonunique Naming assumptions. Let's look at the requirements in turn.

Requirement 1 is at odds with the AAA slogan. The AAA slogan tells us that we cannot keep anyone from asserting a property of anything, so we can't enforce the condition that `hasParent` can only be specified for particular individuals. The Open World assumption complicates the situation even further: Since the next thing we learn about a resource could be that its type is *Person*, we can't even tell for sure whether something actually is a person.

Requirement 2 is at odds with the Semantic Web assumptions. In this case, the Open World assumption again causes problems. Just because we have not asserted a second parent for any individual does not mean that one doesn't exist. The very next Semantic Web page we see might give us this information. Thus, regardless of how we model this in OWL, there cannot be a contradiction in the case where too few parents have been specified.

Requirement 3 is not directly at odds with the Semantic Web assumptions, but the Nonunique Naming assumption makes this requirement problematic. We can indeed say that there should be just two parents, so if more than two parents are specified, a contradiction can be detected. This will only happen in the case where we know that all the (three or more) parents are distinct, using a construct like `owl:differentFrom`, `owl:allDifferent`, or `owl:disjointWith`.

The discrepancy between these requirements and an OWL model doesn't depend on the details of any particular model but on the assumptions behind the OWL language itself. An object model is designed for a very different purpose from an OWL model, and the difference is manifest in many ways in these requirements.

Despite this mismatch, it is fairly common practice to attempt to model these requirements in OWL. Here, we outline one such attempt and evaluate the inference results that the model entails. Consider the following model, which is a fairly common translation of an OO model that satisfies these requirements into OWL:

```
:Person a owl:Class.
:hasParent rdfs:domain :Person.
:hasParent rdfs:range :Person.
[a owl:Restriction;
 owl:onProperty :hasParent;
 owl:Cardinality 2]
```

This model was created by translating parts of an object model directly into OWL, as follows:

1. When a property is defined for a class in an OO model, that class is listed as the domain of the property in OWL. The type of the property in the OO model is specified as the range in OWL.
2. Cardinality limitations in the object model are represented by defining a restriction class in OWL.

We have already seen that this model cannot satisfy the requirements as stated. How far off are we? What inference does this model support? What inferences does it not support?

According to the stated intent of this model, if we assert just the following fact:

```
:Willem :hasParent :Beatrix.
```

The model should signal an error, since only a `Person` can have a parent, and we have not asserted that `Willem` is a `Person`. If we fix this by asserting that

```
:Willem a :Person.
```

then the model should still indicate an error; after all, `Willem` must have two parents, not just one. If we also assert more parents for `Willem`:

```
:Willem :hasParent :Claus.
:Willem :hasParent :TheQueen.
```

then the model should again signal an error, since now `Willem` has three parents rather than two.

Now let's see what inferences can actually be made from these assertions according to the inference patterns of OWL. From the very first statement

```
:Willem :hasParent :Beatrix.
```

along with the `rdfs:domain` information, we can infer that

```
:Willem a :Person.
```

That is, there is no need to assert that `Willem` is a `Person` before we can assert who his parent is. This behavior is at odds with the first intent; that is, we allowed `Willem` to have a parent, even though we did not know that `Willem` was a person.

What about the cardinality restriction? What can we infer from that? Three issues come into play with this. The first is the Open World assumption. Since we don't know whether `Willem` might have another parent, who simply has not yet been specified, we cannot draw any inference about `Willem`'s membership in the restriction. In fact, even if we assert just one more parent for `Willem` (along with `Beatrix`, bringing the total of asserted parents to exactly two) that

```
:Willem :hasParent :Claus.
```

we still do not know that `Willem` really does have exactly two parents. After all, there might be yet a third parent of `Willem` whom we just haven't heard about. That's the Open World assumption.

The second issue has to do with unique naming. Suppose we now also assert that

```
:Willem :hasParent :TheQueen.
```

Surely, we can now infer that `Willem` cannot satisfy the restriction, since we know of three parents, right? Even if there are more parents lurking out there (according to the Open World assumption), we can never get back down to just two. Or can we?

The Nonunique Naming assumption says that until we know otherwise, we can't assume that two different names refer to different individuals. In particular, the two names `TheQueen` and `Beatrix` could (and in fact, do) refer to the same individual. So even though we have named three parents for `Willem`, we still haven't disqualified him from being a member of the restriction. We haven't named three *distinct* parents for `Willem`.

The third issue transcends all the arguments about whether `Willem` does or does not satisfy the cardinality restriction. Look closely at the definition of the restriction: It is defined, as usual, as a bnode. But the bnode is not connected to any other named class in any way. That is, the restriction is not `owl:equivalentClass` to any other class, nor is it `rdfs:subClassOf` any other class (or vice versa).

What does this mean for inferences involving this restriction? On the one hand, even if we were to establish that `Willem` satisfies the restriction, still no further inferences could be made. Further inferences would have to be based on the connection of the restriction to some other class, but there is no such connection. On the other hand, if we could independently establish that `Willem` is a member of the restriction, then we could possibly draw some conclusions based on that. Since the restriction is not connected to any other class, there is no independent way to establish `Willem`'s membership in the restriction class. Either way, we can draw no new inferences from this restriction. The AAA slogan keeps us from saying that this model is "wrong," but we can safely say that it does not support the inferences that were intended by the modeler. Unlike the case of the other anti-patterns, we are not in a position to "fix" this model; the requirements of the model are simply at odds with the assumptions of modeling in the Semantic Web.

Creeping conceptualization (antipattern)

In most engineered systems, designing for reuse is enhanced by keeping things simple. In software coding, for example, the best APIs try to minimize the numbers of calls they provide. In physical systems, the number of connections is minimized, and most common building materials aim for a minimally constraining design so as to maximize the ways they can be combined. On the Semantic Web, the same idea should apply, but all too often the idea of "design for reuse" gets confused with "say everything you can." Thus, for example, when we include `ShakespeareanWork` and `ElizabethanWork` in our model, we are tempted to further assert that `ElizabethanWork` is a subclass of `Work`, which is a subclass of `IntangibleEntity`.

Of course, having included `IntangibleEntity`, you will want to include `TangibleEntity` and some examples of those and some properties of those examples and, well, ad infinitum. After all, you might think that modeling for reuse is best done by anticipating *everything* that someone might want to use your model for, and thus the more you include the better. This is a mistake because the more you put in, the more you restrict someone else's ability to extend your model instead of just use it as is. Reuse is best done, as in other systems, by designing to maximize future combination with other things, not to restrict it.

This kind of creeping conceptualization may seem like an odd thing to have to worry about. After all, isn't it a lot of extra work to create more classes? Economists tell us that people minimize the amount of unrewarded work they do. However, in practice, it often turns out that knowing when to stop modeling is harder than deciding where to start. As humans, we tend to have huge connected networks of concepts, and as you define one class, you often think immediately of another you'd "naturally" want to link it to. This is an extremely natural tendency, and even the best modelers find it very difficult to know when to finish, but this way lies madness.

A relatively easy way to tell if you are going too far in your creation of concepts is to check classes to see if they have properties associated with them, and especially if there are restricted properties. If so, then you are likely saying something useful about them, and they may be included. If you are including data (instances) in your model, then any class that has an instance is likely to be a good class. On the other hand, when you see lots of empty classes, especially arranged in a subclass hierarchy, then you are probably creating classes just in case someone might want to do something with them in the future, and that is usually a mistake. The famous acronym KISS (Keep It Simple, Stupid) is well worth keeping in mind when designing Web ontologies.

SUMMARY

The basic assumptions behind the Semantic Web—the AAA, Open World, and Nonunique Naming assumptions—place very specific restrictions on the modeling language. The structure of RDF is in the form of statements with familiar grammatical constructs like subject, predicate, and object. The structure of OWL includes familiar concepts like `class`, `subClassOf`, and `property`. But the meaning of a model is given by the inference rules of OWL, which incorporate the assumptions of the Semantic Web. How can you tell if you have built a useful model, one that conforms to these assumptions? The answer is by making sure that the inferences it supports are useful and meaningful.

According to the AAA slogan, we cannot say that any of the practices in this chapter are "errors" because Anyone can say Anything about Any topic. All of these models are valid expressions in RDF/OWL, but they are erroneous in the sense that they do not accomplish what the modeler intended by creating them. In each case, the mismatch can be revealed through careful examination of the inferences that the model entails. In some cases (like the objectification error), the requirements themselves are inconsistent with the Semantic Web assumptions. In other cases (like the exclusivity error), the requirements are quite consistent with the Semantic Web assumptions and can be modeled easily with a simple pattern.

Fundamental concepts

The following concepts were introduced or elaborated in this chapter.

The Semantic Web Assumptions—AAA (Anyone can say Anything about Any topic), Open-World, and Nonunique Naming.

Inferencing—In OWL, inferencing is tuned to respect the Semantic Web assumptions. This results in subtleties that can be misleading to a novice modeler.

Competency Questions—Questions that scope the requirements for a model.

Modeling for Variability—The requirement (characteristic of Semantic Web modeling) that a model describe variation as well as commonality.

Modeling for Reuse—The craft of designing a model for uses that cannot be fully anticipated.

Wishful Naming—The tendency for a modeler to believe that a resource signifies more than the formal semantics of the model warrants, purely on the basis of the resource's name.

Model Testing—A process by which the boundaries of a model are stressed to determine the nature of the boundaries of the inferences it can entail.

Expert modeling in OWL

The examples in Chapters 9 and 13 have shown applications of Semantic Web, and the role that models play in those applications. In some cases (e.g., OGP), a very simple model was used to mediate large amounts of data. In other cases (e.g., QUDT and CHEBI), the models were very involved, and a lot of the value came from the complexity of the model itself. A large portion of applications on the Semantic Web can be achieved using the modeling facilities that have been presented in the book so far. But there are occasions where these modeling constructs are insufficient, and more advanced capabilities are required. Many of these have been included in version 2 of the OWL standard. We have already seen (in Chapter 12) some of the advanced counting facilities from OWL 2, and we will outline some of the more fundamental new capabilities here, but the OWL 2 standard is rich in modeling constructs that go beyond the scope of this book. First and foremost, we will provide some of the background you will need to search through the OWL standard documents yourself to explore its rich landscape.

OWL 2 was designed to be fully backward compatible with version 1.0. That means that any valid OWL 1.0 model is also a valid model in OWL 2. But more importantly, it means that all the styles of modeling that we learned for OWL 1.0 are still valid for OWL 2. The new constructs in OWL 2 can be used in conjuction with all the models you've seen in the book so far.

In Chapter 8, we introduced a subset of OWL that we called RDFS-Plus. There are a number of reasons why someone might define a subset of a language like OWL. In the case of RDFS-Plus, we were interested in a subset of the language that has considerable utility for semantic modeling but does not place a large burden on either a modeler or someone trying to understand a model. OWL 2 also includes a precise description of four subsets of the OWL language (each of them richer than RDFS-Plus) identified for various practical technological reasons, often having to do with how OWL relates to other technology. The four subsets are called OWL 2 EL, OWL 2 QL, OWL 2 RL, and OWL 2 DL.

We will describe each subset and the rationale for why it has been identified and named; the details of each subset are given in the OWL specification.[1]

OWL SUBSETS AND MODELING PHILOSOPHY

Normally, when we refer to different subsets of a language, we can list the language structures in one subset that are not found in the other. For instance, RDFS has `rdfs:domain`, `rdfs:range`, `rdfs:subPropertyOf`, and so on, whereas RDFS-Plus has all of those, plus some new language features like `owl:inverseOf` and `owl:TransitiveProperty`. We can define how these two languages are similar or different, based on which language terms are available in each one.

In the case of the OWL 2 subsets, the situation is more subtle. Each subset uses the same set of modeling constructs. That is, if we were to list all the properties and classes that make up (say) OWL EL and then compile the full list for all of OWL, the lists would be exactly the same. In fact, it would be the list of OWL features that you have been reading about in this book. Everything you have learned so far applies equally well to each OWL subset.

So what is the difference? Why is it important to identify subsets of a language, if they have the same constructs and the same meanings? The distinction between these the subsets of OWL are motivated in part by a difference in the basic philosophy of why one builds models for the Semantic Web. We will outline these two basic philosophies—one in which the emphasis is placed on having provable models and one in which the emphasis is placed on making executable models. We examine each in turn, along with the intuitions that motivate them.

Provable models

An important motivation for formal modeling (as opposed to informal modeling) is to be precise about what our models mean. In the context of the Semantic Web, this tells us precisely and without doubt when concepts from two different sources refer to the same thing. Does my notion of a James Dean movie correspond to yours? A formal description can help us determine whether or not this is the case. My definition of a "James Dean movie" is one that stars James Dean, but your definition of a "James Dean movie" might be movies *about* James Dean or movies with the words *James Dean* in the title. How can we tell if we have the name "James Dean movie" as the only indication of these definitions? A formal model makes these distinctions clearer. Then it becomes a simple matter of automation to decide whether two classes are the same, if one subsumes the other, or if they are unrelated.

It is this aspect of modeling that motivates a logical definition of OWL. Each construct in OWL is a statement in a formal logic. The particular logical system of OWL DL is called *Description Logic*. As the name suggests, Description Logic is a logical system with which formal descriptions of classes, individuals, and the relationships between them can be made. The inferences in OWL that have formed the basis of the bulk of this book are formally defined by a model theory based on Description Logic.

Using logic as the foundation of a modeling language makes perfect sense; we can draw upon decades, or even centuries, of development work in logical formalism. The properties of various

---

[1]Details of the OWL 2 standard can be found at http://www.w3.org/2004/OWL.

logical structures are well understood. Logic provides a framework for defining all of the inferences that our modeling language will need. But there is one fly in the ointment: In a computational setting, we would like our logic to be processed automatically by a computer. Specifically, we want a computer to be able to determine all of the inferences that any given model entails. So, if we want to be able to automatically determine whether my notion of a James Dean movie is exactly the same as yours, we must show the set of all facts that are true in one are true in the others, and all facts untrue are untrue.

It is at this point that the details of the logic become important. What does it mean for our modeling formalism if we base it on a logic for which this kind of automation cannot, in principle, exist? That is, what happens if we can't exactly determine whether my notion of a James Dean movie is the same as yours? If we view this sort of provable connection as essential to the nature of modeling, then we have failed. We simply cannot tolerate a logic in which this kind of question cannot be answered by automated means in some finite amount of time.

In the study of formal logic, this question is called *decidability*. Formally, a system is *decidable* if there exists an effective method such that for every formula in the system the method is capable of deciding whether the formula is valid (is a theorem) in the system or not. If not, then the system is *undecidable*. It is not our intention in this book to go into any detail about the mathematical notion of decidability, but a few comments on its relevance for modeling are in order.

The first thing to understand about decidability is also the most surprising: how easy it is for a formal system to be undecidable. Given the formal nature of logic, it might seem that, with enough patience and engineering, a program could be developed to correctly and completely process any formal logic. One of the most influential theorems that established the importance of the notion of decidability shows that even very simple logical systems (basically, any system that can do ordinary integer arithmetic) are undecidable. In fact, it is actually quite challenging to come up with a logical system that can represent anything useful that is also decidable.

This bit of tightrope walking is the impetus behind the OWL DL subset. OWL DL is based on a particular decidable Description Logic. This means that it is possible to design an algorithm that can take as input any model expressed in OWL DL and determine which classes are equivalent to other classes, which classes are subclasses of other classes, and which individuals are members of which classes.

The most commonly used algorithm for this problem is called the *Tableau Algorithm*. It works basically by keeping track of all the possible relations between classes, ruling out those that are inconsistent with the logical statements made in the model. The Tableau Algorithm is guaranteed to find all entailments of a model in OWL DL in a finite (but possibly quite long!) time. Furthermore, it is possible to determine automatically whether a model is in fact in OWL DL so that a program can even signal when the guarantees cannot be met.

Modeling in OWL DL supports the intuition that a model must be clear, unambiguous, and machine-processable. The Tableau Algorithm provides the machinery by which a computer system can make determinations about equivalence of classes.

Executable models

A different motivation for modeling in the Semantic Web is to form an integrated picture of some sort of domain by federating information from multiple sources. If one source provides information about the places where hotel chains have hotels and another describes what hotels appear at a particular place, a formal model can tell us that we can merge these two sources together by treating them as inverses of one another. The model provides a recipe for adding new information to incomplete information so it can be federated with other sources.

Seen from this point of view, a model is similar to a program. It provides a concise description of how data can be transformed for use in other situations. What is the impact of decidability in such a situation? Standard programming languages like FORTRAN and Java are undecidable in this sense. The undecidability of these languages is often demonstration with reference to the *Halting Problem.* It is impossible in principle to write a computer program that can take another arbitrary computer program as input, along with input for *that* program, and determine whether *that* program will halt on that input. Even though these languages are undecidable, they have proven nevertheless to be useful engineering languages. How can we write programs in these languages if we can't automatically determine their correctness or, in some sense, even their meaning? The answer to this question in these cases is what programming is all about. Even though it is not possible *in general* to determine whether any program will terminate, it is usually possible to determine that *some particular* program will terminate and, indeed, with what answer. The skill of engineering good computer programs is to write programs that not only will terminate on all input but will actually perform well on particularly interesting input.

Seen from this point of view, decidability is not a primary concern. Models are engineered in much the same way as programs. If a model behaves poorly in some situation, then an engineer debugs the model until it performs correctly. Since we are not concerned with decidability, we don't need the guarantee that any algorithm will find all possible inferences. This opens up the choice of processor for OWL to a much wider range of technologies, including rule systems, datalog engines, databases, and even SPARQL.

It's also the case that, in many Web applications, the size of data sets we would like to analyze are quite huge, dynamic, or not well organized. The question could be asked as to whether one needs a 100 percent correct model to analyze data that are themselves scraped from the Web by some heuristic program that is not perfect. On the Web, people use Google because it can find good answers a lot of the time, even if it can't find perfect answers all the time. Some Semantic Web systems are targeted at this rough-and-tumble Web application space, and thus provable correctness, as opposed to efficient computation, may not be a key goal.

This executable style of modeling is the primary motivation behind some of the OWL subsets. The meaning of a modeling construct in one of these subsets is given in much the same way as the meaning of a construct in a programming language. Just as the meaning of a statement in a procedural programming language is given by the operation(s) that a machine will carry out when executing that statement, the meaning of an executable model is given by the operation(s) that a program (i.e., an inference engine) carries out when processing the model. Information federation is accomplished because the model describes how information can be transformed into a uniform structure.

OWL 2 MODELING CAPABILITIES

A comprehensive list of the advanced modeling capabilities supported by OWL 2 is beyond the scope of this book, but we describe some of the most important ones here.

Metamodeling

Metamodeling is the name commonly given to the practice of using a model to describe another model as an instance. One feature of metamodeling is that it must be possible to assign properties to classes in the model. This practice causes a problem in OWL 1.0, since OWL 1.0 disallowed treating classes as if they were individuals in this way.

One motivation for metamodeling is that a model often needs to play more than one role in an application: A particular concept should be viewed as a class in one role but as an instance in another role. If we are modeling animals, we might say that `BaldEagle` is an endangered species, thereby referencing `BaldEagle` as an individual. In another application, we could view `BaldEagle` as a class, whose members are the particular eagles in the zoo. Similarly, wine connoisseurs speak of individual wines in terms of `vintage`. For them, the vintage is an individual, but for a wine merchant who is calculating how many bottles he has sold, the bottles themselves are individual members of the class that are indicated by the vintage.

We have already seen some example of this kind of metamodeling in this book. In Chapter 9, we saw how a `foaf:Group` is an individual that corresponds to a class of all the members of the group. In Chapter 11, we saw this in the Class-Individual Mirror pattern.

Another purpose of metamodeling is to imitate capabilities of other modeling systems (like object-oriented modeling) in which the value for some property can be specified for all members of a class at once. The overloading of a resource to refer both to an individual (the species `BaldEagle`) and a class (the set `BaldEagle`) is allowed in OWL 2 through a process known as *punning*.

While punning is allowed in the OWL 2 standard, we recommend against its use for metamodeling. There really is a difference between a species and the set of animals of that species; there is a difference between the desktop and the applications that run on it. The relationship between a bottle of wine and its vintage is different from the relationship between an eagle and its species, and these distinctions could be important to someone who wants to reuse a model. Keeping them distinct in the first place will often enhance the model's utility.

In particular, we recommend the use of the Class-Individual Mirror pattern from Chapter 11 for metamodeling. In that example, the relationship between the desktop and the application was clear (`runsOn`), as was the relationship between the ADA90 and the applications (`conformsTo`). When modeling a class like `BaldEagle`, we recommend determining just what the relationship is between a particular eagle and the class (`hasSpecies`), or the particular bottle and the vintage (`hasVintage`). Just as in our example of the desktop applications conforming to the ADA90, this allows the model to relate these properties to others—for example, modeling `hasSpecies` explicitly allows the model to relate it to other properties like `hasGenus` or `hasPhylum`. Modeling `hasVintage` explicitly allows the model to express relationships to other properties like `madeInYear`.

Multipart properties

In RDFS, we have seen how properties can relate to one another using `rdfs:subPropertyOf`. This establishes a hierarchy of properties: Any relations that hold lower in the hierarchy also hold higher in the hierarchy. There are other ways in which properties can relate to one another. A common example is the notion of *uncle:* A is the *uncle* of B only if A is the *brother* of someone who is the *parent* of *B*. This is called a *multipart property*—that is, the property *uncle* is made up of two parts (in order): *parent* and *brother*. We have already seen how to define relationships of this sort using SPARQL in Chapter 5.

When multipart properties are used with other RDFS and OWL constructs, they provide some powerful modeling facilities. For instance, we can model the constraint "A child should have the same species as its parent" by stating that the multipart predicate made up of hasParent followed by hasSpecies (denoted as :hasParent + :hasSpecies) is rdfs:subPropertyOf has Species. Let's see how this works. Suppose we have the following triples:

```
:Elsie :hasParent :Lulu.
:Lulu :hasSpecies :Cow.
```

Now we can infer

:Elsie :hasParent + :hasSpecies :Cow.

But since the multipart predicate :hasParent + :hasSpecies is an rdfs:subPropertyOf :hasSpecies, we can infer that

:Elsie :hasSpecies :Cow.

One reason that multipart predicates were not included in OWL 1.0 was that they were thought to cause undecidability. Recently, however, it has been shown that under certain conditions it is possible to represent multipart properties in OWL in such a way that they do not endanger decidability. The multipart predicate feature in OWL 2.0 has been designed to guarantee decidability.

Multiple inverse functional properties

Inverse functional properties can be used to determine the identity of individuals based on the values of the properties that describe them. If two people share the same social security number, then we can infer that they are actually the same person. This kind of unique identifier is indispensable when merging information from multiple sources.

Unfortunately, anyone who has done a lot of such integration knows that this kind of merging only scrapes the surface of what needs to be done. Far more common is the situation in which some combination of properties implies the identity of two or more individuals. For instance, two people residing at the same residence with the same first and last names should be considered to be the same person. Two people born in the same hospital on the same day and at the same time of day should be considered to be the same person. Examples of this kind of multiple identifiers are much easier to come by than single identifiers, as required for an InverseFunctionalProperty.

OWL 2 introduces the notion of owl:hasKey for this situation. By analogy to how a relational database can declare multiple primary keys for a table, a set of properties can be associated with a class through owl:hasKey. Two members of the class are considered to be the same (owl:sameAs) if they have the same values for all the identified keys. If we were to define keys :firstName, :lastName, and :address for the class :Person, then two people would be considered the same whenever all of these properties match.

To further complicate matters, in many information federation situations, it is often the case that even these combinations of properties cannot guarantee the identity of the individuals. Two people at the same address with the same name are very likely to be the same person (but not for certain— a father could live with his son of the same name). OWL has no facility to deal with uncertainty, so there is no way to express this sort of information.

OWL 2 profiles

OWL 2 includes one major infrastructural change from OWL 1.0 in the introduction of several *profiles* of the language. The profiles were motivated by the observation that certain technologies can process certain subsets of OWL conveniently. If one has already made a commitement to such a technology, it is natural to ask just what subset is supported by that technology.

There are four subsets of OWL that have been named and identified.

OWL 2 DL. Decidability can be a key driver for model development. In such circumstances, it is desirable to have as expressive a language as possible, while still being decidable. OWL 2 DL is the largest subset of OWL that retains this feature. It includes all forms of restrictions, combined with all of the RDFS forms. It is a superset of the next three profiles. It can be processed faithfully by the tableau algorithm.

OWL 2 QL. Many semantic applications leverage information in relational databases, and need to be built on top of these systems. Such applications fit the profile of typical database applications, in which a fairly simple schema describes the structure of massive amounts of data, and fast responses to queries over that data set are required. OWL 2 QL is the subset of OWL for which this is possible. Queries against an OWL 2 QL ontology and corresponding data can be rewritten faithfully into SQL, the query language of relational databases.

OWL 2 EL. Many ontologies in the life sciences follow the pattern of the OBO Foundry ontologies described in Chapter 13; they include a large number of classes that are defined primarily using `someValuesFrom` restrictions. It is difficult to process ontologies of this size using an unconstrained tableau algorithm. The OWL 2 EL profile was designed for just this case. It walks the line between expressive power and known optimizations for querying such structures. OWL 2 EL allows `someValuesFrom` restrictions to be used, so the OBO Foundry ontologies fit within its limitations. But it is restricted enough that fast algorithms are known for processing large ontologies, up to and surpassing the size of the OBO Foundry ontologies.

OWL 2 RL. Many OWL processors work by using rules-based technology to define OWL processing. In this book, we have often used SPARQL to illustrate the inference rules that define certain constructs in OWL and RDFS. Used in this way, SPARQL is an example of such a rule processor. Rules processors have been around about as long as relational databases, in the form of systems like Prolog and Business Rules engines. OWL 2 RL defines the subset of OWL that can be faithfully processed by such rule systems. Having identified this subset, it is possible to encode the rules for OWL 2 RL in each rule system. This exercise has already been done for the W3C Rules Interchange Format (RIF[2], see below), as well as many proprietary rules processors. Many variants of encodings of OWL 2 RL into SPARQL have been done as well.

---

[2]http://www.w3.org/TR/rif-overview/

It is important to keep in mind that all of the OWL subsets use the very same resources in their models—there is no separate namespace for any profile. That means that any model in any profile can be interpreted as a model in any other—subject to the restrictions of that profile. In this way, all the profiles are interoperable at the RDF level.

Rules

Even with the capabilities added in OWL 2, there are still some limits to the expressivity of OWL. Some of these limitations are best addressed, for the purposes of data management, using rules, and thus the development of a rules language for the Web has been developed in the form of the Rules Interchange Format (RIF).

Rule-based systems have a venerable tradition starting in the days of Expert Systems and are in common use in business logic applications to this day. A number of useful algorithms for processing data with rules have been known for many years, and many of them have been made very efficient.

Many of the issues with OWL presented in this chapter can be addressed with rules. Multipart properties (like the definition of *uncle*) are easily expressed in rules. Multiple inverse functional properties can be expressed in rules as well. There are even a number of approaches to reasoning with uncertainty in rules. Many of these have considerable research and practical examples behind them, making uncertainty in rules a relatively well-understood issue.

Given all these virtues of rules and rule-based systems, why don't they play a bigger role in modeling on the Semantic Web than they do? In fact, one could even ask why there is a need for a modeling language like OWL when there is a mature, well-understood rules technology that already exists. One could even ask this question in greater generality. Why aren't more software systems in general written in rules?

We cannot treat this issue in full detail in this book, but we can outline the answer as it relates to OWL and the Semantic Web. One of the lessons learned from the history of rule-based systems is that software engineering in such systems is more difficult than it is in modular, procedural languages. Although it is unclear whether or not this is an essential feature of rule-based systems, it is undeniable that rule-based programmers have not achieved the levels of productivity of their more conventional counterparts. This has particular ramifications in the Semantic Web. One defense for using an OWL subset other than OWL 2 DL was that the software engineering discipline makes the notion of decidability basically irrelevant for model design. In the case of rule-based systems, software engineering cannot provide this same support. Unconstrained rule-based systems are just as undecidable as general-purpose languages like FORTRAN and Java.

Is there a way to get the best of both worlds? Could a Web-oriented rules language integrate well with OWL? Indeed they can, and this is exactly what we are seeing in the development of things like OWL 2 RL and RIF. Together, they provide a framework that is consistent with OWL, as well as with broader rule-based technology.

SUMMARY

OWL should be considered a living language, growing in the context of the ways it is being used on the Web and in commerce. As shortcomings in the language are identified, the system grows to accommodate them. Sometimes that growth takes the form of additional constructs in the language (e.g., multipart properties), sometimes as connections to other systems (rules), and sometimes progress in a language comes in the form of specifying subsets of the language.

Fundamental concepts

The following fundamental concepts were introduced in this chapter.

OWL—Web Ontology Language, including all constructs in this book and more.

OWL 2 DL—Subset of OWL restricted to ensure decidability; all constructs allowed but with certain restrictions on their use.

OWL 2 EL—Subset of OWL restricted to improve computational complexity.

OWL 2 RL—Subset of OWL restricted to be compatible with Rules processors.

OWL 2 QL—Subset of OWL restricted to be compatible with database queries.

RIF—The Rule Interchange Format, standard format in the Semantic Web for interoperability of rule-based systems.

Metamodeling—Models that describe models, usually requires that classes be treated as individuals.

Multipart properties—Daisy-chain composition of properties.

Multiple Inverse Functional Properties—Uniquely identify an individual based on matching values for several properties.

Conclusions

For those readers who are accustomed to various sorts of knowledge modeling, the Semantic Web looks familiar. The notions of classes, subclasses, properties, and instances have been the mainstay of knowledge modeling and object systems modeling for decades. It is not uncommon to hear a veteran of one of these technologies look at the Semantic Web and mutter, "Same old, same old," indicating that there is nothing new going on here and that everything in the Semantic Web has already been done under some other name elsewhere.

As the old saying goes, "There is nothing new under the sun," and to the extent that the saying is correct, so are these folks when they speak of the Semantic Web. The modeling structures we have examined in this book do have a strong connection to a heritage of knowledge modeling languages. But there is something new that has come along since the early days of expert systems and object-oriented programming; something that has had a far more revolutionizing effect on culture, business, commerce, education, and society than any expert system designer ever dreamed of. It is something so revolutionary that it is often compared in cultural significance to the invention of the printing press. That something new is the World Wide Web.

The Semantic Web is the application of advanced technologies that have been used in the context of artificial intelligence, expert systems and business rules execution in the context of a World Wide Web of information. The Semantic Web is not simply an application running on the Web somewhere; it is a part of the very infrastructure of the Web. It isn't on the Web; it is the Web.

Why is this important? What is it that is so special about the Web? Why has it been so successful, more so than just about any computer system that has come before it?

In the early days of the commercial Web, there was a television ad for a search engine. In the ad, a woman driving a stylish sports car is pulled over by traffic policeman for speeding. As he prepares to cite her, she outlines for him all the statistics about error rates in the various machines used by traffic policemen for detecting speeding. He is clearly thrown off his game and unsure of how to continue to cite her. She adds personal insult by quoting the statistics of prolonged exposure to traffic radar machines on sperm count. The slogan "Knowledge is Power" scrolls over the screen, along with the name of the search engine.

What lesson can we learn from ads like this? This kind of advertising made a break from television advertising that had come before. Knowledge was seen not as nerdy or academic but useful in everyday life—and even sexy. Or at least it is if you have the *right* knowledge at the right time. The Web differed from information systems that preceded it by bringing information from many sources—indeed, sources from around the world—to one's fingertips. In comparison to Hypercard stacks that had been around for decades, the Web was an open system. Anyone in the world could contribute, and everyone could benefit from that contribution. Having all that information available was more important than how well a small amount of information was organized.

The Semantic Web differs from expert systems in pretty much the same way. Compared to the knowledge representations systems that were developed in the context of expert systems, OWL is quite

335

primitive. But this is appropriate for a Web language. The power of the Semantic Web comes from the Web aspect. Even a primitive knowledge modeling language can yield impressive results when it uses information from sources from around the world. In expert systems terms, the goals of the Semantic Web are also modest. The idea of an expert system was that it could behave in a problem-solving setting with a performance that would qualify as expert-level if a human were to accomplish it. What we learned from the World Wide Web (and the story of the woman beating the speeding ticket) is that typically people don't want machines to behave like experts; they want to have access to information so they can exhibit expert performance at just the right time. As we saw in the ad, the World Wide Web was successful early on in making this happen, as long as someone is willing to read the relevant web pages, digest the information, and sift out what he or she needs.

The Semantic Web takes this idea one step further. The Web is effective at bringing any single resource to the attention of a Web user, but if the information the user needs is not represented in a single place, the job of integration rests with the user. The Semantic Web doesn't use expert system technology to replicate the behavior of an expert; it uses expert system technology to gather information so an individual can have integrated access to the web of information.

Being part of the Web infrastructure is no simple matter. On the Web, any reference is a global reference. The issue of managing global names for anything we want to talk about is a fundamental Web issue, not just a Semantic Web issue. The Semantic Web uses the notion of a URI as the globally resolvable reference to a resource as a way of taking advantage of the web infrastructure. Most programming and modeling languages have a mechanism whereby names can be organized into spaces (so that you and I can use the same name in different ways but still keep them straight when our systems have to interface).

With the World Wide Web, the notion of a name in a namespace must be global in the entire Web. The URI is the Web-standard mechanism to do this; hence, the Semantic Web uses the URI for global namespace identification. Using this approach allows the Semantic Web to borrow the modularity of the World Wide Web. Two models that were developed in isolation can be merged simply by referring to resources in both of them in the same statement. Since the names are always maintained as global identifiers, there is no ad hoc need to integrate identifiers each time; the system for global identity is part of the infrastructure.

An important contributor to the success of the World Wide Web is its openness. Anyone can contribute to the body of information, including people who, for one reason or another, might publish information that someone else would consider misleading, objectionable, or just incorrect. At first blush, a chaotic free-for-all of this sort seems insane. How could it ever be useful? The success of the Web in general (and information archiving sites like Wikipedia in particular) has shown that there is sufficient incentive to publish quality data to make the overall Web a useful and even essential structure.

This openness has serious ramifications in the Semantic Web, which go beyond considerations that were important for technologies like expert systems. One of the reasons why the Web was more successful than Hypercard was because the Web infrastructure was resilient to missing or broken links (the "404 Error"). The Semantic Web must be resilient in a similar way. Thus, inferencing in the Semantic Web must be done very conservatively, according to the Open World assumption. At any time, new information could become available that could undermine conclusions that have already been made, and our inference policy must be robust in such situations.

In the World Wide Web, the openness of the system presents a potential problem. How does the heroine of the search engine commercial know that the information she has found about radar-based speed detection devices is correct? She might have learned it from a trusted source (say, a government study on these devices), or she might have cross-referenced the information with other sources until she had enough corroborating evidence to be certain. Or perhaps she doesn't really care if it is correct but only that she can convince the traffic cop that it is. Trust of information on the Web is done with a healthy dose of skepticism but in the same way as trust in other media like newspapers, books, and magazine articles.

In the case of the Semantic Web, trust issues are more subtle. Information from the Semantic Web is an amalgam of information from multiple sources. How do we judge our trust in such a result even if we know about all the sources? To some extent, the same principles apply. We can trust entities that we know or have experience with, and we can trust entities that have gone through some process of authorization and authentication. When we combine information, we must also understand the impact that each information source has on the outcome and what risk we are taking if we cannot trust that source. These important issues for understanding the reliability of the Semantic Web are still a subject of research.

In this book, we examined the modeling aspects of the Semantic Web: How do you represent information in such a way that it is responsive to a web environment? The basic principles underlying the Semantic Web—the AAA slogan, the Nonunique Naming assumption, and the Open World assumption—are constraints placed on a representation system if it wants to function as the foundation of a World Wide Web of information. These constraints have led to the main design decisions for the Semantic Web languages of RDF, RDFS, and OWL.

There is more to a web than just the information and how it is modeled. At some point, this information must be stored in a computer, accessed by end users, and transmitted across an information network. Furthermore, no triple store, and no inference engine, will ever be able to scale to the size of the World Wide Semantic Web. This is clearly impossible, since the Web itself grows continually. In the light of this observation, how can the World Wide Semantic Web ever come to pass?

The applications we discussed in this book demonstrate how a modest amount of information, represented flexibly so that it can be merged in novel ways, provides a new dynamic for information distribution and sharing. SKOS allows thesaurus managers around the globe to share, connect, and compare terminology. QUDT aligns multiple applications so that their measurable quantities can be combined and compared. OBO Ontologies coordinate efforts of independent life sciences researchers around the globe.

How is it possible to get the benefit of a global network of data if no machine is powerful enough to store, inference over, and query the whole network? As we have seen, it isn't necessary that a Semantic Web application be able to access and merge every page on the Web at once. The Semantic Web is useful as long as an application can access and merge *any* web page. Since we can't hold all the Semantic Web pages in one store at once, we have to proceed with the understanding that there could always be more information that we don't have access to at any one point. This is why the Open World assumption is central to the infrastructure of the Semantic Web.

This book is about modeling in the context of the Semantic Web. What role does a model play in the big vision? The World Wide Web that we see every day is made up primarily of documents, which are read and digested by people browsing the Web. But behind many of these web pages, there are databases that contain far more information than is actually displayed on a page. To make all this information available as a global, integrated whole, we need a way to specify how information in one place relates to information somewhere else. Models on the Semantic Web play the role of the intermediaries that describe the relationships among information from various sources.

Look at the cover of this book. An engineering handbook for aquifers provides information about conduits, ducts, and channels sufficient to inform an engineer about the pieces of a dynamic fluid system that can control a series of waterways like these. The handbook won't give final designs, but it will provide insight about how the pieces can be fit together to accomplish certain engineering goals. A creative engineer can use this information to construct a dynamic flow system for his own needs.

So is the case with this book. The standard languages of RDF, RDFS, and OWL provide the framework for the pieces an engineer can use to build a model with dynamic behavior. Particular constructs like `subClassOf` and `subPropertyOf` provide mechanisms for specifying how information flows through the model. More advanced constructions like `owl:Restriction` provide ways to specify complex relations between other parts of the model. The examples from the "in the wild" chapters show how these pieces have been assembled by working ontologists into complex dynamic models that achieve particular goals. This is the craft of modeling in the Semantic Web—combining the building blocks in useful ways to create a dynamic system through which the data of the Semantic Web can flow.

Frequently asked questions

Throughout this book, we have presented examples of modeling patterns, issues, and challenge problems to describe various modeling tasks. In the course of the text, the issues are organized in pedagogical order, starting with the simplest RDFS constructs and moving up to more advanced OWL constructs. Now that you have finished the book, you are familiar with all of these constructs.

This appendix references all the modeling examples through the kinds of modeling questions they answer. It is organized (as much as you can call it "organization") in the form of a FAQ—a list of questions, with pointers for where to find the answers.

FAQ	Challenge	Discussion
How can I represent tabular data in RDF?	1, p. 40	p. 29
Construct: `rdf:type`	22, p. 176	p. 38
How can I transform data using SPARQL?	2, p. 91	
How can SPARQL be used to describe other forms of reasoning?		p. 115
How do I represent IF/THEN logic in RDFS or OWL?	5, p. 139	p. 114
Construct: `rdfs:subClassOf`		p. 128
How do I combine two properties into one more general property?	6, p. 139	p. 128
Construct: `rdfs:subPropertyOf`		
How can I say that two properties are used exactly the same way?	7, p. 140	p. 172
Construct: `rdfs:subPropertyOf`, `owl:equivalentClass`		
How do I merge individuals from multiple data sources into a single class?	8, p. 141	p. 133
Construct: `rdfs:subClassOf`		
How can I use another property instead of `rdfs:label` to indicate the display name of a class or individual?	9, p. 141	p. 133 p. 139
Construct: `rdfs:subPropertyOf`		
How can I filter information based on a value for one or more properties?	10, p. 143	p. 237
Construct: `owl:hasValue`		
How can I filter information based on how it is used?	11, p. 143	pp. 130, 139, 145, 221, 237
Construct: `rdfs:domain`, `rdfs:range`, `owl:someValuesFrom`, `owl:allValuesFrom`		

(Continued)

339

FAQ	Challenge	Discussion
How can I merge information from two sources that are organized differently?	13, p. 157	pp. 133, 156, 159
Construct: `rdfs:subPropertyOf`, `owl:inverseOf`	15, p. 160 16, p. 161	
How do I resolve differences in opinion about how properties should be used?	17, p.162 18, p. 164	p. 150
How do I compute ancestors or descendants?	19, p. 166	
Construct: `rdfs:subPropertyOf`, `owl:TransitiveProperty`		
How can I manage process diagrams in OWL?	19, p. 166	p. 150
Construct: `rdfs:subPropertyOf`, `owl:TransitiveProperty`	20, p. 167 21, p. 169	
How do I merge information from multiple sources?	22, p. 176	p. 175
Construct: `owl:FunctionalProperty`, `owl:InverseFunctionalProperty`, `owl:sameAs`	23, p. 180 24, p. 182	
How do we model prerequisites?	25, p. 189	p. 221
Construct: `owl:allValuesFrom`		p. 266
How do I do classic knowledge representation in OWL?	27, p. 238	p. 237
Construct: `owl:allValuesFrom`, `rdfs:subClassOf`		
How can I import a single database table as multiple classes?	28, p. 241	p. 237
Construct: `owl:hasValue`		
How do I organize information in a taxonomic hierarchy?	5, p. 139	p. 114
Construct: `rdfs:subClassOf`		p. 128
How do I approximate set union/intersection with subclasses?	8, p. 141	p. 133
Construct: `rdfs:subClassOf`		
How do I approximate property union/intersection with subproperties?		p. 133
Construct: `rdfs:subPropertyOf`		
How do I approximate set intersection with domains and ranges?		p. 146
Construct: `rdfs:domain, rdfs:range`		
When are two things "the same" in the Semantic Web?	28, p. 241	170
Construct: `owl:sameAs`, `owl:equivalentClass`, `owl:equivalentProperty`	7, p. 140	
`SPARQL CONSTRUCT`	3, p. 94	
How do I filter out items for which certain data are missing?	12, p. 144	p. 139
Construct: `rdfs:domain, rdfs:range`		

FAQ	Challenge	Discussion
How do I determine when two things are the same? Construct: `owl:FunctionalProperty`, `owl:InverseFunctionalProperty`	23, p. 180	p. 178
How do I select individuals based on their relationship to a particular individual—for example, "the HIGH-priority questions"?		p. 221
Construct: `owl:hasValue`		
How do I express statements like "The players on a team" or "The planets around the sun" in OWL?		p. 250
Construct: `owl:unionOf`, `owl:intersectionOf`		
How do I transfer information represented by one property to another—for example, "The children of Shakespeare are members of his family"?	30, p. 245	p. 244
Construct: `owl:hasValue`, `owl:equivalentClass`, `rdfs:subClassOf`		
I can't decide if something is a class or an individual. What do I do?	29, p. 243	
Construct: `owl:hasValue`, `rdfs:subClassOf`		
How can I assert that I know all the planets? Or all the movies with James Dean? How do I suspend the Open World assumption for a certain class?		p. 252
Construct: `owl:oneOf`		
How can OWL come to conclusions by process of elimination?	31, p. 253	p. 257
Construct: `owl:oneOf`, `owl:differentFrom`, `owl:cardinality`		
Can an OWL reasoner count?	33, p. 258	
Construct: `owl:cardinality`, `owl:disjointWith`	34, p. 259	
	35, p. 262	
	36, p. 265	
	37, p. 270	p. 264
How can SPARQL be used for reasoning?		p. 89
Construct: `SPARQL CONSTRUCT`		p. 86
SPIN (SPARQL Inferencing Notation		pp. 116, 286
How is the Semantic Web used in familiar web sites?		
Facebook OGP		p. 203
Google Rich Snippets and Good Relations		p. 280
RDFa		pp. 55, 53
Data.gov		p. 187
Can I do quantitative calculations in the Semantic Web?	35, p. 262	
QUDT		p. 287
How are SKOS and OWL related?	36, p. 265	
What is an OBO ontology, and how do I query it?		p. 298
How do I find problems in my model?	33, p. 258	pp. 258, 312

Further reading

In this book we focused on modeling in the Semantic Web: how to use the standards and technology to build models that will assist in the interoperation of information in a Web setting. In this reading list, we include pointers to other treatments of issues relating to the Semantic Web, including history, methodology, mathematical theory, business applications, and criticisms of the entire approach. This list is intended to be a starting point for the interested reader and does not claim to be comprehensive.

In addition to the references provided here, a number of tutorials on RDF, RDFS, OWL, and related Semantic Web technologies can be found at http://www.w3.org/2001/sw/BestPractices/Tutorials.

Selected Books

Antoniou, Grigoris, & Frank van Harmelen (2004). *A Semantic Web Primer*. Cambridge, MA: MIT Press.

Bridgman, & Percy, W. (1922). *Dimensional Analysis*. New Haven, CT: Yale University Press.

Daconta, Michael, C., Leo, J., Obrst, & Smith, Kevin T. (2003). *The Semantic Web: A guide to the future of XML, web services, and knowledge management*. New York: John Wiley.

Davies, Johan John, Dieter Fensel, & Frank van Harmelen (2002). *Towards the Semantic WEB—Ontology-driven knowledge management*. New York: John Wiley.

Fensel, & Dieter (2001). *Ontologies: A silver bullet for knowledge management and electronic commerce*. Berlin: Springer Verlag.

Fensel, Dieter, Wolfgang Wahlster, Henry Lieberman, & James Hendler (Eds.) (2002). *Spinning the Semantic Web*. Cambridge, MA: MIT Press.

Geroimenko, Vladimir, & Chaomei Chen (Eds.) (2003). *Visualizing the Semantic Web*. London: Springer-Verlag Ltd.

Hjelm, & Johan (2001). *Creating the Semantic Web with RDF*. New York: John Wiley.

Lacy, & Lee, W. (2005). *OWL: Representing information using the web ontology language*. Oxford, UK: Trafford Publishing.

Knowledge transformation for the Semantic Web, Vol. 95 (2003). In B. Omelayenko, & M. Klein (Eds.), *Frontiers in artificial intelligence and applications*. Amsterdam: IOS Press.

Passin, & Thomas, B. (2004). *Explorer's guide to the semantic web*. Greenwich, CT: Manning Publications.

Polikoff, Irene, Coyne, Robert, & Hodgson, Ralph (2005). *Capability cases—A solution envisioning approach*. Boston: Addison-Wesley.

Pollock, Jeff, & Ralph Hodgson (2004). *Adaptive information: improving business through semantic interoperability, grid computing, and enterprise integration*. New York: John Wiley.

Powers, & Shelley (2003). *Practical RDF*. Sebastapol, CA: O'Reilly.

Selected Articles

Allemang, Dean, Irene Polikoff, & Ralph Hodgson (2005). Enterprise Architecture Reference Modeling in OWL/RDF. *Proceedings of 4th International Semantic Web Conference, ISWC 2005*, Galway, Ireland, November.

Bada, Michael, Robert Stevens, Carole Goble, Yolanda Gil, Michael Ashburner, Blake, Judith A., Michael Cherry, J., Midori Harris, & Suzanna Lewis (2004). A short study on the success of the gene ontology. *Journal of Web Semantics, 1*(2), 235–240.

Berners-Lee, Tim (2003). Foreword. In Dieter Fensel., James Hendler., Henry Lieberman., & Wolfgang Wahlster. (Eds.), *Spinning the Semantic Web: Bringing the World Wide Web to its full potential*. Cambridge, MA: MIT Press.

Berners-Lee, Tim, James Hendler, & Ora Lassila. The Semantic Web. Scientific American (May 2001). http://www.sciam.com/article.cfm?articleID=00048144-10D2-1C70-84A9809EC588EF21.

Brickley, Dan, & Libby Miller. FOAF vocabulary specification. 2005. http://xmlns.com/foaf/0.1/.

BIPM. SI Brochure, 8th Edition. http://www.bipm.org/en/si/si_brochure/.

de Bruijn, Jos, Axel Polleres, Rubén Lara, & Dieter Fenser. OWL DL vs. OWL Flight: Conceptual modeling and reasoning for the semantic web. *Proceedings of the World Wide Web Conference 2005*. http://www2005.org/cdrom/docs/p623.pdf.

Decker, S., Melnik, S., van Harmelen, F., Fensel, D., Klein, M., Broekstra, J., Erdmann, M., & Horrocks, I. (2000). The Semantic Web: The roles of XML and RDF. *IEEE Internet Computing*.

DuCharme, Bob (2011). *Learning SPARQL*. Sebastopol, CA: O'Reilly.

Ding, Ying, & Dieter Fensel (2001). Ontology Library Systems: The Key to Successful Ontology Re-Use. In F. Isabel, Cruz, Stefan Decker, Jérôme Euzenat, & Deborah L. McGuinness (Eds.), *Proceedings of SWWS '01: The First Semantic Web Working Symposium* (pp. 93–112). http://sw-portal.deri.org/papers/publications/ding+01.pdf.

Ellman, Jeremy (January/February 2004). Corporate Ontologies as Information Interfaces. *IEEE Intelligent Systems*, 79–80.

Fensel, Dieter, James Hendler, Henry Lieberman, & Wolfgang Wahlster (2003). Introduction. In Dieter Fensel, James Hendler, Henry Lieberman, & Wolfgang Wahlster (Eds.), *Spinning the Semantic Web: Bringing the World Wide Web to Its Full Potential* (pp. 1–25). Cambridge, MA: MIT Press.

Frey, J. G., Hughes, G. V., Mills, H. R., Schraefel, M. C., Smith, G. M., & De Roure, D. Less Is More: Lightweight Ontologies and User Interfaces for Smart Labs. *Proceedings of the 2004 UK E-Science All-Hands Meeting*. http://www.allhands.org.uk/2004/proceedings/papers/187.pdf.

Fry, Christopher, Mike Plusch, & Henry Lieberman (2003). Static and Dynamic Semantics of the Web. In Dieter Fensel, James Hendler, Henry Lieberman, & Wolfgang Wahlster (Eds.), *Spinning the Semantic Web: Bringing the World Wide Web to Its Full Potential* (pp. 377–401). Cambridge, MA: MIT Press.

Golbeck, Jennifer, Gilberto Fragoso, Frank Hartel, Jim Hendler, Jim Oberthaler, & Bijan Parsia (2003). The National Cancer Institute's Thesaurus and Ontology. *Journal of Web Semantics, 1*(1), 75–80.

Gruber, Tom. A Translation Approach to Formal Ontologies. *Knowledge Acquisition* 5, 2 (1993): 199–200—http://ksl-web.stanford.edu/KSL_Abstracts/KSL-92-71.html. Towards Principles for the Design of Ontologies Used for Knowledge Sharing. In Nicola Guarino & R. Poli (Eds.), Formal Ontology in Conceptual Analysis and Knowledge Representation: Special Issue of International Journal of Human-Computer Studies 43, 5/6(1995)—http://ksl-web.stanford.edu/KSL_Abstracts/KSL-93-04.html. Ontology of Folksonomy: A Mash-Up of Apples and Oranges. Keynote. First *On-Line Conference on Metadata and Semantics Research (MTSR)* 2005— http://tomgruber.org/writing/ontology-of-folksonomy.htm.

Guo, Yuanbo, Zhengxiang Pan, & Jeff Heflin (2005). LUBM: A Benchmark for Owl Knowledge Base Systems. *Journal of Web Semantics, 2*(2–3), 158–182.

Heflin Jeff, & James Hendler. Semantic Interoperability on the Web. *Proceedings of Extreme Markup Languages 2000*. http://www.cs.umd.edu/projects/plus/SHOE/pubs/extreme2000.pdf.

Heflin, Jeff, James Hendler, & Sean Luke (2003). SHOE: A Blueprint for the Semantic Web. In Dieter Fensel, James Hendler, Henry Lieberman, & Wolfgang Wahlster (Eds.), *Spinning the Semantic Web: Bringing the World Wide Web to Its Full Potential* (pp. 29–63). Cambridge, MA: MIT Press.

Hendler, James, Tim Berners-Lee, & Eric Miller (2002). Integrating Applications on the Semantic Web. *Journal of the Institute of Electrical Engineers of Japan, 122*(10), 676–680.

Horrocks, Ian, Patel-Schneider, Peter F., & Frank van Harmelen (2003). From SHIQ and RDF to OWL: The Making of a Web Ontology Language. *Journal of Web Semantics, 1*(1), 7–26.

Kalfoglou, Yannis, & Marco Schorlemmer (2003). Ontology Mapping: The State of the Art. *Knowledge Engineering Review, 18*(1), 1–31. http://eprints.ecs.soton.ac.uk/10519/01/ker02-ontomap.pdf.

JCGM. International Vocabulary of Metrology—Basic and General Concepts and Associated Terms (2008). http://www.bipm.org/utils/common/documents/jcgm/JCGM_200_2008.pdf.

Lassila, Ora, & James Hendler (2007). Embracing Web 3.0. *IEEE Internet Computing, 11*(3), 90–93.

McGuinness, & Deborah, L. (2003). Ontologies Come of Age. In Dieter Fensel, James Hendler, Henry Lieberman, & Wolfgang Wahlster (Eds.), *Spinning the Semantic Web: Bringing the World Wide Web to Its Full Potential* (pp. 171–194). Cambridge, MA: MIT Press.

Mika, Peter Ontologies Are Us: A Unified Model of Social Networks and Semantics. *Proceedings of the 4th International Semantic Web Conference (ISWC), 2005.*

Mika, Peter (2005). Flink: Semantic Web Technology for the Extraction and Analysis of Social Networks. *Journal of Web Semantic, 3*, 2. http://www.websemanticsjournal.org/ps/pub/2005-20.

Motik, Boris. On the Properties of Metamodeling in OWL. *Journal of Logic Computation* 17, 617–637.

Noy, Natalya, F., & McGuinness, Deborah L. Ontology Development 101: A Guide to Creating Your First Ontology (2001). http://protege.stanford.edu/publications/ontology_development/ontology101-noy-mcguinness.html.

Parsia, & Bijan. A Simple, Prima Facie Argument in Favor of the Semantic Web (2002). http://monkeyfist.com/articles/815.

Parsia, Bijan, Evren Sirin, & Aditya Kalyanpur. Debugging OWL Ontologies. *Proceedings of the World Wide Web Conference 2005.*

Shirky, & Clay. Ontology Is Overrated: Categories, Links and Tags (2005). http://www.shirky.com/writings/ontology_overrated.html.

Sirin, Evren, Bijan Parsia, Bernardo Cuenca Grau, Aditya Kalyanpur, & Yarden Katz (2007). Pellet: A Practical OWL-DL Reasoner. *Journal of Web Semantics, 5*(2), 51–53.

Stumme, Gerd, Andreas Hotho, & Bettina Berendt (2006). Semantic Web Mining: State of the Art and Future Directions. *Journal of Web Semantics, 4*(2), 124–143.

ter Horst, & Herman, J. (2005). Completeness, Decidability and Complexity of Entailment for RDF Schema and a Semantic Extension Involving the Owl Vocabulary. *Journal of Web Semantics, 2*(2–3), 79–115.

Thompson, A., Taylor, B. N., & The NIST. Guide for the Use of the International System of Units (2009). http://www.nist.gov/pml/pubs/sp811/index.cfm.

Uren, Victoria, Philipp Cimiano, José Iria, Siegfried Handschuh, Maria Vargas-Vera, Enrico Motta, & Fabio Ciravegna (2006). Semantic Annotation for Knowledge Management: Requirements and a Survey of the State of the Art. *Journal of Web Semantics, 4*(1), 14–28.

Uschold, Michael (2003). Where Are the Semantics in the Semantic Web? *AI Magazine, 24*(3), 25–36.

van Hage, & Willem Robert. OAEI 2006 food task: An analysis of a thesaurus mapping task. Available at http://www.few.vu.nl/~wrvhage/pdf/oaei2006food-results.pdf.

Volz, Raphael, Siegfried Handschuh, Steffen Staab, Ljiljana Stojanovic, & Nenad Stojanovic (2004). Unveiling the Hidden Bride: Deep Annotation for Mapping and Migrating Legacy Data to the Semantic Web. *Journal of Web Semantics, 1*, 2.

Welty, Christopher, A., Ruchi Mahindru, & Jennifer Chu-Carroll. Evaluating Ontological Analysis. Proceedings of the ISWC-2003 Workshop on Semantic Integration. http://sunsite.informatik.rwth-aachen.de/Publications/CEUR-WS/Vol-82/SI_paper_16.pdf.

World Wide Web Consortium Publications on RDF, RDFS, and OWL

RDF/XML Syntax Specification (Revised), Dave Beckett, ed. http://www.w3.org/TR/rdf-syntax-grammar/

RDF Vocabulary Description Language 1.0: RDF Schema, Dan Brickley & R.V. Guha, eds. http://www.w3.org/TR/rdf-schema/

RDF Primer, Frank Manola & Eric Miller, eds. http://www.w3.org/TR/rdf-primer/

Resource Description Framework (RDF): Concepts and Abstract Syntax, Graham Klyne & Jeremy Carroll, eds. http://www.w3.org/TR/rdf-concepts/

RDF Semantics, Patrick Hayes, ed. http://www.w3.org/TR/rdf-mt/

RDF Test Cases, Jan Grant, Dave Beckett, eds. http://www.w3.org/TR/rdf-testcases/

OWL Web Ontology Language Overview, Deborah L. McGuinness & Frank van Harmelen, eds. http://www.w3.org/TR/owl-features/

OWL Web Ontology Language Guide, Michael Smith, Chris Welty, & Deborah McGuinness, eds. http://www.w3.org/TR/owl-guide/

OWL Web Ontology Language Reference, Michael Dean & Guus Schreiber, eds. http://www.w3.org/TR/owl-ref/

OWL Web Ontology Language Semantics and Abstract Syntax, Peter Patel-Schneider, Pat Hayes, & Ian Horrocks, eds. http://www.w3.org/TR/owl-semantics/

OWL Web Ontology Language Test Cases, Jeremy J. Carroll & Jos De Roo, eds. http://www.w3.org/TR/owl-test/

OWL Web Ontology Language Use Cases and Requirements, Jeff Heflin, ed. http://www.w3.org/TR/webont-req/

Index